Dear Valued Customer,

We realize you're a busy professional with deadlines to hit. Whether your goal is to learn a new technology or solve a critical problem, we want to be there to lend you a hand. Our primary objective is to provide you with the insight and knowledge you need to stay atop the highly competitive and ever-changing technology industry.

Wiley Publishing, Inc., offers books on a wide variety of technical categories, including security, data warehousing, software development tools, and networking — everything you need to reach your peak. Regardless of your level of expertise, the Wiley family of books has you covered.

- For Dummies® – The *fun* and *easy* way™ to learn
- The Weekend Crash Course® –The *fastest* way to learn a new tool or technology
- Visual – For those who prefer to learn a new topic *visually*
- The Bible – The *100% comprehensive* tutorial and reference
- The Wiley Professional list – *Practical* and *reliable* resources for IT professionals

The book you hold now, *The Web Testing Companion,* is your inside look at testing Web applications from a leading software tester with wide experience. Suitable for new Web testers, but full of insights and techniques of great value to experienced testers and developers, this book is the only one of its kind: It shows you when and how to test against many platforms, in many languages, addressing larger concerns of performance and security, and provides unique templates and approaches to ensure the best results. Our author has been a tester and has lead web testing projects. Here she outlines best practices and advice learned through experience, and passes her experience along to you.

Our commitment to you does not end at the last page of this book. We'd want to open a dialog with you to see what other solutions we can provide. Please be sure to visit us at www.wiley.com/compbooks to review our complete title list and explore the other resources we offer. If you have a comment, suggestion, or any other inquiry, please locate the "contact us" link at www.wiley.com.

Finally, we encourage you to review the following page for a list of Wiley titles on related topics. Thank you for your support and we look forward to hearing from you and serving your needs again in the future.

Sincerely,

Richard K. Swadley

Richard K. Swadley
Vice President & Executive Group Publisher
Wiley Technology Publishing

Visual™

Bible

DUMMIES

WILEY
Wiley Publishing, Inc.

The Web Testing Companion: The Insider's Guide to Efficient and Effective Tests

Lydia Ash

Wiley Publishing, Inc.

Publisher: Joe Wikert
Editor: Ben Ryan
Developmental Editor: Kevin Kent
Editorial Manager: Kathryn Malm
Managing Editor: Pamela M. Hanley
Media Development Specialist: Brian Snapp
Text Design & Composition: Wiley Composition Services

Published by Wiley Publishing, Inc., Indianapolis, Indiana

Published simultaneously in Canada

For general information on our other products and services please contact our Customer Care Department within the United States at (800) 762-2974, outside the United States at (317) 572-3993 or fax (317) 572-4002.

Library of Congress Cataloging-in-Publication Data is available from publisher.

ISBN: 0-471-43021-8

Printed in the United States of America

10 9 8 7 6 5 4 3 2 1

CONTENTS

There are always people who have affected you in one way or another — those that have pushed a thought a certain way or triggered a different way of seeing things. I want to just publicly thank a few who have opened doors to different ways of thinking for me, those who have been peers and friends, those who have shared, taught, and learned.

My father was the first to get me involved in computers, with a Commodore and a few Apples we borrowed. Whenever I hear a modem connecting with those familiar crackling sounds, I think of the acoustic modem and dad explaining how it worked. Dr. Bernard Barcio, Ray Lawrence, Dr. Lee Ehrman, and Marty Lewinter were some of the most influential teachers a person could ask for. They seem underrated for as many times as I play their voices through my head. Friends rekindled my interest in computers as they started to become a way to pay the bills. Nat Beall, Craig Brozlovsky, Luke Nelson, and many others more than gladly shared information with anyone who could ask the questions. Two people who have taught me more about teams, building teams, and successful teams are Hanzill Dragorr and Usish Baitte. Working with these two people gave more insight into team dynamics than any other experience.

There have been so many peers, testers, developers, project managers, and others whom I have to recognize. Floyd was the first sherpa who I had the pleasure of working with and following. Many former and current teammates must be recognized: Cindy McKelvy, Cathy Selin, Sean Bahner-Guhin, Bob McKelvy, Mike Gahrns, Karim Batthish, Russ Simpson, Bob Gering, Troy Mahan, Brian Mesh, Roy Williams, Brian Deen, Anuradha Rawal, Joel Soderberg, Rob Taylor, Manoj Vasudevan, Jamie Yu, Ping Lin, Craig Thomas, Gerard Reese, Llewellyn Botelho, Chris Gallagher, Rob Long, Neal Noble, Anthony Gavina, Hideto Nakajima, Henrieta Slugenova, Brandon Falloona, Levert Banks, Lisa Baldzikowski, Brendan Fields, Tosh Meston, Arun Narasimhan, Jorge Pereira, Yamin Wang, Aaron Knopf, Ted Scott, and Don Mace. I had a few who have been great sounding boards and have given honest opinions on so many topics, including this manuscript. Jackie McGee, Jim van Eaton, Shawn Bracewell, and Jack Freelander have been great friends and coworkers through the years. I want to thank all of you for together building some great teams.

Throughout the book's writing, Heisenberg, Fermi, and now Neko have faithfully warmed my lap and mashed the keys more than a few times. Nothing is as patient listening to you think through topics as a sleeping cat.

Most of all, my wonderful husband Chris has put up with me, through every one of these sentences (and helped me rethink many of them), and shared those long talks analyzing any number of technical issues. He was the one to suggest putting pen to paper so many years ago. I don't think he knew then what he started.

Thank you all!

Lydia Ash has built her career around practical knowledge of Web testing and test management. In recent years Ash has lead Web testing efforts at Microsoft within the Office and NetDocs divisions. The approaches and techniques that she brings to projects and teams address the needs those teams have to deliver high-quality software on-time and within budget. Ash has a background encompassing many different environments both from a testing and QA perspective and many platforms (including Unix variants, Macintosh, Windows platforms, and Web companion devices). She has implemented several methodologies and used many different languages and technologies. Prior to moving into software testing, Ash held several positions including project management and HTML programmer. Ash holds a Bachelor of Science, is a Microsoft Certified Professional, and a Six Sigma Green Belt. She is also a member of the Association for Computing Machinery and a member of her local chapter of the Quality Assurance Institute.

Guide: *noun*		One who shows the way by leading, directing, or advising
Scout: *noun*		One sent to obtain information
Sherpa: *noun*		A member of a Tibetan people living on the high southern slopes of the Himalayas in eastern Nepal who provide support for foreign trekkers and mountain climbers

Merriam-Webster's Dictionary

Every team has guides, whether it's a software development team or test team or any other sort of group of people working towards a common goal. Some are the managers, but most are just individual contributors who have learned from experience and hard work. Some of these guides are scouts out in front of the rest of the trekkers, investigating tracks and trails and watching for signals, working hard to interpret them properly. These are the guides of the team who will become the sherpas—experts in their area of work who are able, at a glance, to understand the pitfalls and perils involved with various decisions. The sherpas have traveled the paths so many times in so many various conditions that they can guide others through the terrain successfully with the confidence that comes from experience. Both of these types of guides are necessary in organizations; the sherpas are more valuable to the team in the short term, but the scouts are learning fast and will be the sherpas on the next trip.

However, some teams new to the Web and developing Web applications may not have any members who have traveled that road. Many individuals may want to become the scouts, or even sherpas, and are seeking a guide to help point the way. So many times we forget that others may not have the experience that we have. Other times we overestimate our own experience and refuse to request a map.

This book is a guidebook of the terrain of Web testing. It is intended to help identify some good paths and some bad ones to help teams make more successful trips. It does not teach you everything you need to know, but is one tool and will hopefully lead you to more. No craft relies on a single tool, and neither should software testing. A list of other books, articles, and resources is provided at the end of the book in the hope that they will be used when they apply to your project.

Use this book as a guide. Take the parts that work for your team. And enjoy the trip.

I will offer to instruct no man against his will, nor go
about to deserve well of such as understands me not.
—Symon Latham

Why Did I Write This Book?

I have hired full-time and contract software testers, some with testing experience and some without, some with prior development experience and some without. What I have learned is that those factors only loosely correlate with success on the job. What has shown to be a larger factor in success in a project has been the individual's dedication to the profession; interest in the product; ability to learn on the job, retaining the knowledge that is given to him; and a genuine passion to perform. Many times I wished that I could just give new employees a book that would provide a framework from which they can start their work—a basic building block on which many Web testing efforts can build. I spent a lot of time keeping notes and writing just to organize my own thoughts on issues within this topic of Web application testing. At one point, I wrote some short papers on several of those issues and had a great response to them. These papers explained some fundamentals of Web testing, but they weren't enough. What I needed was a more comprehensive compilation of everything—techniques, guidelines, pitfalls, and other specifics of Web testing. This book came about as a response for my own needs for a resource manual. The basic approach of the book is to give testing teams a foundation from which to start planning or testing, or to provide material from which you will be able to start employee training. There are two outstanding features that work together for these goals. The first is that this book starts at the ground level and really explains how to dissect problems and what a tester needs to understand in order to be effective. The second, and possibly the more important, is the raw data in the appendices. The book is an explanation of how and where to use particular techniques; the raw data is provided as what needs to be plugged into these techniques. Even if pieces go out of date, the concepts will still carry over to the newer data. This book comes from the practical experience of testing Web applications and managing Web application test efforts.

Testing is still widely performed as a black art or a craft. It has always had a small constituency that has believed in the standards, certifications, education, and professionalism of the job, like that in any other field. However, it is still ignored and underappreciated as a contributor to software development. Why is this? Businesses en masse do not clamor for testing professionals yet, and our academic institutions do not train them. Very few computer science curricula make even a mention of testing, yet even those working in development spend a considerable amount of their time in this activity. What all this means is that testers are more than likely not those seeking to be testers by design, but rather those who have applied and gotten their foot in the door of a company while seeking other roles in software development—project management, development, and so on—or those who have failed at other roles in software development and settled for being a second-rate tester. Accordingly, this type of person usually is not focused on the true profession, but rather on just muddling his way through and picking up a check. Still, there are the rare individuals who have stumbled into or were drawn to the field and have worked hard to earn the respect of their peers, as well as to educate themselves on their newly chosen profession. Testing doesn't need to be a steppingstone merely to jump into and out of as quickly as possible. Testing, as a profession, isn't a hidden path, and it is available to anyone willing to take it. I want to see some of that knowledge that germinates in a tester stay in testing longer instead of leaping into another area as soon as a minimal bar is reached.

Who Is This Book For?

This book has two audiences, which may appear contradictory.

- The beginning of this book, and of each chapter, is for the novice tester. It explains how things work, what your role is, why things are the way they are, and gives some suggestions on successful approaches.

- The second part of this book delves into deeper issues of performance, and security, and toward the back of the book are appendices full of raw data that provide a goldmine of test cases.

An experienced tester (or anyone experienced in software development) will pick up this book and likely flip to the middle sections, skimming the text to fill in possible holes in their knowledge. Ultimately they will glean test cases from the appendices as they will immediately see how certain ones can be used. The novice will read cover to cover and then see better how to use the various tools, techniques, and test cases discussed.

How Is This Book Organized?

This book is organized in five parts:

Part I: Becoming a Tester.   This part discusses what a tester does on a daily basis and throughout a product cycle. This also walks you through some basic Web technologies and concepts to build a foundation for later discussions.

Part II: Client-Side Testing.   In the second part of the book, I take up the topic of how to go about testing from the perspective of the client, or the browser, accessing the Web application. This includes such topics as HTML, accessibility, localization, and design.

Part III: Server-Side Testing.   Following Part II, I turn to its complementary side to discuss issues that tend to be grouped as server-side issues. These include performance testing and security.

Part IV: Being a Tester.   Part IV concerns itself with larger issues and how you carry out your job. It is not enough to be technical or correct; to do your job in a way that will please you is to do it well.

Part V: Testing Reference Appendices.   Finally, this part of the book is the part that all the rest tries to explain. The rest of the book is a discussion of how to go about testing and why. These are some of the specific cases you will want to use on your own application.

What Will You Get Out of This Book?

My hope for this book isn't that it is a definitive work. Rather this project is aimed at you, the individual, to help you improve your effectiveness. "Work smarter, not harder" may be a cliché, but it does apply. There is no reason for new Web test teams to have to rediscover what is already widely known among those experienced in the field. Just finding one bug from the pointers in this book will easily pay for the cost of the book to the organization. This book then is an attempt at putting some of that experience and knowledge on paper for these teams to use to help them create better, more stable software.

Testing is not strictly an art. Art is unique, original, and not reproducible. Testing is not strictly a science. What works for one group may not work for another, and there is no one formula. It is more of a craft with valid experience and knowledge that gets passed on, even while lacking a truly applicable recipe for every situation. This book will not try to be any sort of formula, but a collection of good tips, experiences, anecdotes, and information that I don't think need to be rediscovered each time anew. There are no magic bullets or tricks, but there are sets of good techniques and approaches that can be passed along. These techniques lower the barrier to identifying the issues that make software of lower quality than it should be. There's no reason for software to ship with commonly known problems. My hope is that the savvy organization will pick up this book and use the information to improve their testing process. I would hope that the managers of any of these organizations would take their new employees aside and hand them this book with their recommendations. There is plenty of room in software testing for more such books and publications of best practices. My hope is that this is another reference to be added to the professional tester's bookshelf, another tool that is useful to you in your projects.

I hope thou meanest to be a learner too, else thou wilt not read much of me.
—Symon Latham

PART ONE

Becoming a Tester

CHAPTER 1

Getting Started with Testing

The journey of 1000 miles begins with a single step.

Though the process of testing is a vital piece in the development of an application, the actual job of being a tester is subject to a great deal of misunderstanding and misinformation. As a person who has been a tester, trained testers, and led teams of testers in large and small projects, I am consistently peppered with questions concerning what is involved in what I do and how it fits in with a software development effort.

- Who are testers?
- Why is testing done?
- What exactly is done?
- What role does the tester play in the overall application development process?
- What differentiates a good tester from a bad one?

The list of questions goes on and on. This whole book comprises the answers to many of these questions, but in this first chapter I want to specifically answer some of the initial questions commonly asked about testing, including who does the testing, what work must happen, and why it's so important.

Quick Overview of Testing

It makes sense to start with a few basic, foundational questions to define a few key terms and clarify some key concepts.

What Is Testing?

Testing can be defined as the operation of an application under controlled conditions in order to evaluate its quality.

What Is Quality?

For testing purposes, *quality* is commonly defined as the benefits of a product (features) minus the problems in it (bugs) *as determined by the customer*. After all, it is the customer who has the final say and either approves of the software by buying it or disapproves of it by selecting a competing product. Since that is too late in the product cycle to identify customer needs and meet them, the test organization must ensure that the product meets the specifications throughout the development process. The product must behave as the customer would expect it to behave. The project managers or business analysts are on the one side of the development effort working directly with the customer to understand the desires, and the tester and the test organization are on the other side working towards the goal of meeting the user's desires. These two groups meet in the middle by refining the organization's understanding of the customer's expectations and the ability of the product to meet these expectations.

Why Is Testing Important?

Testing the software thoroughly early in the product cycle makes software production cheaper in the long run. Bugs can be found at any time in the cycle, from as early as discussions about the potential architecture to as late as a customer calling the support desk regarding a problem that he has encountered. As the cycle progresses it becomes more and more costly to fix the bugs. It is far cheaper and easier to fix a sentence in a proposal document than to change code that many developers have spent weeks working on.

What Does a Tester Do?

The whole point of a tester or a test organization is to find problems and to bring them the appropriate amount of attention. The key phrase in that last sentence is *the appropriate amount of attention*. Some sources define the role of a tester as finding problems and getting them fixed, but this definition ignores the very real situation that you cannot and should not necessarily fix every bug that is found, and that not all bugs will be found. Some bugs are not due to your software, but rather to problems in other pieces of software. Some are just not important enough to fix. You could spend a lifetime testing a single product and still not find all the bugs, let alone get them fixed. The reality of software is that it must ship, and it will ship with some bugs in it. Testers need to make sure that these are very low-impact bugs.

Who Are Testers?

Positions in testing or QA organizations go by a lot of different names: software test engineer, test engineer, tester, software tester, software verifier, build manager, build engineer, configuration manager, release manager, QA analyst, QA engineer, software analyst, and more. Each of these carries with it a certain amount of subtle information about what the particular position is responsible for and how it fits into that company's software development model.

What Is the Difference between QA and Test?

There are two basic breakdowns for the profession: Quality Assurance (QA) and Test.

- **Quality Assurance (QA).** QA tends to be focused on measuring and examining quality and improving the software through process improvements, thereby guiding the release to customers. Although testing activities usually do take place in this organization, the main focus of QA is on the processes and procedures of how software development activities take place. QA is more focused on managing the product life cycle and verifying that the software meets the defined quality standards or customer agreements. QA is less about breaking the software and finding problems than about verifying that it is possible to make the software work under a given set of conditions.

WARNING
QA organizations can get sidetracked by continually making and revising policies. Policies should be written to further the end goal of shipping better software. There needs to be an examination of how people currently go about this task of creating software, but the analysis part of the job can take up much of the team's time if it is allowed to. Like a gas, it can expand to fill the given space. Good management should be aware of this and place the appropriate constraints and expectations on process evaluation and refinement activities.

- **Test.** Testing, on the other hand, may keep an eye on the processes and often owns them, but is far more concerned with finding ways to break the software. Testers are to observe what the software does and to report on the level of quality as well as any serious issues they encounter. Testers must operate under the assumption that there are more bugs out there, and they have to find them. They operate in such a way that they expect to find problems, not just to verify that it is possible for everything to work fine. A good tester is one who is constantly thinking of things that have not been tried and is expected to exercise parts of the software that may be weak or that may not interact well. The whole point of this very critical look at software is to find bugs as fast as possible and get the right ones fixed. There will always be more bugs, but without knowing what they are, a conscious decision cannot be made regarding the software's ability to meet the customer's demands.

Test organizations can become flooded with bad software and drown in bugs if they are not going about their side of the process correctly. This will happen when a test organization becomes too reactive, only catching bugs instead of proactively preventing them. Individual testers may be required, above all else, to find more bugs. However, this focus on increasing the number of bugs instead of increasing the quality of the software can lead to the demise of many organizations. A system that encourages subversion of the ultimate goal—making a software product that fulfills the customer's needs—is not one to adopt. In a problematic system, testers are encouraged to find bugs after the bug has become part of the code base—when it is easy to quantify, and yet more expensive to correct than if it had been caught at an earlier stage. The problem with systems that reward individuals for meeting an intermediary goal is that people will achieve that goal instead of the ultimate goal. The ultimate goal of any software development effort is to ship a high-quality product within a certain period of time and within a certain budget. Tasking individuals to find vast numbers of bugs may appear to be making progress towards the goal of making high-quality software, but that is not necessarily true. It is actually encouraging people to find problems in the software at a very late stage and to concentrate on finding symptoms instead of finding the core source of many symptoms. Although many testers would never take advantage of a poorly constructed system, it still should not be set up in this way because it is not rewarding people for doing what management really wants. Failing to do that will eventually lead to an organization that has lost key members who saw past the reward system, leaving behind an organization that plays to management's set of rewards.

Test organizations that are not effectively communicating with the rest of the software team (development and project managers) will not be aware of proposed changes and will not be able to step in early in the process to prevent problems, which allows a torrential flood of bugs to come back to testers late in the cycle and can end up costing the company time and money. Testing needs to evaluate processes as well as break the software.

What Makes a Good Tester?

A good tester performs the following key functions:

- **Verification.** A good tester can certify that it is possible to accomplish certain tasks.
- **Detection.** A good tester looks for problems that exist, either in the process or the product.

NOTE The tasks of verification and detection are two sides of the same coin. Both exist together, but the ratios of each vary from organization to organization, company to company, and position to position, often changing through the software cycle as well.

- **Prevention.** A good tester identifies potential problems before they manifest themselves.
- **Reflection.** A good tester looks back at how problems and bugs ended up in the product and analyzes this information to learn how to improve the process in the future.

To perform these functions effectively, testers must understand the general technologies used in their product and the product's particular implementation of them. The tester must also have the mindset to break things and ask the questions that will let him learn more.

It makes sense then that one of the key qualities of a good tester is the ability to ask questions—the right questions. Some people let the old saying, "If you have to ask, then you don't understand," prevent them from moving forward. Asking good questions is the best way to learn, though. There truly are no stupid questions, although there are questions asked of inappropriate resources. Identify the right resource to take various types of questions to. One reason why you find so many questions posed and answered in this book is to instill in your mind the habit of creating these questions and then searching out the answers. The best testers are constantly asking questions of the software—interviewing it and interrogating it. Once testers learn this skill they rapidly excel in their profession and exponentially grow their knowledge of the code they are working on. The approach is a Socratic method of learning and helps to teach you how to teach yourself.

Another vitally important, and sometimes forgotten, characteristic of a good tester is tact. Testers see the unfinished side of the company, even the ugly underbelly sometimes. They also directly see where bugs come from and who caused them—architects, developers, designers, or management. A good tester understands that the rest of the company often views their organization as a necessary evil at best (and an unnecessary evil at worst).

Consider the product development situation for a moment. Product and program managers work to correctly identify features and behaviors that have come from customer interviews and studies. Developers labor long hours to make the software, everything from the high level of the user interface down to the complex algorithms that dictate behavior. They need to identify potential error conditions and then handle them properly. Developers build a product very carefully; they put their knowledge and experience and effort into it. Then, this component, which so many have labored to produce, still in its infancy, gets handed over to the testing organization. Test is to pick up that baby and commence with telling the developer exactly how ugly that baby is and how deformed it is. That is a tester's job. No component is perfect; if it were there would be no need for a testing organization. However, the way in which these issues are identified has a great effect on how you, as a tester, are viewed. This, in turn, affects the relationship you have with the other parts of the organization.

Practically, what this means for the individual testers is that they must hold themselves to a high standard of behavior. No finger pointing at the ugly babies! No laughing at the ones you find odd! There is a substantial difference between saying, "My God, Joe! How the hell do you manage to dress yourself in the morning? This code looks like something my cat coughed up," and saying, "The recent billing features that were added are unstable under basic user scenarios. I would like to go back and have the feature implementation reviewed before we continue testing." In the second example, the fault is where it should be—in the code. There is no need to question Joe's abilities. The development manager or the testing manager has the job of tracking down where the bugs come from. Your job is to identify what needs to be fixed, and the easiest way to do that is to not set up an adversarial relationship with those who depend on you.

Here's a real-world example of what I mean. Many projects use a process requiring all bug fixes to be built in isolation and certified by testers before any changes can be checked into the main build tree. In one instance, a developer put five bug fixes together and handed it to one of the testers. The tester found some immediate problems and sent out five emails to the group within 6 minutes, one for each problem with each bug fixed. Such an approach does not encourage a developer to work closely with a tester. In this situation, the tester could have communicated the same information by putting all the issues into one mailing and addressing all the issues at once, instead of pointing at the developer repeatedly in front of the organization.

Your role is to ensure a high-quality, stable product. A good tester makes any developer they work with look good. And a good developer realizes this and values the tester that finds the problems in the code by working cooperatively to identify further issues. Another real-world example illustrates my point. On one team I worked with, testers who found lots of problems would hold up developers from checking in their code to the main build tree. One day, in a discussion about these holdups, I apologized for holding up one particular developer's check-in once again. Very firmly the developer told me no apology was necessary and that what I was doing was exactly what he wanted. He knew that having his code thoroughly tested up front meant that he would probably never have to revisit it. He would not have to worry about a bug being discovered in his code at the very end of the cycle when it would be most visible to management. In that short discussion, I learned that the developers on that team had divided the testing organization into two groups in their own minds—testers who would thoroughly check everything prior to giving the green light, and testers who the developers knew needed to be double-checked. He was one of the appreciative developers who knew how to use Test to his advantage—and he never forgot to thank the testers, even when it was in the late hours that fixes were given our approval. He was also one of the most demanding developers, insisting that testers understand the application they were testing and the technologies involved. Many testers make the mistake of avoiding developers at all costs. This cuts out important pieces of communication: Communicate with the developers and the program managers. Such communication makes you more effective and makes your job easier.

NOTE Remember the whole point of Test—to find the problems as fast as possible and get the right ones fixed.

Who Are All These People?

There are a lot of roles in a software project, and though the names change, inevitably somebody performs these tasks. In a very small organization, such as a one-person development company, all of these roles will be played by a single person. That person designs, develops, and tests his own code as well as markets and sells it. In other organizations, the work may be combined or split between different people, depending on the company and the particular talents of each person involved. In a larger and more formal environment, the organization may consist of hundreds of people. All of the following functions must be filled in any software development effort, large or small.

- **Visioning/management.** There may be a head manager called a product manager, unit manager, division manager, general manager, vice president, or even the president of the company if it is small. But whatever that person is called, somehow all hierarchy leads to that person. That person's role is to understand the marketplace, guide the vision, procure funding, and in part act as a cheerleader and mascot for the team.

- **Planning.** Under this head manager, other levels of management may exist, but some group is responsible for planning. These planners may be called business analysts, project managers, program managers, or some similar moniker. The Sales and Marketing groups might also play a role here. Their combined responsibility is to design specifications on how the software will work, track the schedules of how the project is progressing, communicate with various internal teams as well as current customers, and talk with potential customers to understand how they would like the software to work.

TIP

Seasoned testers will likely groan loudly when I mention specifications because such specifications are usually difficult to get and often appear after the software has been written, serving more as a document of what the software turned out to be rather than documenting the work laid out in front of the team. Development and Test need to stand firm in their requirement to receive specifications and details of the product's behavior prior to the start of coding and testing. Without firm plans of what work needs to be done, how can management identify target dates? How can development know how long the work will take? Test certainly cannot identify how long testing will take without these plans. Management needs to back up their groups to insist that these plans be in good shape prior to scheduling, costing, or work begins. Investigations and discussions can take place, but that is as much as can be expected without firm specifications.

- **Development.** There must be a development organization; after all, there would be no product without them. A development manager or director of software engineering may head up several development leads, each with a team of individual developers or software engineers. This group is obviously responsible for the investigation of the proposed design ideas and the implementations to get to the final product functionality. Developers own the implementation details, and those details should not be dictated in the product specifications. Ideally, specifications detail to the developers what the product does, and developers document from there how it will accomplish those goals. Developers are also responsible for fixing bugs.

TIP
During the process of development, the development organization may also write tools for themselves or for the test group. Some developers are reluctant to share these tools because they do not want to become the support person responsible for each issue somebody identifies with the tool or utility. However, Test can step up and take ownership for the maintenance and support of the tool, thereby giving the developer the credit for identifying a useful tool, creating it, and giving the benefit of a new useful tool to the test team. Such a procedure works out for both organizations. Development is released from the burden of having to maintain the tool, and Test gets the benefit of tools tuned precisely to the product being tested without the hassle of writing the specifications out or having to take the time and write it themselves.

■ **Testing/QA.** Last, there are testers and/or QA. We already discussed some of Test's responsibilities and the general role of the individual tester. The reporting structure may be through any number of organizations, but ideally they would report separately from development and project managers to avoid conflicts of interest. Having a testing or QA organization with as much power as your developers or project managers provides a system of checks and balances.

Some companies have Test reporting to a project manager or development manager, but such an arrangement gives one prong of the organization more control over the product than the others. Project managers want to get on to the next project; as soon as their role in the current project is over, they have usually already begun planning the next one, even if the development group is still writing the code for the last one. Project managers want to ship the product so that the developers can get started on all the neat new stuff they have planned. Fixing the bugs or identifying more will just take more time and push out the ship date. Developers wrote the code. They lived, ate, and breathed that code. They are ready to move on to something new. And, besides, it works on their machine. Test is the only organization that actively holds the product back from being shipped and making money. Setting up a test or QA organization that reports to anywhere except the top level in the hierarchy is setting up an organization to be ineffective. It is possible to have a QA or test organization work in that reporting circumstance, but not likely, and only with the right people in those positions.

What Do You Need from Them?

Once you identify the roles involved in a software project, it becomes important to understand what you need from each of those roles to do your job as a tester most effectively. The next sections examine the expectations you should have of those working with you on a project.

What Do You Need from the Project Management Team?

You need to understand what the product is. The business analysts (or who-ever fulfills that role) are responsible for defining and altering the project, goals, targets, and design.

NOTE Remember that ideally the actual implementation details should not come from this group, but should be left up to the development organization.

The project management team will help you understand the target audience (corporate users? children? senior citizens? technojunkies?) and how the product will be used. Such information, in turn, helps you accurately identify the potential issues to test for and helps you make decisions about which issues should be fixed. The project manager works with all the teams to identify a schedule, but ultimately he usually maintains the documents that describe who will be doing what and when. Test will need to be kept updated on that.

What Do You Need from Developers?

Above all else, Test needs good communication from Development. You need to get some pieces of information from the developers about the actual implementation and about the status of various parts of the project:

- Talk with Development to understand how the components with which you are involved work on the inside. Understand where the "joints" of the product are—where do two components come together? Or where do two developers have their code interface? These "joints," in their interfacing, are where you will likely find problems.

- You need to communicate with developers to have an understanding of code changes. When the code gets changed, Test should be notified of the changes, why they were made, how they were made, what bugs these changes will fix, and what features may not be fully implemented.

TIP Many organizations have a process of sending out a Fix Impact Statement, Check-in Mail, or a Daily Build Release mailing. A sample format for this can be found in Appendix I.

- Test should also expect Development to provide a schedule of work for feature implementation and code changes, and to be notified when that schedule changes.

- Developers also need to communicate with Test on the status of bug fixes. This does not mean that the tester sits in his office surfing the Web until the developer stops by, nor does it mean the tester pops into the developer's office every few hours. There needs to be an open interchange of information between the two parties without one holding up or interrupting the other.

What Do You Need from Management?

Management, whether it is the overall company management or your direct test management, needs to listen to testers and support the testing effort. Many testing organizations have entered the downward spiral of bad relationships or ineffectiveness in the eyes of management. They have been kept around for window dressing so the company can claim a testing effort, but are largely ignored. The test management needs to make sure that it is still an effective organization in the overall company. They should also be clearly tasking the individual testers with achievable and measurable goals and tasks. A reasonable schedule should be a part of helping the individuals prioritize their work and manage each activity they are handed.

What Do You Need from Other Testers?

You should expect the same amount of cooperation from other testers as you give to them. Because of the time crunch that many are under, people are busy and may not have the time to walk you through each point of your job or the product. There is a right way and a wrong way to ask for help, as well as a time to go off and research by yourself. You can expect project-specific information from others on your team—how certain pieces of the product function, where known bugs may be found, where test cases are logged for your team, which other individuals can provide information, what tools will help your test efforts. However, you cannot expect people to drop everything they are doing each time you appear in their doorway. When you do ask for information from them, be clear in what you are looking for or need from that person. Nobody can answer a question that you cannot formulate. If you do not understand the question that you are asking, probably the person that you intend to have answer it does not understand it either. Do your research before asking questions. It will make you look more knowledgeable and help you better understand the answers you receive. If you do not understand the answers, be sure to follow up with more questions. Unless you let your peers know that you do not understand the answer, they can only assume that you do.

What Do They Need from You?

Just as you need others to give you information that helps you do your job, the others involved in a software development project need information from you, the tester.

What Does the Project Management Team Need from You?

Project managers are usually about two steps ahead of Test, and Development is usually one step ahead of Test. Being out ahead, they may not always see what is happening in the here and now. If a slew of serious bugs are discovered or a pattern of security problems is identified, Project Management needs to be involved to solve it and prevent it from happening again. Because much of the schedule is set by this team, scheduling concerns need to be addressed with them.

What Do the Developers Need from You?

Developers need to know the problems that you are finding. If you spend a day focusing on one particular component, or using one particular technique all across the product and turn up several bugs through this, let the developers responsible know. They may not have thought of that before. If you find very serious bugs, let the developers know. The last thing you need is for somebody to come storming into your office wondering why you did not mention that the product crashed when you logged in. The last thing the developers want is to be sideswiped continuously because the testers are not alerting them when important problems are found. Let the developers know what will be tested and when it will be tested. Developers respect a level of communication and will work that line of communication back to you. Communicating a schedule to the developer allows them to plan their time for bug fixes and feature implementation. Let the developers know the test cycle status. If you find a serious bug that they should be aware of, send the owner of that component, feature, or area an email to make him aware of it. If there is a three-alarm-fire bug, you might want to drop by the developer's office to make sure that he can get as much information about it as possible. Above all, communicate with the developers. Don't assume that they dislike you or have no respect for you; some of the best developers I have known were testers at one time and understand the thankless job that it can sometimes be. To them a good tester is very valuable.

TIP Many projects have a requirement that no code can be changed without a bug being associated with the changes. A developer may be stepping through the code and notice a bug that nobody has found a manifestation for. Many developers will give these bugs to a tester with whom they work closely, knowing that the bug numbers are important for the tester and not for the developer. This does allow the developer to avoid having to deal with entering a new bug and following it through the process, and thus frees his time, so there are benefits to both people. Without a good relationship, the developers might as well take care of it themselves. Enlightened self-interest alone is enough reason to build these good relationships.

What Do Managers Need from You?

Testers are really in the trenches day in and day out. As the new tester you will probably attend very few meetings, allowing you to become more intimately familiar with the software than some individuals above you. As an individual contributor, you can still have a large effect on the team's efforts. If you see that the team is spending too much time in the wrong places and is not being an effective organization, you need to address that topic with your management. Perhaps you have some concerns that management is not considering. Perhaps you have some good ideas on how to improve communication or the overall effectiveness of the organization. Share this with your direct management. These contributions are crucial to continuously improving the organization and are the feedback that management needs to hear, no matter how difficult it is to hear it.

Schedule problems are another thing to communicate with your manager. If you have been tasked with completing a test pass in 3 days, do not wait until 5 P.M. of the third day to tell your manager that you cannot make the deadline. Communicate concerns early. If you do not understand something or if something is unclear, you need to communicate that and ask questions. If you do not, your manager will have a set of expectations that you will not be able to meet. Set yourself up to be successful. One of the most honest statements that you can make to anyone is "I don't know," but what management wants to hear is "I don't know yet." If you do not know something, ask management about it, clarify it, and make sure you do come to an understanding with management on it.

What Do Other Testers Need from You?

Although you are a part of a testing team, you will probably spend at least as much time working closely with your development and project manager counterparts as with other testers. Because of the way that testing is broken up, along the lines of functionality, it is easy to become more involved with these members of other teams than with members of your own test team. Keeping up good communication with other testers can be something that is difficult to do, but it is essential. If a process is changed, the testers affected by this need to be alerted. Depending on how the organization is set up, individuals may or may not be rewarded for sharing information. Such arrangements are largely a managerial problem, but as a professional, you need to do the right thing and further the software and the maturity of the organization. Sharing tools, techniques, or product information is crucial to being a professional. Some individuals, in any line of work, hoard information to allow themselves to surpass their peers. Such hoarding may work in the short run, but it does not further your professionalism, the product, or the discipline of testing.

Good relations make for better communication. Knowing what to expect from others and what they are expecting from you helps teams to grow strong and helps each group, and the individuals that make them up, to work together in the best fashion possible.

What Is a Bug?

A *bug* is any unexpected behavior; the software does something and you do not think it is right. This can be anything from the layout of information or a wording of an error message to a crash of an application. A bug is what users would not like or what does not help users achieve their goals with the application. Some of these are:

- A condition in which the software is not handling an unexpected state or input gracefully.

- Any variation from a published standard. These standards are serious and must be followed precisely.

- A deviance from an internal specification produced by the project manager. There then needs to be a review to determine if the internal specification should be changed or the software should be changed. It is very possible that the detailed behavior in the specification is annoying or confusing. It is also possible that there is a disparity in the specification that needs to be addressed.

A Bug by Any Other Name . . .

These problems can also be referred to as *faults*, *failures*, or *defects*, but those terms imply a very serious condition. Referring to your particular problem as an *inconsistency* implies that it is insignificant and noticeable only to the aware user, insinuating it may not be worth fixing. A report of an *incident* usually means that a customer or another team came across the problem and found it bothersome enough to report. Calling these things a *problem*, an *error*, or just simply a *bug* is more generic and less aggressive, and carries far less associated baggage. Telling somebody that you found a defect in his code and mentioning that there was a bug in it are two different things, yet on a very subtle level. Just be aware of the meanings you convey when you use words because each has a precise meaning as well as an implication.

What Happens after Testing?

Once the product has emerged from the testing cycle and been declared fit for consumption, several things can happen, which are discussed in the following sections.

What Is Dogfooding?

Many development houses deploy the software internally in a practice called *dogfooding* or *eating your own dog food*. The idea is that you have created something not yet fit for consumption by external people, but fit only for a dog. You have to eat the dog food you created to know how good it tastes. If it tasted good at this point in the project, it probably would be called eating your own apple pie or something, so it is generally acknowledged that this process will not be a wholly pleasant experience. Dogfooding your own software has some points in its favor:

- It gives management the sense that progress is being made—the whole company is now using the software, so we must be getting somewhere with all this money spent.

- It can catch complex scenario problems—those that involve several domains, child domains, many complex topologies, and then complex actions performed together. If the process catches such problems, however, that is usually an indicator to Test that either they failed to see that scenario, or that they were not given the resources to set up, maintain, and test such real scenarios.

However, dogfooding also has many points against it:

- This practice usually happens too early.

- Many argue that this practice uncovers usability problems, ensures that bugs are found, and ensures that stability is at a known level. However, in most projects the people consuming the dog food do not represent the people who will be using it, so they are blind to the usability problems. If you are a developer or a tester and are having problems with the query interface for the database, you can usually sum up your knowledge and force that interface to do what you want because you know how it works. Likewise, you probably have no other choice and are being forced to use the product, unlike the consumer who will have a choice of several pieces of software that would meet their needs. I have watched forced dogfood-ings where people had to be cajoled or even threatened into using the product. If you have to force your own people to use it, there is probably a problem.

- Advocates of dogfooding also argue that more problems are found because of the process. However, if everyone does see the same error or has to go through the same painful process to get the desired outcome, then one of two things may happen—either everyone may assume that somebody else has already taken care of the error due to its obviousness, or everyone becomes numb to the pain and starts assuming that because they can work around issues like that, then the user will as well.

As is probably clear by now, I am not a big advocate of dogfooding because the loss of productivity is usually more expensive and demoralizing than the process is worth. If you are testing an email service and require everyone to use that system for company communications, but it is down half the time, then has it really saved anyone anything? Have you found problems that you did not find on your test beds? Probably not, and people were unable to com-municate and get their work done. This exact scenario is what happened to Time-Warner when they merged with AOL. The AOL email service was rolled out internally to the corporate environment and failed to meet the needs, resulting in lost mail, lost productivity, and, in some cases, internal strife when people were thought to not have communicated well with others. In this case, the AOL email system was shipping code rather than beta quality; however, it still illustrates my point of forcing tools to be used where they do not fit the sit-uation. The company was trying to use the product as it was not meant to be used and so they gained little and lost much from its use. It has since been removed from the corporate realm.

To Whom Does the Product Ship?

Many different terms exist for the process of shipping out the software product.

- **RTM (release to manufacturing).** RTM has been the most commonly used term. RTM originally meant that CDs called *golden masters* would be cre-ated and handed to a manufacturing department. Copies would then be burned and shipped to customers or other outlets. RTM is still used in the Web-ified software world, but other terms are used as well.

- **RTO (release to operations).** RTO usually means that the server-side operation is internally hosted and the software has been handed over to operations for deployment and consumer consumption.

- **RTI (release to the Internet).** RTI usually means the software or service is now available to users on the Internet; such availability can be internally hosted or hosted by another company specializing in providing these services.

- **RTW (release to the Web).** Usually means the same as release to the Internet—the product is now available to users for download from the Internet. The lag time between when the product is declared ready for RTW/RTI and when it reaches the customer is very short when compared with sending out a product to have CDs created and then taking orders to ship customers a CD.

- **RT?.** Many groups have their own specific terms for whom they ship to, either the name of a specific group or an internal delivery point. There's no need to conform to anybody else's terms as long as everybody involved with the project understands what the terms mean.

There can also be a process of *escrowing* or *hitting the gold master*. Usually these terms indicate a time when all development effort stops. Testing continues, beta testers continue to report on issues they encounter, and unless any priority 1 issues come in before a set date, then the software is declared to have shipped.

What Will You Be Doing in Your Job?

Your role as a tester includes a variety of activities. You will, at some point:

- Write test cases
- Manually perform tests
- Log bugs
- Perform test passes
- Communicate with various of levels of management
- Develop test plans for a component or a product
- Make decisions on whether something is a bug or a design constraint
- Research competition
- Schedule projects
- Allocate resources
- Make crucial decisions about the product
- Possibly automate testing or write tools for the team

Certainly when you enter into any organization, and especially as a green tester, you will not be making sweeping decisions. More likely you will start off running test cases written by others and doing a lot of learning. The value to the organization is twofold:

1. They have somebody who is not terribly valuable (yet) running the monkey test scripts that would waste the time of their more experienced and knowledgeable testers.
2. The work gets you familiar with the product and its workings.

Take advantage of this time. You may be bored, but do not complain; everyone else has had to do it, and the testers who will excel use this experience to their advantage. If you see a way to improve the process or the test cases, take it to your manager. You will be making them look better for having hired someone who works to improve the current state of the team. You will move up, but take advantage of this time to learn different parts of the process. Eventually, you will be assigned tasks such as reading designs and product specifications that can take up a large amount of time at various parts of the product cycle. This can be boring or it can be a good educational experience if you are alert. When you are that manager handing the new "greenie" the scripts to go through, you will be able to more effectively judge their performance, their aptitude, and explain their job to them.

Because your job starts at the ground level, that is where this book starts. Some testing manuals start with test case design, but rarely have I seen an organization that assigns the new person hired to immediately draw up the test plans and schedules for the testing activities. More likely somebody else has already done that, and they need you to go through the grind of performing the tests. Accordingly, the early chapters of this book start the testing discussions there, with understanding and performing the testing; then in later chapters of the book, we will shift the discussion toward the design of test cases and how you can more effectively test your software—a maximum effect from a minimum of effort.

The Theory of Software Testing

Contradictions do not exist. Whenever you think you are
facing a contradiction, check your premises. You will
find that one of them is wrong.

—Ayn Rand

All projects have a beginning and an end and many activities in between. Software products may start with crisply defined events and checkpoints, but more often they do not. Whether the events to transpire are explicitly called out in advance of the project's beginning or not, the same types of activities take place in one form or another.

Product Life Cycle

Where does software come from? Products start as ideas in someone's head. *You know what I need . . .* is how the idea usually begins, though occasionally the idea is more like *You know where we could really make some money . . . .* At this point organizations may take many different actions (based on such things as the size of the team assigned to the project and the scope of the project), but those actions fall into two basic approaches to the product's life cycle:

1. **Send the product designers or architects off to decide how things will work.** In the ideal development world, the ideas are written out on paper as product specifications (also called *specs*), detailing the core components that will be necessary, what each of those will be composed of, and their necessary functions. Development may do exploratory coding in the beginning to help shape the specifications and identify plans that really will work. Test, Development, Project Management, analysts, and others

read through these documents finding places where the framework is not adequately filled in or inconsistencies exist. Once a general architecture is agreed upon and thought through, Development begins creating the structure—the very basics of what needs to be there. For example, if the product were an online retailer, the database structure would need to be detailed as well as the methods for getting information out of it, searching for information, and so on. Once those specifications were stable, plans would be drawn up for what components would be put on top of the basics to extend the product. Would people want to create accounts and be automatically recognized each time they visited the site or just enter their address and information when purchasing items? Would people be able to put items on layaway or order items in advance? Components would be decided upon and filled in one by one, allowing the core functions to remain basically unchanged and stable for the longest period of time. This type of development process employs some clean room techniques by sketching out the plan before the code is written. This first model allows a predictable project to be undertaken. It allows Test to be involved during the spec reviews, the development in code reviews, and more.

NOTE

"Clean room" is an approach to software engineering borrowed from the materials-engineering industries. Among other practices, it sets requirements that designs be written and fully detailed prior to development and that there are to be full documentation of diversions from the plans.

2. **Send a group of developers off to start coding the product.** Unfortunately, this second approach is what usually happens. Typically after the thought *You know what I could really use . . .* occurs, somebody turns to the computer and starts coding up a prototype. That person tells a friend or manager who would join in this adventure. Others join in, and management sees the value of continuing an already started project. Test may be told about it and have resources allocated to it, an architect might get involved, but it would be too late to do anything except a slight rerouting of the plumbing to retrofit some necessary components. The end result of this type of a project is usually a product with several architecture issues, such as security or performance problems, and it usually requires a complete rewrite for the next version.

Whichever way the product starts, it needs to be defined to go any further.

Product Specifications

What does the customer expect? Whether you are working with an interactive application or a static Web site, the customers' expectations need to match the product specifications/definition.

Building Product Specifications

Good product specifications for Web applications will need to cover many different areas in order to ensure that the entire application fits together in the best possible way. There are server-side considerations, client-side technical considerations, and considerations of users' preferences as well as their needs. Some of these considerations are detailed as follows:

- **Design and usability requirements.** Online services need to have a simple design. Losing customers because they cannot figure out how to give their money to you is not a good business plan. Sacrifice trendy for usable. If your service is easily consumed by your target audience, then it increases the probability that it will be successful. Ensuring that the stability and performance requirements are detailed in the design specifications and that the maintainability is considered from the beginning ensures that it will be easier to move from version 1 to version 2.

- **Performance and scalability issues.** Making your service perform well and scale ensures that you can attract and keep the large audience that your company wants. Both performance and scalability need to be clearly communicated in the product's definition.

- **Audience identification.** Is this product for entertainment, for commerce, or purely informational? What are the three key product features? These need to be defined by the customers' values through market research and competitive analysis.

- **Revision information.** How frequently will the site change? How frequently will there be product updates? The key concept is that a Web application is not a shrinkwrapped software package. Freshness counts on the Web, but so does consistency, stability, and quality. If your company has control over the servers, you can roll out product or content versions, updates, and bug fixes on a much faster schedule than if you were producing shrinkwrapped software.

  For example, I have a free email account with an online provider, which is fantastic most of the time. Every so often updates are made to the product, and a function changes or a piece of the UI changes. Inevitably the update is noticeable, and not in a good way. For several days after one such update if I selected items to move into the Trash folder, they would be immediately purged without a chance to recover them. Another time, all of the spaces in the subjects of incoming emails were removed. I lived for weeks with runtime errors popping up every time I logged in. Another time, cookie issues caused the first login attempt to fail, but the second attempt would succeed when I provided the exact same username and password. Further, reporting the errors and identifying the faulty lines of script causing them proved difficult in that there was no way to simply send an error report for a very long time. Errors like these might have been avoided if Test had clear schedules for when updates needed to be stable or had authority to prevent unstable updates from rolling out. The email provider was making attempts at keeping their product fresh but not making Test an integral part of their update process, which likely ended up causing much user frustration.

Specifications need to detail all of this. Development and Test have an opportunity to stand firm together and insist that such specifications be in place before diving into the project. Test and Development have an opportunity to work together, reviewing product details, putting them together prior to coding, and testing the plans. Early collaboration finds many architecture problems, and fixing them educates everybody involved on what architecture is put in place, as well as the reasons behind it. Further, it's helpful if management backs up their team's needs and doesn't let the specification writers ignore their responsibility to the larger effort. Test, Development, and management all have an obligation to be involved through the development of these product definitions.

Testing the Specifications

A bug can be found at any stage in the development process, or can be found later by external beta testers, or by an unfortunate customer after the release. These latter stages are where it gets expensive to make changes, where shipping dates slip, and where the company can lose customers as well as money. That situation is exactly what the second product life-cycle model, discussed earlier in this chapter (where coding begins before any planning takes place) forces a company into. A well-planned development cycle with a fully thought-out architecture allows the company to make software cheaper. It might not feel that way, but decades of studies have shown this to be true.

Having a plan means that you have the luxury of determining the best possible point when certain bugs should be fixed. Finding 100 bugs a year before the product is supposed to be released is not a problem. The work that must be done in order to address the problems can be scheduled in with other work that needs to take place. Finding 100 bugs the day after shipping the product means a very high cost will be incurred to fix them. Not only will they likely be scattered throughout the code, necessitating that many areas be touched, but the changes will need to be redeployed either to the servers hosting them, downloaded to the customers, or even new CDs burnt and shipped to customers. The cost of supporting customers and fielding their calls when they identify the problems prior to fixes being in place only adds to the cost of late bugs.

Looking through the specifications and identifying the areas of risk are ways to improve the overall quality of the product. One of the most recent studies performed by the U.S. Department of Commerce showed that software bugs cost the U.S. economy alone an estimated $59.5 billion a year. Improvements in testing can reduce this cost by a third. Considering that the study went on to show that more than a third of the $59.5 billion was cost-incurred by the development effort or the vendors, a more firm testing effort would reduce that significantly.

CROSS-REFERENCE

You can read the U.S. Department of Commerce study in its entirety online at http://www.nist.gov/director/prog-ofc/report02-3.pdf.

Risk Analysis

Risk analysis is the process of identifying those code paths and functions that are critical to the success of the product as well as those that have the highest potential for failure. It may be a task that business analysts head, that Project Management runs, or that Test takes charge of. The features that are most critical to the success of the product are the ones that must work flawlessly and that should receive more attention from the testing team. These features are the ones that user scenarios, from the high-level product plans and the test plans, should cover and that rank high in the test priorities. For example, an online store has the primary functions of selling items, taking credit card numbers, providing help, and more. If a primary function does not work properly, then the application or business as a whole is not successful. That is why identification of test priorities is such a key issue.

NOTE

It may well be that the code paths that present the highest probability of failure are some of the least-used code paths, but have the potential for causing the most problems to the primary functions of the software. Overall security can also be a piece of the risk analysis inasmuch as the consideration may not be only specific features or code paths, but also the overall application. If the application is an online quotation site where users can create private lists of their favorite quotes, the general interest that it holds to a malicious user is relatively low. If, on the other hand, this application is an online business accepting credit cards, you have some very important data of high interest to malicious users. While overall interest to malicious users does not relate to specific code paths in the application, it does add weight to the security concerns of the overall product and specific areas of the product.

Once the product specifications have been approved by both the development team and the test team, real work on the code can move forward. Investigative coding has been done to help properly guide the designs and specifications. While the developers start coding beyond the initial investigations, they also document their implementation as they go along.

Test should be involved in the meetings related to this process, taking notes on test scenarios and test cases. Test plans need to be written up, defining features to be tested, scenarios to be tested, and areas that will not receive as much attention. As the development team gets functions into working order, Test becomes more involved in a hands-on testing of the written code. Figure 2.1 shows a general flowchart of the product life cycle of a Web application as we have discussed it so far. Note that the activities are very interactive, with Development handing code to Test, and Test working with project managers and developers to identify the right bugs to be fixed.

Milestones

This cycle shown in Figure 2.1 may be repeated several times before the product has all the features implemented for release to the public. Each iteration through the cycle has goals and criteria, which are usually labeled as *milestones*. As each milestone comes to a close, the product must meet the exit criteria in order to enter into the next phase:

- Milestone 0 is usually the term given to the beginning of the project where work begins.

- Milestone 1 may be set aside for getting the core functionality working and may have little or no UI work involved.

- A later milestone may be reserved for working on the integration of the user interface and the back-end server code to ensure that it all hooks up properly.

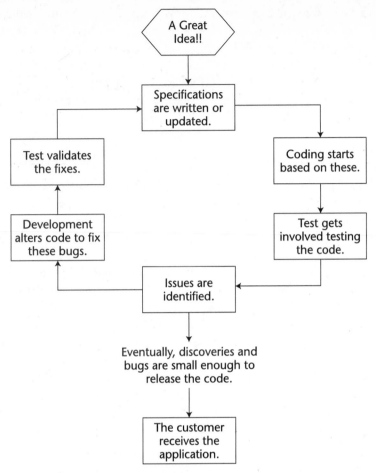

Figure 2.1 General product cycle.

Each milestone needs to be clearly defined with the work laid out, a schedule planned, and criteria examined before work begins. At the end of this milestone, all the features added, as well as ones that existed prior to the milestone, will be tested. Milestones can be measured in weeks or months, and always involve new code, new functionality, and a thorough evaluation by Test. Within each milestone, processes may be put in place to ensure that quality is a part of everyone's work.

Also, just as the product specifications are reviewed by various groups, the test plans should be reviewed by the spec writers and the developers to make sure that there are no gaping holes in the plans for testing. These groups can also help identify some of the high-risk areas and save the test team a lot of time. In addition, code reviews may be put in place as features are written or bugs are fixed so that all new code is reviewed by at least one other developer, and possibly a tester, prior to check-in. In 1962, the Mariner I Venus probe went severely off course, requiring NASA to blow it up. The problem was traced to a single line of FORTRAN code that was missing a hyphen. The mistake cost the agency $80 million, and Arthur C. Clarke called it "the most expensive hyphen in history." This problem is the type of a bug that a code review is designed to catch. No tool or process finds every bug, but it makes sense to use those tools and processes that have been found to be most effective.

Test Cycles

Test has its own cycle that it goes through outside of the milestones. As a new feature is integrated into the code, code tends to break. There is a 30 percent chance that a one-line fix will cause a bug or not fix the bug it was intended to fix. As a general rule in most software efforts, an entire new feature will be bug-ridden for the most part, if not broken altogether. Because of the risk of one of these bugs blocking the rest of testing down that code path, the initial bugs, though low in number, are likely high in severity. Towards the middle of a feature implementation, or a milestone, the bug numbers go up and severity of the bugs varies widely—high- and low-severity bugs are identified. Once the feature has been in testing for a while or the milestone comes to a close, bugs begin to taper off, and hopefully their severity tapers off as well. More fit-and-finish issues are identified, and fewer crashing bugs appear. Because you, as a tester, are involved in different parts of the testing cycle at different times, some days you may be logging 20 or more bugs, and then days may pass where you do not identify any new bugs.

Figure 2.2 demonstrates this fluctuation of bug severity and quantity through-out the testing cycle of a product on the macro-scale, or a single feature imple-mentation on the micro-scale.

1. Here, you see that early in a milestone or feature implementation there are relatively few bugs found—many code paths are blocked by the few very severe bugs.

2. Towards the middle of the milestone or feature implementation you have varying results, but usually there is a rise in the number of bugs, while the severity starts to decrease. The feature has become more stable through the resolution of the very severe bugs, which unlocks more code paths and, therefore, more bugs. Often, very severe bugs are still found in these paths, but the overall stability should be improved.

3. Ideally towards the end of this cycle the severity and the number of bugs taper off, indicating a rise in the stability of the feature or product.

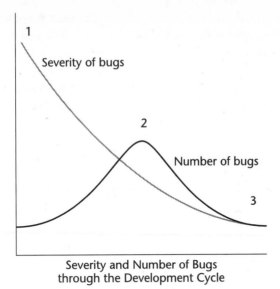

Figure 2.2 contents:
1 — Severity of bugs
2 — Number of bugs
3

Severity and Number of Bugs
through the Development Cycle

Figure 2.2   General correlation of bug severity and quantity.

Many things can affect this chart, and it is by no means applicable to all efforts, but it is a general representation of what many projects experience.

You must keep a few things in mind. Early on, your efforts are focused on verification (asking the question *Is it possible to get this to work?*). At this stage working to answer this question is enough to turn up severe problems in the code. As the feature is stabilized, you become more involved with falsification (asking the question *What else can I do that might break this?*) and detection.

Throughout the cycle, Test works with the entire product team to prevent errors. You work to analyze risk and minimize it by compiling and providing information on the state of the software for management. Some organizations require that all major features be built in isolation, with Test signing off on the changes before Development checks them into the main build tree. Others feel that a code review suffices. Either way, these processes are in place to provide checks and balances. These processes were not put in to make more work for anybody, and especially not for Test.

Be sensitive throughout your test cycle as to whether these processes are working or not. They might need to be adjusted to be more effective, or abandoned entirely if they are found not to work. For example, one organization I worked with had a process whereby everything went through a test cycle before it was checked in to the main build tree. This ensured that build breaks were scarcely seen, even for a development team of a few hundred people, which was great.

It was obviously a very effective process. However, it allowed for some sloppiness to creep in. One developer confided that he found himself not being as rigorous on his own code because he depended on Test to find where he might not have handled a situation. This process was breaking down because testing and testers are not there to absolve developers, architects, or managers from the responsibility when they have created something with a problem. Rather, the development processes that are set in place are to prevent bugs from being incorporated into the product in the first place. Test then checks the product for any bugs that have passed through that first gate of development and catches what it can there. Bugs always slip through the cracks, but a good company and all parts of a good product team are always working to seal up the cracks through better processes and testing.

The Bug Life Cycle

The life cycle of the bug starts with you, the tester, sitting at your desk. You perform an action, and an unexpected response occurs. A bug is found! You can do several things at this point, and as you become more experienced, you will better know what to do for a variety of situations.

Logging Bugs Effectively

When you find a bug, remember what was done to cause the problem. This instruction may sound obvious, but it is the most important point and bears repeating. Being able to break steps down logically and to recall in a step-by-step manner what led to the manifestation of the bug is key to being successful. The very first thing you should do before spending time on any bug is to search the bug-tracking database to see if the issue has already been identified. If the bug has already been entered, it may still be active, but not in the compelling scenario that you have identified. Add that information to the database, and bring it to the attention of the developer responsible, or the test lead. The bug might be closed and identified as one that management is comfortable shipping the product with, or something for which there is no fix. In either case, it still might be worth spending some time gathering a bit more information to include in that bug's information.

The steps that you identify as leading to a bug are called the *reproduction*, *repro steps*, or just simply the *repro*. To log effective repro steps:

1. Find the most straightforward path to trigger the bug.
2. Clearly describe this in your steps.

3. Double-check the steps to ensure that nothing was left out or that you didn't assume something incorrectly.

4. Check, using other machines, if possible, to verify that the bug is reproducible or is dependent on the conditions you believe it is.

Entering duplicate bugs in the database is a tester sin. When it happens, it is usually read as a sign of a sloppy tester. However, it can also be a sign that the original bug information that was entered was written poorly and with little useful detail. It is imperative that a clear, linear, reproducible set of steps be included in the log information. It is okay if you can only get the bug to appear half the time that the steps are performed; just be sure to note that in the report. Think of yourself, at this point, as a detective. You need to gather up all the clues to hand over to the developers so they can identify the problem. For example, say that the software you are working on is a Web community. The bug you identify is that when you log in nothing happens. Here is an ineffective way to log this new entry into the database:

I can't get the community to log me in. I type in my name and nothing happens.

From this description, it would be nearly impossible to determine what exactly you were doing. From an outsider's perspective, you could be doing anything. A more effective entry would be as follows:

I am unable to log in to the community.

1. *Open IE 5.5 on Windows 2000.*

2. *Enter in the community URL (www.community.blah) in the location bar. Hit Enter.*

3. *In the Login: text box, enter the name **user01**.*

4. *Tab to the Password: text box and input the password **123**.*

5. *Click LOGIN to send the information.*

RESULT: Nothing happens, but the IE icon keeps spinning/waving.

From this report, anybody could take a look at the problem and see what happened. And you could even make this entry better if you provided a few other pieces of information. Does this happen with any other user? When was the last time that this user was able to log in successfully? Are you sure this user exists? Are you sure the password is correct? Does this occur on any other platform/browser combination?

CROSS-REFERENCE
███ Chapter 3 discusses writing effective bug reports in more detail.

Using Bug Templates

I strongly advocate the use of a bug template for any team. I keep a text document on my main computer's desktop. As I come across a new bug, I copy out the text, paste it into the database entry, and then just fill in the spaces. It ensures that all bugs have enough information and encourages me to find all the related information at the time the bug report is filed. The last thing I want to do for every bug report I enter is to type in the same formatting and general information each and every time. A process like this ends up saving time and making my life easier. The last thing a developer wants is to play bug tag, assigning a bug back to you several times for more information. It does not help your reputation to be known as somebody who cannot get it right the first time and wastes the valuable resources of another person, or other people, to track down a single bug.

NOTE
Not all bugs found will fit into a template. Often product suggestions, tracking issues, or requests for new features will not fit into this mold, but for the most part the bugs found in testing will be better documented through the use of such a structure.

Assessing Bug Priority and Severity

Most bug databases, whether developed in-house or through third-party tools, have some fields that can be filled in—title, priority, severity, opened by, assigned to, and others. I strongly suggest filling in these fields after the body of the bug report has been created. After writing all of the description, you are more focused on the issue, exactly what the bug is, and how it occurs. You can accurately write a short, pithy title and set a severity and priority for it. Most teams set these values, but they can vary greatly. The *priority* of the bug quantifies how it affects the company internally and, relative to other bugs, when it should be fixed. For example:

1. Fix this first. These are all very important, very noticeable, or very easy.

2. Fix this after all Priority 1 bugs are done. These are important, but don't have as big of an impact as the Priority 1 bugs.

3. Fix these after the Priority 2s. These have an impact on the quality of the product, but not so much that they would stop shipment.

4. Fix these last. Usually these are very minor or corner cases that customers would not encounter in typical use of the application.

The *severity* of the bugs describes the impact that it would have on a customer—the risk and the visibility. The most severe impact is a crash of the product or a loss of data or otherwise undesirable result, made worse if it is caused by a common action. For example:

1. The bug causes client or server machines to crash, hang, lose, or corrupt data.
2. The bug makes a feature unusable or presents a serious problem to the user.
3. The bug causes a noticeable problem, but the user can work around it.
4. The bug represents a trivial issue that is not expected to be a problem. Might be a suggestion or a preference of the tester.

A Bug's Life

Once the bug is logged, a few things may happen to it. The process of the organization may be such that you, the tester entering the bug, directly assign it to the developer or specification writers responsible for that area. Another possibility is that a manager or group of managers may comb through all the bugs and assign the important ones to the developers to be fixed. The first method may seem faster, but the second method ensures that any duplicates, bad bugs, or tester fouls get weeded out. Using the second method, a developer knows that what he is assigned is authorized to be worked on. Managers can effectively load-balance their team and decide at a specific time what will be fixed for the current version of the product, what will be fixed for the next version, and what will never be important enough to bother fixing.

The bug eventually makes it to a developer, who then evaluates it. The bug may require a simple string change or may involve a complex feature request. The developer ends up checking the code changes into the main tree, which is what the builds are produced from. Once that code is checked in, the bug usually has its status changed so that it is no longer active, and it is assigned back to you, the tester, to verify. Once a build is produced that contains the fix, you become responsible for verifying if the changes fixed the issue, caused a regression, or did not address parts of the problem. If the issue has not been resolved, the bug will be reactivated, and the cycle will start all over again. Occasionally, the fix unblocks new code paths, where new bugs are found. In that case, it is usually best to open a new database entry for the new bugs and mention, when you log the new bug, that the fix to the old bug unblocked it. This new bug then goes through the cycle. If all goes perfectly, the life cycle of a bug looks like Figure 2.3.

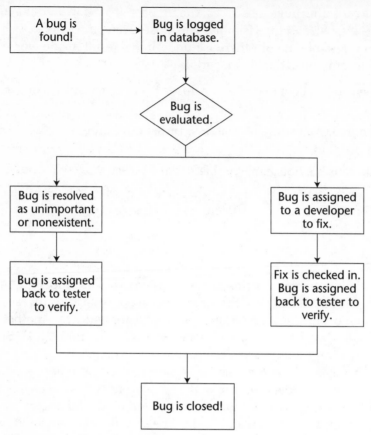

Figure 2.3 Life cycle of a bug.

Maintaining the Bug Database

As I have indicated, some active bugs are left alone; they are active, but not worth fixing at the moment. Test teams often go through the database looking for these active bugs and attempt to reproduce them a month or more after they were logged. Many times these bugs are fixed with various check-ins, but nobody notices or logs the related bugs as fixed. These voodoo fixes may be from a developer noticing a coding problem and fixing that, or from the removal or rearchitecting of a poorly built component. Clearing out these incidental fixes prevents the bug database from becoming stale or having bug counts that inaccurately reflect the quality of the software.

Testing Approaches

There are a lot of theories, philosophies, programs, processes, and standards out there to help organizations reach their goal and produce good software within their budgets. Many companies are trying to sell their own brand of "What You Should Do." Many of these are good or at least have good ideas and approaches. Some of the common ones are the Capability Maturity Model (CMM), Six Sigma, Rational Unified Process (RUP), and ISO approaches (ISO 9000-3 and others). Without adopting any of these, your organization can still be successful. And just because your organization employs one or more of these does not make it successful or effective. If the underlying principles are not understood and implemented well, then the positive effects of following any regimen are lost. There are many "best practices" out there, and everyone agrees that their organization needs to adopt them. However every best practice has a proper application and many scenarios where it may not work so well. The problem is there is no one Best Practice, no matter how much those marketing them want you to believe there is. Best practices are relevant and only apply within the context of a project or to the people implementing it.

Testing Techniques

All of these standard processes or certifications are basically enforcing the same techniques or best practices. Two common ones are:

- Know what you are doing before you start.
- Write it down.

Again, these seem simple and obvious, but I cannot emphasize enough that these two simple practices have positive results throughout the product cycle. So many times other problems in an organization can be traced back to these root causes.

Sometimes the most obvious things escape us. One fairly common mistake is for an organization to neglect to objectively and definitively identify the product release criteria early on. This seems easy, and it is easy enough to say, but doing it is far more difficult. In one case, when working on a product update, the schedule gave 4.5 months to complete and ship the update. Two days before the declared ship date, it was suddenly announced that the date would slip another 2.5 months. Management had finally come to the realization that no one had defined what the update was to accomplish. Each team, and, indeed, each individual, had an idea of what the deliverable was, but put together, the organization had no focus or common goal that they agreed on. The release went on to slip another 3 months and finally shipped more than 6 months after the originally set ship date—more than 100 percent ship slippage. Certainly, there were other factors involved in this slippage, but one of the main ones recognized internally was that we simply forgot to determine what we were doing and rushed ahead to ship.

The same concept holds true for any development effort: Know what the point is. If you cannot go from office to office and ask the team what the intent of the project is and get a fairly consistent response, then either the product has not been well defined or it has not been well communicated. Both cases result in similar effects.

And the first best practice, knowing what you are doing, leads clearly to the second best practice—writing things down! Document the intent and the product criteria. Document as much as you can. Such documentation is not red tape to get in the way of things, but when done correctly, will save time and effort. When you, as an individual tester, start in on a new piece of functionality or a new area of the product, document what you learn. Often, what you learn from various people or documents contains some contradictions. You need to resolve these. While some things you need to learn and remember and store in your head, there are a lot of pieces of information that you and the team will not want to lose, but do not need to always hold in your mind.

For example, you may have several server test beds in your organization. One day, you may be called upon to reinstall one of these. If clearly documented steps for an installation and configuration exist, then you won't have any problems. You wouldn't need to be fully trained and regularly updated on changes to perform the function; just having a familiarity and following the steps would be enough. Think of having good documentation as being prepared for one of those open note tests where understanding the material is more important than the ability to memorize. There is no reason to remember all the minutia of a configuration process that may change as often as weekly, depending on how your build process changes. If all those steps are well documented, the test team saves time and money (and a lot of frustration) by just referring to the documentation.

TIP

It's often useful if a single person owns all the documents that fall into his area of expertise and takes responsibility for writing new documents as well as keeping current ones up-to-date.

Another situation in which documentation is key occurs when a person leaves a team. In many organizations, all the information is stored in people's heads, so that when a person leaves, all of that knowledge goes with him. Documenting things prevents a lot of this loss.

Allow me to make one caveat—merely documenting key information or an important process may not be enough if you don't widely circulate the knowledge that such documentation is available. Consider the following example. I had documented the "blessed" steps for a particularly complex configuration that the team rarely performed. A month later, we started seeing a lot of bugs reported in this area as Test's attention turned to this part of the product. When we tracked them all down, it turned out that the people reporting these bugs had not properly set up their servers, causing the bad behavior. If my documentation of the configuration had been more widely announced, others could have made use of it, and time spent tracking down these issues could have been saved. I could have more widely announced their existence through email or through listing the existing documentation on a team Web site. Ultimately, the aim is to collect all instructions and documentations of interest to the team into one place, where everyone can look when questions come up. Your team can have the best documentation possible, but if nobody finds it or uses it, then it might as well not be there.

Testing Types

Testing gets broken into two types: *black box* and *glass box* (also sometimes called *white box*):

- **Black box.** The idea behind this type of testing is that if the code is in a black box, you can't see the inside machinations of how it works. You see only how you are able to use it as an end user.

- **Glass box (or white box).** The idea here is that if the code is inside a glass box, you can see the internals of the code and poke at the weak points of the functions because you understand how the internals are put together.

The testing process gets further granularized into unit testing, integration testing, functional testing, system testing, end-to-end testing, regression testing, and more. The delimitations between these types of testing are often fuzzy, but can be used to indicate activities and assign ownership. The following list defines some of the more common types of testing you engage in:

- **Unit testing.** Developers create the code—small discrete functions. Once they add more functions, they need to go back and test to verify that the functions interact as a unit the way they anticipated and designed for. This process is the *unit testing*, testing individual atomic units to ensure that they work as expected.

- **Integration testing.** A thorough developer carries the idea of unit testing into testing how their new units work together with related units, integrating them and checking their connections. This usually expands to include testers, who perform the remainder of this sort of *integration testing*.

- **Smoke testing, build verification tests (BVTs), check-in tests (CITs).** The real challenge starts in integration as features that are stable are integrated with new functionality. When code is passed to the test team, it is often verified first through *smoke tests, build verification tests (BVTs), check-in tests (CITs)* or other quick-and-dirty validations of the program's main functions. Such tests are also performed to ensure that the same base level of functionality that was available yesterday is still available today after the latest check-ins.

- **Functional testing.** Putting more of the stable small functions together allows testers to perform *functional testing*, testing a complete function from the user's point of view (as opposed to a code-based single function). In the online bookstore example I use throughout this text, functional testing may mean trying to perform user functions such as logging on or logging off.

- **System testing.** Putting the functions together allows the tester to verify the entire system in *system testing*. This may mean testing pieces of every component available.

- **End-to-end testing.** These tests are usually similar to system testing, but involve a clear user scenario that is being followed to test a user's complete interaction with the system.

- **Sanity testing.** Initial tests to determine if the area or entire product is stable enough to put more time and effort into testing.

- **Regression testing.** Retesting areas after fixes or functional additions to ensure that previously fixed bugs have not reappeared and new bugs have not been introduced (often performed by running the same test case as before or through automation).

- **Acceptance testing.** Final test pass based on specifications, customer agreement, or other such particulars.

- **Load testing.** Testing the software under heavy usage to determine performance degradation or failures.

- **Stress testing.** Testing specific functions while the system is running under high loads; helps determine the mean time to failure and performance metrics.

- **Performance testing.** Determines how much time or cost is associated with certain actions of functions. (How long will a customer have to wait for a particular action to complete? How long does the code spend in a particular function?)

- **Usability testing.** Testing the ability of the software to be used by the identified customer base.

- **Install/uninstall testing.** Testing how product components download, don't download, and work on various platforms, client or server, as well as how easily they can be removed.

- **Recovery testing.** Evaluating how well and how fast the system can bounce back from a crash or other failure.

- **Compatibility testing.** Determining the primary and secondary supported environments (OS, platform, browser, and so on) and the levels of support/behavior/functionality provided on each.

- **Exploratory testing.** A creative approach to learning and evaluating the software; usually informally introduces a tester to the environment.

- **User acceptance testing.** Determining if the software is satisfactory to a customer (usually not performed in shrinkwrapped development efforts).

- **Alpha testing.** Initial incorporation of endusers into the completed program. Involves early adopters or other partners. Design changes may occur as a result of this feedback.

- **Beta testing.** Development and test are basically finished. Finds final problems before the final release. Can be an open invitation to anyone who wants to download the software or try the service.

- **Comparison testing.** Comparing software features and stability to those of competitors.

- **Accessibility testing.** Checking if product or service is accessible to users.

- **Server log testing/report testing.** Examining the server logs after particular actions or at regular intervals to determine if there are problems or errors generated or if the server is entering a faulty state.

- **Security testing.** Testing the potential for accidental or malicious damage due to attacks, denials of service, open ports, and other issues.

- **Memory leak testing.** Testing the server components to see if memory is not properly referenced and released, which can lead to instability and the product's crashing.

- **International sufficiency/localization/globalization.** These are discussed in Chapter 7; however, each one is a distinct testing effort.

  - **International sufficiency.** This involves testing that the product can be localized into the target languages; languages that write from the right side of the page to the left side of the page place special requirements on the user interface as do double-byte languages such as Chinese and Japanese. Testing that the user interface can handle these is a separate task from actually translating the words.

  - **Localization.** This is testing that all the words that the user sees are translated into the specified language properly.

  - **Globalization.** This is testing that all the various characters and combinations from the various languages can be accepted by the system or are properly rejected and that no data conversions or corruptions occur.

- **HTML validation testing.** Specific to Web testing. This certifies that the HTML meets specifications and internal coding standards.

- **SSL testing.** Testing Web site/service over an SSL connection, if that's an option.

- **Bandwidth testing.** Testing a site with a variety of link speeds, both fast (internally connected LAN) and slow (externally, through a proxy or firewall, and over a modem); sometimes called *slow link testing* if the organization typically tests with a faster link internally (in that case, they are doing a specific pass for the slower line speed only).

Overall, you want to move away from *brute force* methods of testing. Sure you could find bugs by blindfolding yourself and randomly hitting keys, but it would take a very long time and be rather inefficient. You will include some amount of *ad hoc* testing in your test activities. Where brute force just bangs on the keys and the mouse, ad hoc testing lets loose your creativity to think more about certain areas and investigate them. This is best undertaken by a tester who knows the software and testing methodologies well enough to see the bug patterns and know where to poke to find more problems.

It's a good practice to keep a notebook nearby and take notes on good test cases, even if they are successful (that is, they don't produce a bug) or if features have not been implemented but test cases for them come to mind. It is also a good practice after running through some ad hoc testing to look through the new bug reports for patterns, creating new test cases from these.

When Does Testing Stop?

There are several ways to determine when testing stops:

- Testing might stop because a deadline has been met, either an arbitrary one or one in a customer agreement. But making software decisions by dates is problematic because it does not take into account the status of the project. At its extreme, features may not be implemented or severe problems may be known to exist in the product. Stopping the project based on the date does not allow the product to evolve and does not take into account additional work detailed, problems encountered, or severe risks that may still exist.

- Testing also comes to a halt when the budget has been exhausted. Such a halt is another very poor end to a software project because product quality is not necessarily linked with the finances allocated to produce the product. However, if the finances have run out, there is rarely any other option.

- Testing might stop when all the test cases have been run and passed or a predetermined percentage have been passed. Such an arrangement is fine if you are sure that you have identified the proper test cases and that the percent that were not run are not your most important ones. If 80 percent of the test cases are always run and that is identified as sufficient, some good questions to ask are *"Is that 80 percent always the same 80 percent? Does the 80 percent contain the really important scenarios and functions? Are there 20 percent of the test cases that have never been run? How important are the remaining test cases?"*

- Testing might stop when a certain coverage percentage is met, either by function or by code paths. This measurement is not a bad metric, but should be used as another way to measure if there are unmined places where bugs could be found.

- Testing might stop when the bug rate or severity falls to a certain point. But such a drop could be due to other factors, such as the test team being given a week off.

- Testing may also stop when a certain metric is met, perhaps 3 months of uptime under stress without a failure. This is a good metric because the needs of the user have been translated into goals of the product. When the product is able to meet these objective goals, it will satisfy the customer.

All of these methods describe various factors that must be considered in any software development effort. Software that drags on year after year without shipping (ignoring the date in an attempt to create perfect software) will fail. Software that ignores its budget is not realistic. Software that does not lay out goals and measurements in advance of the release will not be successful. Each of these must play a role but should not be the sole deciding factor.

Ultimately, testing will not find all the bugs. Testing will not exercise all possible scenarios. Testing will never be able to test everything. (Kenneth H. Rosen walks through this example in his book *Discrete Mathematics and Its Applications*.) Suppose there is a system in which each user must have a six to eight character password. Each character can be an uppercase letter or a numeral, but each password must have at least one numeral. How many passwords would you have to test to make sure that every one behaved properly? You would have to verify 2,684,483,063,360 individual valid passwords. Even at an unreasonable rate of testing 480 passwords per day, it would take 155 years to test all of the passwords.

The trick is to test based on risk. Risk-based analysis of software takes into account both the severity of the bug and the likelihood of failure. For instance, if a particular action is identified as one that 80 percent of all users will perform, then there is a high likelihood that users will exercise this code. Based on this likelihood alone, this area of functionality should be covered well in the test plans. Contrast that with a function that very few users, or perhaps only malicious users, will perform but that has a high potential for causing severe impact. If the outcome has the possibility of being that severe, then this aspect too should be covered well in the test plans.

NOTE Areas that malicious users will exploit are usually difficult areas to identify and get full coverage on, which is why we see so many security problems making it into released software. Security testing is covered in more detail in Chapter 9.

The main idea with testing is to get the biggest bang for the buck. The core tenet of any good testing effort is to use your limited time wisely and get the most effective test coverage.

The Practice of Software Testing

Success is more a function of consistent common sense than it is of genius.

—An Wang

T he practice of software testing carries with it a lot of the theory of software testing, but where theory and common sense are sometimes at odds, the practice must be in line with factors that may seem mundane.

Starting Testing

There are many different ways to start into testing, and many different preferences. Ultimately, starting will be determined by many factors including the testing team, the talents and abilities that each member brings to the effort, the software cycle, and the overall plan to bring the software to market. This chapter discusses many of these issues to help you make better decisions about your approach to the work.

Where Should Testing Start?

So how do you avoid the most costly and noticeable problems? You start testing at the beginning. An ideal testing project starts with the product specifications and architecture. These items start as documentation of how the product is to be created and change over the life cycle of the product to become documentation of how it has been implemented. If you identify problems in the planning stage before any implementation has been done or before the design becomes a standard with components built on top of it, the problems are cheaper and easier to fix. At this point, you need to change only a few documents in order to fix a bug and prevent related ones.

Of course, it is not always possible to catch things at this point. The time it takes up front to do the design or to document the proposed design so that others can critique it is time that does not appear very productive to some management organizations. Though specific people often own this design function—product managers, program managers, designers, and so on— actually getting these people to produce these documents with the necessary detail may be difficult. Still, you, your test organization, and the development team need to work together and make every effort to drive this process, through communication and putting processes in place that further the goal of producing high-quality software. The practice of testing the product specifications and designs has been shown to catch 50 percent of all bugs and to catch them cheaper and faster than any other method. This statistic alone is a compelling argument to make such early testing a most valued part of the software development life cycle in every software production house, but that sadly is not always the case. When organizations do bother to produce these detailed documents, the testing organization is rarely involved. When Test is involved, they rarely understand how to be effective in this stage. The next few sections discuss how to make such a test review of specifications effective and should give you some information to help you make a case to management as to why such testing is appropriate and cost-effective.

Reviewing Product Specifications

When Test reviews the specifications, there are three buckets in which the document can be placed.

1. The design is appropriate.
2. The design is inappropriate and must be changed.
3. There is not enough information or detail provided about the proposed design to determine whether or not it's appropriate.

Be careful of the typical pitfall that many testers fall into at this stage—passing a design that is incomplete or with concerns floating around because you intend to catch these concerns later as concrete bugs. You may have uncertainties if you don't have enough information to understand the proposals, or if there are time pressures and a need to show some progress. The pitfall though is to pass the design to get on with the "real" work. Be tough. Insisting on good and complete proposals will prevent problems and clarify in everybody's mind what will be done and how the plan will be carried out. It is when what will be done and how it will be done are undefined that everyone takes away a slightly different perspective of what the objective is. In that event, the pieces do not match up to give a clear picture, and the software's seams start coming apart, creating more numerous and more serious bugs that cost the organization time and money in the long run.

TIP

Specifications should detail the desired behaviors, not the specific implementation. Developers investigate that and document the implementation in their design documents. The specification proposals should outline the product needs.

Blanket statements usually hide many bugs and need to be challenged. For example, one team made two guiding statements concerning the next release of a product. The first statement was that they wanted a 100 percent improvement in performance. What a great goal (even if it is poorly defined, the sentiment is a noble one)! The second statement was that they did not want to test old legacy code and were not going to make any code changes to it. The problem lies in the fact that these two statements blatantly conflict. You cannot have a performance improvement in the existing code paths without altering the code paths. It is just not possible. Looking for these sorts of blanket statements helps you identify contradictory goals and efforts.

As a tester, you need to look at these product design specifications from two points of view:

1. **Technical.** Is the design appropriately addressing the problem and will it technically work as expected?

2. **Customer advocate.** Is the proposal really addressing the customers' needs and desires?

From the technical point of view, Test needs to catch the scenarios that developers and program managers may not have thought of. Remember, the people who are creating these designs are concerned with how to make the product work. You, as a tester, are in the role of asking the question of how to make it *not* work. One design meeting that I was involved with had development demonstrating what they were intending to write for a particular algorithm. Program Management added in a few scenarios that the customers required be handled. Then, Test got up and started asking the challenging questions and getting no responses. They asked the *what if* questions, showing that there were many scenarios that had not been considered that needed to be handled. Since Test was intimately knowledgeable in how to break the product, they were able to point out their tricks to the developers and program managers in advance so that these scenarios could be handled. Product teams working on large projects with a lot of common scenarios might want to develop a checklist of issues that need to be addressed for the specification to be considered complete. Test has the opportunity to step in and develop such a checklist that the entire team can benefit from and add to.

CROSS-REFERENCE

A sample checklist constructed from the contents of this book can be found in Appendix H.

Development and program managers have been so focused on how to make the product work that they can now turn their attention to solidifying the design, addressing the concerns about what could make the product not work. Obviously such a development process can lead to fewer bugs being logged, but good management should also see that such input by Test early on is a much cheaper way to find bugs and get them fixed, allowing the software to be shipped earlier than if Test were tasked only with getting high bug counts.

Taking the point of view of customer advocate is somewhat more difficult. It requires more research and is inherently more subjective. You do have to remember that for most pieces of software you are not the typical end user. You are far more technically savvy than most consumers and know the internals of the application under development. You know why certain design decisions were made and can work around many problems that you might encounter, both luxuries that your customers will likely not have. Having user profiles and scenarios already written out helps you test the specification from the mindset of the users and with their needs in mind. Again, though, Test needs to stick to their guns and be firm in their decisions. For example, in one project I was given ownership for testing a conflict resolution piece of a program. The proposed design for this piece started from the assumption that the user had created a document and placed it on a server for the user and others to access and modify. In addition to the copy on the server, a local copy of the document was also kept on the user's hard drive. Conflict resolution was needed because either version of the document (the one on the server side or on the client side) could be changed, and somehow this difference in versions needed to be addressed. The design that management decided upon and handed to me specified that if there were a conflict between these two versions, the local copy was secondary and would be moved to a separate directory on the user's hard drive. Then, the newer copy would be pulled down from the server and placed on the user's hard drive, where the user was expecting to find his version. Although this solution sounded good for a few user scenarios, it was inappropriate for many others. (One example I considered was as follows: A user heads out on a business trip and has pulled down a copy of his business report to work on while in flight. He works diligently while flying, and after getting it done, he decides to dial in from his hotel to check for new mail or any status changes in his schedule. Behind his back, and without alerting him, the local copy notices that the copy of the business report on the server was just edited by a coworker a few minutes ago. It efficiently moves his version to another place on his hard drive and copies down the coworker's version to the place where his had been. After checking his mail he falls asleep and wakes up the next morning ready for his meeting. While preparing in the hour before his meeting, he runs through his presentation and the business report to be presented. He is completely surprised to find that, as far as he can tell, all of his changes and work are gone. What will he do? He will most likely panic and call the support line.) After reading and understanding the proposal, I quickly mailed the others involved and described my concern with this design. The management reaction to my concerns was that people would figure out what had happened and come to understand that the conflict detection function was very helpful. I disagreed and decided to press the issue one more time. I remembered having heard support calls on the Internet with people irate and inconsolable over issues like this, so I spent a few minutes surfing to find some. I found one, downloaded it, and attached it to my response insisting that if we implemented the proposed solution, this would be the type of customer we would have, and our support costs would increase. I am not sure which argument it was that helped to tip the balance, but that piece of functionality was cut and soon after so was the rest of the component.

To play customer advocate, the first questions that you want to challenge the spec with are:

- Does this meet the requirements?
- Does this meet the customers' expectations?
- Does this match marketing's promises?
- How will the customer use this?
- What are the risky (critical) areas?
- How will I test this?
- What is missing?

The most basic question to keep in mind while challenging the specifications is *Does this meet the requirements/goals/expectations/promises*? You obviously must clearly know what those requirements, goals, expectations, and promises are to answer this question. But if you do know all that information, and if the product does not meet those benchmarks, then it will be a failure no matter how free of bugs it is. If your users are expecting a way to place items in a shopping cart, check out, and pay online, and you do not accept orders with more than one item, you will likely not be satisfying your customers. It just might be that your software has a fantastic interface, is bug free, fast, and easy to use, but if it does not meet the requirements of the user, then it will not be successful. Part of the job of a tester is to ensure that the software is set up for success. That needs to start from the beginning. If nobody catches this mismatch in expectations until the day before the product ships, a lot of time is wasted and a lot of work has to be undone to correct this. Catch problems early. Save your company money. Your bug counts may not look as high, but they won't be falsely inflated. People will know and understand your contributions to the product's quality.

Who Should Start?

If you are in the position of assigning testers to parts of a project, keep in mind that testing specifications takes a different skill set than other parts of the testing process. Testing a specification takes more experience, knowledge, ability, and technical understanding than testing an application that is already coded and working in front of you. It is unlikely that testers will stumble across bugs in a spec the same way they will in a working product. Because at the specifications stage the application has to be put together in the tester's mind, this task should be assigned to a more experienced tester, or a green tester under the guidance of a senior tester. This type of a project can be rewarding; it is a high-profile task that can be offered to testers to allow them the rare opportunity to receive individual recognition by a larger audience and to work more closely with management. They should not be encouraged to skimp on their time on this task by being held to bug rates. An unscrupulous tester would quickly see that he could "miss" bugs only to "catch" them once the feature had been coded, thereby getting the credit for being a good tester on both ends. However, I have even had experienced testers tell me that they cannot be assigned to the specification testing part of the project because they have no idea what to do at this phase. It is easy to fall into the common trap of agreeing with the proposals without critiquing them. If you are assigning testers to test specifications, assign ones who will challenge the specs. If you are a tester assigned to test specifications, keep in mind all that you can save by taking the specifications to task early in the process.

Applying Testing Techniques

You all have your own techniques that you have developed through practice for any activity that you engage in. These techniques could be for cooking, driving, or cleaning your house. You may not notice even them or may only notice that you prefer the results from your actions to those of others. As a tester, what you want to do is become aware of what techniques you use and identify them. You want to become aware of those techniques that others use so that you can incorporate the best pieces into your own work. You want to identify best situations for various techniques and alter your own modus operandi accordingly. What starts this section is a discussion of some of the most basic techniques that you are probably already using in any number of ways to let you further analyze techniques you use or see around you.

Breaking Tasks Down into Chunks

Breaking tasks into chunks is how any large project is accomplished and especially how software gets written well. It is also a technique that you can use to help you approach the work of testing software. Faced with an insurmountable problem? Start by breaking it into pieces. Don't know how to do one of those activities? Break it down into smaller pieces. Once it is in manageable pieces it is easier to work with—easier to track, easier to hold in your mind to understand, and easier to test.

I realized this lesson when my manager asked me to start in on a project with the development team—a redesign of a very complex algorithm that determined which server a request would go to when you had multiple copies of the requested information. As a relatively new tester on the team, I had never faced this before and was quite apprehensive. So I tried something that I was not used to doing: I jumped straight in.

- I thought about the problem.
- I worked to understand what they were trying to do.
- I researched how previous versions of the software handled it. I read up on what problems they had with it.
- I read outside material on what other solutions there were.

When the meeting came around for the discussion of the proposed design, I was prepared and pointed out areas that Test identified as weak points to consider in our designs and tests. That was a highly successful change that occurred very late in the product cycle, and although I cannot take credit for making it successful, I definitely learned something that I would not forget. Jump in and break things down until you can understand all the pieces. If you cannot coherently explain all those pieces to somebody else or systematically develop the test cases for them, then you need to keep breaking them down and understanding them.

Asking the Right Questions

Even if you do not come to an intimate level of understanding of the software, you can start asking the challenging questions of those who do know and effectively contribute to the software project. It is acceptable not to have the answers. (In fact, I firmly believe that people are not encouraged enough to admit, either to themselves or to their team, when they do not have an answer.) Nobody can be expected to have all the answers or to always be right. But only through acknowledging that you don't know can you start to seek the answer. Sometimes just asking good questions is more appropriate. Asking good questions is also a good technique to help others examine the designs from Test's perspective. It can sometimes be easier to get people to see your point of view if they come to the same conclusion through your posed question than if you tell them the answer outright.

The Five Basic Software Functions

I need to introduce a bit more testing theory before I can further discuss the practice of testing. Software basically performs five functions:

1. Accepts input
2. Gives output
3. Saves data
4. Manipulates data
5. Removes data

One piece of software may only do a few of these, or all of these, but to produce a basic framework for creating test cases and viewing the software, you need to break it down into these small chunks.

Ask the right questions. I cannot stress this enough. I have learned so much from others just by asking, and by their asking me. Why does this happen? Why do we do this? What happens when we do that? When you have to sit down and design tests for new features, you start looking at the various components and asking all these questions. When you do not have all the knowledge to answer the questions, pose them to those who do have the knowledge. Perhaps they have missed scenarios or cases, and, if not, then you will learn a lot from their answers. What happens if we put in 255 characters? What about 256? What if a service goes down, but the server itself is still responding? You learn much and create good test cases this way.

WARNING

Be very careful about constantly asking questions without absorbing the information, or you could get labeled as a randomizer, someone who moves the focus of a software team away from where it should be. One team I knew routinely complained about one of their coworkers. The randomizations had gotten so bad that this coworker had earned the nickname of Focus Hoover due to the way the tester's and developer's focus was sucked away when this person showed up. This type of person is always asking the most basic question such as *What is [insert technology here]?* without thinking about his questions first or finding the most appropriate resource to query (such as a search engine) before asking the team. Once a label like that gets hung on you, it is a hard reputation to rise above. There is a time to listen and a time to ask questions and a time to assert your knowledge. Save your time and that of your peers by asking the right questions of the right resources.

Enumerating Software States

Once you know the five basic software functions you are ready to perform a key testing technique, enumerating the states of the software. Figure 3.1 contains an example of a very simple Web page. This form accepts two pieces of input and can either be cleared or submitted.

In this example, the user is able to put in data and click a button to submit it, probably to a database. You can enumerate three software states in considering this example:

- The form is in a creation state when the user is presented with a fresh text entry area in which to enter data.

- The data then is saved and stored in a database somewhere in the system.

- At some point, the admin retrieves the data and views it.

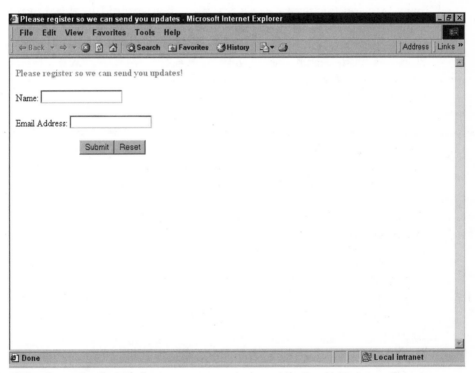

Figure 3.1   Simple Web form.

These three states each need to be tested and covered in the test plans to ensure proper coverage. If the system allowed the user to input data and save it, then revisit the site to view and alter the data periodically, you would have a much more complex scenario because you would have an edit state (starting from the text entry area pre-populated with the previously saved data) and a second save state, where the data was re-saved with and without alterations. Analyze each area of the software for what states are available and how they can be accessed. One product that would have benefited from this was Microsoft's Ultimate TV. This product allowed users to record television programs onto a hard drive to be played back later, much like their competitors Tivo and RePlay. However, Ultimate TV users started seeing their available hard drive space shrinking even though they were deleting items. Some users saw their available space shrink from 30 hours down to 12 hours in a very short period of time. It was discovered that if users deleted a program while they were in pause mode, the listing would disappear from the menu, but the space was not actually marked as freed on the hard drive. The user had no way to record over that space and no way to access it again. Microsoft did fix this, but not before it hit the media and made many of their customers unhappy. More thorough testing and state modeling of the software through identification of its primary functions would have uncovered this type of problem, saving the company from the cost of sending out updates and fielding customer complaints.

NOTE

Many Web sites are static, having only a read state—a user is able to click on links to view more data, but there are no interactions other than that. The data is static, and the user can only request copies of it. However, Web applications usually allow more interactivity, so enumerate the states you are dealing with carefully.

Examining Data Input

Examining data input is another testing practice where understanding the five basic functions of software helps you make your evaluations. Inputting data is something you do all the time. You type and select values without even thinking that you are inputting data. As users such unconsciousness is fine, but as testers it is a crime. Think carefully about the data and the way that it is input in order to test effectively and with the minimum of effort.

A basic type of an input is a text area or a text entry field. It accepts data and probably saves it. However, just saving it is probably not good enough because somebody will want to access it later, which means outputting the data. For example, the most basic input might be a text entry field in a Web page allowing a user to submit comments about the Web site. The user is able to enter data and save it and has no further interaction with the data. However, the site administrator will want to view this data at some point, making the same data that was the input to the customer the output to the system administrator. In this scenario, the data has gone through three states—creation, saving, and viewing. Following the data in this way is the very beginning of creating useful functions and software.

Examining More Complex Data Input

Having a single input for a piece of software is rare and simplistic, but it gives us a starting point. The next complication added to a single data input is having functions or calculations performed on that data. Consider a mortgage calculator provided online. Users are presented with a data entry field to input the amount of the mortgage. They can then click a Calculate button to have the monthly cost of a 20-year mortgage displayed. In this case, the input is the amount of the mortgage. A standard calculation is performed on that number, and the result is then displayed to the user as the monthly payment—the output. Figure 3.2 shows an example of such a form.

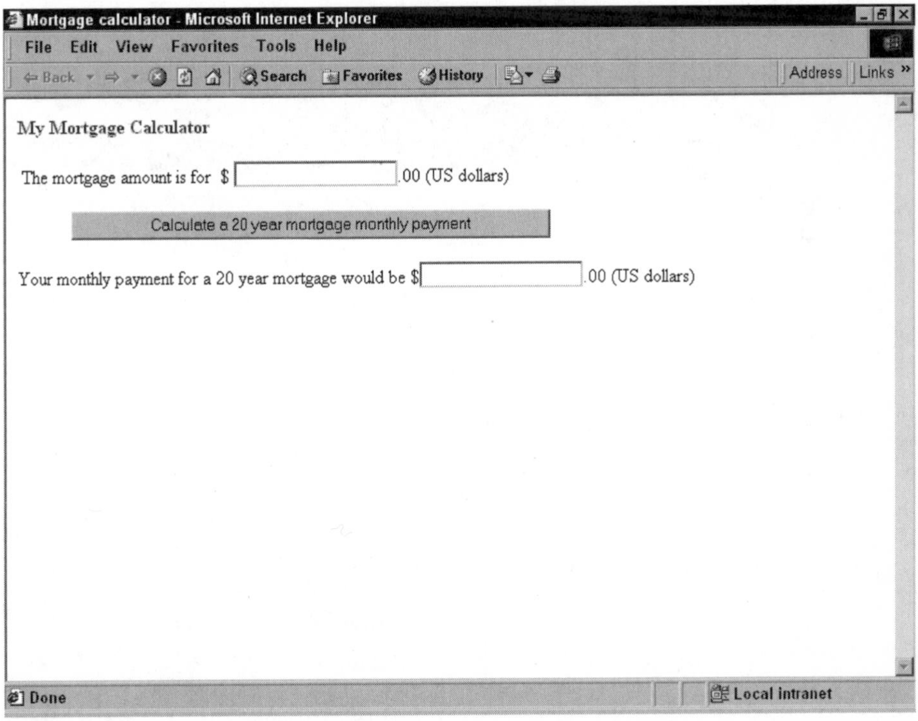

Figure 3.2 A more complex Web form.

This form has one location for data input and a single algorithm that is applied to any input placed there. Many test cases can be created off a page as simple as this. You need to test unique input in the text entry field and the interaction with the button. Can the entry field handle only numbers? Only single-byte numbers? What happens if a user enters a currency sign in front of the number? Can the user enter in a delimiter such as the comma after the thousands place?

To add another level of complication, consider an online calculator (see Figure 3.3).

This particular calculator accepts only two integers and only adds them. From the users' perspective, they type in a number in the first field, type in another number in the second field, and can then click only the Add! button. The output of this computation is then displayed to the users. In total, three points of data are of interest to you as a tester—each of the two inputs and the output.

Testing Data Input

Testing these points of interest is a huge area. Books are written on just that. This section gives you only an introduction to the subject and gives some places to start.

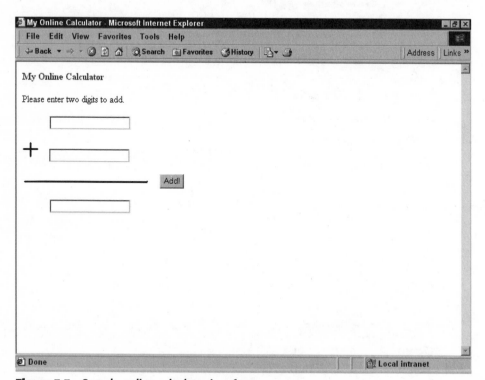

Figure 3.3 Sample online calculator in a form.

To come up with scenarios to test data input you need to create what are called *equivalence classes* of data. An equivalence class of data is data that all goes through the same code path. For example, in the online calculator program I mentioned in the previous section, if you want to test a function by adding 2 + 2 and then test it by adding 3 + 3, you are likely wasting your time. If 2 and 2 add together properly, then 3 + 3 will most likely add together properly, as will 4 + 4. Why is this? These all fall into the same scenario—each has a single digit added to another single digit, equaling a single digit, with none of them being a boundary condition. They are an equivalence class of data and go through the same code path. Rather than choosing data that tests the same code paths, you need to pick the best possible numbers to exercise as many unique scenarios (code paths) as fast as possible. You may want to add 2 + 2 just to ensure that it comes out with 4, but there is no need to try all the numbers. You may initially use this simple case to ensure that the software has at least the most basic case working (validating the software's basic functionality), but after that you want to identify several classes where problems may occur.

- Handling 0 could be a test case, as the first number in the equation, the second number, or both.

- Adding two single digit numbers to get a double-digit number could cause a problem.

- Adding a single digit number to a double-digit number to get a three-digit number could cause a problem.

Table 3.1 contains sample scenarios you might choose to test on the sample calculator program, exercising the use of single- and multiple-digit numbers, forcing the software to change the size of the output from the size of the input.

Table 3.1 Sample Test Cases

FIRST NUMBER	SECOND NUMBER	EXPECTED SUM
0	0	0
0	1	1
1	0	1
1	9	10
1	99	100
9999999	1	10000000

You could even test without entering any numbers by clicking the Add! button without inputting anything. Do you receive an error? Should it be ignored? All of these cases so far have used positive integers, yet the interface allows for negative numbers as well as decimals. You need to come up with appropriate negative numbers to add to positive numbers, as well as negative numbers to add to negative numbers, to ensure that the program is adding properly. The interface also allows for decimals, so you need to find equivalence classes where you add the decimal numbers to yield a whole number, as well as other classes. What would happen if you tried to add 1.5 + 2.5? Should the answer displayed be 4 or 4.0? The specification should guide the proper behavior for scenarios where there can be more than one right answer. Specifications that are missing these crucial details are calling for clarification. Test will need to push to have a clear statement in the specifications saying either that only whole numbers are accepted or that decimals and other numbers are accepted.

NOTE

All of these checks do not guarantee that the software is completely bug free, but they do start to check that it works properly.

You may have noticed in Table 3.1 that 0 + 1 is performed, followed by 1 + 0. Why do the same thing twice? The answer is the two operations aren't necessarily the same thing. In this program, you may need to check how the value of 0 was handled in each place, the first input and the second input. The input order may have made a difference, or the variables handling each of these may have handled them differently. It is entirely possible that although 0 could be an expected and handled input, the output of 0 is not expected and is not

The Intel Floating-Point Bug

Possibly the most infamous bug that this sort of testing would have turned up was the Intel floating-point bug. The floating-point division bug could be uncovered in faulty processors by taking 4195835 and dividing it by 3145727. The result of that operation was then multiplied by 3145727. From that total, 4195835 was subtracted. A faulty chip will not give the correct answer of 0 to this equation. News stories revealed this bug, which only affected scientific software and developers; most home users would not be doing calculations to this extent. The stories around this bug portrayed Intel as being uncaring and unconcerned about their obvious bug with its simple repro. Intel apologized and replaced the faulty chips at a cost to the company of over $400 million.

handled properly, throwing a nasty error to the user. When you can identify individual data points and the states that the data can be in, you can start examining the relationship between these. Is there an expected input order or an assumption that could be made? How can you thwart that and input data in a different way to set the software up to fail?

Testing inputs needs to have a couple other goals:

- **Forcing all error messages.** Clicking the Add! button is an input. What happens if you do not enter in a number and instead click Add! first? Does an appropriate message alert you to this? Does the software freeze as it is attempting to add the nonvalues? You may need to experiment to find out, and certainly if there are specifications for how this should work, you will want to enumerate all the error messages and error states and force the software into these states to ensure that it handles them as expected.

- **Checking the keyboard (and mouse) tie-ins to the interface.** Perhaps your online calculator is more like Figure 3.4, allowing the user to click buttons to input values.

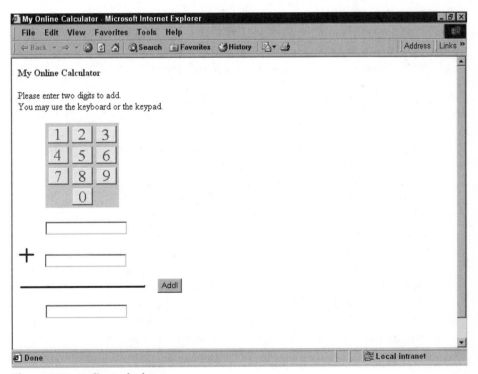

Figure 3.4   Online calculator.

The example in Figure 3.4 should accept both mouse clicks and keyboard inputs. Can I hit the 5 button on my numeric 10-key area of the keyboard or the 5 button on the number strip on the top of my keyboard? Can these buttons be tabbed to and selected by hitting the spacebar or Enter key? Checking the accessibility of these hotkeys and knowing the extent to which your software is accessible is part of testing the interface.

Testing Boundary Conditions

A *boundary* is any constraint that is put on the software or an edge where two different sets of rules may be in place; for example, the calculator program may be able to display only eight places. If that's the case, you need to test inputting two numbers that when added together equal an eight-digit number. You also need to test adding two numbers that add together to be more than eight digits.

Figure 3.5 is a visual representation of the two boundaries on the calculator program.

You have handled the low boundary requiring at least one digit to be input, but now you need to test the upper range. You want to force the software to handle the eight-place limit properly. The interface does not allow more than eight digits to be displayed, but perhaps it is actually taking the input anyway. If you enter a nine-digit number and added 0 to it, what happens? What happens if you add two 8-digit numbers together?

There are also some boundaries inherent in software, such as 256 values. Many pieces of software set this boundary on any number of things and have issues with it. For example, one bug in a messaging system that was caught prior to shipping involved a subject line of 256 characters that was handled properly, but a reply to a subject of 255 characters ended up sending a blank subject. Again, the exact boundary needed to be tested, but then tests needed to be conducted around the boundary as well. The limit that was accepted in that text entry field was exactly 256 characters, so testing 257 was unnecessary, except that on a reply, or a forward, to a message, four extra characters were stuck on—"RE: " the letter *R*, the letter *E*, the colon, and then the space. So test cases needed to send a message with 252 and 253 characters and then reply or forward it to make sure that the extra characters were handled properly. Another boundary where systems may not properly handle a value is 2147483648. This value overflows a signed integer on many machines. These are intrinsic boundaries based on the languages and assumptions in place.

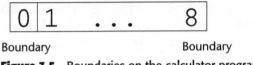

Boundary   Boundary

Figure 3.5 Boundaries on the calculator program.

Further, your software may carry its own boundary conditions, as eBay found out. The online auctioneer implemented a new feature called *Buy It Now*. This feature allowed a prospective buyer to click one button and pay the requested price to purchase the item without going through bidding and waiting several days. Buyers were experiencing problems with this feature and received *Problem with bid amount* errors when it was clicked. As it turned out, the *Buy It Now* amount equaled the opening bid amount exactly hitting the cusp of that boundary. The workaround that was temporarily suggested was to have sellers list the *Buy It Now* amount as $0.01 more than their opening bid amount in order to prevent this error.

You may also find that assumptions have been made as to the size of the data being entered. For example, you may have a place on your Web site for a user to register where they can enter their phone number. The developer, and many testers, will test for a three-digit area code, a three-digit regional part, and then the typical four digits at the end. But what if a person enters the 1 in front of the phone number? Perhaps the user has an office extension to include? Or what about a foreign phone number with a two-digit country code? Since there are so many different formats, it is best not to test for each format, but to test for the largest sizes that will need to be input.

Testing Problem Characters

In addition to boundary conditions, certain inputs can cause problems. For example, consider the place on your Web site I mentioned in the previous section where users enter their phone numbers. Does the text entry field accept only numbers? Can a person format their phone number in any of the following ways?

- (555) 555-1212
- 5555551212
- 555.555.1212
- (555) 555.1212
- 555-555-1212

Does your software handle the parentheses, periods, hyphens, and space correctly? These can all be problem characters in this place, and a client-side script might be useful to validate the input to save the user frustration.

Perhaps your Web application allows users to upload files to the server. Could there be assumptions around what the file names would be that could cause errors? Could somebody, or some function, have assumed everything would be on the Windows platform and would be an 8-dot-3 format? Windows does not allow some characters in the file name that other operating systems allow, and these characters should be tested. Also, older versions of Windows do not allow spaces and long file names, and so these also need to be tested to see how they are handled. Typical characters that are not handled properly here are \ / : * ? " < > and | . However, other characters may not be anticipated, or may have other meanings. For example, if the file is going into a database table, the semicolon, tab, or the comma could be used to delimit the items, and testing input involving those characters may be warranted. File names with other symbols may not be anticipated and need to be tested to ensure that they are handled properly.

There are also reserved characters or character combinations in various languages. For example, the HTML tags <SCRIPT> or <B> may actually be interpreted and rendered by your software if placed in one of your text entry fields. The JavaScript character combinations of \n or \b may trigger your software to actually render these rather than displaying them as a backslash and the letter that was typed in. There could also be the possibility of security issues if your text field actually ends up executing script that is typed in, especially in the case of shared data. Data interpretations like this should not happen, and you, as the tester, need to anticipate these potential problems through test cases and testing to ensure data integrity.

Another area where issues can arise is data conversions, either by the user or by the software. The character " looks a lot like " or even ' or ' and many people will use them interchangeably because, to the user, they may indicate the same thing. If the user does not know the difference between one and the other, it is reasonable to suppose that a well-intentioned user could enter the wrong character. For example, one bug that was caught in a particular server product was in the name resolution. A user could enter a full SMTP address, such as [SMTP: "blah@blah.com"], and the software properly resolved the name. However, if the user mistakenly typed in [SMTP: 'blah@blah.com'], then the server would not handle it properly. A reasonable user did, in fact, put that in, which was how the problem was found. Error checking had to be put in place to prevent that problem. Sometimes conversions can happen where one upper ASCII character will be converted to its lower ASCII counterpart, or a Unicode-only character will be converted to a lower ASCII character. These conversions are sometimes necessary to properly handle issues that may arise, but they need to be done consciously and carefully and always tested.

CROSS-REFERENCE

The discussion on problem characters continues throughout the book and in the International section, but a full list of potential problems is found in Appendix G.

Testing Defaults

Another area to test involves default data, and one place where default data is apparent is in registration forms that a user can fill out with personal information (see Figure 3.6).

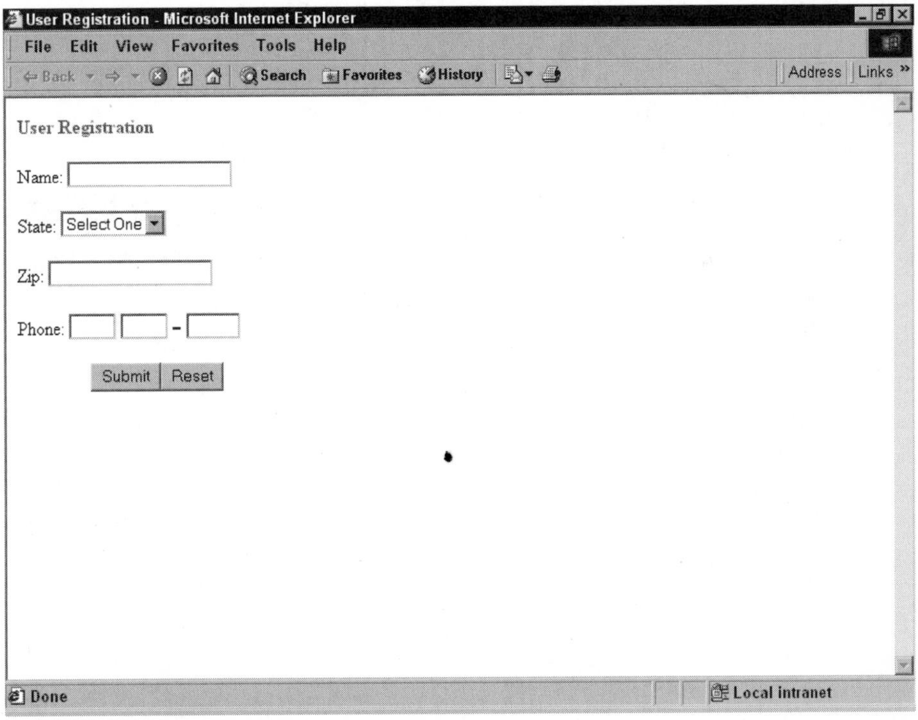

Figure 3.6   Simple online registration form.

In the example shown in the figure, you have a drop-down box with each state's abbreviation or full name in it, and the default selection in the list is *Select One* to indicate to the user to select a state. Your testing should include leaving all these defaults in place and attempting to work through the software with the defaults selected. The result of allowing all the defaults to be selected should be logical and expected. The software should behave logically and consistently and always leave the users in control and with enough information to work their way through situations. Do users not want to input their state of residence? Is it appropriate to allow them to save their registration with the *Select One* option selected? Or should the form check to ensure that an acceptable value has been chosen? The behavior that comes from leaving the defaults in place should be one that the user understands. The software should not allow the users to get five steps past that form and then alert the users that they must go back and select a value.

Testing Data Dependencies

To illustrate the concept of testing data dependencies, I want to continue using the example of a sample registration page (see Figure 3.7). In such a program, you might encounter pieces of data that are related to each other on the screen. Such relationships between data are *data dependencies*.

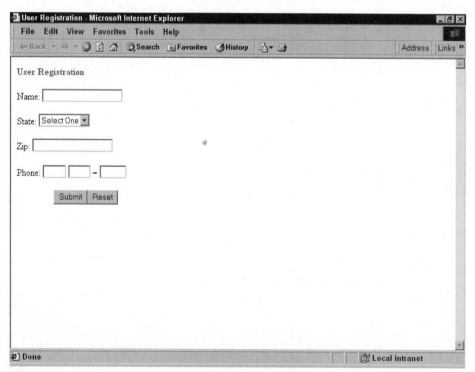

Figure 3.7 Sample form with fields related to each other.

In the form shown in Figure 3.7, the user is asked for a state, zip code, and area code. Will the software perform a lookup to verify that the zip code matches for the state and is valid? The area code for a phone number could be looked up as well. You need to identify these relationships. Make attempts to exploit them in testing, but also raise questions as to the appropriateness of the requirements and the user annoyance factors they may cause. Perhaps another zip code is added to the Post Office's list, and your company does not notice until several users have failed to register with your site. Is the hassle of performing the lookup and maintaining the database, as well as requiring all users to enter a valid zip code, adding any value to the product or the process?

Testing the Sequence of Events

Sometimes the order in which you perform actions or input data can affect the outcome or uncover bugs. These are usually some of the hardest bugs to reproduce because many testers will forget the *exact* steps that they performed or not realize that the sequence is the key. Remember the important steps that caused a problem and enter those into a bug report, but don't include extraneous information that would confuse the issue. The repro steps must be pithy and simple without losing any important information.

For example, in the registration page shown in Figure 3.7, you have a place for the users to select their state and then input their zip code. A developer or tester might make the assumption that the users will always select the state first and then enter the zip code. Functions can be written with this assumption in mind, and these assumptions may not always hold true. Try entering in the dependent information prior to the parent information.

Checking Your Timing

Timing can greatly affect the outcome of some functions. These are called *race conditions* because the conditions are in a race. If the proper one wins, then all works well, but if the wrong one wins you hit the bug. With Web applications, you have several aspects that can affect this race:

- The server speed
- The line speed
- The client machine speed

If any of these are too fast or too slow and the scenarios are not handled, the most common outcome is a script error or a runtime error indicating that the script blocks have not properly finished loading prior to the user performing an action or another function trying to call them. Some might say that these errors are inevitable parts of working on the Web, but they do not need to be so common. If your main user scenario is the home user, you can expect that they do not all have DSL connections and screaming fast machines. In fact, they probably fall at the other end of the spectrum with a 26.6-Kbps or 56-Kbps dial-up connection and a rather pokey machine that is not tuned for high-performance work. Even if your typical scenario is the CEO type, these professionals spend a lot of time on the road and are often at the mercy of airport and hotel kiosks or dial-up connections. And even the 56-Kbps modem has only the potential for a connection reaching that maximum speed. More likely the connection will be around 30–48 Kbps. Jupiter Metrix recently reported that only 28 percent of users on the Web have a broadband connection from work. Only 9 percent have a broadband connection from home.

Such statistics point to a clear need to test over a slow link. A proper test pass runs through the software on the high-end scenario and the low-end scenario, with a trigger-happy tester itching to hit the keys as soon as they can to hit these race conditions.

TIP

Alternately, automation can be used to hit these bugs, but frequently the timing needs to be so exact for the automation to input something at the appropriate time and still hit the window of opportunity that it can be better to have a caffeine-popped tester take a day or two to try to hit these bugs.

Taking the Back Door

Often there is a back door to many pieces of input that is not readily identified in the test cases, but would show up in a state enumeration exercise. For example, in the test registration page illustration, users may be provided with a way to update and edit their information in case their address or phone number changes. This activity is then separate from the initial creation of the data. What happens if you change data to be incompatible while in this software state (i.e., the state and zip code or area code don't match)? What happens if you edit data out of turn (i.e., edit the zip code and then the state)? Many times this back door to the data is an edit state rather than a creation state. Be sure to examine the various data flows to see if this can be a place where unexpected input can occur or where error handling is missing. The error handling could be as simple as an error-checking routine. Many pieces of software check for a condition only the first time and do not conduct the check any time after that. An example of this is a function that checks that an email address is valid. If the user types in **blah**, the function notes that this entry is not a valid format for the address and pops up an alert to let the user know. The user clicks OK on the alert but then doesn't change the address, instead ignoring the warning and submitting it again to the server. The function may not be called again to verify the format because the entry box is in a different state after the pop-up alert, depending on how the form was handled.

Trying Alternatives

Many times there are alternate ways to accomplish the same task. Consider the calculator example discussed earlier in the chapter. In that example, you could use the mouse to click on the 5 button that was presented in the user interface. It was also possible for the software to allow a keyboard input for the value of 5 or tab to the 5 button and hit Enter or Space to input that value. There may be multiple ways to accomplish the same task or to work around the same constraint. Look for these and exploit them by running each through the same paces to ensure that these alternatives do not leave your software open for failure or give the user a frustrating experience.

General Testing Techniques

In addition to verifying that it is possible to get the software to work correctly, you are also trying to set the software up for a failure. This falsification of an application and ensuring it handles invalid input in the best possible way is sometimes overlooked. Some organizations dismiss this, believing that their users are going to input only "valid" data. Who says which phone number is valid, though, (555) 555-1212 or 555.555.1212? If one of these forms actually ends up crashing your service, then does it matter? If you deny the use of any character other than a numerical value in the creation state, but forget to limit it in the edit state, then you are just as likely to have the issue arise. Much like a shirt, software has places where the pieces come together and seams where the pieces are joined. Often unexpected and unwanted outcomes arise from the seams in the software. These seams can be places where one function hands data to another function or where one developer hands off responsibilities to another developer. People often misunderstand each other and miscommunicate expectations. If this has happened, then their seams won't match exactly. If each person makes an assumption on how the other is implementing their part of it, then each may assume incorrectly. As a tester, you are trying to find the loose threads to pull and the weak spots to poke to get the software to hit a state where it should not be or will give an outcome that is not wanted.

These software seams are ripe with the potential for bugs. As testers you should see these seams as prime areas for testing. Data conversions often happen between these seams, and if they are not tested rigorously, bugs can slip through. Shortly after launch on June 4, 1996, NASA's Ariane 5 rocket failed. It was later found that there was a lack of exception handling in the conversion of a 64-bit integer to a 16-bit signed integer. This lack of exception handling resulted in an uninsured loss of over a half billion dollars. The developers implementing the designs are the best sources for identifying these areas of concern and often know of potentially failing test cases that they are not running. Through good communication, they can pass those cases along to the Test department.

This sounds like a lot of work, and it is. Your software is probably so large and your test organization crunched for resources and time that you are thinking *Wow, that's nice, but so unrealistic!* It can be, especially if the test organization is set up poorly or has been spending its time in the wrong places. If you run the exact same test cases every week, and they pass every week, you have not been testing the software. One time, I came into an organization where there were very few functional bugs found due to the structure of the testing activities. Talking with my new reports, the picture I had of some of the issues was validated, and I put a plan in place to work the team out of the testing rut it was in. Each tester had an area or component assigned to him or her and was responsible for it. We started an exercise by which they looked at their component and broke it out into smaller pieces—little bites of this larger component. We reviewed and worked with these lists and then set about testing them. Each tester was able to take one of these atomic units of his or her component and spend a few hours or a few days only testing that area. It created a very limited area so that the tester was not overwhelmed by functionality and could really scour it free of bugs. It also pointed out holes in their test plans where they had missed areas of functionality by doing only verification.

This sort of focused testing exercise reaps many benefits:

- It allows testers to really own their area and to focus on very discrete parts in order to deeply delve into specific functions.

- It allows the testers to train themselves and improve their own skills while learning the mechanics of the code base. For example, if there were code that had changed in an area, a tester could then go back to his small unit distinctions and work only in that area rather than being overwhelmed by the entire system and ending up testing relatively little of it.

- It also allows for tracking which specific areas have been tested and the thoroughness of that testing.

Certainly, if testers hit a wall and cannot work through it, they are able to brainstorm with the rest of the team to get back on track with the testing. This breakdown of testing is another manifestation of the best practice of breaking things into smaller pieces and is a very effective training tool and testing technique.

Reporting Techniques

Testing is not just about mechanically running test cases. Testing is ultimately a job in communication. If you cannot communicate how you found a bug or what the result of a bug is, then you are not going to be as effective as somebody who can. One bug report entered in a database was closed without any intention to fix it with the comment, "Won't fix because there's no way I can tell how much this bug will happen. I'm assuming not much or we would have seen this earlier." Aside from the obvious problems this quote reveals—that leaving the bug was risky and the reasoning for leaving it flawed—the tester had a role (one they didn't fulfill) to more clearly communicate the problems that this bug would cause and further raise the visibility of the bug after it was closed to champion the fix. Clear reporting in the first place reduces the overhead required to obtain a proper resolution and get a bug fixed.

Good Bug Reporting

To report the bugs that you find effectively, one of the best tools you can have in your testing toolkit is a bug report template. If you are new to a team and without a bug template to guide you, look through the bug database and find the bugs that seem to contain the most information in the best format. Copy this format and make your own bug template. The following is one format that I have used in slightly altered forms, which has proven very successful.

```
SERVER CONFIG:
Operating System:  <Operating system and hardware, if applicable>
Software Build:    <Build # of your software>
Topology:          <If you have multiple topologies where you test your
software in house>

CLIENT:
OS:      <Operating system, service packs, other dependant DLL ver-
sions, if applicable>
Browser: <Browser and version>

DESCRIPTION:
    <Brief description of the problem>

Repro:
1. <Very descriptive steps to re-create the problem>
2.

Result:
    <Describe exactly what happens after the last repro step.>

Expected results:
    <Describe what should have happened after the last repro step.>

Notes:
    <You may not need any additional notes here, but a description of
when this was last verified or what this might be related to would be
appropriate here.>
```

You may want to include good supporting documents with your bug report, or at least reference such documents. If your database does not allow for items to be uploaded and attached to bug reports, a public share may be available where you could load those documents and reference them from the bug description. Some useful supporting documents to include are the following:

- Screen shots
- Network traces
- The HTML or JavaScript that the client downloads
- Particular data you used to create a state (for example, 255 Japanese characters), saved off as individual documents and included to make it easier for others to reproduce this state

The discussion of what supporting documents you might create and when it's appropriate to use them continues throughout the book. But this practice is greatly appreciated by test managers and developers because it takes very little of the tester's time and shows thoroughness and consideration for the time of their colleagues. Remember that you are writing not only a report of what happened, but also a persuasive document for why it should be fixed. Not all bugs should be fixed; some just need to be noted, but most will need more attention. If you are unsuccessful in writing a compelling description, then your bug may end up dismissed just as the one in the quote at the beginning of the section was.

Another tip for effective bug reporting involves searching the bug database. A quick search through the database may turn up any similar bugs or related ones that should be noted in the bug report. Linking or otherwise referencing these related bugs helps developers identify if one fix can fix a whole list of bugs. It can also help testers to find the core problem rather than just symptoms. Many test teams keep a count of how many bugs individuals have entered that are exact duplicates of previous bugs. It is best to have a very low number of these. As you become more accustomed to the particular project and terminology used for it, accurate searches will be easier to perform. One thing that testers always kick themselves over is having searched carefully for a bug, found none, and then entered the bug themselves, only to find that in the time that they were writing it somebody else saved the exact same bug. Simply re-querying the database just before saving your entry helps prevent these unfortunate duplications. Taking the short amount of time to search the database properly familiarizes you with the product and existing bugs and ensures that the bugs you enter are unique and productive.

Bad Bug Reporting

What makes a bad bug report? Lack of information is the first thing. One bug in a product database read *When you resize the browser it looks like it got hit by the ugly bus.* The real problem was that the graphics were being wrongly resized, although you could not tell that was the problem from the database entry. The tester was probably also trying to be humorous. However, what the tester might have realized was that the developer who quickly created the graphics for the prototype did not appreciate the offhand critique. Be careful when using humor in text. Saying that *Loading up the new forms pooched my server* may not be understood by everyone the same way. As everyone knows from email, it is difficult to tell when people are joking and when they are serious, and exactly what vocal inflections they are intending as they write. Bug databases are open to all in the team, the company, and sometimes to external customers. These other parties may not understand the relationship between you and another coworker with whom you are joking. For this reason, be careful with humor. One experienced tester owned the area of the individual forms that would appear across the product. Although this area had the title of FORMS, the tester would log bugs referring to it as FORMZ. It may look "cooler" to have this as the title of your area, but 3 months from now it would be impossible to find anything if everybody decided to spell their area in their own way. Follow the guidelines of being professional—no foul language, no rude remarks or finger pointing, and handle humor carefully.

Some bugs do not get fixed or are not fully appreciated in time because of various issues that the testers actually have control over. If the issue is not clearly explained, then it is difficult to focus on the bug because the poor report becomes the focus. If the report or the repro is too complicated or convoluted, people will get lost. They will assume it is a very rare case and will not want to spend time looking into it. If the bug report is poorly worded, people reading it will give up. Watch out for using run-on sentences, slang, and inappropriate terms to refer to the product or the technology. If you click on a link in your product and receive one of the infamous *404 Page Not Found* errors, write that out exactly that way in the bug report. Entering a bug report that instead says *I click the link and nothing happens* is inaccurate, hard to understand, and will not be found on database searches. Putting the exact error strings and error codes into the searchable text of a bug allows you and others to find identical and related issues more efficiently. If you don't take the time to be so exact, finding those identical or related issues is more difficult later when you have several thousand bugs to wade through.

Most of all, before you save your bug report, make sure that you have explained and described your bug in the most compelling way you can. You are selling the bug to management and the developers to get it fixed. You may see distinctly how every customer will be affected by a particular bug, but that may be three steps away from your repro scenario. Others reading the report, in a rush, might miss that. When the true impact of the bug may be lost in an oversight, use a Notes section in your bug report to describe the most compelling scenario where this affects customers, or other relevant comments.

CROSS-REFERENCE
Chapter 2 contains further information on logging bugs effectively and maintaining a bug database.

Making Supporting Documents Useful

The whole point of taking a screen shot is to give others a better idea of what a bug is—a picture is worth a thousand words. Make comments in the shot, draw arrows, circle the interesting parts, paste in several items comparing and contrasting how something looks. Most of all, though, take the shot of only the interesting areas or the areas with the information, and save it with as few colors as possible. If you are dealing with something where the specific colors are in question or there is some other in-depth interface issue, then save it with a higher color palette. Saving as a .jpg or .gif may provide for a close enough match of colors, with some loss, and makes for a much smaller image (useful when entering thousands of bugs in a database where storage space becomes an issue). Figure 3.8 shows a sample screen shot that would not be very useful in a bug report.

This screen shot is not terrible, but it is not great. The problem here is that just by looking you are not sure what the problem is. It would help the shot if there was a comment and the proper images were included to compare the two. Also, the image is much larger than necessary; it would be better to have cropped it, with just the applicable area being provided. Figure 3.9 shows a more effective screen shot.

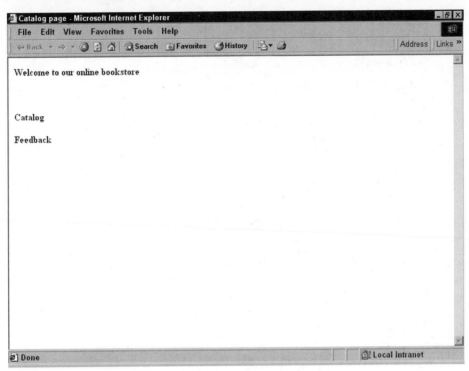

Figure 3.8   Sample screen shot that is of little use in a bug report.

This screen shot shows the issue clearly; the link disappears when you hover over it. The screen shot has comments and points directly to the problem areas.

The cliché is often true: A picture is worth a thousand words. From the picture, somebody who is more knowledgeable about the product can quickly identify if the issue is known, or can prioritize the problem to be fixed. Providing this type of document saves a lot of team time and is a very good habit to get into. When you become one of the product gurus and are wading through a hundred bugs a day, being able to quickly assess what is happening is crucial. If you are a Web-savvy tester, you can take this example one step further and include a comment in the description such as, "the text mouseOver color is set to *0066FF*, which is what the background color is set to, causing the text to disappear on mouseOver."

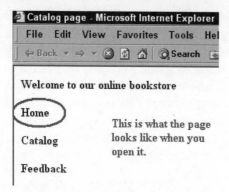

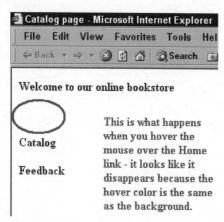

Figure 3.9 Screen shot that is very useful in a bug report.

Tester Fouls

Tester fouls are actions that testers make that, although they may seem to match some intermediate goal, are obviously not furthering the ultimate goal. If I uninstalled the browser and then logged a bug that I could not access the Web community, that would be a clear foul. I have correctly (according to my team's system of rewards) logged a bug, but it does not help us make better software. A tester must always work with a degree of common sense.

Tester fouls come in all shapes and sizes. Another tester foul would be a bug that was entered where the tester describes that if the server gets uninstalled a user cannot access the service. Of course, the customer cannot access the service—because the server is uninstalled. The bug is not that the customer cannot access the service, but rather *how* the server got uninstalled in the first place. If the cause were something other than a security hole, then this situation might be a tester foul because technically the service is behaving appropriately, given that the server is uninstalled. Many applications require that scripting be enabled in order to perform properly. If a user has script turned off in their browser settings and they want to use this service, then the program is not expected to operate properly. A tester who spends time testing in this unsupported configuration is unwise, and bugs logged against this configuration are tester fouls. I cannot take my car to the dealership and complain that it does not fly. It was never intended to fly, and the flight of my vehicle is not supported. If a user has cookies turned off and he wants to use your application, which relies on cookies, then the application is not expected to operate properly. Don't waste time testing unsupported configurations, and bugs logged against such configurations are tester fouls. However, the wise tester might test another option. For example, in the application that relies on cookies, instead of setting the cookies to *Enable* (which the software is expecting) or *Disable* (which is unsupported), the tester may try setting cookies to *Prompt* (see Figure 3.10) and then accept all cookies manually. This setting often causes errors and may be determined to be unsupported by your application after errors are found. But, according to the application specifications, you have accepted cookies and, theoretically, accepting them manually should work. That is an example of some of the settings that can trip up many applications.

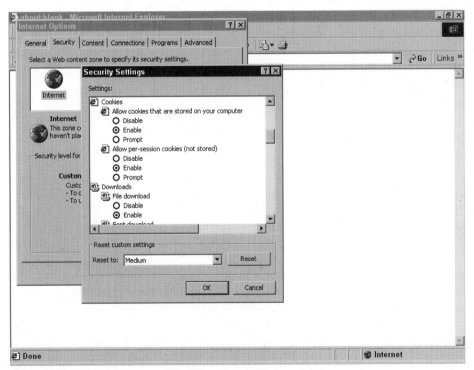

Figure 3.10   IE's security configurations for cookies.

Changing Security Zone Settings

There are five predefined security zones in Microsoft's Internet Explorer: Internet, Local Intranet, Trusted, Restricted, and Local Computer. Changing the security zone settings from Low to High on the appropriate zone can cause problems in applications, especially if your application relies on ActiveX controls or any scripting. Because of these sorts of restrictions, there might be a maximum level of security on the zones supported by your application or there may be certain options that need to be turned on to allow the application to work. These settings need to be well documented not only for your customers, but also for the test and development teams.

Testers can foul in many other ways, too. Championing a bug way beyond its time is a foul. If you disagree with a bug resolution, then take it to your manager or the person who resolved it. Clearly explain the issue and perhaps discuss it with the spec writer, the project manager, or the developer responsible. Do not reactivate the bug five times until somebody calls you a nitwit. Do not harass people or send email in all caps. These are ways that you get fouled. Drop the issue and allow it to come back up at a later date if ancillary issues are found. If they are not found, then the resolution was probably correct. Either way it is not your head on the line, it is your manager's responsibility to make those decisions. If you clearly and calmly communicate it and have it documented, then you can usually be assured that you did your job.

Your job is to find the bugs and campaign to get the right ones fixed. Test cannot fix problems. They can only identify them.

4

Starting on Web Testing

Much learning does not teach understanding.
—Heraclitus

H aving discussed the theory and the practical application of testing in previous chapters, I now want to start to scratch the surface of Web testing. This chapter includes such considerations as where to focus your effort, what considerations could affect your decisions, and how to set yourself up to have the most effective environment. Much of starting a job well lies in the preparation.

Organizing the Work

Many teams organize their Web application testing efforts using a matrix that lists the platforms and browsers and details the level of coverage, that is to say the amount of time and effort to be expended identifying problems and fixing them for various platform combinations. This matrix allows a company to make suggestions to users on how the site is best used or where it may not be supported. The most prevalent platform for a client machine on the Web is Windows; however, there are a lot of different Windows releases—Windows 95, Windows 98, Windows NT 3.51, Windows NT 4.0, Windows Me, Windows 2000 (Personal and Server), and Windows XP. Just testing these platforms could keep a testing team infinitely busy, but you also have to consider a range of service packs, as well as international and localized versions that may or may not affect the behavior of the browser or Web application. Beyond Windows, you also have Macintosh and the various Unix and Linux versions with which to be concerned. How does an organization decide where to test?

Sadly, many do not. They may guess based on one very vocal employee or customer, or there may be a guideline to follow such as the need to support only Windows clients or only Macintosh clients. However, a much better way to decide is to gather real data. Companies such as StatMarket among others deal in data specifically for this. They collect information from as many as a million servers a day and compile it into platform usage (percentages of users on the Internet with each platform), browser versions, line speed, and so on. Individual companies then purchase copies of this information to help them better meet the needs of their audience. Other organizations secure the services of a company to perform a study of their target audience or of their current clientele. Still other organizations use some assumptions to help them target their customers. For example, if your company was putting together software and sets of tools for Macintosh users, then it makes sense that testing your Web offerings on the Macintosh platform would be of the highest importance. However, you might determine that there are also a large number of *potential* customers who were currently using Windows PCs and were planning to purchase a Macintosh. You might want to make sure that they could use the site and have a good experience to pull them into your products.

TIP

If you are running a more general Web site aimed at a broad audience, such as a large news site, more comprehensive data on Internet users will better guide company decisions.

Once the supported platforms have been determined, you will need to rank which are most important to test. If your application does not use any libraries provided by the system, you will probably not need to test various versions of the operating system unless drastic changes were made, such as the difference between Macintosh OS 9 and OS X. If you need to test the various OS versions, your organization may decide that if there are limited changes between versions (Windows 95 and Windows 98, for example) that are anticipated to affect your customer's experience, you will not do a full test coverage on each platform, but will instead do spot checks on each. Such decisions are part, but not all, of determining the matrix of coverage for any product. You also need to determine the browsers that will be supported and where each will be tested. Working on this can be extremely disheartening because some Web applications will have an enormous matrix that will need to be prioritized effectively for the testing process to work.

Browser History

The Web was really developed in 1989 at the European Laboratory for Particle Physics in Geneva, Switzerland. Documents were stored on servers and referenced by hyperlinks. The first Web browsers were text only, like Lynx. These browsers allowed simple browsing of information and navigation through the text-only pages and were usually operated in a Unix terminal session. As the Web shifted to graphical layouts of the text and included images and richer media, the browsers started to take advantage of the new developments. The authors of these richer pages needed to still make sure that their sites were available to the text-based browsers, which were still quite prevalent. Many tags for accessibility come from the retrofit of graphical Web pages for text-based clients. NCSAs Mosaic was one of the first widely available graphical Web browsers, with a first version released at the end of 1994. These browsers were not free; users had to pay to download them, which they would gladly do to access the richness that was appearing on the Web. At this point, Netscape enjoyed an 80 percent market share for their browser. Microsoft saw the booming opportunity and in 1995 shipped the Internet Explorer (IE) browser with their Windows 95 operating system, making the browser essentially free. Microsoft's browser was sorely behind Netscape's. Netscape had more functionality, had better performance, and was a simpler browser that many people were comfortable using, and it was not until Microsoft shipped Internet Explorer version 4.0 with their Windows 95 updates that Microsoft came on par with Netscape. Netscape had to respond to this threat, which was rapidly eroding their lead, and in 1998 they also made their browser downloads free. Currently, IE 6 alone has over 30 percent of the market share, leaving Netscape with around 12 percent of the market, and many others filling in the remainder.

The problem with all of this is that there are a lot of versions of each browser out there, all with different implementations of the World Wide Web Consortium (W3C) standard. For your testing, one helpful bit to glean from all this history is that with the later versions of these browsers being freely available, a reasonable user can be expected to have a relatively recent version of any browser installed or can be guided to installing one. Such availability helps to eliminate older versions from the test and support matrix standardizing the user base. However, with the new PDAs, Web TVs, and other devices adding new browsers to the mix, the matrix is expanding again.

Browser Options

Netscape 7 is available on Windows 98, Windows NT 4.0, Windows 2000, Windows XP, Mac OS 8.6 or later, and Red Hat Linux 6.2 and 7.0. It is available in English, French, German, Italian, Spanish, Swedish, and Japanese. Netscape does have installable versions on the platforms listed in Table 4.1, some of which may not be fully supported:

Table 4.1 Netscape Browser Versions

WINDOWS	MACINTOSH	UNIX
Windows 98 (and SE)	Mac OS 7.6.1 or Higher	Linux kernel 2.2.1.4
Windows NT	Mac OS X	Red Hat Linux 6.2+
Windows Me	Macintosh PowerPC	
Windows 2000		
Windows XP		

Microsoft IE 6 is the latest version of Internet Explorer and is available for Windows 98, Windows Me, Windows NT 4.0, Windows 2000, and Windows XP. Earlier versions are available on the Windows platforms as well as Macintosh and Unix (Solaris SPARC and HPUX). The localized versions shipped for IE 5.5 are English, Arabic, Chinese Simplified, Chinese Traditional, Czech, Danish, Dutch, Finnish, French, German, Greek, Hebrew, Hungarian, Italian, Japanese, Korean, Norwegian, Polish, Portugese (Brazilian), Portuguese, Russian, Slovak, Slovenian, Spanish, Swedish, and Turkish.

MSN Explorer 8 is the latest version of MSN Explorer and is available for download in English, French, and German on Microsoft Windows 98, Windows Me, Windows 2000, and Windows XP.

Alternative Browsers

There are many other browsers in use including text-based ones:

- *Opera* has the third largest user base, with around 4.5 percent of the Web traffic reported as using it. Opera is available on Windows, Linux, EPOC, BEOS, and Macintosh, although it is most common on Linux. It is available in Afrikaans, Celtic, Chinese, Danish, Dutch, English (United States), Estonian, Finnish, French, German, Hungarian, Icelandic, Italian, Norwegian (Bokmal), Norwegian (Nynorsk), Portuguese, Portuguese (Brazil), Romanian, Russian, Spanish, and Swedish on the Windows platform, but only in English on other platforms.

- Omni Group makes a browser for the Macintosh platform called *Omni Web*. The most recent version, 4.1, is available in Chinese (Simplified), Chinese (Traditional), Danish, Dutch, English, French, German, Greek, Icelandic, Italian, Japanese, Korean, Norwegian, Portugese (Brazillian), Portugese (Native), Russian, Spanish, Swedish, and Finnish, with more translations planned.

- Amaya is W3C's open source Hypertext Markup Language (HTML) editor and Web browser project, and conforms precisely to their standards. It is available on the Windows XP, Windows 2000, Windows NT, Windows

95/98, Linux, Sparc Solaris platforms, AIX, Alpha, SGI, and HPUX. Amaya is available only in English, although the spell-checking component covers several languages.

■ Mozilla is an open source organization that works on the *Mozilla* browser. It is similar to Amaya in that it tries to adhere strictly to the standards laid out by the Consortium. Currently, Netscape consumes versions of Mozilla for its Navigator browser. Mozilla is available on Windows 9x/Me, Windows NT 4, Windows 2000, and Windows XP; Mac OS 8.6 or later; and Red Hat Linux 6.x and 7. It can also be built on:

- Solaris 2.7 (sparc), 8
- FreeBSD 2.2, 3.0
- Linux/Intel and Alpha 2.0, 2.1
- MacOS (9 and X)
- Win32
- AIX
- BeOS
- NetBSD
- OpenBSD
- OpenVMS
- BSDI
- HP/UX 10.20, 11.0, 11.2
- OS/2

Mozilla 1.1 is localized into Breton, Simplified Chinese (China), Traditional Chinese (both Hong Kong and Taiwan), Czech, Danish, Dutch, English (United Kingdom), Estonian, French, Galician, German, Greek, Hungarian, Italian, Korean, Lithuanian, Polish, Portuguese (Brazil), Russian, Siswati, Slovak, Sorbian, Northern Sotho, Spanish (Argentina), Tswana, Turkish, Ukrainian, Venda, Xhosa, and Zulu.

Platforms

In general, most consumer machines on the Web are running Windows—although the version will vary. Windows 95 is still a very viable operating system for home consumers and provides much of the functionality that they would want. The Windows platform also encompasses Windows 98, Windows Millennium Edition (Windows Me), Windows NT 4.0, Windows 2000, and Windows XP.

Macintosh is the second most common consumer platform and consists of OS 8, 9, and now X. OS 8 and 9 are very similar, but OS X is a completely different architecture based on the BSD kernel. Mac OS 9 shipped with IE 4.5, although IE 5.0 is available on this platform.

Not very many consumer client machines are running any of the Unix variants or Linux, although your particular consumer group may comprise of mainly this constituency. Many universities and Internet kiosks run Unix machines or terminals. Knowing what your user base will be using in a typical scenario will help shape your testing focus. If your application is an online university bookstore, knowing that the universities you serve have their student computer labs filled with various Unix terminals may affect your support and test configurations.

On top of the various main operating system versions, there are also service packs or QFEs (hot fixes) that may update the browser or vastly change the installation by updating the DLLs (dynamic link libraries) that the browser or other components depend upon. The difference between Windows 95 and Windows 95 SR2 was significant in terms of the changes to Internet Explorer and the underlying DLLs that it consumed. You should check the software documentation to see if the components you rely on are altered in the various updates.

CROSS-REFERENCE
■■■■■■ See Appendices J and M for listings of various software corporation Web sites.

Other Devices

As indicated earlier, in addition to these browsers and platforms, there are now PDAs and other devices that come into play when making testing decisions. Palm OS PDAs are not shipped with a Web browser, although there are some third-party options that provide this. Windows CE platform can carry a version of IE called Pocket IE (PIE) or Generic IE. Distributors of CE can decide which browser to compile in when designing their devices, and currently PIE is the more common one. PIE sends a Mozilla 2.0/IE 3.0.2 user-agent string and is supported as such when server applications render information based on the client. PIE supports the HTML 3.2 standard, but not ActiveX controls, Cascading Style Sheets, Dynamic Hypertext Markup Language (DHTML), downloaded controls, animated GIFs, VRML, or VBScript. It supports 16K colors, cookies up to 4 KB each, JScript 3.0 (ECMA-262 compliant), and can use only Basic authentication. The other version of IE for the CE devices is on par with IE 4.0 and uses that as the user-agent string identifier. It is referred to as Generic IE 4.0 (GENIE).

AOLTV provides a Web surfing machine, Internet access, and AOL client from the customer's television, much like Microsoft's Web TV. Both of these run over a 56-Kbps modem. MSN Companion is a similar Web surfing device offering Web access with a browser through a 56-Kbps built-in modem.

NOTE

The information provided thus far (and provided in the rest of the chapter) is not meant to be a complete or thorough discussion of all operating systems or browsers out there, only of the main ones. And even narrowing the information down this far, by the time that this book is published, this list will be out of date. What will not be out of date is the general idea that there is a huge matrix that can be tested and that you need to test wisely, understanding your dependencies in order to select the right places to spend your time.

The Matrix

To start indicating which platform/browser combinations are the potential ones to support, you create a matrix and gray out the cells for pairs that do not exist. A browser matrix can be depicted as a vertical axis holding the browser and a horizontal axis holding the operating system. Such an arrangement can clearly display all possible values that you can test. Table 4.2 shows an example.

Once the potential platform and browser versions are determined, you can fill in the matrix and proceed with prioritizing which are the most important to your company, product, or Web site. You may even decide to support only one browser or one platform because of technical or international support issues. For instance, Netscape Navigator 3.0 did not support frames. If your application relies on frames, you may want to provide an alternative link to a

Table 4.2   Sample Test Matrix of Browsers and Operating Systems.

	WIN 95	WIN 98	WIN 2000	WIN ME	WIN XP	MAC 9	MAC X
IE 4.5							
IE 5.0		Shipped with IE 5.0b	Shipped with IE 5.01				
IE 5.5							
IE 6							
NN 4.76							
NN 6.01							
NN 7							

nonframe area, or inform visitors of the minimum browser requirements. In that case, you still want to test hitting your Web application with the major browsers that you do not support to ensure that they can view your message regarding which browser/platform to use for your application. PDA platforms are becoming more substantial, but PDAs need close attention because they are still very limited in their abilities. Table 4.3 shows a sample matrix with some testing priority decisions entered into it.

This format easily quantifies which platforms will be tested and shows you where you should concentrate the bulk of your time. This can be done with symbols, numbers, colors, or any other identification method that works for your organization. Calling out different tiers of support helps determine coverage and priority.

TIP

One thing to note is that just because a platform/browser combination does not have a full test pass does not necessarily make it less supported. Often it can be determined that by alternating testing between certain closely related platforms or browsers, such as Windows 95 and Windows 98 or IE 5.0 and 5.01, enough coverage can be attained to ensure that the application is of sufficient quality.

You can take cues from the matrix to rank bugs based on the importance of the platforms the bugs occur on and to determine how and where your time is most wisely spent.

Table 4.3 Sample Browser Test Matrix, Including Test Emphasis

	WIN 95	WIN 98	WIN 2000	WIN ME	WIN XP	MAC 9	MAC X
IE 4.5	×					◆	×
IE 5.0	×	◆	◆			✓	◆
IE 5.5	◆	◆	✓	◆			
IE 6	◆	◆	✓	✓	✓		
NN 4.76	❑	❑	❑	❑	❑	✓	×
NN 6.01	◆	◆	◆	◆	◆	×	×
NN 7		◆	✓	◆	✓	×	×

❑—Not supported, although users may be able to run it from here
×—Low support; brief test pass
◆—Fully supported, but only moderate testing here
✓—Fully supported; full test pass

Another problem you face as a tester when you try to cover your matrix is that you cannot have multiple versions of the same browser on the same operating system installation. A newer installation of the browser will install over the previous one and overwrite the common libraries that each application is otherwise expecting to use. This situation immediately sounds expensive to a team, implying a lot of machines are needed to perform all the appropriate testing, but if testers are each assigned a main machine to work from and then secondary machines are made into multiboot systems, they can cover the matrix more easily. In addition, using switchboxes saves office space and reduces the number of monitors necessary.

Other Factors in Testing Web Applications

Many other factors must be tossed in to effectively test a Web application. Understand these concepts of designing Web applications before beginning the testing in order to save time and spend what little time you do have in the right places.

Considering Screen Resolution

The typical monitor size is currently 15" or 17" for a home user with 19" or 21" becoming more common for the corporate user. But monitor size only gives some guidelines as to what the resolution may be set to. Some users set their screen resolution to 640 x 480, and some crank it up to 1600 x 1200, which is a very large difference in the real estate that your Web application could be given. The lowest common denominator for a supported resolution is still ordinarily 800 x 600.

This information comes from data that is compiled by companies such as Stat-Market, showing that although these 800 x 600 resolutions may not make up the bulk of the audience, they make up enough of it that you cannot afford to ignore them. For example, if you design for 1024 x 768, then the users on the 800 x 600 screen size miss over ¼ of the pixels, which fall off to the right of their screen. If they never realize that they need to scroll to the right, they may never see the Subscribe button or the Purchase button.

The team that foresees this problem might decide to go with the 800 x 600 screen size and pass those specifications on to the designers. The designers see that the design should be 800 pixels wide, so they design a fantastic toolbar that is, as specified, 800 pixels wide. Whoa! That was only the target screen resolution. The canvas size needs to be calculated before starting to design any part of the interface.

Accounting for Canvas Size

The *canvas size* is the actual display area that you have to work with. You can see when your machine is configured to 800 x 600 that the maximum width that is displayed is 800 pixels. When you start any application, the application frames it with a few pixels, sometimes referred to as *chrome* (see Figure 4.1).

Figure 4.1 gives two examples of the same Window. In the first example, you see everything in the Window, canvas area, and chrome together. In the second example, the chrome has been shaded out, leaving only the usable canvas area where the Web page can actually be displayed. Everything outside the square can be considered typical chrome for this application on this platform consisting of toolbars, scroll bars, and window edging.

The chrome eats into the screen real estate, so you have to subtract it out of the 800 x 600, or whatever resolution you are aiming for. Each application has its own amount of chrome, and each application's toolbar can be configured to a different size, not to mention that size varies for each platform. You want to look at the very bare minimum amount of real estate that you can count on being there. Width is more important than height; people are used to scrolling down to see more, but scrolling down and across is annoying and not as apparent to users. If, after considering the issue, you decide to make the choice to exceed the dimensions, at least you have done your research and found what is optimal. Table 4.4 lists general canvas sizes for various browsers in 800 x 600 resolution. (Just as a note, there always seems to be a few pixels worth of disparity between different reports, but the numbers in this table are the ones I have found through investigation.)

The Incredible Shrinking Real Estate

Table 4.4 gives you the guaranteed maximum for each of the platforms. If you wanted to be fully supported on IE 4.5+ on Windows and Mac, then you could set your maximum canvas size to 723 x 395. However, you also have another factor that will creep into the edges of your display area. Each browser has an *offset area*—a blank space allocated between the edges of the window and the start of the display of text or graphics. This offset area is there by default and varies for each browser and each platform (see Table 4.5 for some examples of common offset area values).

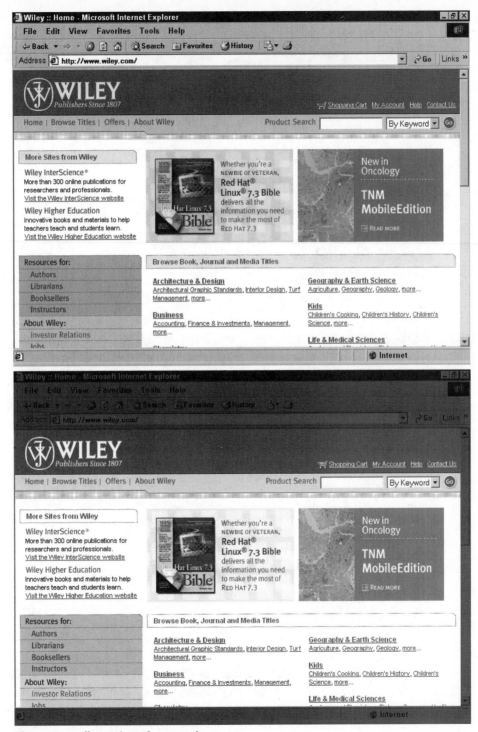

Figure 4.1   Illustration of canvas size.

Table 4.4 General Canvas Sizes for Various Browsers (in Pixels)

	800 X 600 AVAILABLE WIDTH	800 X 600 AVAILABLE HEIGHT
IE 6.0—Windows	778	431
IE 6.0 w/ Explorer bar—Windows	574	431
MSN Explorer—Windows	635	447
IE 5.0/5.5—Windows	760	395
IE 4.0/4.5—Windows	760	395
NN 6.0—Windows	792	423
NN 6.0 w/ sidebar—Windows	630	414
NN 4.5/4.76—Windows	764	414
IE 5.0—Macintosh OS X	764	373
IE 4.5/5.0—Macintosh OS 9	751	442
NN 4.5—Macintosh OS 9	752	429
MyMobileStuff portal—PalmOS	153	145
EudoraWeb—PalmOS	153	120
PocketPC	234	239

Again, if you wanted to be fully supported on IE 4.5+ on Windows and Mac, these offset areas (using the Windows values because they are the highest) would reduce your display area to 703 x 365 (10 pixels from the right and left offsets, totaling 20, and 15 pixels from the top and bottom offsets, totaling 30). The only other option you have is to tweak the BODY tag attributes to not leave the offset margins:

```
<BODY MARGINWIDTH=0 LEFTMARGIN=0 MARGINHEIGHT=
  0 TOPMARGIN=0>
```

Resetting the BODY tag attributes in this way allows you the 723 x 395 that you wanted to have.

However, there is even more you have to consider. If the Microsoft Office suite is installed, it would run a toolbar on the side that would take up another 43 pixels of width. If you are writing a corporate intranet application and know that all internal consumers have this Office toolbar displayed, then you might want to allow space for it.

Table 4.5 Offsets for Various Browsers (in Pixels)

	HORIZONTAL OFFSET	VERTICAL OFFSET
IE 6.0–Windows	10	15
MSN Explorer–Windows	10	15
IE 5.0/5.5–Windows	10	15
IE 4.0/4.5–Windows	10	15
NN 6.0–Windows	8	8
NN 4.0/4.5–Windows	8	8
IE 5.0–Macintosh	8	8
IE 4.0/4.5–Macintosh	8	8
NN 6.0–Macintosh	8	8
NN 4.5–Macintosh	8	8

Of course, all of this discussion should be disregarded when designing for the PDAs or cell phone surfers. Completely different constraints apply there.

What this means to you as a tester is that you will want to test on the minimum standard configuration, but you will also want to test on a higher resolution of something like 1600 x 1200 to ensure that the graphics look appropriate at that setting and are readable. With the introduction of flat screen monitors, high resolution becomes even more critical. With the high resolution that these newer monitors can display, the colors and images of applications that are aimed for traditional monitors may end up looking very bad. A quick pass through the software can identify these problems and prevent shipping a product that looks low in quality.

Additionally, Pocket IE provides an option called Fit to Screen that allows the user to see more of a Web page at one time and actually reduces the dimensions of any graphic by up to 50 percent. Select View in the browser window to test this option.

Testing Color Depth

Another monitor setting to consider is color depth. In the past, an average user could be expected to have 256 colors available. Web pages, which specified anything other than these 256 colors, looked unsightly, and even sticking to safe colors was no guarantee that a page would look good on the user's machine. Now, though it's easy to produce millions of colors. However, just because they look great on your Web designer's machine does not mean that they will look great on your consumer's machine. It depends on the browser, the operating system, the video card, the monitor, and how the monitor is configured (warmth, RGB levels, and so on). The Web safe color palette is only 6 x 6 x 6, which means only 216 colors. If you are specifying a background color or a major color for text, icons, and so on, it is safest to stick with these 216 colors.

WARNING
Designers may feel too constrained by this and decide to venture out of the safe palette, which can be fine. But realize that not all colors look the same on all platforms or render the same through various browsers, and may end up looking quite different on other machines.

Even more issues with colors come with PDAs, which can be grayscale only, or have a very limited color scale. Some users run their desktop machine in High Contrast mode to allow them to read the screen more clearly. This is a setting that is commonly ignored by Test, but can greatly affect your application. If you have a site with a large customer base that you anticipate is running in this mode, such as a site that is selling eyeglasses, you might consider doing a thorough test pass in High Contrast mode to make sure that your particular consumers will not be left out of your site. Often these accessibility settings are ignored, but we will discuss many of them as they apply to Web testing. For instructions on setting your machine to High Contrast mode, see Appendix D.

To cover testing color depth, set the colors down to your minimum supported configuration and then up to the millions. Then, also view your application on other constrained platforms, most importantly the PDAs.

Testing Line Speed

Another large variable to throw in is how fast a connection the user has to the network, also called the *line speed*. Although more users are able to subscribe to DSL or cable modems, and more people are surfing the Internet from work, most home users still have modems for home access. Your test plans need to specify what you expect your user's connection rate to be. If your typical user is one who connects from home, is not at the cutting edge of technology, and uses the computer infrequently, then you can expect that this user will have a connection rate of 56 Kbps at the highest. 56 Kbps is really the low end of the line speed for the testing that most organizations do on a day-to-day basis. At the other end of the spectrum is an internal Web application where all users are guaranteed to be connected via the LAN (probably a T1 or T3). Such arrangements are toward the top end of the spectrum and are where many testers tend to confine their testing. Such connections are faster, easier, and get the job done for the tester. However, if your typical user is a sales professional, he may have a DSL link from home and a LAN connection from work, but because he is on the road a lot he is subject to the slow links from hotels and airports. This scenario requires a pass with both the fast link and the slow link:

■ Set up a screaming fast machine to perform the fast link testing and dedicate a day to trying to hit the *race conditions* for that scenario.

NOTE A *race condition* is when two functions are in a race. If the expected one wins, then all works as anticipated. If the other one finishes first, then unexpected results occur.

■ Hit the other end of the spectrum with a slow chip machine hooked up on a slow link connection with little RAM to verify that runtime errors do not appear for that scenario.

Your application may have no race conditions to be seen, but if the download time for the average user is very slow, they may use a solution that is faster. The typical rule of thumb is to keep a single page below 50K with no single graphic larger than 24K. Such restrictions are not always possible, and there are always exceptions to the rule, but for a basic state, these restrictions are good guidelines.

Revisiting the Matrix

Now you can apply some of your new constraints to your matrix making it more granular to give the most information as simply as possible. You can even break the application into functional areas and present a matrix like the one shown in Table 4.6.

Table 4.6 Sample Test Matrix for Browsers, Importance, and Configurations, Covering the Subscribe Process Function

	800 X 600	1600 X 1200	SLOW LINK (56 KBPS)	FAST LINK (LAN)
IE 4.5—Win 95 ×				
IE 5.0—Win 95 ×				
IE 5.0—Win 98 ♦				
IE 5.0—Win 2000 ♦				
IE 5.5—Win 95 ♦				
IE 5.5—Win 98 ✓				
IE 5.5—Win 2000 ✓				
IE 5.5—Win Me ♦				

(continued)

Table 4.6   *(continued)*

	800 X 600	1600 X 1200	SLOW LINK (56 KBPS)	FAST LINK (LAN)
IE 6 Win 95 ♦				
IE 6 Win98 ♦				
IE 6 Win Me ✓				
IE 6 Win 2000 ✓				
IE 6 Win XP ✓				
NN 6.01–Win 95 ✓				
NN 6.01–Win 98 ♦				
NN 6.01–Win 2000 ✓				
NN 6.01–Win Me ♦				
NN 6.01 Win XP ♦				
NN 7 Win 98 ♦				
NN 7 Win 2000 ✓				
NN 7 Win Me ✓				
NN 7 Win XP ✓				
IE 4.5–Mac OS 9 ♦				
IE 4.5–Mac OS X ×				
IE 5.01–Mac OS 9 ✓				
IE 5.01–Mac OS X ♦				
NN 4.76–Mac OS 9 ✓				
NN 4.76–Mac OS X ×				
NN 6.01–Mac OS 9 ×				
NN 6.01–Mac OS X ×				
NN 7 Mac OS 9 ×				
NN 7–Mac OS X ×				

❑—Not supported, although users may be able to run it from here
×—Low support; brief test pass
♦—Fully supported, but only moderate testing here
✓—Fully supported; full test pass

From this matrix, you can perform your tests, appropriately prioritizing them and checking off each, making comments as necessary. For the best performance and to minimize the time that testing takes, running a scenario such as high resolution, fast link, and high color depth all at the same time saves time and keeps you from getting bored from running the same test cases day after day. You cannot double and triple everything up like this, so there will be some amount of repetition. Tasks where only the user interface (UI) is being evaluated, such as testing High Contrast mode, are often handed to a more junior tester, while automation can cover many of the redundant test passes of the functional verifications on the various configurations.

Considering Other Factors

A lot of other factors can affect your software. You need to find out what needs to be tested, such as access to your application through Secure Socket Layer (SSL) or from behind various firewalls or proxies. All of these other factors (including ones particular to your test projects that I can't anticipate) determine the boundaries of the matrix you generate and indicate to you how the testing effort should proceed.

Basic Web Applications

You see, wire telegraph is a kind of a very, very long cat. You pull his tail in New York and his head is meowing in Los Angeles. Do you understand this? And radio operates exactly the same way: You send signals here, they receive them there. The only difference is that there is no cat.

—Albert Einstein, when asked to describe radio

How does the Web work? The most basic of Web applications is a simple Web site that is not interactive or dynamic. The information you are able to see is exactly what I am able to see and what everyone else is able to see. For example, suppose for this case there is a simple server containing HTML files and images. Other things can be there, but I want to keep this to the most basic of all scenarios as possible. Figure 4.2 shows a very simple scenario, consisting of one client connecting to one server.

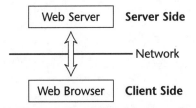

Figure 4.2 Simplistic client/server scenario.

But what really happens in this scenario?

1. As a user, you type in an address such as: *http://www.oursimple application.com.*

2. The browser, in concert with the networking software, which I will leave out of this discussion, then tries to find the domain *oursimpleapplication. com*. Once it finds the domain, it tries to locate the server named *www* in this domain.

3. The server looks for the default page that it should serve up when the site is requested, such as *default.htm*. The server sends back to the client a copy of the file *default.htm*.

4. When the browser receives this, it starts walking through the file character by character and rendering it. It starts off by seeing `<HTML> <HEAD>`...

5. As it walks the document and tries to render each piece that it can, it will likely come across references to images that need to be displayed, which in this case might look like `<IMG SRC="image.jpg">`. The browser does not have a copy of this file in its cache and must send a request to the server for a copy of the image.

6. The server locates the image and sends a copy to the client. The browser then takes the image file and renders it in the proper place in the Web page.

You should understand two crucial points about Web applications from this example:

- The client sends requests that the server then responds to.
- Between these requests and the response, the connection between the client and server is completely cut. The network connection to the client machine could be removed and the browser would still try to render the data, as long as the files had already been sent down to the client. (This point that between request and response the connection between client and server is cut is crucial, but is not always grasped by many in Web development projects.)

Consider this relationship in another way. You want some information from me, so you come to my office, knock on my door, and request a data file. I grab the data printout off my desk and hand it to you and close the door. At this point, you have opened a connection (knocked on my door), the connection was established (I opened the door), you made a request ("Can I get that data file from you?"), your request was answered ("Sure, here you go," and you were handed the file), and the connection was closed (I closed my door and went back to work). You are now standing in the hall with a copy of the data you requested. You can start reading the data, understanding it, or whatever you want to do with it. But, as you start reading this text, you realize that it references a really useful chart. So what do you do? You request it. You knock on my door, I open my door, you request the graphic to add to your collection of data, and I hand it to you and close the door. This example illustrates the way that every request is made to the server. If there are no other files referenced, then that is the end of our communication. However, if you wanted to gather another document, you might start the process over and request another text file, the supporting graphics and images, and so on. Once you have been handed the file you requested, the connection is severed and must be reestablished for the next request. While that connection is cut, I have no knowledge of you standing outside my door, no idea what you want, or what you will request next. The server is in exactly the same position as I am in this illustration. Keep this analogy in mind as I begin to make the sample application scenario more complex and realistic.

TIP A really great exercise to help you understand this client/server relationship is to get a network monitoring tool and install it on your client machine. Start requesting very simple Web sites and watch the traffic that goes across putting together what files the client requested. Look through the HTML as displayed in the browser and identify where these files were referenced. Try to put the whole series together in your mind. Once you feel comfortable with that, continue on through the dynamic Web sections. Links to network monitoring and packetsniffing tools are available in Appendix J.

Complicating the Web Application Scenario

A dynamic Web application can be broken into three parts:

- **The user agent.** The user agent is typically thought of as the browser as operated by a user, but it is really the combination of the operating system and the browser such as IE 5.5 on Windows 2000. There are other user agents on the Web, such as Web spiders, but for the discussions in this chapter, I want to stick with the familiar concept of a user-operated browser.

- **The Web server.** The Web server is part of the server side and receives the transmissions from the user agent. It is typically a Windows NT or Windows 2000 server with IIS installed, or a Unix variant with Apache installed.

- **The database.** The database portion is just that—a database. Not all Web applications have databases, but they are a common part of many Web applications and Web sites. The database can be located on the same machine as the Web server, and in some smaller applications this machine may be the only machine there is serving up pages to the client user agent. In larger applications, there may be several databases and/or several Web servers to handle the requests from users.

Figure 4.3 shows a simple diagram of this three-tier scenario.

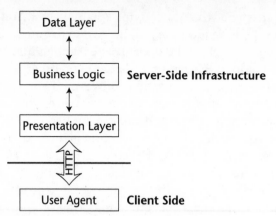

Figure 4.3 Generalized three-tier scenario.

A Bit More on How the Web Works

Every single page or item on the Web has a unique *URL (Uniform Resource Locator),* or *URI (uniform resource indicator).* Figure 4.4 shows a URL format.

The protocol tells the browser how to make the request to the server. The domain name routes the request through the Internet to the correct domain where the host server is located. The file is located on that machine, or on the group of machines serving the content. HTML files live on a server, the machine that is out "on the Internet." Files with extensions of .htm or .html and many others sit in directories and wait to be requested. When a browser navigates to a site, HTML pages are typically being requested from that site. The browser sends a request to the server for a particular URL (for example, *http://www.foo.com/bar).* The server knows that it is the *foo.com* server and that it should look in its bar directory. Many administrators set up a default file for all folders as *default.htm* or *index.htm* or *home.htm* or some similar name. Since there is only a directory specified and not a particular file, the server locates the default HTML file and sends a copy of that to the browser. Once the file is located, a copy is sent to the browser that requested it. The browser starts going line by line through the HTML code and deciphers how to display the content according to the tags. The browser may also request a particular file within a directory so that instead of the server locating the default file for a folder, it finds the particular file that is being requested (for example, *http://www.foo.com/bar/foobar.htm).*

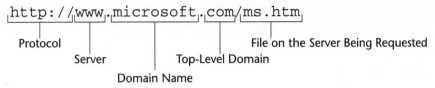

Figure 4.4 Analysis of a URL.

The URL has no one standardized limit but is generally handled at about 4,096 bytes, and that includes any commands or parameters added onto the end. However, IE has a limit of 2K for the URL length. Although this is a long string of data, if your Web site has files many levels deep, long filenames, files with double byte characters that must be escaped, forms that send the information to the server with a GET method, or a lot of parameters on any request, then this limit could definitely be reached. Because of this, the limits should be tested for any Web application.

The browser requests the data from the server by way of this URL. Within the page that is requested, there are usually links to images or scripts. The browser requests each of those as it comes across the reference in the page. The HTML is processed as it arrives at the browser and is displayed to the user. If there are links for images, sounds, scripts, or other files, the browser sends another request to the server for each image referenced. The same process occurs here—the browser requests them, and the server locates the image and sends a copy of it to the browser. The browser then determines where to place images in the page according to the formatting tags. If the browser is unable to handle the file, it is handed to the proper component or application to assist. All script is handed off to the scripting engine (if there is one) to compile and execute. Because of the delay in the receiving of the script, handing it to the engine, and executing the results, script errors can occur when users try to interact too quickly with pages that have not fully loaded.

Requesting a Web Page

When the user starts up a Web browser and types in an address or clicks on a link, the browser sends information to the server using *Hypertext Transfer Protocol (HTTP)*. HTTP is a request/response protocol that is generic and stateless. *Stateless* means that the state of the client is not saved from request to request. There are ways that applications work around this and provide state, but the protocol itself treats each request as a fresh one with no knowledge of prior requests and no information persisting between them. The client's request is formatted into three parts:

- The request line
- The request header
- The request data

The *request line* contains the method being requested, such as GET, SEARCH, or POST. The request line is followed by the URL being requested and the HTTP version. It might look like the following:

```
GET http://www.microsoft.com/  HTTP/1.0
```

The end of this section is marked by a CARRIAGE RETURN-LINE FEED (CRLF) to indicate the beginning of the next section of data. In the raw code point format, this carriage return and line feed will be seen as OD OA indicating the code points of a carriage return and a line feed.

The second part of the request is the *request header*, which typically consists of the name: value pairs such as Accept-Charset, Accept-Encoding, Accept-Language, or User Agent and their associated values. In a request, it might look like the following:

```
Accept: image/gif, image/x-xbitmap, image/jpeg, image/pjpeg, application/
vnd-ms.powerpoint, application/vnd-ms.excel, application/msword, */*
Accept-Language: en-us Proxy-Connection: Keep-Alive User-Agent:
Mozilla/4.0 (compatible; MSIE 5.5; Windows NT 5.0) Host:
www.microsoft.com
```

This request has just told the server what types of files it can receive (it lists the file types, but generally it accepts everything as indicated by the */*), the language that it is using (English—United States), and the browser and OS version that it is running (Windows 2000 with IE 5.5). Between each name: value pair is a CARRIAGE RETURN-LINE FEED to indicate the start of a new name: value pair. A full list of the potential name: value pairs is available in RFC 2616. The request line is concluded with a CARRIAGE RETURN-LINE FEED to indicate the beginning of the request data section.

The *request data* section contains any data that might be relevant to the request such as cookies, the search query, and so on. The entire request is ended by a CARRIAGE RETURN-LINE FEED, followed by a second CARRIAGE RETURN-LINE FEED to indicate the end of the entire request.

Responding to the Request

Once the server has received and interpreted the request, it responds. The HTTP response message consists of a status line with header information and the message body. The status line tells the user agent which HTTP version it is communicating with. If the user agent has requested a higher HTTP version than the Web server can support, then the server responds with the highest version it can support, and the communication takes place on that version. If the server is capable of using a higher version than the user agent, the server degrades to the lower version. The lowest common denominator of the two is chosen if they do not agree.

The HTTP version is then followed by the status code and the description of the reason. Everyone has seen examples of these items many times: for example, the *404 Resource Not Found* message that appears when clicking on dead links. In that case, the *404* is the status code and the reason description is the *Resource Not Found* string, describing the code for you. Most of the codes that are returned from the server are never seen by the user; they are just communicated directly to the browser, describing the status of the requests. The status codes are always three-digit numbers. The first digit indicates the response category:

- The 100 range (1xx) is information regarding the status.
- The 200 range (2xx) indicates that the response is successful.
- The 300 range (3xx) indicates a redirection.
- The 400 range (4xx) indicates that there was a client error.
- The 500 range (5xx) indicates that there was a server error.

Following the code and the reason phrase can be a series of name: value pairs to give the user agent more information, such as the page's age, the date, the content-location, or the content-type. A full list of response codes and response header name: value pair fields can be found in RFC 2616, and a discussion of them can be found in Appendix E. The whole status line is terminated with a CRLF.

The message body is the next part to come across and consists generally of the actual data that was requested. The message body contains the HTML, the JavaScript, or other requested data that the browser interprets into the text, and layout of the Web page. With some large pages, it may take many response packets to transfer all the requested information to the client. At the end of the session that was requested, the server can close the socket connection that this has all been transferred over, or it can issue a Keep-Alive command to keep that socket open. To go back to my office door example, the end of the session is similar either to my closing my office door when I have responded to your request, or to my leaving it open in anticipation of your next response.

Web Application Testing Techniques

The great thing about Web testing is that unless the transmission is encrypted, you can see exactly what is going across the wire—like eavesdropping on the conversation of exactly what is said between the client and the server. Many tools exist to help you to do this. Microsoft has a tool called Network Monitor that comes with Microsoft Systems Management Server (SMS) and allows you to view not only the traffic on your computer, but also the traffic to and from any other machine on the subnet where Network Monitor is installed. Such a tool gives you a great deal of power!

WARNING

A word to the wise. Installation of such software is usually accompanied by a company policy that requires users to use it only for testing purposes, and rightly so. Otherwise, users have the power to watch which sites the vice president surfs when he is between meetings, or possibly watch what emails coworkers are sending. Companies do not mess around with this kind of power, and they regulate its installation and usage. Network Monitor and many other packages like it do announce their presence to the network when they are running, and they attach the machine name to that announcement. If somebody wanted to track down who was watching the VP, it would not be terribly hard.

The real usefulness of any sort of network monitoring or packet sniffer tool is not just watching the data flow as it happens, but having the ability to record the requests from the client and the responses from the server and save off the trace as a file for future reference. These files can be crucial to debugging problems and identifying the root cause of issues in Web applications. Packet sniffers are fantastic tools that teach you a lot about your application and prove very useful in debugging problems.

Including Supporting Documents

I cover the topic of including supporting documents with your bug reports in more detail in Chapter 3, but touching on it here in the context of network traces you generate from packet sniffers is appropriate. These network traces are some of the most useful supporting documents that can be included in a bug report. When you find bugs, you need to give a text description of what you see wrong. Sometimes you have enough information to diagnose the problem, and sometimes you do not. Being able to attach appropriate supporting documents to your issue reports saves a lot of time and effort. After reading your description of what you identified as a problem, a test manager or developer can open a supporting document and quickly see what the issue is. A nice clean trace can quickly point a developer to the exact place where the problem can be located. Show only the information that is applicable to the issue. Don't clutter it with unnecessary information.

CROSS-REFERENCE
Chapter 3 goes into more detail about writing effective bug reports that include supporting documentation.

Dealing with Caching Issues

One problem you face with Web testing involves caching. The browser holds a cache of recent information; if the Web server's copy has not changed as far as the browser can tell, the cached copy of information is used by the browser instead. For users, caching makes browsing much faster as they do not have to download every single item every single time. As a tester, however, you want to absolutely get the latest information off the servers. If a cached copy is available and retrieved, the information you really need to test is not transferred across the wire.

The following steps walk you through what you have to do to take the cache into account and verify problems in a Web application:

1. Suppose you encounter a script error. The first thing you do is see if you can reproduce it.

TIP
You may want to take a screen shot of the problem (if the problem displays like that) just in case it does not reproduce easily. For instructions on taking screen shots, see Appendix D.

2. To see if the error is reproducible, you will need to shut down all browser sessions for that type of browser—if we have IE running, you shut down all IE sessions.

3. Open one instance of the browser and delete all the cached items and local copies (and cookies, if applicable) and then close that instance.

4. Open a single instance of the browser and try to reproduce the problem.

5. If it reproduces, then follow up further. First carefully note all the steps that need to be performed to cause the problem. It can be difficult on some issues to identify what actions contribute to the bug and which ones are irrelevant.

6. Once the repro steps are identified, searching out other conditions of the bug is crucial. Does it only occur on Windows? Only in Netscape? Perhaps only on Netscape 6.00 on Windows 2000?

7. Once enough information has been gathered on the issue to understand it, searching the bug database is the next logical step. Search carefully for bugs that match the issue you have found.

TIP

Be careful of bugs that have been entered with a slightly different term than the one you are expecting; for example, you may call a Web page's location the URL, but somebody else may refer to it as the href, location, URI, or other term. Not all duplicates can be avoided, but many can be by a general search based on the proper terms and names that apply to your project.

8. If there are no bugs currently entered on your issue, proceed with entering one. Collect support documents such as screen shots, network traces, or other information that will help reproduce or debug the problem.

9. Just before saving the bug report, do a quick search for all bugs entered in the last half hour, just in case somebody else entered one just as you were opening yours. More than one tester has been frustrated to have carefully logged a bug only to find somebody else beat them to it by a matter of minutes, but such a check keeps duplicate bugs from being posted.

The process I've just described is a general guideline. Remember that all teams have their own process for handling bugs. Make sure you understand your team's process before proceeding, or you run the risk of potentially frustrating fellow testers, developers, or management.

Just because the bug does not reproduce does not mean it was not a bug. A very specific set of interactions performed not only by you but also by other users testing that server might have caused some unexpected state or a rare race condition to be hit.

As I alluded to at the start of this section, one of the largest sources of false bugs is a tester not clearing his cache. The cache is a very pertinent issue for many teams, yet many do not realize that they are affected by it. There is the commonly known browser cache that can be emptied manually. If you are testing an application that is available over the Internet, there may be firewall or proxy issues to deal with between the application and the customer. Many proxy servers are overly helpful and cache data to help minimize the network traffic. Again, this is great for users, but not for testing. You do not want to get mismatched versions of files just because that is what the proxy server handed you. If your proxy does cache data, be sure that you configure your browser to bypass the proxy when accessing your test servers. Discussions on how a proxy server or firewall will affect customers should occur prior to deployment, though.

CROSS-REFERENCE
■■■■■ Instructions on dealing with both proxy servers and firewalls are found in Appendix D.

Configuring Your Browser for Web Application Testing

Another source of nonreproducible bugs comes from having unsupported configurations, such as having script options turned off. By default, Internet Explorer disables script debugging and will not display script errors for you. Because these errors are exactly what you want to see, you have to make sure that you turn these options on and have a local script debugger installed to debug the errors you come across. Nothing is less productive than a machine without a debugger on it. Ideally you would have the same debugger that the development team standardized on. Appendix D has instructions on how to install a basic debugger that will serve your purposes as a Web tester.

Figure 4.5 displays three settings in Internet Explorer that represent the bare minimum of how your system needs to be set up to catch the maximum number of bugs. These three settings may be located in different places in other browsers, but they are no less important to correctly configuring your machine. They are Disable script debugging, Display a notification about every script error, and Check for new versions of stored pages: Every visit to the page. Many other settings may or may not be supported for your application; for example, your application may depend on the use of cookies and particular client cookie settings.

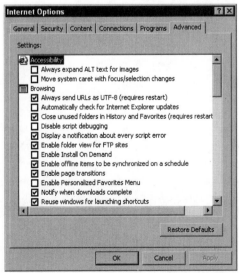

Figure 4.5 Configurations to be aware of on Internet Explorer.

Configuring Other Browser Settings

Browsers have a lot of various configurations that can end up expanding the test matrix.

One setting that users commonly change involves the colors. Although you may really like the colors selected for the application, a color-blind user may have discovered that in order to fully use many sites he must set his own colors for links, text, and background. If you force all users to use your color selections, you could be cutting out part of your target audience. To ensure that you are picking up a user's preferred color settings, reset your machine's color settings and select some hideously obnoxious colors such as orange and lime for text, background, and links. These colors are easy to see and show up well in supporting screen shots to identify hard coded text. Figure 4.6 displays the IE user configuration for colors, which can be accessed through the IE Tools menu. (Select Tools → Internet Options, and then select the Colors button on the General tab.)

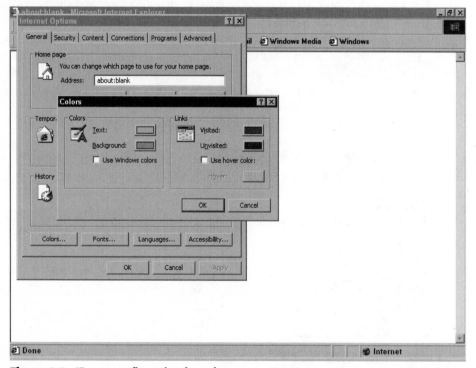

Figure 4.6 IE user configuration for colors.

Text size is another common setting that users adjust to customize their experience. Most users do use their browsers with the text size set to Medium; however, running through your application with it set to Largest and Smallest helps you find strings that get truncated, places where your text is unreadable, and other similar issues. If your user base is primarily the elderly, they may have a need for larger text. In IE, this setting can be set through the browser toolbar (see Figure 4.7), or if you are using IE and have a mouse with a scroll wheel, you can hold down the CTRL button while rolling the scroll wheel to dial the font size up or down.

Another issue that your application could be subject to is the Internet kiosk scenario. If your application will be run in Internet cafés or hotel kiosks, then your application might be subject to Kiosk mode on these machines. Kiosk mode is an Internet Explorer option that forces the browser to take over the entire desktop. Instead of the standard desktop view shown in Figure 4.8, the user is presented with the slightly different Kiosk mode view shown in Figure 4.9.

Figure 4.7   IE's text size selector.

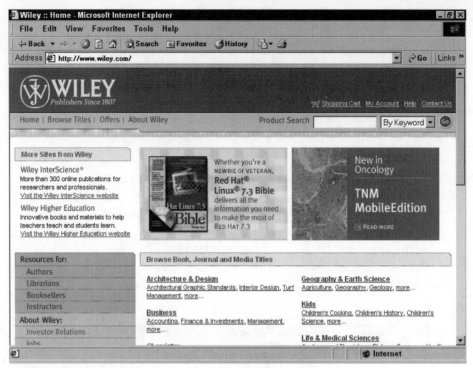

Figure 4.8 Internet Explorer as viewed in Standard mode.

Kiosk mode changes the canvas size so that on an 800 x 600 screen, IE has an available canvas size of 780 x 575 instead of 760 x 398, giving it a much larger space. To toggle between Kiosk mode and normal IE state, with IE as the window of focus, hit the F11 key. The F11 key will display IE in Kiosk mode with navigation buttons. To access IE without these, you can run it from the command line with the command `iexplore -k` *page* (i.e. `iexplore -k www.wiley.com`).To undo this, simply hit the F11 key again, or ALT-F4 if it was invoked from the command line. Several toolbars are missing in Kiosk mode, and your application may not behave the same way or be used as intended without these. If your application has a high probability of being used from a kiosk, then working with the application in Kiosk mode might be part of the design considerations and testing process.

Of course, all of the issues that have been mentioned should be specified prior to the beginning of coding; however, that rarely happens. Doing a quick check of your software in these settings is very useful in the long run. Many teams have not worked with Web development or Web testing, so an overview like this in the spec stage can help to prevent potential problems before they even become a permanent part of the code base.

Figure 4.9   Internet Explorer as viewed in Kiosk mode.

CROSS-REFERENCE
Guides provided in Appendix D walk through setting many settings for Internet Explorer and Netscape Navigator.

Testing Web applications is not just verifying that all the links are active and all the graphics show up. As this chapter has shown, there are a lot of other areas, and you are just starting to get into them. Application usability, content and design, performance, security, and international issues are all discussed in subsequent chapters of this book. This chapter has given you an introductory discussion of the manual process of verifying Web applications. Many tools exist to make this verification easier and faster so that testers can be freed to truly test the application rather than just verify it. However, learning to do something manually is essential to understanding how to effectively operate a tool to get that same job done.

CROSS-REFERENCE
■■■■■ I have compiled a discussion of tools and automation in Chapter 10 and made mention of tools throughout the chapters in this book. Additionally, a checklist of questions to consider while testing has been compiled from the contents of the book. This checklist is available in Appendix H.

But remember, tools and checklists, ultimately, are no replacement for a knowedgeable tester.

PART TWO

Client-Side Testing

CHAPTER 5

Testing HTML—The Static Web

Ignorance of all things is an evil neither terrible nor excessive, nor yet the greatest of all; but great cleverness and much learning, if they be accompanied by a bad training, are a much greater misfortune.

—Plato

To test something, you have to know a bit about it. You cannot judge without criteria, and you cannot develop a good set of criteria without possessing knowledge about that which you wish to judge. To effectively test a Web application, you need to know a bit about how it works and what goes into it. The level of your knowledge as a Web tester will vary, depending on what your position is and what the focus of your job is. A tester who is developing tools for a Web testing effort needs to know much about the inner working of the application under development, as well as the general technologies being employed for it. A QA professional who is auditing a development effort will not need to know nearly that level of detail about the inner workings of either the technology or the application to be effective (however, a professional should make every effort to improve his knowledge).

To start this Web application testing discussion, I turn to the static HTML of the Web. The content in this chapter lays the groundwork for further discussion about dynamic applications and script later in the book.

Coding in HTML

HTML (HyperText Markup Language) is the language used to publish items on the World Wide Web. It is the language of the Internet. It supports text, multimedia, various scripting languages, style sheets, tables, forms, and, of course, hyperlinks. The most recent version set out by the W3C (World Wide Web

Consortium) is version 4.01, although most browsers in the market currently are standardized on version 4.0.

The Basics of Tags

HTML uses tags to tell the browser how to format text and graphics as well as how to behave. A tag consists of an element and possibly an attribute, or several attributes, of that element. An attribute can also have a value. Most tags come in pairs, with an opening tag to tell the browser to begin a formatting style or behavior and a closing tag to tell the browser to end that formatting style or area affected by the behavior. The special characters < and > distinguish the tags from the rest of the text.

Figure 5.1 illustrates tags consisting of elements, their attributes, and values.

One example of an opening tag is <B>, which is the bold tag, indicating to the browser that all text following this tag should be in boldface. Since you want to be able to control what is put into various formatting styles, you also have a closing tag, which in this case would be </B>, telling the browser to stop using boldface for the text. This example then introduces the third special character, /, for this language, which always indicates a closing tag.

Leaving off the closing tag is one of the more common bugs found in Web testing, along with leaving off the closing greater-than sign >.

There are tags for which there is no matching closing tag, such as the break tag <BR>. This tag simply tells the browser to insert a break in the text. Not all opening tags have a corresponding closing tag; however, all tags that begin with a slash are closing tags. Another common tag is the comment tag <!--, finished with a -->. This tag allows the programmer to make comments directly in the text for future reference, reminders, or to explain what he was thinking as he wrote it, but not have them rendered in the Web page. It tells the browser to not render the contents of that tag, and as a result, there is no closing tag to it, just the --> end of the tag. This addition to the language also adds two more special characters, the exclamation mark (!) and the dash (-), and it also increases the number of character combinations that we are likely to find problems with.

Commonly, if only part of a page loads, it may be that a comment tag was not closed properly.

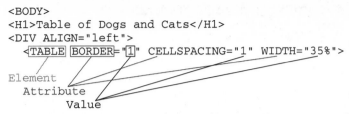

```
<BODY>
<H1>Table of Dogs and Cats</H1>
<DIV ALIGN="left">
   <TABLE BORDER="1" CELLSPACING="1" WIDTH="35%">
```

Element
  Attribute
      Value

Figure 5.1 Illustration of the relationship of an element, an attribute, and a value.

Careful HTML Coding

Other than a handful of single tags, all others have corresponding closing tags, and should have closing tags in your code. Programmers can get away with not closing all tags, but if closing tags aren't used regularly, code will be sloppy and prone to errors.

One mark of clean, careful code is closing the tags in the proper order. Conversely, the practice of mixing the order in which tags are closed can lead to problems. In general, tags should be closed in the reverse order in which they were opened. This guideline prevents overlapping in the code, which can cause rendering problems in some browsers. For example, table tags are notorious for causing problems if they are not coded properly. Opening a second table tag before the first one has been closed, when embedded tables are not intended, definitely causes rendering problems on various platforms (see Figure 5.2).

In the figure, you can see the difference in the way that the browser renders the two tables, based on the faulty HTML. IE displays the first table laid out as a four-box structure, and then cannot render the second table as a table. Netscape does not even render the first table, and can only render the second one as four values rather than in a table format.

As another example, consider a paragraph showing several samples of text in various formats. It may look like this:

This sentence has examples of **bold Arial text**, *italicized Bickham*, and regular Dragonwick.

The code for this sentence could be messy:

```
This sentence has <b><font face="Arial">bold Arial text</b>,
<i></font><font face="Bickham Script" size=20>italicized Bickham</font>,
</i>and <font face="Dragonwick">regular Dragonwick.
```

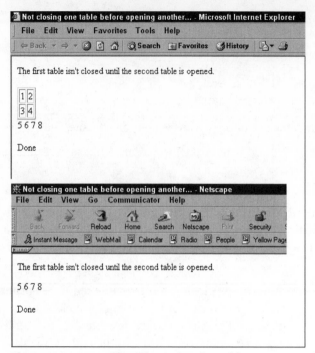

Figure 5.2 Same file with overlapping table tags opened in Internet Explorer (top) and Netscape Navigator (bottom).

Or the code could be neat and easy to read:

```
This sentence has <b><font face="Arial">bold Arial text</font></b>,
<i><font face="Bickham Script" size=20>italicized Bickham</font></i>,
and <font face="Dragonwick">regular Dragonwick</font>.
```

There is not much of a difference, except that in the first sample tags are not necessarily closed in the right order, and the closing font tag is missing. Such a coding error may not be noticed if the code is intended for the end of the document, but if more text will be added later, this type of coding could create problems in the case of forms, tables, or other styles. But regardless if the coding will be noticed, it is poor practice.

NOTE

Nonstandard code creates problems and is the source of many bugs. Being a tester who can read the code, whether you are using C, C++, script, or just HTML, makes you more effective and gives you an advantage in finding and accurately reporting bugs.

Conforming to External Coding Standards

High-quality HTML is standard HTML; that is, it conforms to the standards laid out by the W3C. Standard HTML is HTML that matches the World Wide Web Consortium (W3C) standard 3.2 or 4.01. The W3C is a neutral standards body that is a forum for these standards discussions and that serves to set new standards. Many people are surprised to learn that there is a standards body that standardizes how HTML works, which tags are supported, and how they should be used. It is no wonder then that confusion sometimes results because each browser interprets the standard a bit differently and because each browser tends to define its own tags once in a while. Many tools are available that can run through a site and flag nonstandard code and potential problems. For example, the W3C provides a tool called Amaya (see Appendix J for location information). This is a tool that allows HTML editing as well as viewing and is available on the Windows, Macintosh, and Unix platforms. The W3C provides other tools that will validate CSS and more. The more standard the HTML is, the less chance that your Web application will run into browser specific problems. Just because something works by chance does not mean that it is a good idea to rely on it. A new browser or operating system version could be released that breaks the hack that you have done. No development team wants to have to scramble at the last minute to get their entire site working again.

One bug that I wrestled with for quite some time fell into this bucket. It manifested itself as a random color change in the text, but only on the Macintosh IE browsers. All other browsers neatly and dependably displayed the text as black, but the IE browser on the Macintosh platform would sometimes display sections of the text in blue or green. Refreshing the page might or might not change the behavior. It took me quite a while to realize that the culprit was the text color attribute of `color=0`. All other browsers looked at this and defaulted to black text, but IE on the Mac would randomly spit out a few other colors on occasion. The fix was to go back through the code and change all the color attributes to `color="#000000"`. After that, there were no more problems. As another example, Microsoft's Internet Explorer supports the BGSOUND tag, but Netscape Navigator does not. If a site design includes the playing of sounds in the background when a user navigates there and the BGSOUND tag is used for this, then no Netscape user will hear the sounds. Personally, I would prefer to never have another sound start playing when I open a Web page, but some sites may have found that users prefer the sound used to advertise special offers or some similar function. Just be mindful that Netscape Navigator users and many others will not be able to hear these enhancements to your visual site. In contrast, Netscape Navigator supports the BLINK tag, while IE does not. (In my opinion, we could drop both of these and not miss much from the Web.) Keep HTML standard, and make that task easy by using available tools to identify nonstandard places.

Maintaining Internal Coding Standards

Everyone wants to put their own particular stamp onto that which they create. However, code should not be the place for that individualism, unless a person's stamp is marked by clean, tight, easy-to-read code. Each company typically has its own set of coding standards to ensure uniformity and maintainability across their products. These may be very rigid documents describing the exact syntax that must be used, the use of GOTOs, or anything else. It may also include the use of comments, vocabulary, and formatting. With HTML there is very little that can get too complex, but some users of the language make efforts to produce code unreadable by anyone else. Since all the code can be seen by any client or competitor able to access it, those users can claim there is some validity to their obfuscation, but on the whole they are hurting themselves far more than helping their company. The time spent in having another developer try to understand what was done, format it in his own way, and then update it is wasted time.

Set out a clean standard ahead of time and adhere to it. QA departments typically work with the development departments to draw up such standards and help the standards to be a tool rather than the red tape that everyone abhors. A coding standard should be applied evenly to everyone in the organization, including being used as a guideline for test automation code.

Some organizations may have testers involved in the code reviews. Your role in this sort of review is to look for those seams we've mentioned previously—the places where the code will not match up to other pieces of code. You are watching for nonstandard techniques and general logic problems as well. Just because something happens to work does not mean it is correct. In code reviews you may spot attributes that are nonstandard and know that they will not work for platforms or browsers other than the one it was designed on. Tags that are supported by only one particular browser should be watched for as well. Outside of code reviews, there are many tools that you can use to make this job easier. The W3C has HTML validators that will look for nonstandard coding and flag it for your review. Using these to identify potential problems and then understanding what has been flagged for you can go a long way to making a standard Web application.

There are many other tools available for validating your source code, as well as for script verification. Appendix J has listings of tools for these and other purposes.

For HTML, internal standards for formatting and coding start at the level of the layout of the code. Internal standards build on external standards. Your internal development team will likely have a preference about the arrangement of the code, commenting styles, and more. The reasons behind the preference may relate to maintainability, security, performance, or accessibility. Holding maintainability of code to be of primary importance means that some functions may not take the most optimized form and that code will be written in a neat fashion rather than in the most optimized fashion. For example, if your Web site featured a count of the dogs and cats in the local areas formatted into a table, the table could be rendered like that in Table 5.1.

Table 5.1 Table of Dogs and Cats

TOWN	DOGS	CATS
Bothell	500	1000
Redmond	865	2032
Bellevue	1005	1232

The code for that table could be messy:

```
<HTML><head><title>Table of Dogs and Cats</TITLE></HEAD><BODY><h1>Table
of Dogs and Cats</h1><div align="left"><table border="1" cellspacing="1"
width="35%"><tr><th>Town</th><th>Dogs</th><th>Cats</th></tr><tr><td>Both
ell</td><TD>500</TD><td>1000</td></tr><tr><td>Redmond</td><td>865</td><t
d>2032</td></tr><TR><TD>Bellevue</td><td>1005</TD><td>1232</td></tr></ta
ble></DIV></body></html>
```

Or it could be neat:

```
<HTML>

<HEAD>
<TITLE>Table of Dogs and Cats
</TITLE>
</HEAD>

<BODY>
<H1>Table of Dogs and Cats
</H1>
<DIV ALIGN="left">
  <TABLE BORDER="1" CELLSPACING="1" WIDTH="35%">
    <TR>
        <TH>Town</TH>
        <TH>Dogs</TH>
        <TH>Cats</TH>
    </TR>
```

```
      <TR>
        <TD>Bothell</TD>
        <TD>500</TD>
        <TD>1000</TD>
      </TR>
      <TR>
        <TD>Redmond</TD>
        <TD>865</TD>
        <TD>2032</TD>
      </TR>
      <TR>
        <TD>Bellevue</TD>
        <TD>1005</TD>
        <TD>1232</TD>
      </TR>
    </TABLE>
  </DIV>
  </BODY>

  </HTML>
```

Which one is easier to read and maintain? Since HTML treats a carriage return as a space, and all but the first space is ignored, these can be tossed in to neatly format the code without affecting the layout when it is rendered in the browser. Since HTML is not case-sensitive, putting all tags in capital letters may also be an internal standard, making it easier to distinguish the code from the content. Having tags (both closing and opening) placed on a new line also makes for cleaner code, and indenting may help everyone who reads it or needs to maintain it.

However, if performance is held as the primary issue driving the development standards, the first example would be preferred because it is tighter code. Security as a concern could limit the technologies you select to use or how you choose to use them. For example, when ActiveX controls are a part of an application, calling them, scripting to them, and relying on users not to enter faulty data that requires error handling would all be concerns of security guidelines. Accessibility requirements in a standard would set requirements that all elements have appropriate labels, tags, IDs, or text alternatives, among other guidelines. No one concern will be the overriding one in determining coding standards, but each should play a part in the coding standards that will go in place for your application under development.

A complement to the issue of quality is that of appropriateness. Your application is one of the major interactions that customers have with your company. If you allow slapped-together code that is difficult to understand to pass through, the application will not appear to be professional or stable. Since this code is HTML, any user can right-click the page and choose to view the source. If there are offensive or unprofessional comments in the code, the company might lose customers or fail to engage potential clients.

Your internal coding standard will likely identify questionable words or phrases that you do not want outsiders to see. Some of these would be your run-of-the-mill swear words, but also error messages or comments such as <!-- this is such a hack I can't believe it works --> or <!-- todo later...-->. Do a search through all the HTML and script files for any of these words and then log bugs to get the phrases removed. Include such things as *hack*, *todo*, *crap*, and other words that might cast doubt on the product, team, or company in the eyes of a customer.

NOTE You could also spell-check the string database if you externalize strings in a manner that allows that. Spell checking the code just to make sure that the comments are spelled correctly is probably going a bit overboard since most of the tags would be flagged, and nobody cares too much if your comments happen to be misspelled.

Questionable words and phrases can be tolerated in code that is compiled before users see it, but that is not the case in HTML.

NOTE The discussion here on HTML is not intended to teach you how to code in HTML or how to publish to the Web, but rather to serve as a reference to basic HTML-testing issues and to help you find problems in HTML code and be able to debug those problems on a basic level. If only part of a page is rendering, a good investigation would include looking for opening tags without the corresponding closing tags. If an entire page is bold or italicized, a good thing to look at is if the relevant tags were closed properly. Being able to understand the basics is essential to effectively testing any application. Once you find problems, knowing the language helps you to identify the source of the bug and understand related issues better. Plenty of great books teach HTML and provide complete references on the language. The material here is just a small reference to testing an application that uses HTML.

Testing Design on the Web

It used to be that people would find a cool or popular site and then just copy the format, or even the code. However, if a business is planning an online retail business and copies a popular news site, the site will probably not fit the purpose very well. The problem is that in that example the *design* and layout are being confused with the *information architecture*. The first distinction that needs to be made is between the design of the page and the organization of the content. Since the organization of the content for the news site is so different from that of the e-business, and the customer goals are different, the design of one cannot just be imposed on the other with the expectation of a successful outcome. To make the distinction clear, think of it this way:

The *design* is the color choice, the type of graphics, the placement on the page, and basic layout of the data. The organization of the content is the *information architecture* of the site.

Information architecture is the combination of navigational features and content. Failing to properly provide these as the customer demands them can mean a failure for a Web presence. Consider the following example. Sabre had a competitive application that was widely used by travel agents in travel agencies to book tickets and reservations. When Sabre branched out to the Web with Travelocity, their target audience shifted from the travel agents to their end users—the travelers themselves. However, Sabre did not change their information architecture. Independent usability studies have shown that many users were confused by the architecture, navigational features, and defaults set by the site and ended up booking one-way tickets when the objective was to purchase a round-trip ticket, or became confused by airports in London, England; London, Ontario; and London, Wisconsin. With an estimated 32 percent of shopping carts abandoned prior to purchase (see http://ecommerce.internet.com/news/insights/ectech/article/0,,9561_448381,00.html). No site can afford to lose more revenue simply because the users cannot figure out how it give their money over.

NOTE As a tester, you ideally will be involved in the design stages of a Web site where you can keep problems like user frustration from ever occurring by keeping a few concepts, discussed in the next few paragraphs, in mind and in front of the design group. Remember, a key part of being a tester is being a customer advocate. However, even if you are not involved in the design, the application will eventually be handed to you, at which time you can comment on the design and the information architecture.

The best approach in design is to gather content, or at least ideas for the content, and organize the information first. This stage may include working with user groups to test ideas or paper prototypes, but it will give feedback on how users are expecting to find information and what information is the most important to them (and thus should be closer to the site's entry point). From this information, a successful design may become more apparent, or at least be influenced, and constraints to be placed on it may be recognized.

WARNING If the design is set into place first and the information is forced into it, it may look cool and snazzy, but it will frustrate people and be difficult to use.

Sacrifice the graphic design for the content. No matter what, get good content. Content is what keeps consumers returning to a site, not the pretty colors. Avoid designing on the bleeding edge of technology. Forcing users to download plug-ins only annoys them and prevents them from accomplishing their task—which is hopefully paying you money for whatever you are selling. Why throw up barriers to this purchase? Simply allow the customer to get through that task easily. If you absolutely must provide content that requires a plug-in, provide it in multiple formats (for example, if you provide an online catalog in Adobe PDF format, consider providing a copy in HTML format as well for users without the Acrobat plug-in).

Many sites fall not only into the design trap, but also into the animation trap. Advertisers cite the fact that animated advertisements have twice the click-through rate of nonanimated advertisements. This statistic is true if the user is just surfing a bit aimlessly. However, this statistic doesn't hold up if the user is looking for information. If a site primarily provides information, it has been seen in studies that many users will mentally, if not physically, block out any animation, even going to the length of putting their hands on the screen over the animated areas to be able to read the content unbothered. Flashing is another Web site technique that borders on making a site inaccessible. Flashes at various intervals can be linked to seizures in rare instances. The Pokemon incident in Japan in 1997 illustrated this when a particular rate of flashing in a cartoon induced mass seizures in the population that was watching the show on television. Flashes on the screen need to be set at the same rate that the cursor is set to blink, but to be absolutely safe, flashes should just be avoided.

In other words, know what you are designing for and avoid irritating the user. If the user can get the same quality of content elsewhere without constantly being harassed with pop-up ads, animations, or other interruptions, they will likely go there for their content.

When reading over the design proposals, know the canvas size and the offsets that your product will be subject to. Have these in mind prior to further design to ensure that the important buttons or links, such as the Help link or the Buy Now link, are not left off the user's immediately viewable area in the lowest supported settings. Not accounting for the difference between the resolution and the canvas size has damaged more than one product, and it is a very easy problem to correct early in the development cycle.

Cleanliness is Next to Godliness

In design, cleanliness really is next to godliness. Cleanliness in design includes consideration of such issues as icon sizing and color scheme, as well as the page layout. For example, many books insist that you must leave a lot of white space on your individual pages—*white space* being areas of the page that do not have text or graphics on them. However, this prevailing wisdom is rapidly being challenged as more sites are succeeding with less white space. The reason for this success lies in good information architecture and clean designs. Users can tolerate a lack of white space if they are presented with what they need. It may take a lot of the page to display a news story containing both the text and a few graphics; little white space may be left, but the user interaction right then is a desire to read the story. The user has found what he is looking for. Don't underestimate the proper use of white space, but use it judiciously. Leaving areas of white space just because you have not left any on the page yet is not a good enough reason to invoke this technique.

Notice in Figure 5.3 that the area of text and graphics has been grayed out leaving the areas of white showing through. The "white space" need not actually be the color white; in the figure you can see shaded areas that indicate other colors in addition to white. What should be apparent is that although there is not a large amount of white space, good organization of information with clear descriptions results in a design that does not require as much separation between chunks of information. Users can clearly read and find the information they are looking for and ignore the rest.

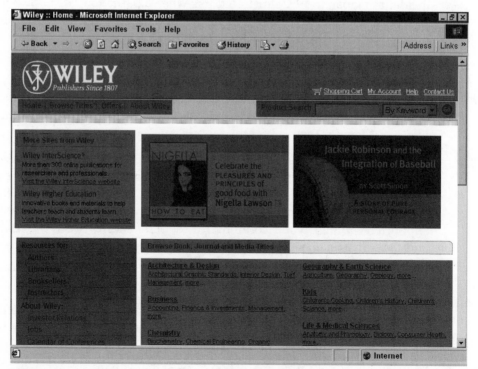

Figure 5.3   Example of white space, using the John Wiley & Sons, Inc., Web site.

Consistency is another design principle to keep in mind as you help plan a clean Web site. If all links internal to the Web site open in the same window and all links external to that site open in a new window, the user has an expectation of how the site will work. They will also be kept at your site for the maximum amount of time. If, however, sometimes a link opens in a new window, sometimes the toolbar is different, or sometimes the page layout changes, the user will begin to wonder if he has navigated away from the site and who owns the site he is now viewing. Consistency is one of the most important tools of good design. Even a poor design can be usable if it has internal consistency. Though double-clicking on items is not a normal part of Web interactions, consider the following: In some Web email programs users are presented with a list of their email items with an interaction model whereby a single-click selects the message and a double-click opens the item. Usability studies have shown that users are not confused by this—they interact with the program as though it were a traditional win32 program. They do not question the interaction model because it gives them the results that they expect. I offer this example not to say that applications you are a part of designing should set out to break conventions, but that if your design strikes upon a slightly unconventional model that works for your users, give it a try. As long as your product has internal consistency, it will probably continue to work for users. This internal consistency includes consistent mouse usage across the product, consistent interactions, and a consistent UI. Above all, as a spokesperson for the user's point of view, work to make the design clean.

Testing for Other Design Concerns

Several other concerns may play a role in formulating some of the early questions you as a tester pose to a Web site's design:

- Will users be able to print? Many users want a hard copy of information and the ability to print out pages of news stories, catalogue offerings, or other bits of information they find interesting. If the design of your site or application does not allow for neatly printed copies, consider placing a link on major points of interest to a printer-friendly version or a text-only version.

- Will there be a Help page? Will there be a whole Help section for the Web site or only a phone number for the user to call the company? Should the Help open in a new page to allow the user to continue working through the application while referring to the Help section?

- Will the application employ the use of hotkeys? The use of hotkeys is prevalent in many platform native applications, but not yet widely used in Web applications. Will the users actually want to use them, or will they even discover them? If the site is an informational Web site, with a wide variety of users, probably not. However if the site is an internal site for employees to use on a regular basis (for example, a time-reporting tool), then they will quickly become used to the interface and will want ways to expedite their usage of the application. Hotkeys may be appropriate there. These keys can be added with the attribute of ACCESSKEY to an element. Will the product be localized? If so, then the hotkey choices will need to be revisited for each localized version because the identifying strings will change. You also cannot have duplicate hotkeys on a page. Two strings that start with the same letter cannot both have the same hotkey as a user might reasonably expect, so one of the strings will have to have another letter selected to represent its hotkey. Such a situation can be very problematic as well as time and resource intensive.

As one example, the Danish localization of the Macintosh operating system presents the user with a set of options when restarting. The option *Genstart* is the Danish localization for restarting. In English, this string is ***Restart*** and has *r* as the shortcut to put focus on that button. Since the product was localized into Danish after being created in English, the shortcut keys were also localized, but this one was missed. A Danish user would expect to hit the *g* key to set focus on the Genstart button, but that does not work. Instead, the *r* key sets focus to that button. This example is from a non-Web application because there are few shortcut keys on the Web currently, but it shows one example of the problems that hotkeys present. Remember, too, that hotkeys cannot overlap with those reserved by the browser or the operating system; for example, the Ctrl+N hotkey opens a new browser window on IE and Netscape Navigator. Because of this, your application could not also use Ctrl+N as a hotkey without taking this known function away from the browser. A new version of a browser or OS could break some of your existing hotkey functionality, too. Similarly, if there are several frames loading, or if each has its own set of hotkeys, whichever frame has focus will try to handle the hotkey being entered. Users can become easily frustrated or confused when their hotkey entries are ignored or work inconsistently simply due to focus issues.

- What tab order is set for the page? Hotkeys may be deemed unnecessary on your particular application, which is fine; however, discussing hotkeys raises the very important issue of tab order. The tab order must allow access to all elements on the page and must be in a logical order. The focus for any one page should default to the most logical place—usually the first text entry field. If the tab order is not logical throughout the page, the user will be frustrated with the page navigation. Tab order can go logically down the page in columns or skip across from left to right as it goes down the page, or it can be another pattern that works for your application. Including the attribute of TABINDEX allows the tab order of a page to be specified in IE, although some versions of Netscape Navigator have some quirky behavior here. When setting the tab order for your application, make sure that the tab order includes entry fields or drop-down boxes and not just link elements.

Testing a Design with Graphics in Mind

Design includes not just the layout, but also the graphical elements of the site. Your initial inspection of any Web application should check that all the graphics show up and ensure that there are no broken image tags. It is easy to handle images improperly, causing much frustration for users. Graphics can add so much to a site or an application, yet they can be so cumbersome to users with low bandwidth when they are used inappropriately. Images should be reduced as much as possible—not the physical dimensions of the image displayed on the screen, but the file size of the image. A rule of thumb is for no single image to exceed 24K (with a much smaller image preferred), and no full page to exceed 50K if it is a main page for the site.

NOTE If the user is deep within the site and requesting scanned images of works of art, there is an implicit understanding that these images are large and will take more time to download. Your users may have similar expectations of certain parts of your application.

You want the user to receive all the information as fast as possible. Most monitors display roughly only 72 dots per inch (dpi). (Actually, this can vary from between 40 to 165. 72 is usually a standard.) Because of this, graphics that are intended to be viewed only on a monitor do not need to be at any higher quality because they will just be degraded when viewed. If your site sells art reproductions, then users may want to print out a sample to view prior to purchasing. In this case, certain images may need more detail and may need to be saved at a higher resolution. For example, the two graphics shown in Figures 5.4 and 5.5 are virtually identical.

Figure 5.4 Heisenberg on the monitor in a bitmap graphic.

Figure 5.5   Heisenberg on the monitor in a JPEG graphic.

The first image is a bitmap (BMP) and is 702K. The second image is a JPG and is only 40K. Just saving it as a JPG made it $\frac{1}{17}$ the size of the original. The GIF image shown in Figure 5.6 was saved from the BMP image as well.

The loss of information fails to give a clear picture in Figure 5.6, leaving you with an unpleasant graphic. On top of that, the GIF format image is actually larger than the JPG graphic in this instance. It may take a bit of trial and error to reduce the image to where it has no perceived loss of information and yet is small enough not to take too much time to download. Saving an image in a TIFF format gives a good image that is about 484K. Saving it as a PNG file also gives a true image that is only 316K. In this example, the JPG image was the best quality for the smallest size. Playing with the images in various programs may allow you to reduce the size further with no noticeable loss of quality.

Figure 5.6   Heisenberg on the monitor in a GIF image.

Reducing the color depth can also help to reduce the file size of an image. If you are displaying graphics for a mathematical formula, saving the formula in a format with millions of colors is unnecessary because a simple black-and-white image will suffice. Tools are commercially available that can reduce the size of graphics to optimize them for the Web. A list of some of the popular ones can be found in Appendix J.

As you test your Web applications, consider the following additional issues concerning graphics:

- Users do not want to wait on the Web. To minimize the page load time, avoid using images as the primary navigation device. Users will not wait for the images to download before assessing their options and clicking on a link. Including the WIDTH and HEIGHT attribute on all images allows the browser to format and display the text for the user to read while the images are being transmitted. Including the ALT and TITLE attributes allows the textual description to be displayed in the place of the graphic until the image can be downloaded and displayed. This technique helps minimize the perceived page download time.

- Putting important information in graphics is generally not a good idea. If users are sight impaired, have graphics turned off, have low bandwidth, have small form factor devices, or have the text read to them through the use of screen readers, they will not receive this information. Search engines that index text from sites will also not be able to index this information in relation to your site, and users will not be able to search your site for this information or do a Find through an individual Web page to find the information.

- One technique that can be used for a graphic like a color block is called a *pixel shim*. This pixel shim is a simple 1 pixel x 1 pixel image of a particular color. A WIDTH and HEIGHT attribute is then added to the image tag to force it to tile, giving the appearance of a block of color. This technique allows a site to have more control over color than the technique of filling in a table cell with a color code that may look different on various platforms. Additionally, pixel shims still have a very fast download and render speed as compared to a graphic of the size that is wanted.

- Reducing the number of graphics and the size of the graphics going across the wire improves your performance, both for the client and for the servers. Reusing the same graphics on the same page or throughout the site also helps improve the performance and load time for each page and the application as a whole.

Designing a Web site graphically to win a Webby is fine, as long as the application is usable by your audience.

Testing a Design for Usability Issues

Making something usable means making it easier to use and easier to understand. However, ease of use does not necessarily mean fewer clicks. Putting all the links for all of the Web pages on the home page does not make your site any more usable just because every page is only one click away. Consider the command-line interface contrasted against the window concept. In a command line, you are only one line away from anywhere and can easily string together commands to quickly accomplish a task. However, the average user does not use this model. Users will gladly double-click through folder upon folder to access information taking more time and effort because they clearly understand the result of each step and where to navigate next to reach their goal. One system is not necessarily better than the other, but each is an approach with its own constituency and uses. Knowing your target audience helps you to make your product usable by them.

Once the architecture of the information and the site design have been determined, the usability needs to be checked. Usability is a huge area and is the silent culprit for many Web failures. Cool, hot, snazzy, sleek—if the user cannot figure out how to purchase something, you will not make money. An airplane cockpit is functional, has a lot of information, and looks pretty cool, but the average person cannot sit in one and perform many actions. Then again, the average person off the street is not the target audience for an airplane cockpit.

Testing Usability with Prototypes

Usability testing is a highly underrated part of development. Usability testing can come at many points within the development cycle. Once the information architecture is set, usability specialists can create a paper prototype from this and work with customers or potential users to identify what works well and what should be altered prior to coding even beginning. A *paper prototype* is literally a set of pages with drawings of the proposed site design, a little cutout pointer of a mouse, pieces cut out for the various drop-down boxes, and so on. A user is given the paper arrow or finger pointer and asked to perform certain actions on the paper as though he were in front of the screen. When the user "clicks" on an element such as a drop-down box, the usability specialist steps in and places the cutout of the drop-down box on the prototype. The user can be a tester working with a program manager to smooth out the proposed designs, or he can be an outside person who represents the target audience and has been recruited for a few hours to walk through the application. This technique is a very primitive way of conducting a study, but it can give some great feedback through the interactions of the specialist and the user and by identifying inconsistencies in the overall application. Moreover, it is cheap and can take place very early in the cycle, when little time has been spent on development efforts.

Other methods of usability testing may include a more realistic mock-up, still nonfunctional, but equipped with enough of a feeling of the software to provide an idea of how it would work. These mock-ups can be produced using almost any application, although plain HTML is quick and easy to produce, either through coding by hand or through coding with one of the many authoring environments available. Teams may use Excel, PowerPoint, Visio, or even VisualBasic, depending on the tools and expertise that are available. Any of these environments can get the job done, and none is really better than the other. They can all work well, or they can all fail, depending on how they are used. As with anything else, these are just some sample tools and techniques, offering some ways to refine the proposed designs.

Composing Effective Links

Some sites have tried to make themselves more usable by making every bit of information on them more readable, using links that are complete sentences. If presented with either of the sets of links shown in Figure 5.7, which one seems easier for you to use?

With the first set of links, you have to read the entire sentence to understand where a link leads. Although the links in the second example lead to the same places as those in the first example, it is easier to understand the outcome of clicking on them and they are much faster for the user to comprehend. Users do not *read* on the Web when they are looking for things, they *skim*. Consider your own Web behavior. You do not want to read a paragraph about each and every link to get an idea of where it will lead. What you want are short, pithy, accurate details about where a link will take you.

Welcome to my web page!
Click here to visit Microsoft's corporate site and view their latest news and products.
The Macintosh computers may interest you more, so try them!
Click here to visit Netscape's site and read all about them!

Welcome to my web page!
Microsoft
Apple
Netscape

Figure 5.7 Examples of two ways to provide information about your links.

TIP

Abbreviations are not as easily skimmed as whole words are. If you were visiting a government site and clicked on a link for the DOE, where would you expect it to lead? That would depend on where you were trying to go. If you were searching for the Department of Education, you would reasonably expect to be taken to that page. If you were searching for the Department of Energy, then you could expect to be taken there. Including the full and proper name or a short description allows users to more easily navigate the site.

Testing Web Site Search Capabilities

Many Web sites provide a way to search the entire site for information. Unfortunately, many of these sites do not help the user when data is returned. Users have little use for filenames being returned; a title and a description helps them hone in on the information much faster. Conversely, some sites are overly helpful providing multiple searches through various search engines. This presents the users with several search UIs and tends only to confuse them. Pick one search engine and present that to the user.

Developing Effective Error Messages

Error messages are historically a problem for users. Error messages that refer to code or are too general give users no idea why there was a failure and leave them helpless to handle the problem or understand what caused it. On the other hand, errors that are too specific may confuse users or present a potential security problem. Some studies have found that up to 33 percent of all support calls relate to error messages (see http://www.ecommercetimes.com/perl/story/4557.html among other sources)—the user received an error message and was not sure how to proceed. Sure, the user is in trouble before the message pops up; otherwise, the message would not have appeared. The fact that users cannot determine what the problem really is or what they need to do about it from the messages that the software provides is an indication that more information should be provided in these messages and that they need to be more useful to the user. The support costs alone come to millions of dollars for large applications, not to mention the lost revenue when frustrated users fail to upgrade or purchase further services or products from the company that gives them these unhelpful messages. Error messages do cost a bit to develop—they must be planned into the product and implemented by developers, the conditions which fire them off must be tested, and they need to be localized. However, weighed against the cost of product support calls, lost sales, customer dissatisfaction, and an increased difficulty in diagnosing problems remotely, such development of error messages results in a savings in the long run and moves the industry towards a more professional state.

Implementing Accessibility

Accessibility rarely gets mentioned unless a large percentage of the client base will make use of these accommodations. Until recently accessibility was just considered to be extra overhead. In the United States, accessibility of software is not mandatory. However, if your company plans on selling software or software services to the government, then it must attempt to meet the accessibility guidelines set out by Congress. In 1998, the Workforce Investment Act of 1988 was amended to include Section 508—the Rehabilitation Act Amendment (RAA). This amendment requires that everybody have the same access to all federal agencies when they develop, procure, maintain, or use electronic or information technology. What this means for a software manufacturer is that the government is required to consider these guidelines when purchasing software or services. Recently, this legislation went into effect and has changed many corners of the Web. The Section 508 guidelines are designed to allow users who cannot hear, see, or move the ability to access the same information as those who can. These guidelines cover such issues as not relying on color or sound for conveying information because a person who is blind, colorblind, or deaf cannot receive that information, including the ability to tab to all elements (removing the requirement to use a mouse), or adding text tags that screen readers can read in place of information that appears in a graphic. Many disabled users have third-party software that allows them to use alternate means to get at information, if sites and Web applications have been designed to allow their use. Section 508 suggests that manufacturers meet their responsibilities by allowing these third-party tools to access the information. Support for tools such as voice recognition and narration software packages that plug into software may need to be tested, among the other considerations involved with adding such support.

NOTE This category of third-party software is referred to more generally as assistive technology (AT). Assistive technology is any technology (hardware or software) that allows users to perform an action that they otherwise would not be able to do, as, for instance, a screen reader does. Without a screen reader, a blind person could not use a Web application. However, with the use of an assistive technology, such as a screen reader, that person is now able to gather the same information as if he were sighted.

Several approaches to testing this accessibility can be taken:

- You can write your software package and then test it with some of the plug-in tools to discover where your software does not work smoothly. This approach is costly and a large amount of third-party assistive technology software exists.

- You can hand your software over to a contracted third-party testing agency that already possesses the assistive technologies and the knowledge of how they interact with Web applications. This way is expensive and time-consuming. Further, both of these first two approaches focus on the back end instead of setting accessibility criteria up front and then coding to match that criteria.

- A better approach than either of the first two is to plan the accessibility requirements up front.

Planning accessibility requirements up front provides development goals to be met when creating the software (instead of having to revisit every area, potentially creating bugs) and ensures that you meet accessibility requirements regardless of possible bugs in other software. Providing such additional attributes as ALT attributes for images and links allows narration software to pick up the description and read it to the user. It also allows users to view the text description of the image if graphics are turned off, are not supported, or users are on a text-based browser, and it allows screen readers to read the alternate text description instead of the hyperlink listed. Software development with the user in mind takes a little extra time up front but opens up a large potential user group for your product.

Although an important one, the ALT attribute is not the only one that can be provided. The TITLE attribute allows a tooltip to be displayed to give more information about the object or the result of interacting with it. These additions should not just be reiterations of what is already there, but should be supporting descriptions. One Web page on your site may allow for users to fill out a form and post the information to your server. The button provided to post may be labeled *Send*, but an effective tooltip description for it could be *"Click to send your feedback to Company X."* Providing this type of information on top of document titles, as well as frame, table, and column labels, not only helps users see where they are, but also allows search engines to more accurately locate your pages and represent them to the users.

Consider users who cannot move. They may not possess the ability to type using a keyboard, and may instead be using mouth puff and sip tubes in order to select one key at a time to type. If your application has a 20-second timeout period, this person may not be able to type in his login or password without being timed out. Users utilizing a reflective headset that allows them to shine a pointer light on the screen instead of using a mouse also face the same timeout issues the puff and sip tube user does.

Consider users who cannot see. Assistive technologies that plug into the operating system or the hardware can output the screen text in a special Braille display, or visual cues can be represented as audible signals. Users could also be using a screen reader that reads the screen text and accessible tags to the user. If all of your strings are externalized and your tables, images, and frames are labeled with a real name, users with voice plug-ins can experience and interact with your application. Using full words allows these users to interact with your software. If acronyms are used such as the *DOE* example mentioned earlier in this chapter, a screen reader reads that as "doe" instead of "D-ee O-h E-ee," as it would normally be spoken. Other shortened versions of words such as using *txt* instead of *text* will cause the screen reader to pronounce what is spelled instead of what is meant. Screen readers are also not able to apply logic that might be applied when a check box enables or disables regions of the screen, so using a navigational method that displays or hides parts of the application, based on these check boxes, can lead to accessibility problems. Other concerns for users with vision problems may be having a high contrast mode for users with some limited sight, or color choices indicating information that could leave colorblind users without access to the data.

Consider users who cannot hear. The software cannot wholly rely on sound to indicate errors or give information. There is no guarantee that even the part of the audience that can hear has speakers or has them turned on.

Many companies push this group of disabled users to the side, but it is a large group and growing larger still. Further, many times it is not the user who cannot take advantage of some of the software features, but rather the platform that a user is using. Users accessing your application through a PDA will likely turn off graphics and not have speakers or sound capabilities. Users over a slow modem might turn graphics off in order to more quickly navigate to their desired destination and then turn the graphics back on. If for no other reason than enlightened self-interest, making your software accessible allows you to sell it to a larger potential audience.

Designing for User Interactions

There are many ways users can interact with software and direct their experience. The simplest and safest way is for a site to dictate the possible interactions and to allow the users only to make selections, which can be done with links or other objects that just take a click. Consider the following types of input:

- The most simple input method is a radio button. This button is a type attribute of the INPUT tag, having the TYPE="radio" format and is one of the simplest interactions because only one radio button in an area can be selected at a time.

- The menu also has its contents specified prior to the user selecting an item, and only one item can be selected at a time. It is also a type attribute of the INPUT tag, with the format of TYPE="menu".

- The button is another simple type attribute of the INPUT tag, having the format of TYPE="button". A drop-down box allows the user to make only one selection, and a button is either clicked or it is not. Both of these states allow for a very traceable experience that can easily be diagrammed, coded, and verified. No user-defined input is allowed; no space is set aside for the user to put in anything other than what the application has already offered.

- The reset type simply returns all form options to their default state. It is also a type attribute of the INPUT tag, as in TYPE="reset".

- The check box is more complex because several combinations are possible, and there are many more code paths that could occur from this. The check box is another valid value of the INPUT tag, as in <INPUT TYPE="checkbox">.

Even these "safe" inputs can have their problems. Runtime errors still occur if the software gets into unexpected states. Not selecting options or leaving them set to the default can cause script errors. For a site containing only this type of predefined options, simple verification testing, accessibility, usability, and server-side concerns (performance, security, etc) are probably all that will be necessary. Including such things as radio buttons or check boxes opens up the application to errors such as incompatible data selections or race conditions, but still leaves a very limited scope to test. Eliminating the possibility of user-specified input is one way to make your application more stable and easier to test, and there are fewer security concerns with applications that limit input. However, remember that input limitations also place stringent limits on the capabilities of the application.

Selection boxes that allow the user to Shift+Click or Control+Click to select multiple items open up the software to a further customizable experience; however, all the options are still defined prior to the user ever entering the site and can be closely controlled. The users cannot type in anything they want, and aside from a few supported keyboard interactions, such as tabbing, the keyboard is generally not used to interact with the software.

Few Web applications provide such a limited interface for users, though. Users really begin to interact when they can type in their own data, and this is when the software really opens itself up. Careless coding can allow unwitting or malicious users to wreak havoc on their account or your system. Once you open up your system to this type of user input, you open the floodgates. Most applications have text input boxes, text areas, or even content-editable DIVs that do just that.

Examining Text Inputs

Input on the Web is typically handled in forms. Scripts on the server interact with the HTML forms to do something relatively simple; they take the named identities of objects in the form and the values that have been entered and perform a function with them such as saving them to a database, sending mail, performing calculations, or printing them out.

A typical form has three main parts:

- **The form tag**. The *form tag* consists of the *form method* (what to do) and the *form action* (reference to the code that does it). The method is typically a POST, but it can be a GET. A form will typically begin something like `<FORM METHOD="POST" ACTION="script.js">`. The form action is the link to the script, which will act on the data entered. The link can be a relative or absolute path to the script file on the server.

- **The form elements**. Following this form tag are any number of elements with input types and areas that we will discuss later in this section. A text area, radio button, check box, text entry box, or others exist here to allow the user to put in information that will be acted upon.

- **Method to submit**. The last requirement of a form is the ability to submit the information. This submission is typically performed through a button to commit that would read `Submit` or `Send`, or some other indicator that the data will be acted upon. A `Clear` button might also be present to reset all fields back to their default (blank or default selections). A closing `</FORM>` tag ends the form.

Starting with a very basic input, I want to look at some of the questions that you, as a tester, need to ask about user input. A useful sample application for this illustration is an online stock brokerage. A typical application of this type allows users to log in to their account, view their current holdings, and buy and sell stock. Just by focusing on the buy and sell pages, you can assume there is most probably a text input field for the user to input the amount of stock to be bought or sold. Consider the questions you need to ask to test these types of text input fields:

- Is this amount in currency or number of shares?

- If it is in currency, does putting a currency sign ($ or € or £ or ¥) in front of the number break it?

- Does it allow a decimal such as the value $1054.32?

- Does it allow more than two decimal places, since some stocks are valued to a more precise amount?

- If the value is for number of shares, can a number less than 1 be entered (a decimal or fraction)?

- How large of a number can be entered in either position?

Testing the boundaries and some simple errors that can be made (inputting the currency sign when none is needed or expected) helps ensure the robustness and usability of your system.

From the usability side, it can be very confusing working in an application within an application, such as a Web application hosted in a browser application, if there are no clear delimiters. If you provide a toolbar environment for your application within the browser, are all of the user's needs satisfied by the options presented? If your form does not present some of the obvious options, such as a link to return to the previous set of data or other points of interest, you are encouraging the users to use the browser navigation methods of Back or Forward or just type in URLs to try to get to their destination. Presenting users with a form that doesn't satisfy all their needs and expecting them to use it frequently will be frustrating as opposed to a slightly more robust form that has considered the user interactions. If your application does not give users explicit navigational means, they will likely be forced to use the browser's Back button to navigate, or constantly return to a known place in your application by typing an address into the Location Bar, constantly retracing their steps. Perhaps a user enters the wrong amount into the BUY fields and clicks the BUY NOW! button. If the program encourages the user to rely on the browser for navigation, can a user reasonably expect that clicking the browser's Back button will undo or reverse his command? In a hosted environment like this, great care needs to be taken so that users do not confuse the two applications.

I want to move away from simple fields where only numbers are accepted, and a limited amount of them at that, and address more complex scenarios. There are many places where an application needs to take in a string rather than anticipating what the user wants to select. An application that allows users to search for jobs usually has several ways for users to begin their search. Typically, one of these options involves a place to enter a string. Two different approaches to this type of user input can be seen in Figures 5.8 and 5.9.

Figure 5.8 A search input field with little user guidance.

In the Figure 5.8, the same searching functionality is allowed as in Figure 5.9; however, no user guidance is provided. The display of the radio buttons help users customize their search and indicate what type of search logic is applied. The text entry field in Figure 5.8 is less intuitive than the one in Figure 5.9, forcing users to come up with their own mechanism to work around the search dialog. Not helping users customize their searches could mean they will perform multiples searches, which translates to more load on your server when, in reality, there is no difference in the output of the searches, and that extra load in unnecessary. If users are searching for a software tester position, would they enter *test* or + *"software"* + *"test"* or *test**? Not knowing how the search criteria will be applied causes users to guess, and perhaps it is this guessing that will choke your server. If the server absolutely cannot handle an asterisk and users logically enter it in order to search on wildcards, then your site will be brought to its knees rapidly. It takes only one confused user. I'm not saying that a user using a page like that in Figure 5.9 won't enter the wildcard character even if an explanation is provided—these special characters must still be tested. However, since an explanation of the search is provided, it reduces the user confusion and the likelihood of unwanted input.

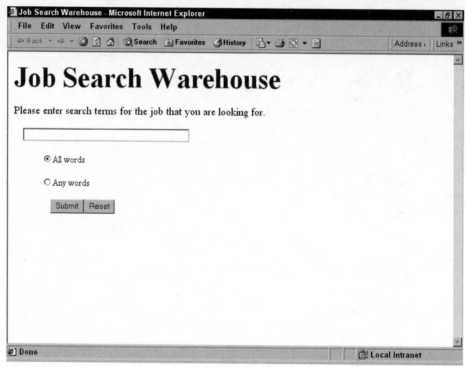

Figure 5.9 Search input field with more user guidance.

For example, one email server product encountered this type of issue before it shipped. Mysteriously a server crashed one day. In debugging it, it was found that a user had entered the fully qualified SMTP address format of 'user@ company.com' instead of "user@company.com". The end result of this was that the code, not expecting the single quote in this place, did not handle it well, and that entry resulted in the server crashing. It was an honest user mistake that had terrible consequences.

The questions you have about the text boxes included in your application should have their answers detailed in the product specifications. Since the users are allowed to enter a string, how long of a string can they enter? Can the users enter a space and have multiple terms typed in? Is the search function case-sensitive? Will a search on the word *test* also return matches for *tester* or *testing*? Text entry fields can be limited in their length. It is best to specify their limit in the design specifications so that all components agree on the size of various variables. If the box is not limited and a user inputs more information than a downstream function is expecting, you are facing a buffer overrun situation.

Testing Other Inputs

The largest input areas are a text area, a custom control, or, with recent versions of Internet Explorer, a supported tag called <ContentEditable DIV>. These are multiline input areas, as might be found on a comment form for a site. For such entry boxes, the boundaries become very important. For example, for a text area with the tag of <TEXTAREA>, Netscape 4.76 for Windows has a 64K limit on text being entered into a text area, and Macintosh IE 4 or 4.5 has a 32K limit on typed-in text. Boundary testing these aspects, and testing functions that will act on the input, ensures not only that the program works as expected, but also that buffer overflows, data loss, and corruption of data do not occur.

There are many other HTML tags that allow for user input.

- A simple text entry field is an attribute of the INPUT tag and is specified with the TYPE="text" attribute. This field has a default size of 20 characters, but can be changed with a SIZE attribute or a MAXLENGTH attribute.

- There is a PASSWORD field that is also an attribute of the INPUT tag. This type of entry field does not display the actual text typed in, but rather masks it.

NOTE

Both the password type and the text type need to be tested in similar ways, looking for valid cases, invalid cases, and valid but unexpected cases. The specifications should detail these classes.

- The last area I touch on here is a form that allows a user to upload a file, perhaps a Web-based support page that allows a user to upload a file for the support personnel to use in diagnosing issues. A form that allows a file upload must be of the method POST and cannot be a GET. The code for this form appears something like <form method="POST" action="upload.cgi"> File Path: <input type="file" name="filepath">. The length for the text entry box provided for users to enter the file's path has a default length of 20 characters. This length is quite short, and you will probably want to raise this considerably with the SIZE attribute, again testing the limits to ensure that functions that deal with the output from this field accept the limits appropriately.

  Suppose a *Browse...* button is located on the form for the users to browse (using the operating system provided browse function) and select the file that they want to upload. This file could be on any local drive (for example, C:\, A:\, F:\), could be on a network share (for example,

\\server1\public\file.txt), or could be on any other resource that can be seen from the machine. In this case, not only must there be test cases to test the entry box using long pathnames, paths with spaces, and paths with problem characters, there must also be test cases to test that the files are dealt with in the appropriate manner. (Remember this application could be accessed from various operating systems and each has its own set of reserved characters.) Do all types of files come through properly? Do large and small files come through properly? If a user types in a path and filename that does not exist, is the proper error handed back? What if the filename is not in the typical DOS 8.3 format? Is there a limit placed on the file size and is it obeyed? If your server-side function checks the file size after it has received the entire file, a user could try to upload an enormous file (such as one greater than 4 GB) potentially bringing down the server. What if the server allows for a 10-MB file to be uploaded, and there is only 5 MB of space left on the server? These are all good places to start in testing the robustness of your application in reaction to this sort of user input.

Testing for Performance

Performance is another issue to consider in your HTML testing. Although not terribly controllable with HTML, there are some things that affect it. Many generated Web pages from WYSIWYG (what you see is what you get) environments include far too many tags, usually the <font> tags to declare face and style. Having too many of these bloats even the simplest of HTML code, forces the server to store and send larger files, and delays the client's output because of the transfer rate. Redundant tags may sound small on the surface, but multiply their effect times a million users and the numbers start adding up. Removing redundant tags helps alleviate this problem. Two code samples can help illustrate this point. The first sample, HTML file dogs_fonts.htm in Listing 5.1, contains unnecessary, but often included, font tags.

```
<html>
<head>
<title>Dogs and Cats - font</title>
</head>
<body>

<p><b><font face="Times New Roman">This is in bold</font></b></p>
<p><font face="Times New Roman">this is not bold</font></p>
<p><font face="Times New Roman">This is a new line</font></p>
<p><font face="Times New Roman">This is another new line</font></p>
<p><font face="Times New Roman">Table of Dogs and Cats</font></p>
```

Listing 5.1 dogs_fonts.htm

```
<div align="left">
  <table border="1" width="80%">
    <tr>
      <td width="33%"> </td>
      <td width="33%"><font face="Times New Roman">Dogs</font></td>
      <td width="34%"><font face="Times New Roman">Cats</font></td>
    </tr>
    <tr>
      <td width="33%"><font face="Times New Roman">Bellevue</font></td>
      <td width="33%"><font face="Times New Roman">237</font></td>
      <td width="34%"><font face="Times New Roman">483</font></td>
    </tr>
    <tr>
      <td width="33%"><font face="Times New Roman">Bothell</font></td>
      <td width="33%"><font face="Times New Roman">192</font></td>
      <td width="34%"><font face="Times New Roman">384</font></td>
    </tr>
    <tr>
      <td width="33%"><font face="Times New Roman">Redmond</font></td>
      <td width="33%"><font face="Times New Roman">220</font></td>
      <td width="34%"><font face="Times New Roman">452</font></td>
    </tr>
  </table>
</div>
</body>
</html>
```

Listing 5.1 *(continued)*

The version of this in Listing 5-2, dogs_fonts2.htm, which was coded by hand, does not have unnecessary font tags.

```
<html>
<head>
<title>Dogs and Cats 2 - font</title>
</head>
<body>
<font face="Times New Roman">

<p><b>This is in bold</b></p>
<p>this is not bold</p>
<p>This is a new line</p>
<p>This is another new line</p>
<p>Table of Dogs and Cats</p>
<div align="left">
  <table border="1" width="80%">
    <tr>
```

Listing 5.2 dogs_fonts2.htm *(continued)*

```
          <td width="33%"> </td>
          <td width="33%">Dogs</td>
          <td width="34%">Cats</td>
      </tr>
      <tr>
          <td width="33%">Bellevue</td>
          <td width="33%">237</td>
          <td width="34%">483</td>
      </tr>
      <tr>
          <td width="33%">Bothell</td>
          <td width="33%">192</td>
          <td width="34%">384</td>
      </tr>
      <tr>
          <td width="33%">Redmond</td>
          <td width="33%">220</td>
          <td width="34%">452</td>
      </tr>
    </table>
  </div>
 </font>
 </body>
 </html>
```

Listing 5.2 *(continued)*

The difference between these two files is that the first one is twice as large as the second one. It may not seem like much when the files are this small, but scale this out and imagine thousands or millions of users requesting all that extra, unnecessary information. That is a lot of extra traffic and bandwidth to pay for, and potential performance problems could arise when bandwidth is taken up with unnecessary information. In this case, the extraneous tags have doubled the size of the data being requested. Ignoring some other sources of overhead in Web applications, this illustrates a case of almost half the bandwidth in use being used for unnecessary data. Bandwidth is an expensive part of any Web application, and controlling extraneous tags is one way to control the bandwidth consumption.

Frames and tables each take more time to render than plain text as the browser must read in the entire frame or table markup in order to start rendering it, although tables are not terribly bad unless they are embedded. Nesting a table within a table should be avoided because they do not tend to render properly on many browsers. Frames have built-in performance problems. First, an initial frameset file needs to be downloaded—one request and one small response of a file. This action references at least two more files that need to be requested and downloaded. Immediately, there is a performance difference between using frames and not using frames. However, if only small sections of the page are changing after each user action, then the difference between requesting the entire page of data again for each action and requesting the small area of data that has changed may actually be a performance improvement. It is up to testing to discover which is optimal for the application under test.

HTML may seem old, stale, and out-of-date, but it is the foundation of the Web. Static content is not as interesting as dynamic content. It does not have nearly the complexity or the risks. Static Web sites are hardly Web applications, so they need less testing. However, static content is a starting point, a point of origin that you can begin to branch off from. Understanding the technologies at the heart of your application makes you a much better tester and professional.

CHAPTER 6

The Dynamic Web

That which is static and repetitive is boring. That which is dynamic and random is confusing. In between lies art.
—John A. Locke

Plain HTML does not allow for a truly interactive and tailored user experience. Script, controls, and other technologies add this richness to the Web, but add complication to testing efforts.

Providing a Rich Experience

HTML in and of itself constitutes the basic framework of most Web sites and can provide some interesting information in a pleasant format, but to make a user's Web experience interactive and customizable, you need script. With only HTML, the Web is static. When User A requests a particular page from a site, he receives the exact same page that User B is given. Dynamic Web pages that allow user interactivity must employ technologies other than plain HTML in order to achieve a level of customization. Script can run in three places:

- It can reside on the server-side only and be executed there.
- It can be downloaded to the client machine and run there.
- It can use a combination of the two methods.

In the case of *server-side script*, the script lives and is executed on the server. The browser sends the information to be processed by the script up to the server and waits for the output. The server is responsible for making decisions and processing the information. This approach possibly means more traffic if the scripts are small, with a large amount of data being passed, or if data is passed multiple times due to user error. It also means more load on the server. Typically, server-side script is used by the Web server to access the databases, files, or other applications. Server-side scripting technologies include Active Server Pages, JavaScript, and VBScript. Other server-side technologies that create a rich experience are CGI programs or ISAPI programs, which are actually compiled programs.

Client-side script sits on the server and waits to be requested by the client. At that time a copy of the script is downloaded to the client to be interpreted and executed there. Client-side script can be used only with browsers that contain a scripting engine; otherwise, the browsers cannot interpret the script. These browsers are called *scripting hosts*. The interpreter may be a core component of the browser, or it may be a plug-in that is separately downloaded.

NOTE

Since most browsers, and therefore most users running browsers, are scripting hosts, this issue is not normally a constraint on Web applications, but it may be when supporting alternative devices such as PDAs or Web-enabled phones.

In the case of client-side script, processing and decision making are carried out by the client browser, taking a load off the server. If the scripts are very large and the data being passed back to the server is very small, this method can cause some high traffic. JavaScript and VBScript are two scripting languages that can be used either as client-side script or as server-side script. Java and ActiveX technologies enrich the user experience and are compiled programs downloaded to the client and processed there.

Examining Application Architecture

Because of the need to provide good response times and scalable servers, many Web applications are developed with a separation between the database and the processing of the data that must be done. Since the database server(s) have the bottleneck of accessing the hard drive to obtain the data, adding additional stresses onto the database server(s) would only slow down the user's session. Separating out the data from the processing or presentation also allows for the service to be upgraded providing a fresh user interface (UI) without touching the user data. A typical three-tier model of this architecture is shown in Figure 6.1.

The three-tier architecture model is composed of a client to handle the rendering, a front-end server to handle business logic and presentation, and a back-end server to handle data storage. The client with a browser sends out a request. This request is routed through the Internet to its destination server. At that point the server application takes over to understand and respond to the request. The front-end server deciphers the request and formulates it in such a way that the database can understand it. The database retrieves the information that the front-end server is requesting and sends it to the front-end server. The front-end server takes the data and adds presentation information to it. That entire set of data and presentation information is then handed to the client machine. There could be a four-tier architecture, splitting the front-end server so that the business logic layer is separate from the presentation layer. The *databases* make up the data layer and could store user data, such as the items being ordered or data that the user is requesting, such as a company catalog. The *data layer* is responsible only for receiving, storing, and manipulating the data. The *presentation layer* is responsible for formatting the data into a readable, and hopefully usable, format. It is responsible for generating the HTML, CSS, or other code that will be sent to the browser to instruct the browser on how to lay out and display the data. The *business logic* is an interface of rules that details access to the data and particulars on the presentation side. Being able to split up the work between several servers provides a performance improvement if the software is written correctly. It also provides redundancy—if one server goes down, performance may suffer, but the application as a whole is still available to users.

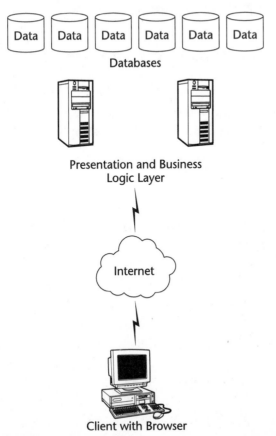

Figure 6.1 Generalization of a basic three-tier architecture.

Your Web application will likely have an architecture that fits into this model in some way. Each of these large components will have particular attributes and will require certain techniques to test. The aim of this discussion is to start taking the large black box of the Web application and start pulling out each of its components, labeling them, and discussing their attributes so you can be a more effective tester.

Script

JavaScript and VBScript are scripting languages used to enrich the experience on the Web, and both languages are discussed in more detail later in the chapter. But before turning to those languages, I want to examine a bit about how scripts are referenced in HTML, which is something you as a tester will want to understand.

Referencing Script

When a page is loaded, a script may be referenced in two main ways:

- Referencing script inline
- Referencing a script file to be downloaded and interpreted

Each method has characteristics that you, as a tester, need to be familiar with.

An inline reference comprises a few script tags inline with the rest of the HTML code for the page. Consider the following code sample:

```
<HTML>
   <HEAD>
     <TITLE>Hello World-Inline JS</TITLE>
   </HEAD>
<BODY>
<SCRIPT LANGUAGE="JavaScript" TYPE="text/javascript"><!--
document.write('Hello world')
//-->
</SCRIPT>
</BODY>
</HTML>
```

In this example, there is just an inline script statement. When the browser sees that there is script, it hands that entire piece to the proper script interpreter to be interpreted and executed. The <SCRIPT...> tag indicates the beginning of the information to hand to the interpreter, and the </SCRIPT> tag indicates the end of that section. Everything between the script tags is called the *script element*. There can be many of these sections in one Web page.

Also note the `<!--` and `//-->` HTML comment tags within the `<SCRIPT>` tags. Since the HTML comment tags are between the `<SCRIPT>` and `</SCRIPT>` tags, they will not be rendered by the script interpreter and will not even be seen by a browser with a script interpreter. However, they serve a very important purpose; browsers without a script interpreter can have problems with the `<SCRIPT>` information and will ignore that tag. Wrapping the script itself in the HTML comment tags ensures that browsers that cannot handle the script ignore it. On the last line, the `//` tells the script interpreter to ignore the HTML comment of `-->`. The HTML comments out the script for browsers that cannot handle it, and the script cancels out the HTML for the interpreter. It is just another piece added to your application's code to make sure it is robust, useful, and safe for all users of your application.

Additionally, another HTML tag can be placed after the `</SCRIPT>` closing tag. The `<NOSCRIPT>` tag is used to add a comment like the following:

```
<NOSCRIPT> Your browser is not script enabled. Please upgrade your
browser or use our 1-800 number (1-800-555-1212) to place an order.
</NOSCRIPT>
```

By suggesting the use of the `<NOSCRIPT>` tag to display a line of text like this to a browser that cannot render the script, you can save the company from having to deal with customer service calls, and help retain customers who might otherwise become frustrated or be lost.

The other option for client-side script is to reference a script file to be downloaded and interpreted, as in the following example.

```
<HTML>
   <HEAD>
      <TITLE>Hello World - Reference JS</TITLE>
   </HEAD>
<BODY>
<BR>
<SCRIPT LANGUAGE="JavaScript" SRC="hello_world.js">
</SCRIPT>
</BODY>
</HTML>
```

This piece of HTML code references a script file named hello_world.js. That script simply contains the following:

```
document.write ('Hello world')
```

The browser behaves in much the same way for both methods of referencing discussed here. In the first example as the browser reads in each line of HTML, it comes across the `<SCRIPT>` tag and hands off everything that follows to the interpreter until it hits the `</SCRIPT>` tag. It then resumes interpreting the HTML and displaying the information contained in it, while the interpreter does its job with the script.

In the second example, the example in which the script file is downloaded and interpreted, much the same thing happens, except that instead of several lines from the same file being handed to the interpreter, the interpreter is handed a different file that contains only the script. This other file has to be downloaded and handed off to the interpreter to be executed.

The coordination of two pieces of script or script and HTML can lead to some problems. If the HTML has all been rendered, to the user it appears that the page is ready to interact with and receive information or actions. However, if the server has not sent all of the script to the interpreter or if the interpreter has not finished interpreting the script, then you can experience race conditions. These race conditions typically manifest themselves on slower systems connected to the Internet with modems, or fast machines with fast connections. Unfortunately, the slow connection is the typical user scenario. Because of these race conditions, testing needs to happen with a high-end machine and a slow machine, with fast and slow connections, in order to catch these problems. Race conditions can be very serious but also very difficult to catch because they are dependant not only on the system, network, and hardware, but also on the tester or script running against the application.

CROSS-REFERENCE
Race conditions are discussed more thoroughly in Chapter 3.

JavaScript

JavaScript is a hot buzzword of the Internet; however, it is misunderstood. JavaScript has nothing to do with Java or JavaBeans. Java is a programming language created by Sun. JavaScript is a scripting language developed by Netscape and was originally called LiveScript. Netscape licensed the name Java because of the Internet hype and applied it to their language. Netscape shipped JavaScript 1.0 in their 2.0 version of Navigator. Microsoft jumped into the JavaScript fray with their own version of the language called JScript. Although the languages are very similar, there is still an industry standard— ECMAScript. The European Computer Manufacturers' Association (ECMA) standardized the scripting language with their publication ECMA-262, which, as of December 1999, is in its third edition. ECMA-262 was adopted by the Internet Organization for Standardization as standard ISO/IEC 16262:1998. JavaScript is now in version 1.5, which shipped with Navigator 6. JScript shipped version 5.5 with Microsoft IIS 5.0, and version 5.6 with Microsoft IE 6.0. Both Netscape Navigator 2.0+ and Microsoft IE version 4.0+ browsers are JavaScript script hosts. Netscape's Navigator 4.0 supported JavaScript 1.2, but it was not fully ECMA-262 compliant. Microsoft's Internet Explorer 4.0 supported JavaScript 1.2 and was fully ECMA-262 compliant. Because each

The Therac-25 Bug

One of the most famous race conditions, and the most tragic, was the Therac-25 bug. The Therac-25 was a medical machine designed to deliver a specific dosage of radiation to patients. It had two settings—filtered radiation and unfiltered. At rest, it sat in an unfiltered state. When it was ready to be used, the operator would enter the instructions as to whether the dosage would be delivered filtered or unfiltered. The machine would set itself appropriately. The operator would then enter the dosage amount, and the machine would deliver it. Operators became so proficient that they could type in several lines of instructions, leaving the machine to catch up with them. The problem that this caused was that the machine would start to switch to the filtered state and err on the next line of instructions not expecting them so soon. As everything was working properly, the operator would dismiss the error not knowing that the filter had not been moved into place. The machine would then deliver the requested dosage, except in the unfiltered state. Between 1985 and 1987 this bug that could have been fixed in several ways and could have been caught through testing caused eight deaths. This incident is a grim reminder of the responsibilities that our software may carry.

version of the language has its individual interpretations of the standard, each will behave differently given the same pieces of script. Therefore, you need to make certain that code matches the standard and then is tested on each supported platform.

NOTE Microsoft's JScript cannot be run on the client side by the Netscape scripting host without plug-ins. On the server side, JScript can be run only under Microsoft's IIS server and as Windows Scripting Host (WSH) scripts. Because of these limitations, JScript has not had the following that JavaScript has gained.

JavaScript is case-sensitive, unlike HTML. In HTML, you have the ability to use the bold tag as <b> or <B> and have it all mean the same thing. You can even mix the cases, closing the <b> tag with </B> . or mix cases within the same tag, as in <A href...> or <a hRef...>. In JavaScript, you need to be far more careful because it is case-sensitive. A variable named FOO is different from one named foo or Foo. As far as JavaScript is concerned, there are three different variable names in that last sentence, and accidentally hitting a Shift key can break your program. The browsers themselves have even had trouble with this point. For example, in IE 3, all client-side script was interpreted as case-insensitive, which meant that if your Web application had the preceding three variables, it would have a lot of problems because the browser would interpret them all the same. IE4 shipped properly, interpreting JavaScript as case-sensitive. However, in Netscape Navigator 4, JavaScript style sheets are case-insensitive. All these browser inconsistencies basically boil down to a simple concept to apply to your testing: Do not rely on creating different variables by just changing the case of letters in the same word. There is no telling when a browser from another third party will ship with a nonstandard implementation based on a different interpretation of a standard and break your JavaScript application.

As is described in Chapter 5 on static HTML, certain characters, and sets of characters, are reserved or may be read with a secondary meaning. These make great test cases as subjects for input in text boxes, hidden form fields, and any other place where users can dictate the data. You are looking for places where the string of characters that you put in is not what is read out, and the string of characters is instead interpreted to mean something else.

Table 6.1 shows some of the special characters found in JavaScript.

VBScript

VBScript is properly called Visual Basic Scripting Edition, but is more informally referred to as VBScript or VBS. VBScript was developed by Microsoft in answer to Netscape's JavaScript. It is very similar to Visual Basic (VB) and Visual Basic for Applications (VBA), which immediately lends it a programming base with at least some familiarity. Microsoft's Internet Explorer has a built-in script interpreter for VBScript; however, Netscape's Navigator does not, which is an immediate downside to any Web development project planning to use VBS and has hindered the VBScript adoption as a client-side scripting solution.

NOTE
Netscape does support several plug-ins that can interpret VBScript that can be downloaded from various third-party providers.

Unlike JavaScript, VBScript is not case-sensitive. In the example in the previous section, I showed how in JavaScript FOO, foo, and Foo were three separate variables, and the problems that this could cause in different browsers. In VBScript, these three words would all reference the same variable. This characteristic can cause problems when using VBScript if developers are not used to the case insensitivity and inadvertently end up referencing the wrong functions in their code. Even when case sensitivity is not an issue, efforts should be made to remain consistent and always reference variables in the same way.

Table 6.1 JavaScript Special Characters

CHARACTER SEQUENCE	INTERPRETATION
\"	Escape sequence for a quote character; similar syntax for other characters.
\xxx	Latin-1 octal encoding for a character—for example, \101 would be interpreted as A.
\xxx	Latin-1 hexadecimal for a character—for example, \x41 would be interpreted as A.
\uxxxx	Unicode hexadecimal representation for a character—for example, \u0041 would be interpreted as A (not supported in Navigator 4).
//	Comment tag—comments to the end of the line.
/* */	Comment tag—beginning and end tags.
;	End line of JavaScript operations—separates statements.

Test can act as a watchdog for this type of coding standard and identify casing issues during code reviews.

VBScript has its own set of reserved characters that can be interpreted with a meaning particular to that language. Again, these strings of input make excellent test cases for applications written in this language or any application that can use a browser that might automatically attempt to interpret the strings' meaning rather than simply pass and display these characters.

Table 6.2 shows some of the reserved special characters in VBScript.

Table 6.2 VBScript Special Characters

CHARACTER SEQUENCE	INTERPRETATION
'	Comment tag
Rem	Comment tag with no code preceding it in that line
: Rem	Comment tag in a line of code
:	Separates statements

Recognizing Script Problems

There are three major types of script problems.

- Errors that occur on compilation
- Errors that occur at runtime
- Logic errors

Errors that occur on *compilation* manifest themselves as soon as the page is requested. Figure 6.2 shows this type of error.

If you have a debugger installed, you may see an error such as the one in Figure 6.3, though.

The errors in both figures are pointing to the same problem: The Web page has not loaded yet because it is completely stopped by this compilation error. Notice also that in the lower-left corner of your browser window (refer to the lower-left corner of Figure 6.2) there is a small alert that there was an error on loading the page. Any time that you see this alert, you can double-click on the icon, and it will display the exact error that was encountered.

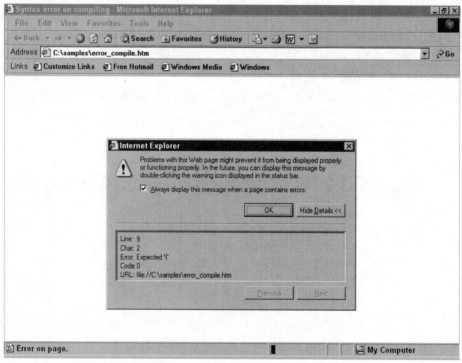

Figure 6.2 Error at compile time as Internet Explorer displays it.

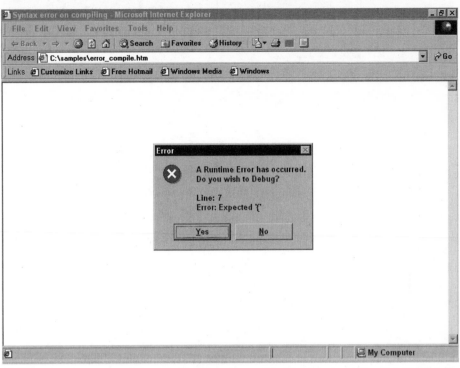

Figure 6.3   Same error in Internet Explorer if a script debugger is configured and installed.

WARNING

If you do not have your browser configured properly, you will not receive the pop-up alerts that errors have been encountered and will see only the small icon in the lower-left corner of the window, which can easily go unnoticed. See Appendix D for directions to ensure that these errors are not missed.

Compare that behavior with the graphic in Figure 6.4.

As you notice in that file the first line of the text appears, and then the error is displayed. This happens because the faulty line of JavaScript was moved below into the BODY section instead of the HEAD section. The browser was able to display some text before the interpreter hit the compilation error in the JavaScript. The root cause of both of these errors is the same—there is a missing brace { for the Alert function. This missing brace represents a syntax error because the syntax of the language requires that this brace be there. When the JavaScript interpreter attempted to compile the lines of script that were handed to it, it saw that there was a brace missing, and compilation failed before interpreting the script.

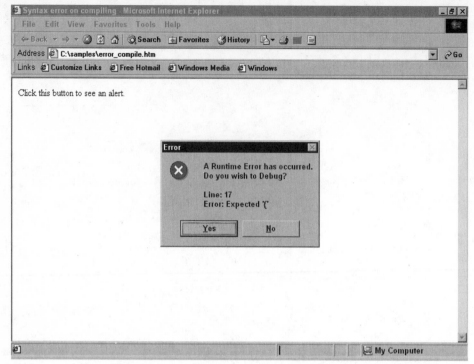

Figure 6.4 Here, the compilation error is in the middle of the page of HTML.

A *runtime error* is very similar. The page loads without error, the engine interprets the script without any syntax problems, but a function has a problem and will give an error when it is entered. For example, if the user clicks the button, a runtime error is received, like the one in Figure 6.5.

The page loaded and the user action was accepted, but on entering the function that would handle that user action, the script engine encountered an error—in this case, the function name is misspelled `Alrt1` when it should be spelled `Alert1`.

A *logical error* happens when the script engine enters functions, most usually due to a user entering a value that is not expected or a variable not being handled correctly. The malformed function causes the browser to choke on the function and time out or have other logical errors. The result of a logical error may not be an error message, but it is an unwanted behavior nonetheless.

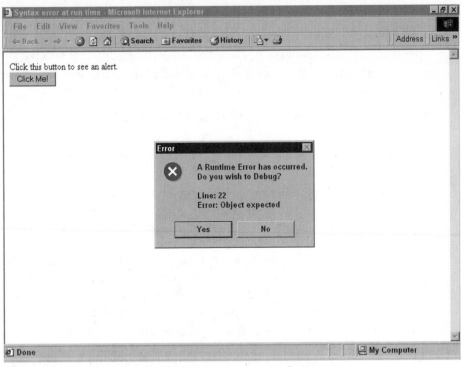

Figure 6.5 Runtime error as displayed In Internet Explorer.

Testing Script

There are a few pointers to testing script in Web applications.

Checking for Cache Issues

Since copies can be stored on the client in the browser cache, when a problem is encountered, it may not be a true problem with the application, but only a problem that a tester would encounter. The version in the cache may not be compatible with other data that is being retrieved from the server and, therefore, cause errors. For example, say that early in the day you start testing your Web application. You take a coffee break and come back to continue testing the application, only to find errors all over that had not been there before. Unknown to you, somebody loaded an old version of the application onto the servers for testing. If your browser is using the files from the cache, there will be a mismatch between the versions and this will likely cause errors.

When a problem is encountered, there are a few things you can do to try to track down the problem:

1. If you receive any kind of error, the best thing to do is immediately take a screen shot of the error and save it with comments about how it was encountered.

2. If the error is reproducible through those same steps, close all instances of the browser.

3. Open a single instance of that browser, dump the cache, and close the browser again.

4. Open a single instance of the browser and try the repro steps again. If you do not encounter the error, then there is a good chance that your browser had cached the data and that was causing a problem.

Following up with development will help to identify the exact problem, but most likely if clearing the cache fixes the problem, then there was a cached version clashing with files on the server. There is also the consideration that a proxy server has cached the content much as the browser will do. If there is a proxy server between your client machine and the server under test, make sure that your settings are such that your client does not go through the proxy server if it can be helped. A client going through a proxy server leads to many false bugs and a lot of wasted time otherwise. Appendix D has steps and screen shots to help you correctly configure your client machines.

Data Validation for Error Handling

Data validation is one function that client-side script can be used for. There are three main types of data validation employed by scripts.

- *Form-level validation* is handled either by the onClick event or the onSubmit event and returns a pop-up to the users alerting them of the invalid data. This type is typically used if two fields on a form could disagree, such as an address where the state and the zip code are incompatible. This validation is typically the easiest to have, but is usually employed too late to effectively warn users; their attention has already gone to other places on the form by the time that they are alerted.

- *Field-level validation* is the next most granular type of validation employed in Web applications. This type of validation uses more handlers than the form-level validation, but it alerts the user when the focus leaves a field or the form changes its state. The field handler fires a warning, and an alert pops up to let the user know that the information is invalid. An example of this might be a text entry box asking for a user's email address. If the user entered *asdfasdf*, on leaving the field the handler would fire an alert that it was not a valid email address. What the validation might be look-ing for in this case would be anything with at least an *x@x.x* format, where there had to be at least one character before the @ sign and one character after the @ sign, followed by the period and at least one charac-ter. The user could still enter any invalid address such as *asdfasdf@asdf .asdf*, but the form insists on some validation that the format was correct, perhaps enticing users to enter their real email address.

- *Key-level validation* attempts to stop users from typing in certain key-strokes. An example might be a user name entry field that allows only letters and numbers, but no symbols. A valid entry would be *user123* but not *user_123*. Key-level validation prevents the underscore keys from even being accepted in this text entry field and ignores the input.

In order to test any of these types of validation, you need definitions from the specifications outlining what is acceptable input and what is not, as well as how much input is accepted. These characters and boundaries need to be ver-ified by Test to ensure they are disallowed without an unexpected behavior. Related test cases should be performed, verifying that the appropriate content is blocked and testing the form's ability to handle certain content.

Looking for Back Door

One place where many applications get twisted into problems is through a back door. The user creation entry field may disallow underscores and allow only 10 characters, but if there is a user profile editing form and the program-mer of that component did not realize the limitations, unacceptable input could be entered there with unpredictable results. Always look for another way to alter the data to force it into an unexpected state.

Checking Performance

The performance of script is tricky to judge. The server receives a request for an item, an HTML page containing inline script, for example. The browser itself deals with the HTML, but has to hand the script to the interpreter. The interpreter has to start, receive the script, interpret it, and execute it. If the script is very complex, the server may have transmitted all the data to the client browser, but the interpreter may not have finished executing the code and may not be ready to interact or receive input. Because of this, a low-tech test may be of use; grab a stopwatch and see how long it really takes for a page to load all of the data, applets, animations, and script and to be ready to interact with the user. If network traces show that the page downloads rather quickly, but it takes 20 more seconds for it to be ready to receive input, then as far as the user is concerned there is a performance problem. Analyzing the network traffic of your application can help identify performance issues. Consider the following questions:

- Are certain files too large or unnecessarily downloaded?

- Are functions inserted into several areas of script, providing the opportunity to consolidate them into a single function to improve maintainability and performance?

- Are there vestigial functions in the code that were once used but no longer are?

Errors Dependent on Display Size

Your browser's display size may matter to the script.

- Try changing the browser window's size so that it is very tall and skinny and would basically only display one pixel width of the canvas area. Try to perform an action at this point. (You can set your action up by filling out the online form, setting focus to the Submit button, resizing the browser window, and then hitting Enter.) Did you get an error? Try this adjustment for each frame as well, allowing only a single pixel of a frame to be displayed.

- Try the opposite—change the window so that it is very wide and short and displays only one pixel height, either in the entire window or in one frame that will be reloaded. Can you hit errors in the script with this display?

- Resize the browser so that once the script runs, the frame of interest will be exactly no size. Does this give you a script error?

- Resize the browser when you get to a particular page of interest, and then hit F5 to reload it.

Although these are not the most likely of user scenarios, they are potential ones and will test the robustness of the application.

Testing Active Server Pages

Active Server Pages (ASP) is a platform for building, deploying, and running Web applications. Active Server Pages are just text files of script commands with an .asp file extension that hook into Microsoft's Internet Information Server (IIS) by way of the Internet Server Application Programming Interface (ISAPI) interface. There is usually also HTML code in these files to format the Web pages. The default output of these files is HTML or HTML and script to be processed on the client. These files are processed only by Microsoft Web servers (IIS) on the server side. Microsoft originally shipped this server-side technology with the Windows NT 3.51 IIS component in 1996 and has its most recent version in Windows 2000. ASP allows Web programmers to write server-side scripts as powerful as the CGI scripts, but with a simpler syntax. This server-side script would be referenced in a way such as this in a form with the code:

```
<FORM METHOD="POST" ACTION="order.asp">
```

To test Active Server Pages you can start with simple proofreading. Read through the code and check for misspellings that lead to misnamed variables or functions. Verify ASP in several different browsers. ASP also retains session state information, which is very useful for such features as a shopping basket for a Web site; however, it also has limitations and can cause scalability issues as well as memory problems. ASP has stringent requirements for URL construction and necessitates always using the same case in URLs. Session state should be disabled if it is not core to the function of the Web site or of frames within the Web application. ASP also has serialized execution, which means that it will completely finish one task before starting on the next, possibly causing a perception of performance issues.

Testing the performance of ASP on your server is very important, as is stress testing the ASP server. Consider the following:

- When testing, read through the various event logs that are written. The server may not have crashed, but there may be unwanted events occurring. Using such tools as Microsoft's Web Application Stress Tool (also known as Application Center Test, formerly Homer) or the IIS exception monitor helps you to track down these issues. This session state also does not persist to disk, so if a server in a server farm goes down, a user's session could be left stranded. The sessions time out at 20 minutes by default and require that cookies be enabled on the client browser. If this application is to be used for a high security site, such as a financial application, using the session state may not be an option.

- ASP also offers caching on the server side, which is great if there is a lot of static content because the content can then be served up out of memory instead of accessing the disk and processing the data. But if the core of the application is dynamic content, then this caching can result in a performance issue.

- One issue that can come up in responses is the response timeout. Many applications use a Response.Expires property of 0. Using a negative number here forces the content to expire, and because 0 is the current time, a negative is preferred. `Response.Expires=-100000` ensures that the application is properly expired, as does a "no-cache" header.

- In order to test everything around an .asp application, rename the file from *.asp to *.astm, which will allow you to see everything including all #includes and data sizes.

All these tests for stress breakages and performance are some of the most important piece of testing ASP applications. Look for memory leaks from these components.

Testing CGI

Common Gateway Interface (CGI) is a server-side technology that allows for a customizable user experience. CGI is actually a protocol that specifies how compiled programs on the server interact with the Web server (typically other files or the databases). It is actually more like a collection of standard variables for communication between the client and the server. The interface that it standardizes is the one in the server's HTTP server application that serves data to the client browsers and other applications or files on the server. It basically provides a standard way that information can be sent between the HTTP server and the script. CGI programs are compiled programs on the server and can be written in any programming language that allows direct access to the STDIN and STDOUT functions on the Web server, languages that include AppleScript, Perl, TCL, VC++, VisualBasic, and others. The server that CGI files sit on and interact with could be a Microsoft IIS Web server, a Netscape Web server, an Oracle Web application server, or another type. When you compare this against Microsoft's Active Server Pages, which works only with Microsoft's IIS server, you find a larger potential platform of support for CGI.

CGI works much as ASP does. From the user side, the user fills out a form and clicks SUBMIT or some other action. If the <FORM ACTION...> tag has an .asp file referenced, then an Active Server Page server-side technology will be handling it. If there is a .js referenced, then there is a JavaScript script handling the data. If there is a .exe referenced, then it can be assumed that it is a CGI application on the server side. The browser sends up the data to be processed to the Web server. The Web server holds the data in memory and instantiates an instance of the CGI application. Once the CGI executable is ready, this data is handed to it to be processed. The output is handed back to the Web server, where it is held in a memory location as the CGI executable terminates. The Web server reads the output and sends the data back down to the client browser to be formatted and displayed to the user. Instantiating a new instance of an executable each time data needs to be processed can be very expensive on performance if the applications are not written carefully. Careful stress and performance tests need to be performed against CGI applications just as they are against ASP applications.

CROSS-REFERENCE

While ASP and CGI, discussed in the next section, are server-side technologies, they are nevertheless technologies that enrich the Web experience on the user side, which is why these two technologies are discussed in this chapter on dynamic Web technologies. More on performance testing ASP is found in Chapter 8.

Testing ActiveX Controls

ActiveX controls are a client-side technology and are really just OCX controls like those in any win32 program. Because of what they are, ActiveX controls have inherent limitations, concerns, and benefits. When testing ActiveX controls, keep the following in mind:

- ActiveX controls can be used only on a Windows client. Although Netscape does not natively support them, there are plug-ins available. These types of audience limiters should be examined when technical directions are decided on.

- Because ActiveX applications are compiled applications downloaded to the client machine to be run, there are some security concerns. ActiveX applications need to be signed and verified. Many users have become more conscious of security risks and will deny the downloading of ActiveX or other components. If this is an Internet application, a significant part of your potential audience could be omitted if you use any technology that a user does not trust or cannot access. However, an intranet application can benefit significantly from various technologies that are known to be secure since they originate from within the company. Unless absolutely necessary, avoid marking your controls as safe for scripting to prevent other malicious users from exploiting potential problems in your controls.

- The fact that a control downloads and installs can mean that you end up testing an old version of a control for a long time without realizing yours is out of date. Unlike HTML pages, graphics, or script files, which are cached and checked for freshness on request, the ActiveX components are actually installed. They need to be uninstalled and reinstalled to test each new version. Check the version number before testing.

- Since ActiveX controls install themselves, also check for a hard-coded install path (for example, C:\...). Many users now have multiples drives, and a hard-coded install path and other such assumptions could be incompatible with their system.

- Test the downloading and installation on a dirty system (one which has an old version that is out of date) and on a clean system to help you verify that both methods work properly.

- Be sure to test the uninstall process—all files need to be deleted, and the registry needs to be cleaned of any references to the control.

- Verify the registration of the control when it is installed.

- Verify the usability of all the pages in your Web site or application with the control installed and without it installed. Many users will not download the control or cannot download it. To prevent losing portions of your customer base, there must be at least some scenarios that allow them to have a full experience with your application, if not a rich experience, even if they don't have the ActiveX control installed.

- One of the concerns that has plagued ActiveX technology is viruses. Always check your control for viruses. Spreading viruses to your customers is not a good business practice and will not win more customers.

- Be sure to also have your control signed. Signing makes for a safer download and helps your users feel comfortable downloading it. It also makes the application more professional.

Some simple cases for testing ActiveX controls include clicking the browser's Refresh button while the control is active or clicking the browser Back, Stop, or Print button while it is active. The application specifications should detail what the behavior is for these actions. Microsoft's Internet Explorer 3.0 had an issue with ActiveX controls, where navigating four pages away from the control crashed the browser if the control was written improperly. The crash was due to an IE internal three-page cache that would unload at four pages. It has since been changed to be more tolerant of various ActiveX controls. Another test to try is to disconnect the network cable or modem connection while the control is active. This disconnection can cause unwanted behaviors if the control intermittently polls or downloads data from the server.

Most Web applications strive to provide a rich set of features, allowing users a wide range of functionality. The technologies that can be used or combined to create this functionality are varied, and each carries its particular set of weak points and specific test cases. As with other software, detailing the behaviors and interactions of the features, as well as how the user will interact with the software, helps to create seamless software that works as expected.

CHAPTER 7

Testing Character Sets, Code Pages, and Glyphs

A little inaccuracy sometimes saves a lot of explanation.
—H. H. Munro

G ood input is the heart of good testing. To select good test cases and target your cases at the actual types of problems your software is susceptible to, you need to understand input. All input breaks down to characters, which are really just code points as far as the computer is concerned. This chapter serves as an introduction to understanding input, languages, problem ranges of input, and the underlying reasons why some things are problematic. The information in this chapter allows you to then develop your own set of targeted cases, aimed at your application and technologies. Without this knowledge and forethought, we're all just making guesses.

A Few Definitions

It will make it easier to discuss an unfamiliar area if I give some working definitions from the beginning. A more complete list of definitions is in Appendix O.

- **Character.** A single distinctive mark, letter, or symbol such as the letter A or the exclamation mark ! or the backslash \ or the space. This term actually refers just to the value of that character (for example, *A* equates to the value 0x41 on the single byte code pages or [U+0041] in Unicode the name LATIN CAPITAL LETTER A).

- **Charset.** The combination of a code page and the encoding method applied to that particular code page. Shortened name of the term *character set*.

- **Encoding.** Encoding is the process of taking bytes and converting them into characters.

- **Code table.** A table showing the characters allocated to each bit combination. Sometimes called a *code page*.

- **Code point.** The unique location of a character on a code table. This character will always be located in this spot for this table or page, and the code point serves as a way to reference it, a mapping. The code point is referenced in a way such as 0x41 or [U+004D] or [9F/FC].

- **Glyph.** The graphic representation of a character. This is what you would write on paper. You can think of this as the picture of the letter that the computer decides to show you when you request a character. The computer takes the value of the character and matches it to the appropriate glyph.

- **Font.** A collection of glyphs constitutes a *font*. In a more technical sense, as the implementation of a font, a font is a *numbered* set of glyphs. The numbers correspond to code positions of the characters (presented by the glyphs). Thus, a font in that sense is character code dependent and arranged around a language.

Displaying Characters

Remember when you were a kid and you got a secret decoder ring in your box of cereal? Remember how that worked? It had letters arranged around the ring and then numbers associated with each letter such as A-1, B-2, C-3, and so on. You were then able to send secret messages to friends if they had the same ring. For instance, you could send the message *8-5-12-12-15, 10-15-5. 23-8-1-20 4-15 25-17-21 11-14-17-23?* Your friend would receive your numeric representation and proceed to match up the numbers with the letters to understand the message. He would get *HELLO, JOE. WHAT DO YOU KNOW?*

You can take that concept and start to make it a bit more complex and add in cases and symbols, as shown in the following list:

A-1   a-27   [space]-53

B-2   b-28   !-54

C-3   c-29   "-55

D-4   d-30   #-56

E-5   e-31 $-57

F-6   f-32   %-58

G-7   g-33   &-59

H-8   h-34   '-60

I-9   i-35   (-61

J-10   j-36   )-62

K-11   k-37   *-63

L-12   l-38   +-64

M-13   m-39   ,-65

N-14   n-40   --66

O-15   o-41   .-67

P-16   p-42   ?-68

Q-17   q-43

R-18   r-44

S-19   s-45

T-20   t-46

U-21   u-47

V-22   v-48

W-23   w-49

X-24   x-50

Y-25   y-51

Z-26   z-52

This list displays a very simple arrangement. I started with the number 1 and then counted up, assigning a particular letter or symbol to each number. Using this updated list, the same message created earlier would be a bit different and would look like the following: 8-31-38-38-41-65-53-10-41-31-67-53-23-34-27-46-53-30-41-53-51-41-47-53-37-40-41-49-68. This updated list allows me to add cases to my letters and punctuation so that my message would come out as *Hello, Joe. What do you know?*

This simple illustration reveals exactly what a code page is. If you can use a secret decoder ring, then the code page is just one step up from that. The code page, instead of arranging things in a line (one dimension) as in the previous example, where you have the numbers incrementing by one for each new item, arranges information in a table (two dimensions). Once the information is arranged in a table, you need a coordinate system to find items—a map of sorts. The code page is a standard 16 x 16 matrix (shown in Table 7.1).

Once you have the matrix, you can start filling in your letters and symbols and then refer to any spot on this map using the coordinates. The matrix will start to look like Table 7.2.

Table 7.1   Standard Single-Byte Code Page Matrix

	COL 0	COL 1	COL 2	COL 3	COL 4	COL 5	COL 6	COL 7	COL 8	COL 9	COL A	COL B	COL C	COL D	COL E	COL F
Line 0																
Line 1																
Line 2																
Line 3																
Line 4																
Line 5																
Line 6																
Line 7																
Line 8																
Line 9																
Line A																
Line B																
Line C																
Line D																
Line E																
Line F																

Table 7.2   Standard Single-Byte Code Page with the Printable Lower ASCII Characters Filled In

	COL 0	COL 1	COL 2	COL 3	COL 4	COL 5	COL 6	COL 7	COL 8	COL 9	COL A	COL B	COL C	COL D	COL E	COL F
Line 0																
Line 1																
Line 2	space	!	"	#	$	%	&	'	(	)	*	+	,	-	.	/
Line 3	0	1	2	3	4	5	6	7	8	9	:	;	<	=	>	?
Line 4	@	A	B	C	D	E	F	G	H	I	J	K	L	M	N	O
Line 5	P	Q	R	S	T	U	V	W	X	Y	Z	[	\	]	^	_
Line 6	`	a	b	c	d	e	f	g	h	i	j	k	l	m	n	o
Line 7	p	q	r	s	t	u	v	w	x	y	z	{	|	}	~	
Line 8																
Line 9																
Line A																
Line B																
Line C																
Line D																
Line E																
Line F																

If I wanted to encode my message with the information from Table 7.2, I would refer to each individual spot in the character page by the point that it occupies in the map. For example, the point for the letter *A* is 0x41 (line 4 column 1) and the space is 0x20. The location of the characters is designated by the two characters after the *x*. The first character is the row, or line, on which the character exists, and the second character is the column name in which the character exists. The *0x* preceding this map point is conventional notation. So each of the letters, numbers, or symbols has a mapped point, as well as an official name. For example, the space has the formal name *SPACE*, and the *A* has the formal name *LATIN CAPITAL LETTER A*. Using the formal character name standardizes each character and meaning associated with a code point.

NOTE

Characters can be looked up with many tools, in the documents created by standards bodies, or through the Windows utility Character Map. The Character Map gives not only a graphical representation of the character, but also its value and formal name. Appendices J and M discuss various tools and references.

Table 7.2 contains 256 blocks where you could put letters, numbers, or symbols. The first half (line 0 through line 7) is referred to as Lower ASCII, and the last 128 (line 8 through line F) are referred to as Upper ASCII or the Extended Range. Figure 7.1 shows the characters that occupy these blocks.

```
LOWER ASCII RANGE
0x20: !"#$%&'()*+,-./:0x2F
0x30:0123456789:;<=>?:0x3F
0x40:@ABCDEFGHIJKLMNO:0x4F
0x50:PQRSTUVWXYZ[\]^_:0x5F
0x60:`abcdefghijklmno:0x6F
0x70:pqrstuvwxyz{|}~□:0x7F

EXTENDED RANGE
0x80:€□‚ƒ„…†‡ˆ‰Š‹Œ□Ž□:0x8F
0x90:□''""•––˜™š›œ□žŸ:0x9F
0xA0: ¡¢£¤¥¦§¨©ª«¬-®‾:0xAF
0xB0:°±²³´µ¶·¸¹º»¼½¾¿:0xBF
0xC0:ÀÁÂÃÄÅÆÇÈÉÊËÌÍÎÏ:0xCF
0xD0:ÐÑÒÓÔÕÖ×ØÙÚÛÜÝÞß:0xDF
0xE0:àáâãäåæçèéêëìíîï:0xEF
0xF0:ðñòóôõö÷øùúûüýþÿ:0xFF
```

Figure 7.1 Lower ASCII and Upper ASCII ranges.

However, not all of the lower 128 are used, only 127 are, leaving a total of 255 places for characters. Lines 0 and 1 are control characters (for example, the bell, end of line, backspace, and so on). These are not printed characters and, therefore, may not be shown in code pages; however, they are constant across all the ANSI pages.

If you want to display more than 255 characters, you need to have multiple charts. To go back to my example, I could tell my friend which chart to use to look up the message contents that I sent him. Again, that process is exactly what happens with the code pages. When there are many code pages, you have to identify which one you are using to properly input information and then read it back out.

Character Standards' Histories

The original character standards were set in place in 1968 by the American National Standards Institute (ANSI). This standard is called the *American Standard Code for Information Interchange (ASCII)*. The original ASCII standard documented 127 places, the lower ASCII, for letters, numbers, and symbols. This standard was later extended by adding another 128, the upper ASCII, for a total of 255 allocations.

As computing spread, the need for more characters, symbols, and language support became necessary. A larger standards body, the International Organization for Standarization (ISO) adopted the ASCII standard, and the ASCII standard was incorporated into the ISO 8859 standards for characters.

NOTE There is a separate ISO 8859 standard for each breakdown of the languages. ISO 8859-1 covers set 1 of the Latin characters. This roughly covers the Western European languages such as French, Spanish, Catalan, Basque, Portuguese, Italian, Albanian, Rhaeto-Romanic, Dutch, German, Danish, Swedish, Norwegian, Finnish, Faroese, Icelandic, Irish, Scottish, and English, and incidentally also Afrikaans and Swahili. ISO 8859-6 covers Arabic. ISO 8859-7 covers Greek.

Many companies like to customize their offerings to the public for different reasons. Originally, IBM developed the DOS implementation of these standards. Microsoft later developed their implementations of these standards, which have since become more widely used and are the foundation on the Windows platform. These implementations are all based off the ISO standards, but companies pick and choose what they want to support or add in. The differences are small, but it is from these small differences that large problems can occur. Take a look at Figures 7.2 and 7.3, which show the IBM and Microsoft implementations of the 1252 code page.

```
LOWER ASCII RANGE
0x20:  !"#$%&'()*+,-./:0x2F
0x30:0123456789:;<=>?:0x3F
0x40:@ABCDEFGHIJKLMNO:0x4F
0x50:PQRSTUVWXYZ[\]^_:0x5F
0x60:`abcdefghijklmno:0x6F
0x70:pqrstuvwxyz{|}~⌂:0x7F

EXTENDED RANGE
0x80:Ç éâäàåçêëèïîìÄÅ:0x8F
0x90:É`'""òûùÿÖÜ¢£¥₧ƒ:0x90
0xA0:□íóúñÑ──¿⌐¬½¡«»:0xA0
0xB0:░▒▓│┤╡╢╖╕╣║╗╝╜╛┐:0xB0
0xC0:└┴┬├─┼╞╟╚╔╩╦╠═╬╧:0xC0
0xD0:╨╤╥╙╘╒╓╫╪┘┌█▄▌▐▀:0xD0
0xE0:αβΓπΣσμχΦΘΩδ∞∅∈∩:0xE0
0xF0:≡±≥≤⌠⌡÷≈°••√ⁿ²■:0xF0
```

Figure 7.2   IBM implementation of the 1252 code page.

```
LOWER ASCII RANGE
0x20:  !"#$%&'()*+,-./:0x2F
0x30:0123456789:;<=>?:0x3F
0x40:@ABCDEFGHIJKLMNO:0x4F
0x50:PQRSTUVWXYZ[\]^_:0x5F
0x60:`abcdefghijklmno:0x6F
0x70:pqrstuvwxyz{|}~□:0x7F

EXTENDED RANGE
0x80:€□‚ƒ„…†‡ˆ‰Š‹Œ□Ž□:0x8F
0x90:□''""•––˜™š›œ□žŸ:0x9F
0xA0: ¡¢£¤¥¦§¨©ª«¬-®¯:0xAF
0xB0:°±²³´µ¶·¸¹º»¼½¾¿:0xBF
0xC0:ÀÁÂÃÄÅÆÇÈÉÊËÌÍÎÏ:0xCF
0xD0:ÐÑÒÓÔÕÖ×ØÙÚÛÜÝÞß:0xDF
0xE0:àáâãäåæçèéêëìíîï:0xEF
0xF0:ðñòóôõö÷øùúûüýþÿ:0xFF
```

Figure 7.3   Microsoft implementation of the 1252 code page.

As you can see in the two figures, the IBM 1252 implementation is very similar to the Microsoft 1252 implementation. The lines 2–7 are the same, but the control characters and extended ranges are implemented differently. The Windows pages are sometimes also called the ANSI pages in the vernacular (although technically this is not accurate) and are the code pages 1250–1258 that most people think of, as well as the 874 Thai, 932 Japanese, 936 Chinese Simplified, 949 Korean, and 950 Chinese Traditional. Various corporations take the ISO standards and interpret them, creating a code page and defining which encoding method is to be applied to it.

NOTE

There are many other pages for various other systems, but I just want to discuss how the main ones I've mentioned work and leave the minutiae of each page up to more detailed discussions in other sources. If you are more concerned with the Apple code pages or others, then you will want to do more research in that area to understand how they affect your software. Although this discussion does not cover those specific pages, the concepts discussed in this chapter apply to them equally.

Reading Code Pages

Now that I've had a chance to introduce the concept of code pages and some of the character standards that use them, I want to take a closer look at how some actual code pages work. A good place to start is with the Windows 1252 page. Table 7.3 is a representation of this code page.

Again, 0x20 is a space, and 0x41 is the letter *A*. If I wanted to send my sample message from earlier in the chapter to my friend, it would be 0x48 0x65 0x6C 0x6C 0x6F 0x2C 0x20 0x4A 0x6F 0x65 0x2E 0x20 0x57 0x68 0x61 0x74 0x20 0x64 0x6F 0x20 0x79 0x6F 0x75 0x20 0x6B 0x6E 0x6F 0x77 0x3F, and my friend would get *Hello, Joe. What do you know?*

I could even start to use the extended range. For example, the word *résumé* would be 0x72 0xE9 0x73 0x75 0x6D 0xE9. I could also refer to these letters by their official names because in common discussions that may be immediately more meaningful than trying to discuss code points:

r   LATIN SMALL LETTER R

é   LATIN SMALL LETTER E WITH ACUTE

s   LATIN SMALL LETTER S

u   LATIN SMALL LETTER U

m   LATIN SMALL LETTER M

Table 7.3　Windows 1252 Code Page of Printable Characters

	COL 0	COL 1	COL 2	COL 3	COL 4	COL 5	COL 6	COL 7	COL 8	COL 9	COL A	COL B	COL C	COL D	COL E	COL F
Line 2		!	"	#	$	%	&	'	(	)	*	+	,	-	.	/
Line 3	0	1	2	3	4	5	6	7	8	9	:	;	<	=	>	?
Line 4	@	A	B	C	D	E	F	G	H	I	J	K	L	M	N	O
Line 5	P	Q	R	S	T	U	V	W	X	Y	Z	[	\	]	^	_
Line 6	`	a	b	c	d	e	f	g	h	i	j	k	l	m	n	o
Line 7	p	q	r	s	t	u	v	w	x	y	z	{	|	}	~	□
Line 8	€	□	‚	ƒ	„	…	†	‡	ˆ	‰	Š	‹	Œ	□	Ž	□
Line 9	□	'	'	"	"	•	–	—	˜	™	š	›	œ	□	ž	Ÿ
Line A		¡	¢	£	¤	¥	¦	§	¨	©	ª	«	¬		®	¯
Line B	°	±	²	³	´	µ	¶	·	¸	¹	º	»	¼	½	¾	¿
Line C	À	Á	Â	Ã	Ä	Å	Æ	Ç	È	É	Ê	Ë	Ì	Í	Î	Ï
Line D	Ð	Ñ	Ò	Ó	Ô	Õ	Ö	×	Ø	Ù	Ú	Û	Ü	Ý	Þ	ß
Line E	à	á	â	ã	ä	å	æ	ç	è	é	ê	ë	ì	í	î	ï
Line F	ð	ñ	ò	ó	ô	õ	ö	÷	ø	ù	ú	û	ü	ý	þ	ÿ

The extended range is the only part that differs between Windows code pages; the lower ASCII always remains the same. Just as your friend would have to have the same secret decoder ring as you, your friend (or the computer) has to be using the same code page as you to make sure the message comes out as expected. For the lower ASCII characters, identifying the code page being used does not matter so much as those characters and mapped points are exactly the same across all the ASCII code pages. If your message used any characters that fell into the extended range (or upper ASCII), you would need to identify the appropriate source code page because this range changes for each page. For example, Figure 7.4 places the Windows 1252 code page (on the left) by the Windows 1253 code page (on the right). Take note of the difference between the extended ranges.

You can see how the lower ASCII range is the same, and much of the extended range is the same, but not all of it. If you intended to send your friend the word *résumé*, you would send the code points 0x72 0xE9 0x73 0x75 0x6D 0xE9 to your friend. If you forgot to tell your friend which code page to use to reference and your friend used the Windows 1253 code page instead of the Windows 1252 code page, your friend could end up with *rısumı*. And while this change seems like a small one, and you can still tell what is meant, larger problems can come of this sort of miscommunication. Those are discussed later in this chapter.

```
LOWER ASCII RANGE
0x20:  !"#$%&'()*+,-./:0x2F
0x30:0123456789:;<=>?:0x3F
0x40:@ABCDEFGHIJKLMNO:0x4F
0x50:PQRSTUVWXYZ[\]^_:0x5F
0x60:`abcdefghijklmno:0x6F
0x70:pqrstuvwxyz{|}~□:0x7F

EXTENDED RANGE
0x80:€□‚ƒ„…†‡ˆ‰Š‹Œ□Ž□:0x8F
0x90:□''""•––˜™š›œ□žŸ:0x9F
0xA0: ¡¢£¤¥¦§¨©ª«¬-®¯:0xAF
0xB0:°±²³´µ¶·¸¹º»¼½¾¿:0xBF
0xC0:ÀÁÂÃÄÅÆÇÈÉÊËÌÍÎÏ:0xCF
0xD0:ÐÑÒÓÔÕÖ×ØÙÚÛÜÝÞß:0xDF
0xE0:àáâãäåæçèéêëìíîï:0xEF
0xF0:ðñòóôõö÷øùúûüýþÿ:0xFF
```

```
LOWER ASCII RANGE
0x20: !"#$%&'()*+,-./:0x2F
0x30:0123456789:;<=>?:0x3F
0x40:@ABCDEFGHIJKLMNO:0x4F
0x50:PQRSTUVWXYZ[\]^_:0x5F
0x60:`abcdefghijklmno:0x6F
0x70:pqrstuvwxyz{|}~□:0x7F

EXTENDED RANGE
0x80:€□‚ƒ„…†‡□‰□‹□□□□:0x8F
0x90:□''""•——□™□›□□□□:0x9F
0xA0: ˆ΅Α£¤¥¦§¨©□«¬-®—:0xAF
0xB0:°±²³΄µ¶·Έ'ΉΊ»Ό½ΎΏ:0xBF
0xC0:ΐΑΒΓΔΕΖΗΘΙΚΛΜΝΞΟ:0xCF
0xD0:ΠΡ□ΣΤΥΦΧΨΩΪΫάέή ί:0xDF
0xE0:ΰαβγδεζηθικλμνξο:0xEF
0xF0:πρςστυφχψωϊϋόύώ□:0xFF
```

Figure 7.4   Microsoft 1252 and 1253 code pages.

Some of the main code pages that group sets of characters in the ASCII standard (ones that you will likely have to deal with as a tester) are as follows:

- **1250.** Windows code page that covers English, Polish, Czech, Hungarian, and Slovak

- **1251.** Windows code page that covers English and Russian

- **1252.** Windows code page that covers English, French, German, Spanish, Portuguese, Italian, Dutch, Danish, Swedish, Norwegian, and Finnish

- **1253.** Windows code page that covers English and Greek

- **1254.** Windows code page that covers English and Turkish

- **1257.** Windows code page that covers English, Estonian, Latvian, and Lithuanian

- **1258.** Windows code page that covers English and Vietnamese

NOTE

English, as you will notice, is covered in each page. This is because English only needs the lower ASCII range, and since that remains the same for every page, English can be written fully with any of the pages.

Each code page carries with it an implicit encoding method that it applies. This combination of the map of the characters and the encoding method applied to that particular arrangement is called a *character set*, or a *charset*. There is usually only one encoding method specified for each page, but a particular encoding algorithm may be used for several different code pages. Again, it is not necessarily important at this point to know each of these encoding methods or to be able to describe them, but just understand that they are present. To most people they are silent and invisible, yet they are very important. Knowing what code pages are and how they can affect your application is the important part. You want to be able to select well-reasoned test cases based on knowledge. Lacking this type of knowledge leaves you guessing at what input would appropriately exercise your application.

The thing to remember is that you must not only specify your code points, but which code page you are using to avoid data loss, conversion, or corruption. There is a short discussion later in this chapter on specific issues, but just know that there is a specific encoding method applied to each code page.

Understanding Glyphs

If you take a look back at Figure 7.4, you may notice that there are small blocks displayed in the text. These are there because somehow the computer does not know what glyph to show us. A *glyph* can be thought of as the picture of the character. For example, the character Latin Capital Letter A can be displayed many different ways—cursive, flowery, blocky, and so on. The value and the character name are the same, but the representation is slightly changed. A is $\mathcal{A}$ (is $\mathcal{A}$ is **A** is $\mathbf{a}$). All those ways are still the exact same code point (0x41) being displayed and are still the same name, value, and meaning. The only change is that the glyph, or picture, used to display the value is different. You can control which glyph to display by changing the font face for the selected text. A font family usually covers a code page or several code pages. For example, if you wanted to display the 1253 code page characters (Greek letters), you could select from a number of fonts including Arial, Tahoma, and Sylfaen and still be able to completely display the printable characters of the language.

NOTE

Remember how I defined *font* at the beginning of the chapter: A collection of glyphs constitutes a *font*. In a more technical sense, in the implementation of a font, a font is a *numbered* set of glyphs. The numbers correspond to the code positions of the characters (presented by the glyphs). Thus, a font in that sense is character code dependent and arranged around a language(s).

Let me return to those boxes that appear in the text displayed in Figure 7.4. In the case of the code point 0x7F, that is the DELETE code point. There is no visible printed glyph for it, yet it is a valid code point. Therefore, the computer substitutes the default box, sometimes displayed as a thick black line. Formally, this character, displayed to indicate the presence of a nondisplayable character, is called the REPLACEMENT CHARACTER because it is displayed in the place of other characters when necessary. You can think of it as the computer saying, "Gee, I know that this is a valid character, but I really have no idea what you want me to show here, so I'll show you this to indicate that there is something here." Seeing the boxes can also mean that the *font* that you have selected does not have a corresponding glyph for that code point and not necessarily that the character is nonprintable. The computer again may substitute the box to indicate that. Seeing the box is not necessarily bad; it can just mean that there is a configuration problem or that the code point cannot be displayed.

In Figure 7.5 you see the exact same set of code points displayed twice, with only the font changed between the two illustrations. Notice that the 1253 Greek code page is not fully supported in the Browallia New font face—the 0xC0, 0xD0, 0xE0, and 0xF0 lines are not supported as opposed to the Courier New font, which supports almost all of the printable characters. In the figure, the replacement character boxes that are displayed can be rendered as meaningful characters simply by changing the font face from Browallia New to Courier New.

A better indication that you have a problem is when you receive question marks (????) for data you have put in while testing. If you know that you have input the string ΑΒΓΔΕΖ, and after saving the data you try to view it again only to receive ??????, then you might have a corruption problem. Receiving question marks means that there has been a data loss, corruption, or a conversion, causing the computer to say, "I haven't the faintest clue what this is, but there is data here. I'll show you the question marks to indicate that something was here." It can also be an indicator that you need to change your encoding method or the font selected in your browser settings to appropriately view this data.

CROSS-REFERENCE

Sometimes changing the configuration will not help to display the data correctly and you have found a true instance of data loss, conversion, or corruption. Some general guidelines on this topic can be found in Appendix D.

LOWER ASCII RANGE

0x20: !"#$%&'()*+,-./:0x2F

0x30:0123456789:;<=>?:0x3F

0x40:@ABCDEFGHIJKLMNO:0x4F

0x50:PQRSTUVWXYZ[\]^_:0x5F

0x60:`abcdefghijklmno:0x6F

0x70:pqrstuvwxyz{|}~☐:0x7F

EXTENDED RANGE

0x80:€☐,ƒ„…†‡☐‰☐‹☐☐☐☐:0x8F

0x90:☐''""•—☐™☐›☐☐☐☐:0x9F

0xA0: ˜Ά£¤¥¦§¨©☐«¬-®‾:0xAF

0xB0:°±²³´µ¶·ΈΉΊ»Ό½ΎΏ:0xBF

0xC0:ΐΑΒΓΔΕΖΗΘΙΚΛΜΝΞΟ:0xCF

0xD0:ΠΡ☐ΣΤΥΦΧΨΩΪΫάέή ί:0xDF

0xE0:ΰαβγδεζηθικλμνξο:0xEF

0xF0:πρςστυφχψωϊϋόύώ☐:0xFF

LOWER ASCII RANGE

0x20: !"#$%&'()*+,-./:0x2F

0x30:0123456789:;<=>?:0x3F

0x40:@ABCDEFGHIJKLMNO:0x4F

0x50:PQRSTUVWXYZ[\]^_:0x5F

0x60:`abcdefghijklmno:0x6F

0x70:pqrstuvwxyz{|}~☐:0x7F

EXTENDED RANGE

0x80:☐☐,ƒ„…†‡☐‰☐‹☐☐☐☐:0x8F

0x90:☐''""•—☐™☐›☐☐☐☐:0x9F

0xA0:☐☐£¤¥¦§¨©☐«¬-®☐:0xAF

0xB0:°±²³☐µ¶☐☐☐☐»☐½☐☐:0xBF

0xC0:☐☐☐☐☐☐☐☐☐☐☐☐☐☐☐☐:0xCF

0xD0:☐☐☐☐☐☐☐☐☐☐☐☐☐☐☐☐:0xDF

0xE0:☐☐☐☐☐☐☐☐☐☐☐☐☐☐☐☐:0xEF

0xF0:☐☐☐☐☐☐☐☐☐☐☐☐☐☐☐☐:0xFF

Figure 7.5 The 1253 code page displayed with two different fonts (Courier New font on the left, Browallia New font on the right).

Dealing with Bidirectional Text

One of my father's favorite quotes was from a football coach yelling to a player. The quarterback was supposed to catch the ball and run to the left, but the quarterback caught the ball and ran to the right instead. The coach tried to get the player's attention by jumping up and down on the sidelines yelling, "No! Your other left!" Bidirectional text is, in a way, a lot like that, going left and right, zigging when it should zag.

English and most Western European languages, are written starting at the upper-left corner of the page and writing in straight lines across to the upper-right corner of the page. New lines are started directly underneath the first on the far-left corner. In other words, text is written *left to right*, or *LTR*. Some other languages are written from the upper-right corner across to the left-hand side, so they are *right to left*, or *RTL*. Two common examples of RTL languages are Hebrew and Arabic.

However, taking Hebrew as an example, you cannot assume that all the text in a page of Hebrew text is starting on the right and marches to the left without variance. Hebrew can have parts of its text written from left to right, such as numbers and any English that might be inserted. These pieces that are inserted that have different directions are called *segments*. Because of the potential for segments, when the user interface allows these languages to have embedded segments, these languages are more accurately referred to as *bidirectional*, or *BiDi*.

Figure 7.6 shows an example of LTR text.

In the case of this sample written in English, the text has been entered in the same order that it is being displayed. The arrow shows the direction that the text is being displayed (left to right). It was also the order in which the text was entered (left to right). First, the *T* was typed, then the *h*, and so forth.

Conversely, Figure 7.7 shows a string displayed as right to left. The character on the far right was the first character typed, and the character on the far left was the last character typed.

Finally, Figure 7.8 displays a string of text written from right to left with an embedded segment being displayed from left to right.

This is left to right

———————————▶

Figure 7.6   Example of LTR text.

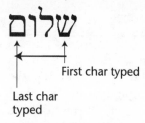

First char typed

Last char
typed

Figure 7.7 Example of RTL text.

 This is left to right שלום

Figure 7.8 Example of bidirectional text.

In the context of dealing with text direction, there are two ways to store the data:

- **Logical order.** The text gets stored in the order in which the user types it in, no matter which direction it will be displayed. Order marks are then used to indicate to the computer which direction to display text. In this case, the program needs to read and interpret these orderings and then display the formatting of the text accordingly.

- **Visual order.** The text is reversed if necessary as it is typed and then stored appropriately. The program display needs to do very little when it is displaying this data because the data is in the correct display order already.

Most current browsers assume that all text is LTR and cannot handle RTL, let alone the bidirectional embedded segments that may be included. Because of this, tricks have to be used to convince the browser to display the text correctly. Usually this means manually creating the visual order storage by inputting the text and manually reversing all of the RTL text. This technique results in the text's being correct when read from the right to the left, even though it is displayed from the left to the right by the browser. However, this trick backfires when some browsers are a bit too smart and reverse the text that was so carefully put in. Some browsers, once they identify that the characters are Hebrew, flip the text for display, text that was already formatted for the LTR browsers. To work around this type of a smart browser, the code would have to specify a font that could display the Hebrew characters, but that the system would not recognize as an RTL font. Line wrapping can also cause a problem, but is easy to prevent through the use of the <PRE> tag. The HTML 4.0 standard allows for right-to-left languages and bidirectional text. The attribute of DIR can be applied with the value of either *RTL* or *LTR*. A single paragraph could then have its direction reversed with <P DIR=RTL> . . .</P>. This tag is supported in Internet Explorer 5.0 and above on the Windows platform, and on some earlier localized versions. There is also a new tag in the W3C HTML standard, called the Bi-Directional Algorithm tag <BDO> . . .</BDO>. It has attributes of lang="language code" or dir="LTR" or "RTL".

If your application localizes the user interface into any right-to-left language, or if it supports right-to-left input, knowing the particulars of the display issues around it will help you more effectively test the application. Many problems are not identified in applications that currently exist because many of the testers working on these applications are not aware of how to test the particulars of RTL displays or RTL input. Many more times the noise-to-signal ratio of the bugs being identified is too high because what is thought to be a problem in the application under development is actually a configuration problem, where the browser has not been set up correctly or the appropriate fonts have not been installed.

Handling Complex Script

Bidirectional text is just one component of *complex script*. Complex scripts are scripts written with no assumptions of a linear layout. As you saw in the case of Arabic and Hebrew in the previous section, pieces of script can be placed in different directions that do not follow a straight left-to-right or right-to-left directionality. English and Western European language scripts are examples of simple script; they all assume that text will be written left to right until the end of that line, with the next line beginning directly under the place where the previous line began. However, some of the European languages use diacritics or combine characters to make a unique shape. One example of this sort of combination is the combining cedilla. Alone it is not a symbol, but can be used in combination with other characters to create a unique character. The lower ASCII Latin Letter C looks like this when printed alone c. When used with the combining cedilla, it instead looks like ç. The character is unique here, having the cedilla trailing off the bottom. Other languages use combining characters and diacritics in similar ways, most notable are Arabic, Hebrew, and Indic. When particular symbols are placed next to each other, they will combine to make a different shape. Arabic and Indic languages also go one step further and have contextual shaping of individual characters, depending on the characters they are near. Such complexities greatly affect the layout of text and the ability to cleanly and accurately process it. This type of input is what needs to be tested in the appropriate text input fields for your application because it is likely to trigger different code paths or uncover frailties in your product. If your application is localized into several different languages, testing the UI in other languages, such as German or French, has a higher likelihood of pulling localized strings and populating the UI with these extended characters and combined characters so you can test the interface's ability to handle and properly display them.

Single- and Double-Byte Character Sets

As I have discussed, characters are arranged into sets, usually by language requirements (called code pages). There are character sets whose characters consist of single-byte characters and there are character sets whose characters do not all consist of one byte. A character set that is made up of one byte characters is called a *single-byte character set (SBCS)*. A set that does not fall into this category is called a *double-byte character set (DBCS)*. A simple SBCS character is what most Americans are used to seeing. Characters such as *a* or *9* are single byte, and so are characters such as © or *å* or « or \. So far everything we have discussed has been single byte.

Dealing with Double-Byte Character Sets

Dealing with DBCS is a bit trickier, first because the name is a misnomer. Not all of the characters in a DBCS set are really two bytes—some are actually only one byte. These sets are sometimes called *multibyte character sets (MBCS)*. It is not as common of a term as DBCS; however, it is more correct. Because of the assumption that all DBCS characters take up 2 bytes, interesting problems can occur when combining the *single-byte* DBCS characters with the *double-byte* DBCS characters, or the SBCS characters with the DBCS characters. As a tester, knowing how to carefully select test cases based on knowledge of these issues will make your testing more effective.

NOTE Other code pages such as GB 18030, developed by the People's Republic of China as a replacement for the 936 code page, create more problems because not only do they have characters which are two bytes, they have characters that are four bytes. If your application is going into the Chinese market, it will likely need to meet a minimum standard of compliance with the GB 18030 code page, and this set of issues is one to be aware of.

DBCS code pages are much longer than SBCS code pages; DBCS code pages have two bytes worth to play with and can create a lot more variations, but still not enough to contain all the characters for some languages. Nevertheless, the advent of double-byte sets was inevitable since there are far more than 255 characters in any of the Asian languages. The following line contains just a few characters in the Japanese 932 code page:

限　餅　★　隠　No.　仝　鄰

You may note that some of the Japanese characters, the Kanji range for example, look like the Chinese characters, but they are different and have distinct meanings.

Often these code pages contain glyphs that would appear in an SBCS set. These glyphs look as if they are single-byte characters from the ANSI code pages, but they are actually double-byte characters with completely different names from their single-byte look-alikes. Consider the following examples:

$　£　G　d　Φ

All of the characters in the previous line are truly double-byte characters; two bytes determine the code point for each of them.

Conversely, the four characters in the following line are all *single-byte* characters, yet they exist in a double-byte character set:

ケ　カ　。　゜

That single-byte characters can exist in a double-byte character set is a very important distinction that is rarely realized and often confuses people. Because of faulty assumptions, developers implementing a text box under the assumption that only *single-byte* characters will be entered will have a problem when they try to globalize their software, as will developers who expect all DBCS characters to be two bytes.

Referencing Double-Byte Characters

Since I have already discussed what a single-byte character is, the character sets where they are arranged, and how they are mapped, I just need to ask you to extend your decoder rings another step in order to understand the double-byte sets. To lay a foundation for this discussion, I want to start by looking at the Japanese Windows code page (932).

The single-byte characters are relatively simple looking such as:

ケ　カ　。　゜

These characters start with the code point [A1] and continue through [DF]. The true double-byte characters have two parts—a *lead byte* and a *trail byte*. The character code points are written conventionally as [81/40], where the point 81 is the lead byte and 40 is the trail byte.

It happens that [81/40] is the very first character in the Japanese double-byte code page, which happens to be the full width space. The Japanese Windows 932 implementation has two double-byte ranges. The first range starts with the lead byte of 81 and continues through lead byte 9F. The second double-byte range is from lead byte E0 through lead byte FC. The double-byte characters are generated by selecting a lead byte (for example, 81) and then iterating through trail bytes (for example, 40, 41, 42, and so on). When the end of one lead byte range is reached (for example, [81/FF]), the lead byte is incremented up one, and the process is started over (for example, after [81/FF] we would go to [82/00]). Table 7.4 shows lead byte ranges for various Windows double-byte code pages.

One interesting point about the 932 code page is the section of Latin-looking characters called Romaji or Romanji. These are double byte but look like they are regular single-byte characters. If I wrote the message that I used earlier in the chapter with these characters, it would look like the following:

```
[82/67][82/85][82/8C][82/8C][82/8F][81/43][81/40][82/69][82/8F][82/85]
[81/44][81/40][82/76][82/88][82/81][82/94][81/40][82/84][82/8F][81/40]
[82/99][82/8F][82/95][81/40][82/8B][82/8E][82/8F][82/97][81/48]
```

And it would produce the following result:

```
H e l l o ,    J o e .   W h a t   d o   y o u   k n o w ?
```

It is important to note these are *not* the same characters that I sent earlier in the chapter. Though to my friend they carry the same meaning, these characters are not the same data and are not necessarily interchangeable with my original message. The individual characters also have different official names, for example:

H   FULLWIDTH LATIN CAPITAL LETTER H

e   FULLWIDTH LATIN SMALL LETTER E

l   FULLWIDTH LATIN SMALL LETTER L

l   FULLWIDTH LATIN SMALL LETTER L

o   FULLWIDTH LATIN SMALL LETTER O

Table 7.4 Lead Byte Ranges for Some Common Windows DBCS Code Pages

CODE PAGES	LEAD BYTE RANGES
932 Japanese	81–9F and E0–FC; single-byte ranges from A1–DF
936 Chinese Simplified	A1–FE
950 Chinese Traditional	81–FE
949 Korean	81–FD

Nippon   Single-byte Latin characters

Ｎｉｐｐｏｎ   Double-byte Romanji characters

Figure 7.9 Space comparison of single and double-byte characters.

Even the space is allocated two bytes: [81/40]–IDEOGRAPHIC SPACE. FULL-WIDTH means that the character is given the full width of 2 bytes. A character that is named HALFWIDTH is one of the single-byte characters in the DBCS set. One interesting fact is that this new version of my message takes up twice as much space as the previous message—an important point for many text entry field test cases. For example, in Figure 7.9 you can see the same word written in single-byte Latin characters from the 1252 code page and in double-byte Romaji characters from the 932 code page. Both of these are displayed in the MS Mincho font face, so they are comparable. Notice how much more physical space the double-byte characters actually take up.

The other DBCS character sets have regions of these Latin-looking characters and they are often the culprits responsible for various problems. The next section discusses how to test for these problems.

DBCS Testing Techniques

So what techniques will cause double-byte problems to show up?

- Place your cursor in a string of DBCS characters. Using the arrow key, move one character at a time both forward and backward. You should not jump over characters or be able to cut a character in half. This technique shows if certain assumptions have been made about the character sizes in the field.

- Place your cursor in a string of DBCS characters, use the backspace, and delete key to eliminate one character at a time. You should not eliminate half of a character leaving question marks for the other half, or delete two characters at once.

- Compile a string of full-width double-byte characters. Place some half-width DBCS characters in the middle. Are they combined into two characters, or are the characters otherwise altered?

- Compile a string of half-width DBCS characters. Place a string of full-width DBCS characters in the middle. Are these split into two or otherwise altered?

- In each field of your application, insert strings of DBCS characters (for example, a user name). Allow your view of it to show only part of the string so that the rest has been truncated off (for example, a text display field that has part of the field left off). Is the last character correct? If it was a full-width character, has it been split into a single byte? Does this show a corruption? Try slightly shifting where the truncation location occurs to see if you can cause this scenario.

When problems are encountered, you need to do a bit of investigation to identify if the problem is an operating system limitation, a browser issue, or a bug in your application. DBCS problems are common, yet some concentrated testing techniques can rapidly identify the problems, likely stemming from a handful of core causes in the application. With these fixed, your application is more robust, and your prospective audience grows larger.

Unicode

Unicode is supposed to make all of these code pages and dependencies obsolete. Instead of only having space for 255 characters, or roughly 8,000 characters as in many of the DBCS sets, Unicode supports 65,536 characters. Unicode is just one enormous decoder ring. It provides an absolute unique numeric reference to a character, no matter the platform, code page, or language it is used in. Where the single-byte sets had the same numeric reference that could point to several different characters, depending on the code page, Unicode has no such issue. Each and every character is referenced uniquely so there should never be any conversion. If all software supported Unicode, it would be like everyone using the same giant secret decoder ring; everyone would be able to communicate without concerns that somebody else's decoder ring would decode a message incorrectly. Nobody would have to carry a pocketful of decoder rings just to read messages sent from different friends.

Unicode basically has two parts:

- UCS, or the Universal Character Set
- UTF, or the Unicode Transformation Format

There are several implementations of each. There is a UCS-2 and a UCS-4, and each carries an implicit encoding, much as our code pages did. Each of these can have an encoding called the Unicode Transformation Format applied and may be UTF-1, UTF-7, UTF-8, or UTF-16.

- *UTF-1* is not found many places any more.
- *UTF-7* is used in SMTP and MIME and many legacy code bases. It was designed to be mail safe, but there are some characters that are not validly transmitted with this encoding.

- *UTF-8* is backwards compatible with UTF-7, but is a far superior encoding and much more widely supported. However, UTF-8 is not a cure-all and is not wholly universal. IIS 5.0 supports UTF-8 for Response.Write only, and the JavaScript pop-up alert does not support UTF-8 content. Because of these sorts of limitations, specific workarounds may be necessary for areas of the content, for example using `<%@codepage%>` in ASP if the string contains characters from code pages that might not be the default on the machine.

- *UTF-16* is not widely supported yet, but is becoming more widely used.

ANSI code pages each has an implied encoding method and that is the only encoding method used on that page (but may not be the only place where that encoding method is applied). When the Windows code page 1251 is specified, the implied encoding method of Cyrillic is carried along with it. In contrast, Unicode characters keep their numeric references (points) regardless of the encoding method (UTF-*x*) applied to them. Therefore, encoding methods cannot be assumed when Unicode is used. In the ANSI code pages, there was an implied encoding method carried by each page, but in Unicode, there can be several options for encoding the information.

Unicode values are not the same as those in DBCS; there are no leading or trailing bytes. Unicode values start at [U+0000] and go through [U+FFFF]. It cannot be stressed enough that these values are not two 8-bit values put together. This value is standard and has a continuous flow through all the characters. There is no need to indicate byte order (little Endian versus big Endian) with UTF-8 encoding, and it is safe for file systems and network protocols. It is also completely backwards compatible with the ASCII standards.

Just as various applications can natively support Unicode, operating systems can natively support it. The Windows 9*x* family was not natively Unicode, but could support Unicode applications. Windows 95 is natively written for ANSI applications run with the system code page. With Windows 2000, the operating system added support for the Armenian, Georgian, Hindi, Konkani, Marathi, Sanskrit, and Tamil ranges of Unicode. With Windows XP support for Divehi, Gujarti, Kannada, Punjabi, Syriac, and Telegu was added. This varying support can be seen in places such as the window title bar for Internet Explorer. In Windows 2000 the Unicode Hindi characters in the title bar will be displayed properly; however, on Windows 9*x* systems, they will not and will instead appear as boxes or as question marks. The Windows NT code base is able to convert text that is in the system code page to and from Unicode for the application (the system code page is determined by the system default locale setting). Not all operating systems or browsers support Unicode. Specific devices like many Web-enabled phones are unable to receive and make sense of this data. Because of these device limitations Unicode may not be the solution for every one of your product scenarios. Knowing your target audience will help you identify the appropriate technical solutions.

So, if I get out my super Unicode decoding ring and send the message I've been using as an example throughout the chapter to any of my friends who also had this super Unicode decoder ring, the message would look like the following:

```
[U+0048] [U+0065] [U+006C] [U+006C] [U+006F] [U+002C] [U+0020] [U+004A] [U+006F]
[U+0065] [U+002E] [U+0020] [U+0057] [U+0068] [U+0061] [U+0074] [U+0020] [U+0064]
[U+006F] [U+0020] [U+0079] [U+006F] [U+0075] [U+0020] [U+006B] [U+006E] [U+006F]
[U+0077] [U+003F]
```

And it could be decoded as:

```
Hello, Joe. What do you know?
```

In the section on DBCS, I mentioned that DBCS characters that looked like Latin characters were actually completely different characters. By looking at the Unicode points for the DBCS characters used in the sample message, you can clearly see what I mean. The DBCS version of the message was displayed in the following way:

```
Ｈｅｌｌｏ，　Ｊｏｅ．　Ｗｈａｔ　ｄｏ　ｙｏｕ　ｋｎｏｗ？
```

The Unicode code points for these characters are as follows:

```
[U+FF28] [U+FF45] [U+FF4C] [U+FF4C] [U+FF4F] [U+FF0C] [U+3000] [U+FF2A] [U+FF4F]
[U+FF45] [U+FF0E] [U+3000] [U+FF37] [U+FF48] [U+FF41] [U+FF54] [U+3000] [U+FF44]
[U+FF4F] [U+3000] [U+FF59] [U+FF4F] [U+FF55] [U+3000] [U+FF4B] [U+FF4E] [U+FF4F]
[U+FF57] [U+FF1F]
```

The Unicode code points clearly show that these characters are not the same as the original ones, even though you or I can read them as giving the same message.

TIP

An interesting issue with UTF-8 that many people do not realize is that characters can be encoded as 1, 2, or 3 bytes. This reality can give rise to buffer overflow issues and is a great place for test cases. Sample test cases can be found in Appendix G.

Unicode carries with it many issues, not the least of which is the 3-byte range of UTF-8 encodings. There are some characters that do not exist anywhere except in Unicode. There are other characters that are traditionally not handled well and are downgraded to other characters by many applications. Appendix G has lists of these characters and strings of problematic characters to be used in your testing. Not all the suggested test cases will identify problems, and your own application will be found to have strings peculiar to it that are problematic. These are just some starting points to begin thinking of problem strings and identifying more in an effort to make your application more robust.

Font Linking

Earlier in the chapter, I mentioned that you may have to manually set fonts to display certain characters. In recent versions of Microsoft's Windows operating system, fonts are automatically linked with text using DLLs. An example of this in action would be pieces of text written in English side by side with pieces written in Japanese. If there were no font linking, you might see

English ☐ ☐ ☐

The system would display the boxes indicating that it was not able to display the proper glyphs for the characters specified.

However in Windows, font linking steps in and splits the text along the lines of which scripts are being utilized. In this case, there are two parts, the English script and the Japanese script. The font-linking DLL allows the currently selected font to display the English text because the current font is able to handle it. However, since the currently selected font cannot display the Japanese text, the DLL looks for the default font used for Japanese text. For Windows, this is MS UI Gothic. The DLL then applies this linked font to the section of the text. Our text string now looks like this:

Englishケカ隠

If the default font is not available, then another DLL steps in to pick another font that supports the Japanese script.

Netscape's browser does not take advantage of this linking, so although the encoding may be UTF-8, you will still have to manually configure the font selected in the browser to whatever one the Web page should be displayed with.

CROSS-REFERENCE
Appendix G illustrates how to configure Netscape Navigator or other browsers that do not take advantage of font linking, in order to display Web pages appropriately.

Exploring Character Input Methods

If you wanted to input the character *a*, you would immediately know to hit the *A* key on your keyboard and would expect the letter *a* to be displayed on the screen. If you wanted to input the character *A*, then you would know to hold down the Shift key, hit the *A* key, and then release the Shift key. In this example, the Shift acts as a keyboard modifier, modifying the input. So how would you input Ä or ë or 似? There is no keyboard key marked for these, so what do you do? There are four main methods to input particular characters (and each of these is discussed in one of the following sections).

1. The ALT key plus the character's numeric reference
2. Character map
3. Input Method Editor (IME)
4. Cut and paste

Alt Key Input

The Alt key allows you to modify input just as the Shift key modified the *A*. To use this method, you need a chart of the various numeric references for the characters you want to input. To input any character, hold down either of the ALT keys and type the numeric reference using the 10-key numeric keypad on your keyboard. When you release the ALT key, the character is displayed on the screen. This method will not work by using the numbers that are above the letters on your keyboard, and your number lock must be turned on for this method to work.

For example, to input the letter *Ä* you hold down the Alt key and type the numbers *1 4 2* on the numeric keypad. When you release the Alt key, you will have the character *Ä* printed on the screen (assuming that you are using your computer and keyboard as English with the US configuration).

Character Map Input

To use the character-mapping utility that comes with Windows:

1. Go to Start → Programs → Accessories → System Tools → Character Map.
2. A dialog box similar to that in Figure 7.10 appears.
3. Each font that you have installed will be an option in the top drop-down list. Select the font that contains the character glyph you want to input. In this case, select Times New Roman, although there are a lot of font faces that contain this glyph.
4. Locate the character you wish to enter and click on it.
5. You can then click the Select button to select this character.
6. Click Copy to place the character, or string, in your clipboard. Then just paste it into the application where you want the character to be placed.

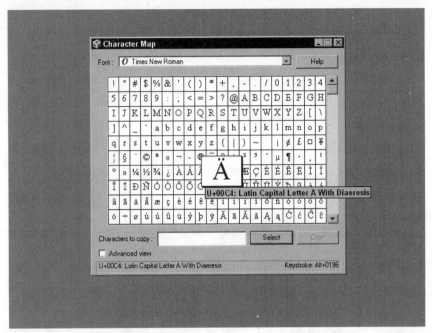

Figure 7.10 Character Map program.

This method works for any of the languages as long as you have the proper fonts installed. You are given all the font's glyphs and are allowed to select ones to input. The great thing about this method is that the Unicode point is given on the bottom of the Character Map dialog box at the far left, with the name of the character following it. This information allows you to absolutely accurately select which character you want to input.

TIP You can also search for characters by value, or input various characters to perform a reverse lookup in order to find out what they are.

Input Method Editors (IMEs)

The Input Method Editor (IME) is the easiest way to input characters, if you know how to use it. You need to install an IME for each language you wish to input characters from. IMEs are available on the system installation CDs or can be downloaded from Microsoft's corporate Web site. For each of these languages, there are usually several keyboard layouts to choose from. As an example, install the Greek IME (see Appendix D for installation and setup instructions). Once you have installed an IME, it appears in your tray next to the system clock (see Figure 7.11) and indicates which IME is currently in use.

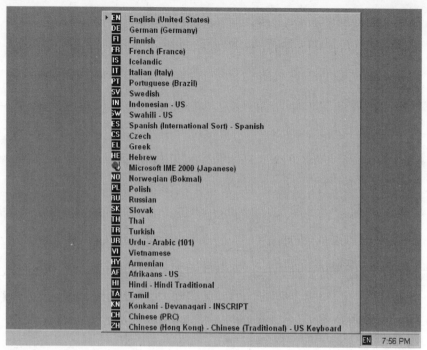

Figure 7.11 Input Method Editor as it sits in the system tray.

Single-clicking on that icon brings up the list of all the IMEs you currently have installed and allows you to select another one to use. Right-clicking on the icon allows you to change the properties of the various IMEs or to install others.

If you set your IME to Greek, then your keyboard layout has changed as far as the computer is concerned. If you hold down the Shift key and type *g* and then release the Shift key, you will see the Greek letter gamma. Type the *e* key, then the *i* key, the semicolon, the *a*, the *s*, the *o*, and the *y* keys. The result should appear as *Γειάσον*, which is *Hello* in Greek.

CROSS-REFERENCE
Appendix C has keystrokes to try for inputting valid content through various IMEs for many languages, and Appendix D has instructions on installing the IMEs.

Switch to the English IME and verify that the keyboard layout is set to US. Start Notepad, hold down the Shift key, and type in the two characters " and *a*. You will see both of these displayed in Notepad. Change the properties of the English keyboard to set the keyboard layout to *United States - International*. This setting will present a different set of keyboard modifiers. In a new Notepad document, hold down the Shift key to type " and *A*. You will get the *Ä* character input. In the case of the *US - International* keyboard, the double quote acts as a modifier. Various other keyboards have keys, such as the right Alt key, that act as modifiers to allow easy input of extended characters, which are common for users those locales.

One group of problems in localization occurs when hotkeys or accelerators are put into the user interface, such as mapping Alt+S to save. On the other keyboard layouts that are standard for the localized versions, the left Alt key may work as anticipated by the developers and testers, but using the right Alt and the *S* key may input the modified character or may save. Another example is the Alt+a input on a Polish keyboard, which will input the character *ą* and should not be a hotkey for some other action. Which is the user expecting it to do? Which is the correct behavior? The best advice is to avoid hotkeys for an international Web application, because they will step on these very common keystrokes and are not really common in Web applications. There are many common keystrokes for various languages that you will need to be aware of to successfully market a product in other countries.

Cutting and Pasting

The final way to input characters is to cut and paste. You may find that the code pages provided on the Web site companion to the book are a good resource to grab characters from. You may have a character generation tool, or you may create a Web page referencing each character in the HTML code by the &#*decimalnumber*; Unicode reference, &#x*hexadecimalnumber*; Unicode reference, or &#*name*; name reference to display that character in a browser window. You would then copy out the specific characters that you wanted. In the case of the character Ä, you would create a short HTML doc, and in the body, put in the text Ä or Ä or Ä to have the character rendered in a browser.

NOTE To specify case for the name reference, just switch the case of the letter specified. In the case of the Ä character, ä specifies the lowercase letter a with an umlaut (ä) and Ä specifies the capital letter A with an umlaut (Ä).

Table 7.5 collects all this information in a sample chart form, and there is a more extensive sample chart of these values included in Appendix L.

Table 7.5 Sample Numeric Reference Chart

CHARACTER	HTML DECIMAL REFERENCE	HTML HEXADECIMAL REFERENCE	HTML ENTITY NAME	CHARACTER NAME
Ä	&#196;	&#x00C4;	&Auml;	Latin Capital Letter A with Diaeresis

Applying Pseudo-Loc

Pseudo-localization, or *pseudo-loc*, is a highly effective technique used by many companies to reduce the costs of having software localized. The typical cycle of software localization is to use an outside vendor who has native speakers that specialize in software translations. This cycle proceeds as follows:

1. The software reaches a point where all the strings are in various tables and is then shipped off to the vendor.

2. The vendor translates all of the strings and ships this back to the software company.

3. The software company does builds of this with the translated strings and has their test team make test passes to ensure that everything looks and acts correctly.

4. Some strings may not have been externalized and given to the vendor, which is very common. These are then sent back to the vendor for translation, and the process is started over again.

This cycle is a lengthy and costly way to translate software, and there are some good techniques to reduce both the time and the cost.

One of the most common problems with localizing a particular piece of software is *string expansion*. When a word or phrase is translated, the translated words are not usually the same length as the original text. Take, for example, the word *New*. In Swedish, this word is translated to *Ny* and takes up less room on the screen. However, in French, this word is *Nouveau* and takes up considerably more room on the screen. In this example, it can easily be demonstrated that there is a 130 percent string expansion. If all screen layouts have been planned for English only, then these French-speaking users may see only *Nou* on their screen, with the rest of the word truncated. This truncation is something that needs to be taken into account before all the layouts and wordings have been completed—the earlier, the better (and cheaper).

The other common problem that can be encountered with localization is that the interface is not written to accommodate extended or double-byte characters or right-to-left/bidirectional text. This problem is evident in such cases as when the product comes back from the vendor localized into Japanese with the string translated to

新規作成

but the interface cannot handle it. The result here is that it displays question marks or otherwise corrupts the display so that it cannot be read as it was entered.

Pseudo-loc catches these types of problems early in the product cycle. Pseudo-loc is a simulated localization. The strings are not really translated, but are pseudo-translated. A tool is run on the strings to simulate the effects of translation. The strings are still readable in English (or the native language of the software team). However, the pseudo-loc tool applies the appropriate character set or position range for the various localizations. It also applies the appropriate string expansion estimations; for example, for German it might be estimated as high as 70 percent average string expansions. From these few rules you can catch the following:

- String expansion problems; testers will see truncations.

- Strings that have not been localized and strings that are hard coded that need to be externalized for the vendor.

- Issues with extended or DBCS characters that are not handled properly, or with BiDi, if you are localizing for those markets.

- Overlocalizations—a file name or an HTML tag may be incorrectly externalized in the string tables, usually resulting in 404 errors being returned when incorrect file names are requested.

The benefits of this process are that it ensures that all appropriate strings are externalized for localization, it ensures product localizability and globalizability, it saves time and money by reducing the number of handoffs and the number of localization-related bugs, and globalization bugs are found earlier, fixed earlier, and verified earlier. No language skills or special knowledge of the target language is required; each tester just needs to know the set of rules being applied to the pseudo-loc build.

When you receive a pseudo-loc build of the product, each string appears in one of four forms:

- **Real language strings.** (For example, *New* is translated properly to *Nouveau*.) These are usually strings that are left over from an earlier version of the product or have already been translated for various reasons.

- **Pseudo-loc strings.** I discuss these more following this list. These may be corrupted or otherwise not displayed correctly, but the first step of externalizing the strings has been completed. Enabling the UI to display the localized content and layout (globalizing the interface is the second part).

- **English strings that should be there.** These include things such as the product name.

- **English strings that should not be there.** These are your bugs, which need to be logged to externalize those strings.

When a pseudo-loc build is created, a tool runs on it that takes all externalized strings (for example, tooltips) and parses through them, replacing lower ASCII characters with extended characters for languages other than English. However, the characters are still "readable" in English. The end result is that these strings are not translated, but rather that it is easy to ensure that content from the various code pages is supported in these areas and that all appropriate strings have been externalized. An example of this would be a pseudo-loc build of a product that is being tested for Greek. In English, the page might read *New User*. In a pseudo-loc build where the Greek built strings are requested, this might read *Νέώ ΰser*. The strings are not translated and are still readable as English strings. However, characters have been replaced to indicate that the pseudo-loc tools picked them up, and the strings are verifying that extended content from the 1253 code page is supported in the interface. Characters were selected from the Greek code page of 1253 extended range and substituted in for the 1252 ones where they could be. Most pseudo-loc processes also prepend and append the string with a unique character throughout the product, for example, a *Q* or *V* or *Z*.

TIP

Some organizations may build using a symbol for this unique character. That can work; however, some fields may only support letters.

After the string is wrapped in the unique characters, the pseudo-loc strings for Greek would look like *VΝέώ ΰserV*. This character is then made known to all testers so that if a tester does not see the unique characters at both ends, he knows that there has been some string truncation.

To estimate the string expansion, make an educated guess about (or study) the amount that a particular language expands from an English translation for your set of words. For example, Greek may be identified as having a 30 percent string expansion. You then pad the strings with some extra characters (such as *MMM* or *XXX*) to simulate the string expansion that occurs during translation.

WARNING

Some groups may use a character such as the letter *I*. The problem with this is that the letter *I* is a very narrow character unless you are using a fixed-width font. Using such a narrow character defeats the purpose of padding on the expansion amounts to your strings.

A fully pseudo-localized string for Greek when the process is all done might look like *VΝέώ ΰserMV*. There were eight characters in the string *New User*. Estimating a 30 percent string expansion would add on 2.4 characters, 2 characters were added for the beginning and the end, and then just to be safe a third extra character was tacked on, rounding up the estimated 30 percent expansion. Often DBCS and BiDi languages are handled by appending a few of the characters particular to those languages on the end, so this product pseudo-localized for Japanese might look like *VÑëw Ûsër鸙鶴V* using the extended characters from the 1252 page, with the characters from the selected language tacked on to the end.

Escaping Reserved Characters

In HTML, XML, C, C++, or any other language or protocol, there are characters and character combinations that have very specific, and *reserved*, meanings. For example, the / in a URL is a path delimiter. When it is in the path, it is recognized as not being part of the name of a file or folder, but as a symbol with another meaning. Excellent test cases can be gathered from understanding which characters or combinations are reserved for usage. In the case of a URL, *% escaping* (also called *wire escaping, URL encoding, URL escaping, %encoding*, and a variety of other terms) is typically used to escape these reserved characters. In wire escaping, a character that is not allowed in a URL, such as a less-than sign, is escaped so that instead of < you see %3C in the URL. As an example, suppose that you wanted to provide a link to a file named Cæser.htm, a valid file name, but not a valid URL. Since the URL cannot have the æ character in it, you would need to refer to it in another way. When your URL encoded it, the new URL would end up referencing C%C3%A6ser.htm. The extended character is handled and encoded into lower ASCII characters.

If you are creating an application where URLs are generated from user input, wire escaping is an area that will need much testing. RFC 2396 lays out the guidelines for valid URLs and invalid ones and should be referred to.

CROSS-REFERENCE
Appendix G lists some of the problem characters that can be issues in many Web applications.

What Makes a Character a Problem?

Many different things can make a character a problem. For example, the previous section discussed reserved characters. They mean something special and have been set aside for that purpose. If you try to name a file in the Windows operating system, you cannot include certain characters in the name; \ / : * ? " < > and | are all reserved and disallowed. Back a few years, you were limited to eight characters and expected to have a period followed by three letters for the extension. Since then you have been allowed spaces, longer file names, and four-letter as well as two-letter extensions. Even more recently five-letter extensions have been used. But a lot of assumptions can be made from the original parameters, so knowing that they existed and understanding what they were helps create intelligent test cases. The Macintosh and Unix file systems allow characters in the name that Windows does not allow. If a program is to work on multiple platforms and access files, you need to plan for this and test it.

Other pieces of software may have characters or sets of characters that are used to send instructions. The character referenced at 0x5C is the backslash \. This character is reserved in many places and often reveals problems when used in testing. People often confuse this character with the forward slash character /. They are two separate characters, both potential problems, and both reserved characters in various circumstances. The forward slash is used in every URL, yet I have met many testers who are not sure which one is which.

TIP

As a slight aside, here's a mnemonic device so you will never have to pause to recall which one is which again. Imagine you are walking along this text—from left to right. You would be facing forward towards the next word. If you stopped walking and leaned backward towards the previous word, you would look like a backslash \. If you leaned forward to the next word, you would look like a forward slash /. Learning the symbols that are used to communicate in the technical world helps you, as a tester, recognize what characters may cause an application problems.

As another example, the character referenced at the code point 0x7F is the delete command. What if you have a text entry box and attempt to put in this code point? In DOS the 0xE5 code point is the DOS delete marker (essentially the same as hitting Ctrl+Z). In Novell NetWare, the 0xAA, 0xAE, and 0xBF code points send disconnect signals. These characters could lead to unwanted results if somebody were using your application and attempted to send the registration mark (®), which is the code point 0xAE on most of the single-byte code pages.

Parsers are commonly at the root of such issues. These inputs or character combinations can trick a poorly written parser that is looking for a particular character or code point. Sometimes it is the interaction of a few characters that can cause problems. Some of these are easy to see. For example, in JavaScript the escape sequence for a new line is \n. If this sequence is improperly read in, will your program throw a new line feed in? Knowing the context of your particular user-defined input and how the parser is stepping through the information can alert you to potential problems or test cases to run.

CROSS-REFERENCE

Chapter 9 discusses the subject of parsers in more detail.

Recall that the DBCS character sets have two points in the mapping designation. For example, instead of 0xE3, each bit is mapped out—[9F/FC]. The problem with DBCS is that now, instead of having just one code point that can cause a problem, you have two.

■ One class of problem DBCS characters are those with a potential problem in their lead byte. Earlier I mentioned that the point 0xE5 was the old indicator for the DOS delete marker. With DBCS, you might investigate what would happen if instead of just sending that code point as 0xE5 you used a DBCS character with the lead byte of E5, as in the characters 華 [E5/40] ([U+8541]) or 蚪 [E5/70] ([U+86AA]) on the Windows 932 code page.

■ The complement to this class is the set of characters that may cause problems due to the code point of their trail byte. Also earlier, I mentioned that the 0x5C point is the backslash. A program may assume that when it encounters the 5C code point it should automatically act as though it were a backslash. As a good tester you need to ask the question of what would happen if someone used a DBCS character that had the trail byte of 5C. Other characters that could have been used here would include _ [81/5C] ([U+2015]) on Windows 932 and 乗 [81/5C] ([U+4E57]) on Windows 936.

The single-byte DBCS characters are also a problem, creating either bad behavior or display issues, as are the boundary characters that fall on the edge of these ranges. There are also a few characters on several code pages where two different glyphs share the same code point. Often inputting one of the glyphs outputs the other, resulting in data loss since you did not get out what you put in. Knowing a moderate amount about what types of problems occur when using a double-byte character set and how to identify lead byte and trail byte potential problems makes you a very effective tester.

CROSS-REFERENCE
A more thorough list of some common problem characters and a discussion of each can be found in Appendix G.

Recognizing Corruption

So what is corruption? *Corruption* comes in many forms from many different causes, but it is generally recognized as a loss of data.

■ For example, you may have entered the string 圧斡扱宛姐虻飴.

However, a corruption of this string might show up as *???????*.

The system had no idea what those characters were and, therefore, displayed question marks. Such a case may be an example of true corruption.

- An example of conversion would be splitting those DBCS characters into SBCS ones so that this 圧幹扱宛姐虻飴

  might end up looking like this ï»¿åœ§æ–¡æ‰±å®›å§è™»é£´

  In this case, the code points may not have necessarily been lost, but the user cannot read the output properly.

NOTE

Such conversion may be more of a display issue than a data-handling issue, but perceived data loss is just as bad to the user as real data loss.

- A simple data conversion may also occur. When dealing with the extended character range, many characters can end up being downgraded so that *á* would become *a*, or *Ë* would become *E*. Such a conversion may be the result of the design of the software or it may be a bug. If this stems from the design of the application, it should definitely be documented because that could not only generate a large number of false bugs, but could also be a very limiting issue if there were ever plans to bring that application to an international market or to localize it.

- One common problem that parsers can fall into is just looking at the first character of a string to determine if the input is single byte or double byte. If a single-byte DBCS character is first and is then followed by several double-byte DBCS characters, those double-byte characters could end up being split in two. The reverse can happen as well—if the first character is a double-byte character, followed by a string of single-byte DBCS characters, the single-byte characters may be merged into double-byte characters. Merging two single-byte DBCS characters into one double-byte one or splitting a double-byte character is another form of data conversion.

CROSS-REFERENCE

Several test cases covering this sort of conversion are listed in Appendix G.

One type of problem that is mistaken for corruption is when the string 圧幹扱宛姐虻飴 instead is displayed as □ □ □ □ □ □ □.

Such a case is not true corruption, but rather the system telling you, "I know what these characters are—their code points are valid as far as I am concerned; however, I don't know what glyph to display for you, so I will show you this default one." This problem is usually due to your configuration. Either you are asking for a font face that does not contain a glyph for this code point or the encoding is incorrect. Correcting your configuration often sets this problem straight.

CROSS-REFERENCE
■■■■■■ A more complete list of potential problem characters, character combinations, and strings can be found in Appendix G.

Understanding characters and being able to manipulate them not only helps when working on software being localized for various markets, but it also helps you test software that never had any business plan to work in anything but one language. Understanding problematic characters and character combinations for the target language or for the audience that will use the software helps you create better test cases with far less effort than randomly hitting keys. Creating smart test cases targeted specifically at your software turns up far more bugs faster than just guessing at how best to exercise your product.

PART THREE

Server-Side Testing

CHAPTER 8

Performance Testing

Fast, Cheap, Good: Choose any two.

Performance is one of those issues frequently cited as the source of customer frustration and rising costs. I'm sure you can think of an instance where poor performance has hindered your use of an application. However there are several facets to this issue to keep in mind, perception being just one of them. Performance can be defined as the amount of time spent in a particular function, it can mean the cost of a function, or it can mean the number of functions that can be run simultaneously. These definitions can be drawn out to illustrate some examples.

- The amount of time spent in a function can be measured at the code level or at the user perception level—how long does a user perceive it takes them to complete a function?

- The cost of a function can be measured at the code level in units of cycles on the CPU, or on the user level for how much any user-defined function costs in terms of CPU, memory, bandwidth, or any other unit of measurement.

- The number of functions that can be run simultaneously can be measured on the microscale of the code by measuring how many individual functions can simultaneously be run before the CPU hits a particular usage amount, or how many users can simultaneously perform certain actions.

Since there are many aspects to performance, many considerations, and many factors, it warrants a more detailed discussion.

Making Performance-Based Decisions: Deciding When and What to Test

Performance is one area that all users identify as crucial to a satisfying experience with any software product. A small performance problem existing on the user's client machine is just that—an isolated small problem on the client machine. However, a very small problem on a server will be magnified thousands of times into a large problem affecting every user of the system. If a function call on the server is a few megacycles too expensive, and every user operation calls that function, then those few extra megacycles need to be multiplied by the number of times it gets called to see the true expense. A small memory leak on the server eventually snowballs into a very large problem.

However, there are trade-offs that can be made here. A little more expense on the client side, forcing the client to process information, may relieve the server of some functions, but it could ultimately be a much slower experience for the customer because more bytes need to be pushed down the wire. Performance tuning is an exercise in making trade-offs. The better the decisions made for the trade-offs, the better the performance. But even good decisions cannot completely compensate for bad architecture or other problems in the foundation of your software. The goal of performance testing is to identify problems and get the right ones fixed.

For the purposes of this discussion, I use a sample application of an online retail bookstore. This application has pages of pure information, pages regarding our company, forms to submit comments, and an online catalog and storefront through which users can purchase books and have them shipped to their homes. The user scenario might be:

1. User navigates to company Web site.
2. User requests several informational Web pages.
3. User navigates to the catalog.
4. User performs three searches in the catalog before settling on a book (simple searches, one book is not found).
5. User places one book in shopping cart.
6. User performs two more searches, reads commentary on the second book, and purchases this book.
7. User places two copies of this second book in shopping cart.
8. User clicks Checkout to purchase books.
9. User purchases all books.

However, another user scenario might result in the user abandoning the shopping cart. Each of these scenarios might be developed as a script and automated to test the software.

One of the most common reasons that performance testing of an application is not successful is that the wrong scenarios were tested. Not every line of code or possible interaction needs to be benchmarked on every build. Identify the critical places, the most frequent code paths, and the most expensive ones, the ones that are most important to the user, and spend the precious test time here. If there is more time left over, spend it on any code paths that have been added since the last release. Testing the wrong thing is a miserable legacy to have to work out from under. Using specifications and locating the actual part of the system or application where the performance problem lies are two approaches to planning performance testing that can help you avoid testing the wrong things.

Using Specifications to Guide Performance Testing

During the design phase of the software development, performance and stability need to be defined. If no explicit definitions are set as targets to determine a pass or failure, then Test can only identify failure points, where the load has crashed the server or the performance is so poor that the client-side connection has timed out. It is crucial that the specifications lay out precisely the behavior that is expected; otherwise, Test cannot make objective claims and must dole out subjective judgments on the software's ability to meet the customer's needs. What will be accepted? What is anticipated? If this is an internal Web application for a small company, then can we tolerate less stability? Consider the following scenarios:

- If the application in question is a tool internal to the company such as a time-reporting utility, then stability or performance might not be so crucial. You know that a predefined number of people will be logging on and performing a well-defined set of actions. Should something fail, it can easily be handled within the company—people can just report their time later in the day or during the next week.

- If this application is an online retail Web site, you need a much more stable uptime and cannot have users turned away just because you didn't think they would want to purchase as much as they do.

- If this application is an Internet service provider, then the agreement may stipulate the number of hours per week users can be logged in or the amount of data that they can transfer. You, as the tester, would then need to keep those stipulations in mind when you tested.

- If your company is hosting Web sites, you may not expect to have high traffic because your clients might all be individuals and not companies. What would happen when one user puts up one really interesting graphic or article and a million users try to access it?

TIP

Whatever your estimates are for the average traffic and stress that will be placed on the server while it is live, the application needs to be tested with double that amount to ensure that it can withstand peak loads. Under these peak loads, what should the performance be? These performance numbers should be for various server components such as server response times, database query times, and so on, and can even include the client interaction times.

The specification needs to call out areas of potential concern based on the application's design. Calling out these areas allows Test to focus on them even before coding has begun and keeps the entire team aware of the risks they carry. The company loses money if they ignore these users' needs. Without specifications that spell criteria out, data can be collected and be absolutely accurate, but cannot be determined to be acceptable because there are no criteria by which to judge the data. If there are no definitions of the acceptable, desired, or unacceptable ranges, then Test cannot identify a pass or failure rate, but only identify points when the server stops responding or is otherwise unusable.

Locating Performance Problems

Your whole application may seem so complicated that it is hard to see where to start in on this. Walking through the basic client/server interactions is the appropriate first step.

1. The client sends a request to the server.
2. The server must process this request and formulate a response.
3. The response must be sent to the client.
4. Then the client must parse the response and display or execute it.

Walking through these interactions, you will find that the client request is almost never the performance bottleneck. The only time you might find a bottleneck in the client request is when the user is sending up large amounts of data, such as a large form or file, to the server. In that case it would be worthwhile to investigate if the client should be sending up that much data.

The time that it takes the server to formulate a response may be the bottleneck. Server-side performance testing can determine if this is an issue and precisely where the issue is. The server hardware may contribute to the problem, and most likely the CPU will be the bottleneck in this case. If it is anything other than the CPU, then the server hardware should be reconsidered, unless there is no bottleneck by realistic definitions.

Sending the response to the client machine is another likely point of bottleneck. If the server CPU is not the limiting factor in application performance, then bandwidth is likely the limiting factor. In that case, the files that are downloaded, the graphics, HTML, and script, are very large and take a long time to transmit. Much can be done here to ensure that this performance hit is minimal, but again, testing needs to identify where the problems are. Client rendering may be a limitation if this is an application on a corporate intranet and there are very complex scripts that the scripting engine must process, but otherwise it is more likely that the server CPU or the bandwidth are the limiting factors.

It is necessary to do a preliminary investigation to identify where the performance limiting factors are. Without this, performance improvements may be put into place, but if they are not applied to the proper place, they will not alleviate the bottleneck. At some point there is a theoretical limit of how good the performance will be. It would be great if all our servers responded instantaneously, bandwidth was infinite, and response times were negligible, but that is not the case. At a certain point your return on investment in continuing to optimize the software will not be worthwhile and will be without perceived improvements (either on the server side or in the user's perception). At this point, turn your testing resources to other areas.

Performance Testing Overview

There are basically three ways to conduct performance testing:

- **Ad hoc performance testing.** This is what every tester should be doing when they are testing the application. As the tester interacts, he needs to be alert to whether the application is responding sluggishly. Bugs should be logged on the users' perception with follow-up from developers. These bugs are based on common sense and are very general in their nature. Ad hoc testing does not indicate where the problem is, but only that one exists.

- **Observational testing.** This uses some tools to identify firmer numbers. Even simply using a stopwatch and tracking the amount of time it takes before one can interact with the page gives a clearer idea of how the application is performing.

■ **Measured testing.** This has the goal of identifying objective measurements rather than subjective ones. This may mean having the developers insert performance markers, watching the network packets and communications, or otherwise monitoring the performance with objective means. *Performance markers* (perf markers) are small bits of code at the beginning and end of code blocks. When a code block is entered, the perf marker is noted, and as the block is exited, the elapsed time can be logged giving a count of the amount of time spent in the code block. Automation can take advantage of this and look for various functions, logging the elapsed time to find the performance of various functions. If it is determined that such markers will help your application, Test may need to ask development to put perf markers into the code. If the code execution speed is not the problem, then this will likely be an unnecessary piece of work. More likely in Web applications the bytes over the wire and network traffic are the limiting factors. Performance Monitor, Network Monitor, or other tools may be watched to get measurements of the performance of the application and the user's interactions with it, which gives absolute numbers for particular functions and helps to identify costly functions.

Given these three areas, there are many ways to spend the test effort and time in performance testing. Some teams can rathole in any of these areas for the entirety of a release, waiting for their efforts to pay off. However, for the most part, a small amount of checks in each area is the best use of the time and money that is available and helps to easily cover 80 percent of user scenarios, far surpassing what most companies do.

Time should be spent understanding the performance of the builds over time as a basic starting point. However, not every build needs to be profiled, or even profiled fully. Again, spend time in the places that make the most sense for your organization. Areas that should be examined are bytes over the wire, user-perceived response time, stress, load, mean time to failure, scalability, and memory leak testing. Formulas can be employed such as transaction cost analysis (TCA) whereby the product of these measurements is inserted into equations to estimate the total cost of rolling out the application. These formulas are only as good as the guesses that make them up and only a little time should be spent on them. TCA carries the assumption that there is no (or very minimal) underlying state sharing or other interactions taking place on the server. This assumption may be inaccurate, but any type of predictive methodology is only a tool to make an educated guess and save some manual labor. Some manual labor will need to be expended in order to verify the guesses, but in the end any analysis should save the team time and produce a number with a high degree of confidence. Many formulas cannot be filled in until late in the cycle because the software is not mature enough to make predictions. Laying out a commonsense plan helps ensure that all areas are covered and no one area ends up wasting the time of the test organization.

The last point to mention is that performance testing should not be done solely on debug builds. Debug builds are going to be slower than ship builds as they need to resolve asserts, if any exist, and possibly contain code that was left in at compile time. Debug builds will not be seen by the outside world, and the performance of these is unimportant. Running a stress pass or a mean time to failure pass on a build near shipping may turn up a very rare assert or other problem, so there may be value if the testing organization has the time to do testing at this point. Performance testing on a debug build will not accurately reflect the performance of the retail code of an application.

NOTE

Asserts are verifications that a condition exists, or does not exist. In debug builds of programs, these are present to help identify potentially problematic conditions and erroneous assumptions. In retail builds, these are excluded. It takes effort on the part of the server to fall into this code and then resolve the assert. These are very valuable in testing because developers may mark areas for conditions that they believe cannot occur. When an assert is fired during testing, it may need to be tracked through a bug so that code goes in place to handle the condition.

Selecting Performance-Testing Machines

The machines used for performance testing need to be carefully considered. There are a few different ways to line up the equipment. The first is to exactly match the hardware that will be rolled out when the application goes live. This method allows constant and real-world measurements of how the application will perform when live. The downside to this method is that it is very expensive to purchase many of the more expensive boxes for testing. If the application is under development for a long time, there could be a lot of hardware changes that you will want to take advantage of when actually deploying it. In that case, expensive machines that had been purchased based on the thinking that they were the exact machines you would roll out on may need to be replaced by the deployment machines that turn out to be something different.

The second way to set up the test environments is to buy high-end workstations dedicated to performance testing. As long as the measurements are consistently collected on the same configuration of machine, the actual model of machine should not matter much. Prior to shipping, the actual machines with the configuration that the applications will run on should be purchased and have some tests run to ensure that the assumptions about the application's performance do hold true. Using this second method is really very useful since early on in the development cycle your application is nowhere close to what it will be when it is done. Eventually, a pass will need to be done on the real machine configurations, but money can be saved by selecting a different type of machine first and stocking up on more of these than would otherwise be the case. The entire purpose of performance testing is to understand what the application is capable of (stress loads, maximum users per server, etc.) and to ferret out potential performance problems. To find the hidden problems, it won't matter what machine you use as long as you are looking in the right places and using the numbers to understand where problems may exist.

When your software enters the phase where it is capable of running full scenarios, the actual configuration of the machine may need to be adjusted. This process can be time-consuming, but it pays off in the long run. If the right regkeys and other configurations are adjusted, then fewer machines may be needed, or more users may be supported per server.

Checking Configurations Before Performance Testing

There will always be a bottleneck. It just depends on how your application is written and what kind of hardware you have installed as to where your particular bottleneck is. Given enough "stuff" to cram through the system, you will find a bottleneck in the disk I/O rate, the network, the memory paging, the database, or your code, but it will exist somewhere. Eventually all unacceptable bottlenecks will be found and resolved, and there will be only acceptable bottlenecks left—ones where the amount of "stuff" crammed through is highly unlikely and, therefore, represents an acceptable risk to release with. You may see through the instrumentations that at a particular point although load balancing across machines improves performance, increasing the number of processors per machine does not.

The areas of concern you focus on, and which metrics you choose to follow most closely, will depend on the technologies employed by the application. For example, if you are using CGI on a Windows NT machine, there are most likely going to be performance issues to be solved since CGI scripts require a new process, and process creation is more expensive on a Windows machine than on a Unix machine. The CGI application would be expected to have better performance on a Unix machine than on a Windows machine. An ISAPI application on the Windows machine can have some of its own performance issues because it interrupts the requests between the client and the server, so no solution is absolutely perfect. Other factors to consider include the line speed (56-Kbps modem or a T1 LAN), the client machine (for example, PIII 733-MHz CPU with 256MB RAM), the operating system and browser, and any router, proxy server, or firewalls that the data must travel through.

Verify that the hardware is load balancing properly if there is load-balancing hardware (or software) installed. If your software is not properly written to work with the load balancers, you might find problems here. Some load balancers look for any response from the servers they are distributing requests across. The first server that responds to the balancer is assumed to be the one with the ability to handle the request the fastest, and the request is routed to that server. However, a feedback loop can be entered if the server that responds fastest is responding to the server immediately to tell the balancer that it is overloaded and *not* to send it any more requests. The balancer misunderstands and instead of not sending the request to that server, it sends the request to that server. The server becomes more overloaded, and when the next request hits the load balancer and the balancer is looking for the machine that responds the fastest, the overloaded machine again responds quickly to identify itself as overloaded, and subsequently receives the request. This type of feedback loop can be fixed if it is identified, but without testing real-world scenarios, it cannot be identified until the application has been deployed.

Because of the complexities of performance testing, each of these components needs to have its pulse checked while the server is being exercised. Tools can help with these checks, and again, the particular tools will depend on your application and the technologies it has implemented.

CROSS-REFERENCE
Appendix J is a reference to many useful tools, including performance-related testing tools.

In the beginning stages of testing the server side, take the following configuration steps:

- The configuration of the server(s) needs to be tweaked to ensure that it is performing at its peak capacity. Make note of any resource deadlocks that are encountered.

- Prior to any testing, the hardware should be configured and reconfigured to find the optimal configuration. More than two configurations should be tried, and the attempts and data should be documented, as well as the most successful solution.

- Identifying that the memory or the network is the bottleneck immediately tells you that more memory needs to be installed in the server and the network connection needs to be upgraded. The CPU should be the only bottleneck that you see unless the identified bottleneck is so far beyond expected user loads that the risk is mitigated.

- Before topologies are further tested, take one individual machine configured as the performance topology machines will be and run the scripts and tests against it. This process gives you one baseline for reference and allows you to determine if the application is scaling out as expected when those individual machines are combined into a topology.

The first step in drilling into performance problems is to certify that it is, indeed, your code that is the performance bottleneck. If you do not pay attention to topology configurations, registry keys, services, and other settings that affect your server, you could be trying to solve performance problems in the wrong places. Eliminate your system and topology configurations as potential sources for performance problems before continuing with performance testing.

Starting Performance Testing

The toughest part of any task is starting. Before you start performance work, the work seems so overwhelming that it appears that it can never be brought under control and can never pay off for the amount of effort put into it. This does not need to be the fated course of the project. If the testing activities are well planned and are started at the appropriate times, then the effort will be well worth it.

WARNING

One trap with performance testing is the feeling that numbers are impressive. You will feel large pressure to present them, graph them, and show them around as proof of the effort paying off. Remember, all these measurements do is track the current status of the software. They are to point to potential problems that need to be fixed, understood, or reaffirm the hypothesis of how it should look.

Profiling the Application

The first task is to identify what needs to be profiled. You want to build up a profile of a healthy application. For this profile, you need to decide on two things: what actions you care about and what metrics should be gathered for those actions. Since the application is not yet mature, many of the actions that are of interest will not be able to be performed yet. Identify all the actions that will be of interest from the beginning, but understand that not all of these will be able to be run, and bugs may pop up blocking code paths later in the maturation. A list of the actions that you care about in the sample online retail bookstore may look like the following:

- Logging in
- Browsing static pages (stipulate pages)
- Searching for books (complex search and simple search)
- Opening a blank commentary form

- Saving a commentary form with 10K of text
- Replying to somebody else's posted commentary form
- Reading a large commentary thread
- Adding books to the shopping cart
- Purchasing
- Abandoning shopping cart

These actions are the atomic units that make up our identified user scenarios. Stringing these together in various ways creates our user scenarios. The testing starts with a single server (or the simplest configuration), with a single client as a single user session on the server. Starting this simply lets the most clear numbers be collected, pointing to the areas in the code where problems may exist. Eventually the testing becomes more complex, but it needs to be kept very simple to start with to pick off the low-hanging fruit of the performance problems.

Taking Measurements

For each of these actions identified in the profile, you should take measurements to understand how expensive the actions are. Some of the common performance measurements may be the following:

- **Megacycles (MCs).** The megacycle cost measures the number of megacycles an action costs to complete, which can be different when one action is requested a single time and when 1,000 of those actions are requested. Since each server has a finite number of megacycles, you need to understand how expensive each major action is in order to estimate the number of users that each server can support and the total number of machines that are needed for the server rollout. The basic equation for devising this cost is:

```
CPU Cost = CPU Utilization * number of CPUs * speed of CPU (in MHz) /
transaction requests per second
```

NOTE

Be aware that doubling the number of processors does not double the number of megacycles you have available, especially if the code does not take advantage of the additional processor. The best that can be hoped for is about an 80 percent gain for each additional processor put in (that is, a dual-processor system would actually be worth 1.8 that of a single processor system). This figure is really just a rough estimate, but it helps get the point across that there is not a full additional processor available.

- **Memory footprint.** The memory footprint is the peak memory consumed by the application while running. Depending on the technologies your application is using, this may or may not be interesting. If your application is serving up only static HTML Web pages and graphics, there will be a very low memory footprint. If your servers are having to take user input, create formatted queries from them, issue these to a database, and then parse the response, there will be a higher memory footprint and higher megacycle cost. Certain languages such as Java and C# are more memory intensive as well.

- **Bytes over the wire (BoW).** The bytes over the wire is a count of the number of bytes that are passed between the server and the client. There are two major ways to measure this value: initial action and cached scenarios.

  The *initial action* means that the user has no cached images, script, or pages on their machine because the request is a fresh request to the server. That request is, therefore, expected to be more expensive.

  The *cached mode* means that images and pages are cached on the client with only the dynamic information needing to be transmitted for these subsequent actions. That request is, therefore, much cheaper, but perhaps a far rarer scenario than an initial action, depending on your application.

- **Time to last byte (TTLB).** Time to last byte measures the time between the request's leaving the client machine and the last byte of the response being sent down from the server. This time does not take into account the scripting engine that must run in the browser, the rendering, and other functions that can cause a user to experience poor performance. If the client-side script is very complex, this number and the user-perceived response time can be wildly different. A user will not care how fast the response reaches their machine if they cannot interact with the page for an extended period of time.

- **User-perceived response time.** The user-perceived response time is how long it takes for the page to be completely rendered and ready to be interacted with. This time includes all images loading and scripts executing. This time is greater than the time-to-last-byte measurement because there is overhead after the last byte is received; the code is then parsed and rendered, and the user realizes that the application is ready to interact.

Two of these measurements (megacycle and memory footprint) are really server-side measurements that need to be collected on the server machine. The two others (user-perceived response time and time to last byte) are measurements inclusive of the network transmission.

The purpose of all measurements is to improve the users' experience and the cost of running the application. All of this testing may be able to be done simultaneously by writing the right automation and coordinating the client and the server so that the server is logging the measurements that you are interested in while the client performs the actions and counts the bytes received as well as the time to last byte. Depending on how frequently baselines are taken, this automation may or may not be of good use. I highly recommend test teams starting off performing all this testing manually to become familiar with the tools and the rudiments of this area of testing. Again, I believe it is difficult to understand the technologies and issues at hand when you are too far removed from them by many layers of automation and tools. Start with a hands-on approach and add in the necessary layers as a full understanding is achieved. Moreover, automation is fragile and can be more effort than manual testing. However, automation can perform the exact same test in precisely the same manner as many times as you ask it to. Because of this capability, it is an invaluable tool in many efforts, but not the right solution in many others.

CROSS-REFERENCE

There are many tools out there for these various actions, and these are discussed in Appendix J.

As I mentioned before, only a few of the many identified actions can be performed at the start because code for the others will not have been written yet or is not completely stable. However, the starting point is to get baselines identified and logged so that they can be watched over time. As you start collecting these baselines, your logs might look like Table 8.1.

The table can then be graphed to show the changes over time. For example, Figure 8.1 graphs the action of logging into the site.

Table 8.1 Sample Megacycle Costs for Various Actions

ACTIONS	BUILD 1100	1101	1102	1103	1104	1105	1106
Log in	12	12	12	13	12	25	33
Browse page	2	3	2	2	4	2	2
Complex search							22
Simple search					15	17	17
Open new commentary	4	5	4	5	5	4	5
Save commentary	9	8	8	9	9	8	9
Reply commentary							28

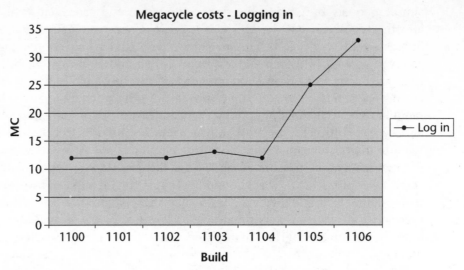

Figure 8.1 Graph of megacycle costs for the action of logging in to the site.

In the figure and in the table, you can see slight fluctuations in the cost of logging in between builds 1100 and 1104, followed by an almost doubling in the cost in build 1105. This jump could be attributed to a check-in that added functionality or a check-in with a bug that costs the server many megacycles. Either way the measurement needs to be understood and resolved against known changes in the code. The additional functionality may not be worth the cost, but at least it can now be quantified and that decision can be made—the result of astute tracking of performance measurements.

Take note also of how certain cells in the table remain unfilled, certain functionality was not available, on certain builds; the cost for those actions was not measured because the code was either not written or had been broken. Since the ability of the software is highly limited in the beginning, your team gains an excellent opportunity to explore the tools available to you, work with the developers to give you the information that will help you identify problems, identify what format the data is most useful in, and refine the process of gathering the measurements. The numbers are not that critical in the beginning as the code churn is so volatile. The real purpose of starting early is to give quick turnaround to developers on specific measurements and to become very skilled in gathering these measurements with high confidence. Once all of the actions are functioning, tests can be completed for the entire series of actions for a "day in the life" of the user interacting with the application or to run user scenarios to determine the total cost of MCs (or bytes over the wire, or other measurements) per user session.

Continuing with Performance Testing

So you have your machines configured, you have some baseline numbers showing how your software behaves, you have your user scenarios, and you have some automation to test the software. The testing has begun! Now, you need to collect data—a lot of data. Performance testing involves a lot of measurements. Although you have a few baseline numbers to compare to, you need to collect benchmarks for a variety of things. As you start to stress the machines by adding virtual users, you need to collect the performance numbers for this and track the results. As you scale the servers out or up, you need to track the performance to see the effects that this has. As you optimize the code and estimate the effects on the performance, you need to gather data to see what the effects really are. If the real improvements are too far off from the estimated gains, then what is the reason? Is there another issue that was not identified that should be fixed instead?

Considering More Than Performance Alone

The performance testing of a server ties in with other areas. Performance alone is meaningless. Your server may perform with lightning speed when there is only 1 user connected, but how does it perform when 10 users are connected? Or 10,000? The performance numbers that answer questions like these two are going to come from the standard user performance test scenarios that you built originally for the single-user scenarios, and there may be one or several of these scenarios you want to generate. Typical performance metrics that are analyzed are:

- Performance versus users
- Performance versus time
- Hits per second (transactions or requests per second)
- Errors per user interaction
- Errors per unit of time
- Kilobytes per second
- Average amount of data downloaded per user visit

Measuring some of this may feel daunting, but the measurements can be broken down any way that the organization would like to examine them. For example, typically, the cost per transaction is an important number. It may be figured as follows:

```
MHz cost = Np * Sp * avg(Pt)/avg(Rps)
Np = number of processors
Sp = speed of processors
Pt = Processor time (System: % Total processor time)
Rps = Requests per second
```

To show you how to use this formula, I want to assume that you have two Web servers, and each one has two processors running at 400 MHz. Your number of processors is 4, but Np will be 3.6 (Np = 3.6 here; 1 + 0.8 + 1 + 0.8 = 3.6) because the second processor on each machine can only be counted on for roughly 80 percent of its potential. The speed of the processors is 400 MHz (Sp = 400). These numbers give you a total of 1,440 MHz available (Np*Sp = 3.6 * 400 = 1,440). If you assume that this processor time will tax the server, on average, at 60 percent (this is the assumed average processor time from your specifications), then you multiply that number times the total MHz available to find how many are used during any one time.

```
1,440 MHz available * 0.60 average load = 864 MHz at use during average
times
```

You can make some guesses from the specifications as to how many requests you will receive per second. Your specs might tell you that you will receive 30 requests per second. You can divide the average MHz in use by the average requests per second to find how many MHz will be used per second.

```
864/30 = 28.8 MHz in use for each request
```

So if you have a total of 1,440 MHz available for your complete system, then you can estimate that you can reliably serve 1,440/27.2 or a total of 52.9 copies of this particular page delivered per second.

You should know from the specifications what the expected loads are on the server, what the minimum performance requirements are for the expected loads, and the maximum failure rate. These values might be expressed as number of user hits per unit of time, percent failure rate that users will encounter, or some other expression. You need to verify that the application meets these goals and that other metrics are identified. The server response times under average expected loads needs to be measured, as does the average database query response times. A requirement may read that a page should take no longer than 6 seconds under double the anticipated loads and over a 56-Kbps modem. A framework like that gives you a good average profile of how the application performance should be experienced.

Performance never exists in a vacuum; it is dependent on many factors. These factors may be determined to be important, but not under your control, and therefore are omitted from the testing. Other factors may be selected to be adjusted in order to isolate the appropriate variables. When numbers are reported, these factors need to be stipulated in order to accurately convey the state of the application.

Optimizing for Bandwidth

The work so far in this chapter has focused on identifying and correcting problems on the server itself. However, you need to also be concerned with how data gets to the server and back to the client because that is the other major potential bottleneck. Users are expecting an application to be near instantaneous, even though that is not possible. Still, you need to bring your application as close to ideal as you can.

The point of diminishing returns was mentioned once, but it bears repeating. Traffic between a client and a server is a lot like letters between you and a friend. There is the interesting data within the letter that could be very short or very long, and then there is an amount of data that needs to be included to get your letter from you to your friend. If your friend had a really long name and a very long address, this could be a lot of data that you would need to send on each and every letter. If you only had a short message to your friend, then this overhead of addressing and identification could far eclipse what was in the letter. At that point it would not make sense to optimize the short messages very much. However, if you are sending very long messages between yourself and your friend, the overhead of addressing and identification is only a tiny part of that. In that case there might be some great optimizations to be had. Of course, optimizing also depends on the frequency that these messages are sent back and forth. If the small messages are transmitted thousands of time and some amount could be shaved off them, then that might equate a sizeable improvement. Most likely, with the percent improvement per message, a user would never notice the difference, but an administrator who was managing a system where millions of these messages had to pass through could see a real savings in the bandwidth.

This scenario with the addressing adding to the overall amount of information you send your friend is the exact situation seen in packets transferred between clients and servers. A certain amount of overhead has to be passed to identify the client and its abilities and to properly address the server so that the packet makes it to the proper destination. The packet overhead for a single request-response pair depends on a lot of factors. I've found a decent estimation for this to be roughly between 700 b and 1 k for basic authentication without any encryption. If your application uses another authentication mechanism, cookies, or encryption, your average overhead for a request-response pair could be much higher.

Optimizing the Use of Graphics

In optimizing your use of bandwidth, the first thing to examine is the size of your graphics and the number of graphics you use. There are many tools available to crunch your graphics. Photoshop allows you to save a file optimized for Web use. Compression here can be up to 90 percent, depending on color depth. Load all the graphics your application uses into a single Web page and examine it to see if there are any duplicates. This is easy to do by selecting all the images and dropping them into FrontPage. You can then proceed with matching up any that are identical or near identical to see if some can be removed from the application. The problem is not that an extra graphic exists on the server (they take up very little space) or that the user downloads one extra graphic, but the cost of the overhead of that transaction and the port being occupied by an unnecessary request.

Good Web graphics come out rather small. A rough overhead of the client GET and the server response is around 700–1000 bytes, depending on the server name and various other pieces of data being transmitted in the request and response. Many times, this overhead is larger than the graphic or the real data being transmitted. If there are many contiguous graphics being displayed, it may be of more use to combine them into one larger graphic so that there is one hit of the overhead and then the image is downloaded. The image size will be larger, but the overall bandwidth consumption may break even, or better, depending on the circumstances. Adding up the total cost of the download when the graphics are separate and then when they are grouped helps to eval-uate if changing your graphics in this way is worth the effort. Eliminating overhead here helps make a better-performing server and application. These gains seem small (500 bytes here and there), but eventually they add up for a user who has a 56-Kbps modem. And when you have several hundred thou-sand users, multiplying out the excess really amounts to a lot of extra data being shoved over the small amount of bandwidth available.

Optimizing Code

Look in the directories where all the HTML, script, and controls are kept on the server and examine the largest of these files. Many times these text files can be optimized further by removing comments and white space (tabs and returns) from the code. This process runs the risk of making it less readable, though. Some teams employ tight coding standards whereby they use very short func-tion and variable names, again to keep the total file size small. There are tools available to strip not only the white space out, but to remove duplicate or unnecessary tags, such as the `</p>` or replace the `<strong>` with the `<b>` tag. If your HTML is generated by any WSYWIG program such as FrontPage, Word, or the like, there may be extraneous FONT tags surrounding each piece of text. Sometimes the only good way to correct this is to spend the time to edit it down by hand. Readability, maintainability, and proper coding practices should be balanced here against the potential performance gains that could be had.

Optimizing by Compression

As an additional measure, IIS and other tools allow the content being sent over the wire to be compressed as it leaves the server. The cost of the decompression by the client is minimal compared to the cost of downloading a bloated file. However, this method may only be an advantage to users connecting with a means other than a modem as modems all ready are compressing the data. Any data encryption that occurs may negate this mode in compression, but that depends on where the encryption takes place. There are also third-party tools that can help reduce the bandwidth requirements by compression or lossy transferral. If you apply one of these tools, you want to test the cost of employing it to ensure your server performance does not degrade beyond an acceptable amount. The server impact varies depending on the Web application and the configuration; however, such compression or lossy transferral may be a worthwhile investment of time. In some applications the costs of monthly operations are largely wrapped up in the bandwidth, and potential compression rates of 77 percent are attractive enough to investigate.

Optimizing with User Scenarios

The user scenarios come in very handy as you seek to optimize bandwidth. The user scenarios map out the most common of the user actions. Take network traces of these actions and dissect them carefully. Consider the following points:

- How many 401 responses does the server respond to the client with? Each of these is a significant amount of data passed and takes up time. These should be eliminated.

- Are any files downloaded more than once? Often the browser sees that a file is required and starts to download it. If there is another reference to it and the file has not been placed in the cache yet, the browser requests the exact same file again. The double GETs need to be eliminated because they put extra strain on the server and add to the amount of data that needs to be sent over the wire.

- Make sure that the cache control has the header and the expiration set correctly. Under SSL the settings may not work as expected, so be sure some testing is done with this scenario if it is supported in your application.

- If the file being transmitted is large, meaning that the user must wait for every last byte to be received in order to start interacting, can it be split into several different files? In contrast, if there are many tiny files, can they be pulled into one large file to save on the overhead of each request and response? There will be a balance of these two techniques for your application. If it is a script file, are there pieces of script that are not used until later that can be split out? Is there a way that large, and necessary, files can be pre-fetched? One way to pre-fetch is to start the request while the user is at the main page, is logging in, or is performing other actions, such as reading requested information.

- Take the traces of the user scenarios as both uncached and cached to see the difference. Both initially need to be examined because the uncached version may have errors such as re-requesting files that should be in the cache, forcing the server to send back a 304 and adding to the cost of the overhead.

- If your application allows different ways to authenticate a user, try to use basic authentication because other methods may tack on more overhead that can eclipse the operating costs that you have control over. Testing can help identify if this is the case.

- Finally, running a parser on the traces gathered to pull out the total number of bytes over the wire of HTTP traffic for each of these traces helps point to problems and serves to mark in the sand a starting point on which to improve.

If much time has been spent by developers and testers to improve the performance without any measurable results, then the wrong changes may have been made.

Reading Metrics

Metrics can be tricky. They can lie for you or to you. If you handle them correctly from the beginning, then they should be good, but one false assumption can invalidate them all.

Consider the following situation. I remember seeing a performance analysis done by a team on their Web application. It compared their application to three others—two were external products in the marketplace and one was another being internally developed. This particular team had taken the other internal team's code and put in performance improvements. This report was to substantiate that effort. There was an astonishing 36 percent improvement in the performance found in their modified code. Management was ecstatic that the efforts had been so successful. I read through the report and noticed one particular paragraph that discussed the test setup. Since the team was testing two external services, they created accounts on those services (live on the Internet) and ran the automation scenario against it. This meant that the requests went out of the building, through the firewalls and proxy servers, over the Internet, and to the other service, and then back. This service was live and under usage by real customers and subject to network traffic. The report never said what time of day or what day the numbers had been gathered on, but that seemed to be okay as the team's code far surpassed these services. The team also tested the user scenarios against the other internal team's code base. Since this too had been deployed on a live site, that was used so as not to arouse the suspicion of the other team. These requests also went out of the building, through the proxies and firewalls, onto the Internet, and then back into the building to the live servers. However, the paragraph mentioned that since their newly updated code was not deployed on any production server, the team had to settle with testing their code on the servers down the hall, which meant that their virtual user was the only user on the servers at the time the sample data was taken. A full 100 MB internal network in the building was available to take the requests and responses there and back; the requests and responses did not have to travel through any proxy servers or firewalls, and certainly were not subject to Internet traffic. I would bet good money that almost any product could show a substantial improvement in performance given those scenarios without modifying a line of code.

Some of the numbers you may need to track are:

- **Round-trip time (RTT).** The time it takes for a request to leave the client machine's browser and for the server's response to reach the browser; similar to TTLB, but slightly different.

- **Round-trip count (RTC).** A count of the number of round-trip request/responses necessary for any single action or scenario.

- **Client response times (CRT).** The amount of time necessary for a user to wait to interact with any particular page.

- **Bytes per request (BPR).** The number of bytes transmitted from the server per request from a client; if much data is being passed from the client to the server in hidden fields, then measuring the size of the requests may be of use to your application as well.

- **Bytes over the wire (BoW).** The total number of bytes transmitted across a connection for any request/response pair or scenario; this may need to be done in cached and uncached scenarios (bytes from the client to the server plus bytes from the server to the client).

Once you settle on the hardware configuration, the first stages of the testing activities can be started. During the hardware configurations, part of the team may be working on the hardware, while the other part is working to write the automation scripts and tune those appropriately. If the scripts are too complex or are written poorly, then they can skew the data one way or the other.

Some main performance counters need to be observed on the server side. In Windows NT code base servers, these can be found in the Performance Monitor (PerfMon) utility that comes with the system. Some of the counters to watch here are:

- For processors:
    - Watch each instance of the *% Processor Time* to gauge the server activity (there will be one for each processor).
    - Watch the *Working Set* of the CPU utilage of the component being tested.
    - Watch the *Private Bytes,* a subset of the Working Set, of the component being tested to identify its CPU utilage.
- For memory:
    - Watch *Pages Input per Second.* This value should not be too much lower than the Pages Output per Second.
    - Watch *Pages Output per Second.* If this value is significantly higher than the Pages Input per Second numbers, then there could be a memory leak.
    - Watch the *Available Megs* to make sure that you don't run out of memory or that memory isn't the bottleneck. If you run out of memory, then you wrap up your resources in paging data back and forth from the disk to the memory without actually performing many tasks.
- For the physical disk:
    - Watch *I/O.* It can be difficult to measure, especially across machines.

TIP

PerfMon is particularly useful because it lets you monitor the resources not only of the local machine, but also of any other machines you have access to on your network, and alerts can be set for various states. More on this, and other tools, can be found in Appendix J.

When a performance parameter is tracked, it should be seen to increase linearly as the stress on the box increases. If the performance starts to flatten or lose the rise, then a bottleneck has been hit, which means that one or more resources have hit 100 percent utilization. One common problem you may run into is that the tools and utilities you use to take your metrics themselves are taking up resources and causing a bottleneck. As with any system, once you start observing it, you alter the outcome. The act of observing disturbs the observed. The performance tools and load generation tools may be the bottleneck. If the tools you are using on the server use up more resources than they should, then you will observe the peak performance to be lower than it really is. If client-side tools are being used to apply loads, it is very possible that each client that is attempting to simulate multiple clients has struck an upper limit on what it can simulate. Although you may dial up the number of simulated users, the client machines cannot output more simulations. In this case, the observed server flat line in a graph is not due to server-side bottlenecks, but client-side tools. To alleviate this scenario, you need to add more client machines in order to simulate more simultaneous client connections. Using the server logs and network logs can help to identify and understand the problems. If the performance is not as high as expected, perhaps errors in the system log can help identify the problem. If the network drivers are not working properly or at their peak, then they will turn out lackluster numbers.

You also need to watch network traffic to identify the bytes over the wire being transmitted, the response times, and the concurrent connections that are allowed. The network traffic analysis is one of the most important functions in performance testing. It allows you to identify unnecessary transmissions, transmissions that are larger than expected, and those that can be improved. The response times can pinpoint if requests are being received by the server, and then if processing is taking longer than expected before responses are sent out. Slow response times can be due to many different causes, but are yet another potential problem that needs to be searched for.

Performance testing is about being detailed and thorough, detailed enough to recognize all of the factors that are in play that affect a given measurement and thorough enough to come to an understanding of each of those factors. Since many of the factors can't be controlled by you, you must apply common sense as well. You have absolutely no control over how fast your application renders on a user's machine. You can have some influence over it, though. The user could be using a 300-baud modem, be downloading a video and a music file, and have a 286-MHz machine. You have no control over any of these factors, each of which will affect how the user perceives your application's performance. What you do have control over is how much stuff you are pushing to the user and how responsive your servers are to the user's request. Both of these factors directly influence the user's experience.

Load and Stress Testing

Load testing is sometimes called *stress testing* and is similar to stability testing; however, duration is not really a factor in load testing.

CROSS-REFERENCE
Stability testing is discussed in more detail in the next section of this chapter.

Rather, load testing applies heavier and heavier loads in order to induce a failure in an application. The load testing may include the load's being balanced between several servers in a test bed. These test bed scenarios can be tested by increasing the number of client connections being simulated, running all virtual user requests through SSL, only exercising the most expensive actions, or otherwise taxing the system to a state of failure. Load testing is primarily focused on identifying a breaking point in the application that is independent of time. The load testing needs to verify that applying twice the expected average load of average user actions does not cause any adverse effects on the service, which means taking the current load that the application has on it (if there is a current user base), adding the expected growth that will occur before the next release of the product, and then multiplying that times two. This sort of testing helps ensure a stable application or service even through peak unexpected loads, and especially if some servers have to be taken offline during peak hours. Load testing is done to help identify what the load profile for the service is under a load. Knowing this sever profile helps you identify when the server in a live production environment is about to break or crash.

NOTE

Database-driven Web sites particularly need to take several profiles of the software under a variety of loads to identify what the effect is on the performance.

The best way to apply load is through the use of a client side tool. Conventionally, one client is the master or controller of others. All of these clients point at a single server (or set of servers later in the test cycle) and send out a specific number of requests. The sorts of requests applied in this kind of test need to be drawn from your user profiles. The best way to mimic the real-world scenarios is to use several different user scenarios that each client machine rotates through, inserting random data where applicable. The scenarios should be run for 30–60 seconds to allow the server to achieve a steady state (all objects are created, all initialization overhead is accounted for), and then allowed to run for anywhere between 5 minutes and 30 minutes.

NOTE

If there are memory leaks, then over time the performance counters will show degradation in performance, but the purpose of this set of tests is not to identify those leaks. You will focus on those with other efforts. Be crisp about what you are looking for in each set of tests and then ensure that your focus is there. Memory leak testing is a related area, but can distract from the main purpose of this type of testing. Tools, scripts, and information will be common to both efforts, but each needs to be focused on separately.

As was the case in the metrics gathering discussed earlier in the chapter, you need to carefully chart the information you gather through load testing to create a profile of a healthy and an unhealthy environment and understand where the point of failure (POF) is. One way to do this is to chart requests per second sent to the server versus the server's CPU utilization (remember that because of configuration prior to the start of performance testing, your CPU is the only possible bottleneck remaining, so it should be the first indicator that something is wrong). The graph of what you may track may be something like the one shown Figure 8.2.

In the figure, you can see a healthy server that has a standard, level overhead cost as the only cost for up to 450 requests per second. The highest CPU utilization for peak usage should be about 75–80 percent. Using that estimate as a guide, this server can safely service 1,250 requests per second before moving beyond the highest CPU utilization estimate.

Another way to view load is by looking at how long it takes to service the request. Just because our server is not completely falling over at 1,250 requests per second does not mean that the user is having an optimal experience. Because of this reality, when considering load, you also need to apply some constraint, such as no page should take longer than 3 seconds for the TTLB measurement over a 100 megabit LAN (not what home users will have, but it provides a standard of measurement for our purposes). In this case, you may see a graph like Figure 8.3.

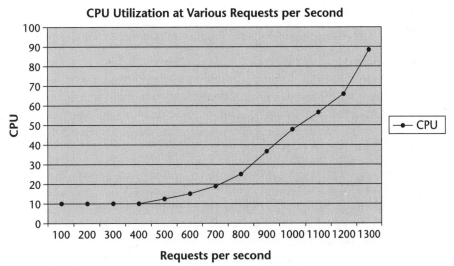

Figure 8.2 Sample graph of CPU utilization for a variety of requests per second.

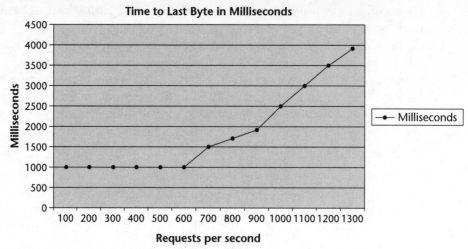

Figure 8.3 Sample chart of time to last byte.

In this figure, again, there is a fixed overhead of the amount of time it takes to receive the request, process it, and respond. It lasts until 600 requests per second, though. At the stated goal of a 3-second response time, the application is servicing only 1,100 requests per second, which is less than the 1,250 that we can service, according to our processor. So, to satisfy both constraints, both CPU utilization and the 3-second TTLB, the application can service only 1,100 requests per second. You can, however, go back and reconfigure your boxes or purchase lower-end machines in order to save on costs, but remember, that necessitates another round of testing.

For one last example concerning load testing, refer to the graph in Figure 8.4.

In this figure it looks like 1,500 requests per second is a threshold, and at 1,600 some code must kick in and you have great performance! In reality, the server probably had a service crash somewhere or a lock and is just returning an error. And it is much faster to send an error than to really process a request and then formulate a response. That explains the sudden perfect performance time seen here—the server fell over.

Essentially, load testing allows you to understand how many users a server can support and how many servers you need in order to roll out an application for an estimated number of users. Estimating incorrectly is very easy, but very expensive. The more accurate you can make your load testing, the less expensive the deployment will be.

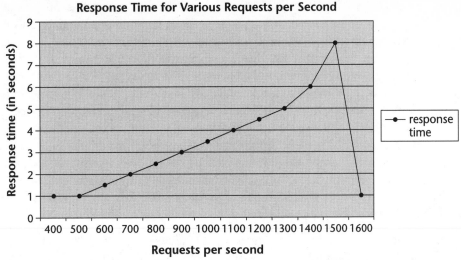

Figure 8.4 Response times at various requests per second loads.

Testing Reliability and Stability

Reliability and *stability* are quantifying generally the same thing—how much uptime does the system have under certain conditions? The types of questions this sort of testing answers are:

- What is the uptime under real-world loads?
- Can the application handle 1,000 user requests in a second?
- How many users can it reasonably handle?

Every management team would like to enjoy 100 percent uptime, and marketing could have a heyday with those numbers, but the reality is that uptime at that level is very expensive. One specification I read specified that the system have 99.999 percent uptime. A deployment manager very quickly jumped on this number and told the authors of the spec that it needed to be changed to, at the most, 99.9 percent. The difference in production cost involved in that one change would mean tens of thousands of dollars. But what really is the difference? Given that there are 24 hours in a day and 365.25 days per year, there are 8,766 hours in a year. A 99.999 percent uptime allows for 8765.91234 hours of uptime per year, or stated otherwise only 0.08766 hours of downtime, about 5 ¼ minutes, a year. A 99.9 percent uptime allows for 8,757.234 hours of uptime or downtime equaling 8.8 hours per year. It is far easier to debug, troubleshoot, upgrade, or restore servers in 8 hours than in 5 minutes, and far more realistic and cost-effective. Further, if your application markets itself with a higher uptime than it can realistically provide, it could raise potential legal issues for your company when paying customers do not receive what they have paid for. Although products need to strive for stability and reliability, there is a realistic threshold that comes into play. If you are creating a medical system that monitors patients, a 100 percent uptime is crucial. If you are providing an online music service, users may want a 100 percent uptime, but it is not nearly as crucial. Many online businesses have learned the stability lessons the hard way. Crucial applications have failed, and even large, well-funded companies running important applications, such as E*Trade, Quick and Reilly, Charles Schwab, and TD Waterhouse, have experienced server crashes bringing down their applications.

Reliability/stability numbers can be misleading, as well. If the reliability/stability topology has been sitting untouched in a locked lab, then it will show near 100 percent uptime when running the software. What actually needs to happen when testing the software is to deploy it in an internal lab and stress it with the automation scripts simulating the virtual users and with the CPU holding at about 75 percent or 80 percent for an extended period of time. Time is the crucial factor in this piece of performance testing. Many problems go undetected for the short term, but contribute to crashes or data corruption over a long running time. Since you want your servers up and running in production for an extended period, it is critical that these tests take place without administrative intervention (rebooting and so on) for a long period of time.

This long-term reliability/stability testing helps to turn up memory leaks, among other issues. Memory leaks are an enormous problem for software. *Memory leaks* are tiny bits of memory (or sometimes large chunks) that are not properly released to allow them to be used again. Because the memory is not released, over the long term more and more memory becomes inaccessible to the system and this affects performance, stability, and more. Memory leak testing is really looking for double frees, low memory situations, and memory not being released. Often these problems do not show up with short-term tests unless the server and application are properly set up to catch them. The application needs to be run full force with virtual users performing as many different actions as possible continually, to turn up many of these types of errors. Every scenario and action should be performed at least once to check for any leaks. There are many tools that help isolate individual memory leaks, but this sort of long-term reliability/stability testing is one practice that will help to identify leaks across the user scenarios and across time. When failures start happening, and they will, then you have found your uptime numbers. The machines can then be wiped clean, redeployed in the lab, installed with new builds of the software, hopefully with the leaks fixed, and the stability can be tested again. A part of the testing may also include just resetting the machines (as they would be in any real production environment), restoring the data, and continuing to stress them to find more stability numbers.

Another question to ask in the course of stability testing is if there are DLLs that are used but are not loaded at startup. Some applications may load a DLL only when it is necessary. Loading only what is necessary may sound like a great idea, but it is also increases the potential to crash. If the server has been running for a while, there may be very little contiguous memory left. If this DLL is larger than any contiguous memory, it may fail to load, putting your server at risk for a crash. If you are running servers that you own, then the time to start up is not terribly important—even an extra 5 minutes to load all the DLLs at startup is not bad compared with the potential for a crash. Examine the DLLs that are used by the system to ensure you are not at risk for this.

Again, the specifications need to detail the expected behavior and the objective standard for acceptability. A spec should tell if there is an expectation of 1 error for 100 virtual user purchase interactions, or 2 percent errors allowed for 200 virtual users. It should detail if the response time is no more than 8 seconds, while under the maximum number of virtual users being tested (2x the anticipated load). The specification also needs to detail the amount of uptime—will the application run for 500 hours with a 75 percent CPU utilization load before needing attention with no evidence of corruptions or crashes? If the specifications do not lay out measurable points for the software and instead rely on phrases such as "will not crash unexpectedly," then Test cannot effectively identify issues and get the right ones fixed.

Testing Scalability

On average, software with scalability problems costs an organization an average of $115,000 to fix in some way, and not necessarily the right or best way. Because of the complexity that is usually a part of server-side issues, half of all deployed applications do not scale as they were expected to. It is far easier to fix a simple client-side JavaScript issue than a server-side core function simply because of the inherent complexities in the server technologies and the fact that any small problem is amplified when it is a server-side issue.

Scalability testing really overlays the other topics in this chapter and occurs on a complete system instead of on an individual server (unless your application will only ever require a single server). There are two ways that a system can scale—it can scale up or out.

- If a system can *scale up*, that means that making changes in the current machines to produce bigger machines will alleviate a problem. This can mean changing the CPUs for better ones, adding more processors, adding more memory, or other accommodations. The problem with scaling up is that it does not add any redundancy to the system.

- *Scaling out* means that more machines are added to the topology to offload the processing. Such additions may complicate matters because sharing state across machines is very difficult to manage, reproducing and resolving bugs may be more difficult (especially race conditions), and from an administrative point of view, the topology is more complex. However, scaling out provides redundancy in the case of failover scenarios, where if one machine completely crashes then the others can take up the balance.

NOTE

Capacity testing can be focused on a single server to identify the capacity that that server can accommodate, and scalability testing can be done by scaling an individual server up; however, scaling out requires more than one machine.

Several dimensions of scalability need to be tested. Among them are:

- **Uptime.** Can you have the system stay up for months at a time?
- **Data items.** What happens when your database has hundreds of millions of items?
- **Clients and users.** What happens when you have millions of customers?
- **Machines.** Can you add another machine and improve the scenario?
- **Processors.** Can you add another processor in the servers and improve the scenario?
- **Memory.** Can you add more memory and have it effectively taken advantage of?

Any application can scale to almost any degree, given enough money, but that is not the point of scalability testing. Doubling the number of users should not double the cost of running the application. The cost per user or cost per transaction should go down. Scalability is the ability of a system to accommodate an increased number of users without increasing the cost per user and while maintaining the system responsiveness. Any system can scale, given enough money or lax enough requirements, but no organization has that much money to waste, so you need to develop and test with cost and requirements in mind.

Testing Active Server Pages Performance

Active Server Pages (ASP) are a very common Web application technology. However, there are some common tips that teams new to using ASP may not realize until late in the process. This section lays out some of this knowledge simply.

Active Server Pages are a resource-intensive technology. Because of this, performance becomes a big issue, and some simple efforts can be made to improve the performance and minimize the cost.

- The operating system can greatly affect the performance. Windows 2000 Server with four processors running in-processor makes a huge difference in the performance of the server application.

- You also have several database formats to select from. Choose the right technology for the job. Know what options you have available to you, but know their particular strengths. Avoid using Access for a Web application server database. It just is not built for that job. SQL Server performs far faster and better. Use SQLs Query Analyzer to analyze the queries being done and index the common properties. However, minimizing the data access and caching the transformed outputs will help improve the hits on the database. CSS, remote scripts, RDS, and XML can help to offload some of the processing work to the client machines and relieve the servers of that necessity.

- Since some users may abort before they have finished all of the interactions that your application is expecting, using Response.Write at the top of an expensive page sending a small bit of data (such as a space) to the client followed by Response.IsClientConnected and do Response.End to check if the client machine is still connected before continuing with the transaction. You can have a Response.Flush in case client buffering is enabled. If the client is not connected, the data will not be sent. This strategy minimizes needless transactions.

One good ASP testing technique is to place Response.End in the middle of various ASP scripts. When the next measurement is taken with the performance tool, if the performance is the same, then the performance is dictated by the first half of the page. If the performance is greatly increased, then it is the second half of the page that dictates the performance. Comments can be added to scripts to detail the results and the Response.End can be moved up or down in the page to more locally isolate the performance blocks until they are identified.

ASP page performance should always include a measurement with the server in high-load scenarios to identify the performance issues. Be sure through all of this testing that the IIS exception monitor is turned on to catch any exceptions thrown here. Most likely in ASP applications the CPU is the limiting resource, so be sure to monitor it carefully.

CROSS-REFERENCE
See Chapter 6 for more information about testing ASP.

Automating Performance Testing

Server-side testing can be easy to automate, but it is difficult to automate properly. Much of the testing is dependant on well-reasoned assumptions and user scenarios. If these are incorrect, the test effort can be nullified. Consider the following process:

1. Typically the test effort can start with a quantification of common user actions and user actions that require the most resources. The resource-utilization factor needs to be weighed against the frequency-of-request factor to come out with the most expensive and common interactions. Formulas such as megahertz per request per second can be used to reduce these down to simple numbers to compare apples with apples. This process helps identify the most expensive pages in your application.

2. You can then start to ask the important questions. Can you have 1,000 simultaneous users? Can you have 100,000 simultaneous users? What if you run a sale on one particular item and have 1,000 users simultaneously log on and attempt to purchase that same item? Can 1,000 users simultaneously log on and purchase 1,000 different items? In order to answer these, user scenarios need to be developed.

3. Once the user scenarios are developed, they are likely automated through the use of scripts. This should help pinpoint the location of the expensive or problematic functions. For example, if the application is an online music service, it may be determined that the logon process is not expensive, nor is the uploading or downloading of files. Rather, the searches for individual music files are what really cost the servers. If the average user logs on once, performs several searches before finding the desired file, downloads one, performs a few more searches, downloads another, and then logs off, the overall user session is very expensive. The evaluation in this example should point out that performance improvements for the online music service need to be made and that it is not worth making them in the upload/download code. Instead, the effort is better spent on the search code.

Once you've identified a problem area, the automation script that was initially written may not be suitable for continuing with the testing. Many times a lot of values are hard-coded to quickly create automated scripts. Randomizations need to be thrown in because a static scenario simply does not represent how users interact with software. Throw in randomness and track the effects. Write up several more user scenarios that differ from each other—some long and some short. Throw in variables to pull random numbers for everything—the number of searches performed, the number of items purchased, even the amount of wait time (latency) between the user interactions. When this scales out to thousands of virtual users randomly running a script or a user scenario with a random number of searches and purchases, you obtain data that is a lot more reflective of how the application will behave when in use in the real world.

Teams that forget to randomize the data may find something undesirable when the application is deployed live to real users. For example, one team was finishing the performance testing of their online software that did mapping of addresses. The performance that the software showed was far beyond anybody's hopes or the bar set in the specifications. It was an incredibly fast application! Performance miracles do not happen, and further investigation revealed the real problem. The application had large maps available. When a map of a position was loaded, such as New York City, then the state of New York would be loaded into memory and decompressed. The exact location would then be found on the decompressed map and would be given to the requesting client browser. That map would remain open in memory until the memory needed to be freed at which point the map would be closed. All of this meant that if the same address were requested multiple times, the system would need to do the work of locating it and serving it up only once; all subsequent times would be almost "free" as far as the server's expense was concerned. Once the mistake was realized, the data was randomized, and real numbers were found. Luckily, the real numbers were found to be very good as well. Had they been found to be unacceptable, it would have been quite late in the project to do much about it.

There are many packages available that you can use to automate testing and many different approaches. As with any other effort be sure to identify how the automation fits a need in the testing and how it will be used in the short term as well as in the long run before committing to the effort.

CROSS-REFERENCE
There are too many performance automation and general testing tools to go into here (there are entire books written about them). However, Appendix J lists many that are available.

Key Performance Testing Tips

This section outlines a few tips that some organizations might not recognize for this stage of the testing, some of which I've touched on throughout the chapter, all of which are important to keep in mind as your test team deals with performance testing:

- **Define up front the expected results.** Know in advance what will determine a pass or failure on the part of the software.

- **Be realistic with the schedule.** Server-side testing takes a lot of time and effort and requires running the exact same test multiple times in order to find trends and to have enough data for the results to be meaningful. Avoid the mistake of planning on doing more than can actually be done.

- **Do not install the browsers onto the servers and run the performance, load, or stress tests from there.** Although it might be possible for your application servers to act as both the client machine and the server, such an arrangement will not give accurate numbers.

- **Set up an isolated performance lab early.** Be very careful doing stress or load testing while on the corporate intranet because this will fill the bandwidth with the stress requests, slowing the network for everyone. Setting up an isolated lab prevents network pollution.

- **Stability problems need to be identified prior to deployment.** Once the application has been rolled out to the users, it is too late to do many fixes, and each fix becomes far more expensive. The application needs to be tested with real-world expected loads, usage scenarios, and topologies. Double the expected load to ensure that peaks can be withstood. If the weakest points of the application are known before deployment, then while it is deployed, it can be watched for any signs of imminent failure.

- **Create many user scenarios derived from the most common and most intensive user actions.** Run these randomly on different client operating systems and browsers, and with randomized data. Test the performance of the retail builds, and if time allows, perform a quick stress test on the debug build. Many code asserts are missed when the testing department does not use debug builds, and I have known teams who learned their lessons by only testing debug builds, not wanting to waste time on the retail builds. So testing debug builds is important; it just does not yield genuine performance measurements. One-sided testing efforts lead to shipping applications with large problems because Test never tried to find issues through the avenues that they should have.

- **Although security is always a concern and can be a necessity, minimizing the usage of SSL or any encryption saves money.** Encryption is expensive to put in the hardware or software; it degrades performance and requires more servers to get the job done. SSL may be necessary in the part of our application that asks for the users' passwords or credit card numbers, but is it really necessary for their lookups in our catalog? Perhaps. If the site is a job search site, the big selling point may be that users can look for jobs while at their current employer because all the data transmissions are encrypted. If we are hosting a catalog of various silverware patterns, it is entirely likely that our catalog might not need encryption for the protection of our users.

■ **Analyze your performance numbers after your performance tests are complete.** Isolate the performance factors such as proxy servers, connection speed, or firewalls and acknowledge them. Check for memory leaks and other problems that build over time. Conducting the tests many times takes very little actual time. Your time will be spent in resolving code changes against changes in the measured performance. Analysis is expensive, detailed work and must be done carefully.

Above all, performance is every tester's concern. You may not be the person running the tests in the performance lab, but you still need to be aware of any performance issues you come across and raise the concerns with the appropriate people.

Improving Application Performance

As I state in other chapters, the whole goal of testing is to identify issues and address the appropriate ones. Most of the issues that your software encounters will be unique to it. However, this section identifies some common types of issues that you may quickly identify as being potential issues in your application. Being able to learn such lessons from others' efforts will save your testing organization time and money.

■ **Minimize the number of round-trips and the data flow.** You can minimize the data flow by reducing the size of the graphics transmitted, which will help performance. You can also reduce the amount of multimedia data sent across the wire. Animations, large graphics, or sound files may be unnecessary or may be able to be reduced in size. Also use server-side caching and client-side caching to reduce the hits to the database and optimize the data flow.

■ **Apply distributed and redundant architecture.** Distributed and redundant architecture is likely a requirement in your production environment. If your application is an internal Web app for a small company, then perhaps you do not have the resources to have multiple servers, which is appropriate for this situation. You can perform due diligence through regular backups and contingency plans for the internal server. However, in a larger environment or a mission-critical application, the architecture needs to be distributed and redundant. Failover testing needs to be done by systematically crashing or otherwise pulling a machine from a test topology while in the middle of testing. A few requests may be delayed, but the remaining machines should pick up the extra load without noticeable degradation of performance, and the balancing needs to be equal across all machines. Load-balancing hardware may be necessary if your software does not balance the loads itself.

Redundant network connections will be a necessity as well. There should be no single point of failure and that includes network connections. While at work one day, all of our mail services went down suddenly. Nobody had the ability to find people's office numbers, phone numbers, or send and receive email. It was discovered later that a network serviceman, while working in the server room, tripped over the fiber connection connecting everyone to the servers. It had gone unnoticed and unsuspected for a while, and although everyone was up and running again later that day, how many man-hours were wasted or lost? Time directly corresponds to money. Can your corporation afford to lose money when a problem like that happens during peak hours?

- **Consider redundant power supplies and generators.** Although energy crises, such as the recent rolling blackouts in California, are not common, what would something like that do to your business? Could your business withstand a natural disaster that knocked out local power, even for a week? Although nobody can prevent these disasters, plans can be made to handle them. Perhaps your company has a backup facility on the other coast or somewhere else in the United States to use in an emergency. If the application is crucial enough, this sort of redundancy may be an appropriate solution for you.

- **Monitor your software after deployment.** All of this performance testing helps you to identify what a healthy profile of your software looks like under loads. It should also help identify a profile of what the service looks like just before it falls down and breaks. Once your software is deployed, install and use Web-monitoring software. Use a log analyzer. Products such as WebTrends, Microsoft Operations Manager, or Site Server Express Usage Analyst can be a great help in monitoring the ongoing health of your software.

TIP

A mistake many organizations make is keeping the development and test teams separated from the deployment and administration personnel. This communication breakdown prevents those on the front line, who are responsible for keeping the software up and running in the live environment, from knowing what the signals of an impending server meltdown looks like.

- **Keep the software design simple.** The simpler the design is from the beginning, the easier the software will be to maintain, upgrade, and administer. Think ahead about the evolution of each feature, and plan for the next version. Development costs are not the only costs. If the software is difficult to upgrade from version 1 to version 2, how will the production servers be upgraded? How expensive will it be? Will there be a lot of downtime? The object of Test here is to save the company money in the long run through good-quality software.

The key to keeping performance testing in perspective is to really understand why the measurements are being taken and what they mean.

Why are the bytes over the wire being measured? Because, in the deployment, the cost of pushing many bytes over the wire will likely eclipse other costs, and it is a critical factor in improving the customer's experience.

Why are the megacycles being measured? There are a finite number of megacycles available on any processor, so no function can bloat too far without negatively affecting the rest of the system.

Do these measurements need to be taken for each and every build? Maybe. The test organization will have to make that determination.

The whole point of taking these measurements is to point out problems in the code, and to identify areas that need to be improved. They are simply used to provide a rough idea of how the software will eventually perform and how many servers will be necessary for the expected number of users. The better quality the test effort here, the more probable it is that the measurements reflect the deployed scenario with real users. As with all other testing efforts, start small (single user, single server) and snowball to a more expansive effort (many servers, clients, and users). Performance testing can be extremely rewarding. When the right problems are fixed, the results are immediate, drastic, and measurable, providing that crucial feedback that the right decisions are being made.

CHAPTER 9

Security Testing

There is no security on this earth, there is only opportunity.
—General Douglas MacArthur

T he idea of doing security testing is enough to send most testers shirking to the back of the room hoping somebody else will be assigned to the job. Oh, it sounds fascinating and thrilling! Hacking at software! Finding major holes! But where to start? And how?

The real problem with security testing is that it needs to be done from the very beginning—from the start of the project when everything is still being discussed, even before any plans are actually written down. Security needs to be thought of before anything else. Including security testing from the beginning of the project prevents the security issues from ever making their way into the product and is far more effective than sending a team of testers in to blindly hack at the software for weeks on end. A well-architected application with smooth seams will not have as many loose threads just waiting to be pulled. The biggest stumbling block to achieving this early planning is that not enough testers (or developers or managers) know where to start. There are two parts to the security equation.

- *Architectural problems* are the first part. If your customer database *by its very design* does not require a password to access it, then it is very insecure. Other architecture decisions may not be as obvious contributors to security issues.

- The other side involves *coding problems*. Even if your architecture is absolutely perfect (which is impossible in and of itself), poor coding decisions, poor practices, and simple mistakes will open security holes. If your database requires a password, but your password verification code forces only the first password entered to be checked, allowing through any subsequent attempt, then it is not properly verifying the user's credentials.

Both of these together make up the vast amount of bugs and security issues.

Who Are We Up Against?

The common thought is hackers, but many legitimate users can stumble across the right combinations of input and actions that produce very undesirable results. The term *hackers* has changed meanings to now mean something completely different from what it meant originally, so I prefer to label these people as *malicious users*. They have the aim of finding the one problem in your system that can gain them the most access, or the most press. They typically have a lot of time on their hands and many have a considerable amount of knowledge and resources in the form of machines, scripts, information, and tools. The other point here is that there is not an equal number of testers to malicious users. Your team has a budget and a set number of people who are examining the application before releasing it. There are easily orders of magnitude more malicious users who can focus on your product than there are internal resources to prevent problems. Because many of the specifications for Web products come directly from industry standards, malicious users have open access to these blueprints. These individuals have the priority of finding one bug over the next 3, 6, or 9 months. Contrast that with your own testing position. If you found one bug in 6 months, and that was all you were doing, you would probably be out of a job in short order. Still, it really doesn't matter if the person on the other side of your application is a malicious user or a legitimate but unlucky user—the end result is that something bad happened to your software, and you now need to clean up the mess. If the mess could have been prevented in the first place, then there wouldn't be as much need for a cleanup squad.

Security issues are a huge concern to any company. There is a responsibility that all software companies have to ensure the safety of their customers' data, as well as maintain their servers' integrity. This data may be information such as the customer's credit card number or just the email from their mother, but there is a responsibility on the company's part to consider security and think of the information assurance of its customers.

NOTE

Some companies have tried to follow a model for security testing that bases their testing on a perceived idea of the importance of a company or service. The thought is that a less important company or service will not be as interesting to a hacker or other malicious user. While this assessment does provide some sort of framework to help in assessing the software, beware of allowing it to lull the organization into a false sense of security and complacency. I personally do not care for this method because it allows for incorrect assumptions and a false sense of security. Quickly reading through any security forum should alert you that there are all kinds of hackers. Just because your company is not involved in pollution, politics, or anything else that might make it an obvious target, the fact that it has machines connected to the Internet is enough to put a big bull's eye on all of your servers. There are hackers who concentrate on particular companies, but there are many others who use the tools and techniques created by their more knowledgeable counterparts to blindly run scripts against any server they can find. These *script kiddies* can be just as dangerous as the real knowledgeable users, and sometimes more so. Some knowledgeable individuals bring security issues to the attention of the company to fix prior to publicly announcing them, but that is not always a courtesy companies are afforded or one that the companies take advantage of. Approach security testing with the mindset that attempts will be made to breach your security. The rest of this chapter is dedicated to this approach.

Choosing Your Security Test Tactics

Remember, your product is on the defensive, having the tactical need to protect every line of code at every moment. In military tactics and in business, this is referred to as the defender's dilemma—the need to defend every piece of everything all the time. As the defender gains more and more that is desirable, he is also gathering attackers and gathering more that needs defending. These attackers, by nature of their position, have certain advantages—attacker advantages. All they need to do is find one piece that is not completely guarded, and they can potentially invade and own the entirety. As I have indicated, there is a certain assumption that could be drawn that the less desirable that which you are defending is, the less likely it will be attacked. But that doesn't mean it will never be attacked. Just as small businesses and homes are robbed, small applications are targets just by virtue of existing.

To be completely safe, your software would have to be perfect all the time. You will never achieve this; your product will always have problems, but there is much you can do to safeguard against them and prevent being an easy target.

Organizations have two potential approaches concerning who performs the security testing, or really any specific testing:

- Have an individual (or team) who specializes in this type of testing test for these types of problems
- Have each feature's owner test his feature for these types of problems

Depending on the complexity of the software, the level of the individual testers, and many other factors, one method will make more sense for your organization than the other. But who does the testing will not change the basic approach to the software and the security issues that the software has.

I want to back up and review the sample application that has been an example throughout this book. Remember that the application is an online bookstore where users can buy books, read reviews of books for sale, or post their own reviews of books. In order to perform security testing on this sort of application, or any testing on any type of application, you need to have a plan of where to start. But how do we start this plan?

One very effective technique to deal with security problems is to essentially audit the software as it progresses. This approach means auditing the plans as they are designed, auditing individual features or components as they are coded, and finally auditing the software as a whole as it is integrated. An approach from this direction ensures that problems are prevented before they start, and that problems are chased out at each stage of the software development cycle. This approach also solves security problems at the cheapest point because most are prevented, and the ones that slip through are found soon after they are created.

The best way to approach security problems that I have found is to classify security problems into logical groupings and then evaluate the software's potential to have problems of that type. There are many ways to evaluate concerns and security compromises. For example, you can evaluate attacks aimed at other users versus attacks aimed at the hosting servers. The approach discussed here helps greatly when creating test cases because you can identify what the risks and expected outcomes are for various actions. It also helps not only in securing your borders, but also in keeping your customers safe.

Coordinating the Security Effort

Initially, you want to audit the proposed design of the application and architecture to identify potential security problems. Those security holes that cannot be eliminated through design should be tested for once code is in place.

TIP

The more complex a system, the more likely that there are unknown security bugs. If there is only one door into a room, then it is very easy to watch it and monitor it for only approved traffic. However, if there are many doors and windows, and some hallways, it becomes far more difficult to ensure that all traffic in and out is legitimate.

Coordination is required to test the application and architecture through the various stages of its development:

- **The first steps need to be taken by the product designers.** They need to be aware of laws around privacy issues and security and ensure that the software will comply. They may be able to prevent some security problems in their designs; however, because problems are introduced when the code is actually implemented, this is only the first line of defense. Their role here is to be aware of the larger security concerns and privacy issues and ensure that the system architecture is able to *be* secured. Features such as anonymous access to the database may or may not be a concern. The designers need to do the research on how much data should be collected on users, if it needs to be encrypted, and how it can be secured. Particular techniques can be identified and explicitly documented as not to be used because of a known potential for exploitation. Some of the techniques to avoid are: the use of GETs to send form data to the server, placing user data into the URL (usually invoked as a mechanism to maintain state), hidden form fields, or using client-side scripts to validate data being sent to the server. While designs are still on paper, your job as a tester is to identify assumptions and ambiguities that increase the probability of mistakes in the implementation.

- **The developers take the first steps towards ensuring that their code is safe by employing best practices when writing code.** Some of the problems that may be found here are:
  - Marshalling data from an untrusted part of the application to a trusted part without verification
  - Marshalling data from managed to unmanaged code
  - Fully trusted code making calls to partially trusted code or code marked as no trust

Many tools exist to verify code is written to a fair degree of security (functions are correctly called, buffers sizes are checked). Many of these tools are available only for native code (C or C++) and not for managed code, but since managed code can be written with unsafe functions as easily as not, it is susceptible as well. Developers may have processes whereby they review each other's code before it is checked in. Having team standards that are enforced in code reviews can take this activity a step further. Such an approach may prevent problems if it is used as the best practice it can be and not treated as overhead.

In addition, the people responsible for actually building each of the builds can increase the warning level on the build tools in order to catch potential problems early. (Certain problematic warnings could be disabled if they give too many false positives.) Warnings can be forced to be errors so that at build time builds will give failures instead of just displaying a list of errors. Having a low threshold for what constitutes a warning and a failure applies more stringent requirements on your software to conform to certain standards and requirements.

- **Testers are only the last line of defense in this attempt to lock down secure code.** Test may not have been directly responsible for any of the stages to this point, but they can always act in a guiding role helping to shape current processes into better ones. Test will become directly responsible for the latter stages of security testing.

Developing Your Approach

From the black box point of view, our application looks rather like Figure 9.1—an opaque box with unknown contents.

As you progress through these exercises in auditing your software for security problems, the application starts to become more transparent and begins looking more like Figure 9.2, a gray box.

In Figure 9.2 you can clearly see the components and their interactions, what components communicate with what other components, inputs and outputs, and their relationships in the whole of the application.

Input   Output

Figure 9.1 At first, the application is an opaque box, where only input and output are identifiable.

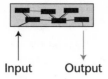

Input   Output

Figure 9.2 On closer examination, you start seeing the inner workings of the application.

When you take an individual component and look at it, it will at first look like the opaque black box in Figure 9.1. As you begin examining it and understanding its inner workings and individual features, the interfaces and data flow become apparent, more like the box in Figure 9.2. With each new level that is examined, the box becomes clearer and clearer until, finally, on the most atomic function level you are, essentially, white box testing (or glass box testing), where the application is completely open for you to look at the most basic of its inner workings—the code. It is essential for security testing that you have some degree of vision to the inside of your box. The complexity of your application and the abilities of the organization will affect your approach to the security auditing exercises.

The first part of the approach is to enumerate the various components of your application. In the sample application involving the online bookstore, the enumeration of components may look like the following:

- SQL database
- Book section (read only)
- Review section (read and write)
- Search
- Sign-up and account management
- Purchasing and checkout
- Third-party ads

Most of these have a user interface component to go along with the data that is sent back, but there are other pieces to this application that lack a visible interface for the user. There is an operating system that is used on the servers that run the software, configurations of these servers when they are deployed, and perhaps specialized components on top of that. These other components most likely are not under your control and, therefore, are *dependencies*—things you have no control over but must rely on.

TIP

Listing each of these dependencies helps you to identify other potential problems and helps when the application is actually deployed.

Each individual area needs to be broken down in several ways. The first way to start breaking an area down is to identify how the user will use the feature. User scenarios of the expected interactions are the first step. In the example of the online bookstore, you might start with users logging in, probably searching for a particular book, adding it to the shopping cart, and then purchasing it.

Mapping what data is passed, from where, and to where, helps you in identifying what can be attacked or where weak points exist. Even if not all of the underlying pieces are understood, just knowing where data is touched and by what code helps in planning tests. These maps should also detail all entry and exit points. If a user can give you data, then a malicious user can give you malicious data. As part of the security test plan, you will need to examine the flow of data to determine if layers could be bypassed. For example, the users are expected to use a browser to connect to the rendering servers, which will then request data from the databases. Certainly the browser can be bypassed and tools can be used to send requests or data to the servers. Are there holes that would allow other tools to directly communicate with the databases? Tracing the data flow through the system seems like a Herculean task, but it will be very much worthwhile. The process of tracking down the data flow clarifies in everybody's mind how the program is structured, and it serves to educate testers on their product. In tracking the data flowing, be sure to list any of the technologies that the application uses. A good specification contains this information, or it should. Program managers may have this duty fall to them, but Test can also collaborate with development, analysts, and others, to document the technologies used. Some of these might be:

- Parsers
- Converters
- ISAPI filters
- DLLs
- Script (client-side script that is generated and sent to a client, as well as server-side script—can be JS, VBS, Perl, Mocha, or any other language)
- ASP
- CGI
- COM objects

In addition, list all the files, as well as any registry keys and values, that are looked at by the server.

For the client side, list out what the application is putting on the client or is retrieving from the client. This could be files or values such as:

- Temporary files (include where they will be located and name)
- Controls downloaded—ActiveX

- Script
- Registry settings and values
- Cookies—including values
- Command-line commands accepted, including arguments

Each major action will end up having a data flow diagram associated with it. A data flow for the online bookstore application could end up looking like that pictured in Figure 9.3 and explained in the numbered list that follows.

NOTE The task of mapping a data flow will probably fall to the data analysts, project managers, or others who document or plan the way the product works.

1. The user types in `http://oursamplecompany.com` to navigate to the Web site.
2. The request is sent from the browser over the Internet to the Web server.
3. The Web server responds, sending the browser the standard Web page that allows the user to search for a book (list files sent).
4. The browser receives the response and displays the HTML and script.

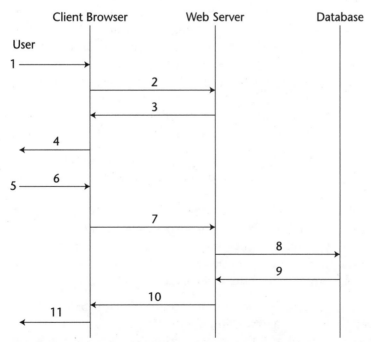

Figure 9.3   Sample trace of the requests and responses through the request life cycle.

5. The user reads the welcome and types into the search field the title of a book.

6. The user clicks the Search! Button.

7. The browser sends the input and search request to the Web server.

8. The Web server formulates a query and sends the query to the database.

9. The database runs the query and sends the results back to the Web server.

10. The Web server formats the response and sends the appropriate HTML and results to the client.

11. The client receives the response and displays the results for the user.

WARNING

Most applications tend towards the Pareto Principle, or the 80/20 rule—80 percent of the actions tend to follow the same code paths (in whole or in part). There will be a minority of potential interactions that use completely unique paths of the code. These interactions are important because they do not get much focus in regular testing efforts and are at high risk for security holes.

Once the data has been traced through the system, take each component and enumerate the various states in which it can exist. State-based modeling of the data and forms helps the team to understand even more about the application and provides better coverage without duplication of effort. In the case of the Review Opinions section of the sample online bookstore, there is a read form, a fresh review entry form, and perhaps a reply form to respond to another user's commentary, which means that the data can be in a read-only state, an input mode (create), and an edit mode (reply to another's commentary). Once you determine that information, it is much easier to identify how the data can be accessed, in what state it can be used, and how it can be used. The states also usually illustrate unexpected accesses to information that should be checked.

Once the areas of the software are listed and their individual inner workings are understood, they can be audited for their potential risks. The best way to go about this auditing is to take the specifications for each component and walk through each security risk with each component, creating test cases and auditing each of those components for security concerns. This auditing can be done while in a meeting discussing the various ways that the component could be designed, or it can be done after the code is written to create the suite of test cases. Ideally it will be done at each point.

Essentially, you want to prevent problems in the designs before effort and time have been spent implementing inherently faulty designs. If proposals with flaws can be identified and the flaws eliminated, then both time and money have been saved as opposed to identifying these issues much later in the process.

NOTE

Unfortunately, many people believe that all security bugs have to be proven to do something malicious to be counted as a security issue and warrant fixing. Consider this scenario: Suppose in the online bookstore application that a user can enter an opinion of a book. The user-provided commentary is unescaped, and data is passed through exactly as it is entered. The tester may use one of the cases suggested in any of the security sections of this chapter and see that JavaScript alerts will execute. The tester could spend large amounts of time examining exactly how malicious a user could get with this weakness and how badly it could affect a genuine user. But really that doesn't matter. The bug is that the data is not properly escaped, allowing HTML and script to be rendered and executed instead of the plaintext that was input. As testers, you need to identify the bug, not the exploit. Fixing the bug will prevent the exploit.

Testing for Types of Security Problems

This list is not exhaustive because there are many more technologies available than space to dedicate to them. This list covers the main types of security concerns for Web applications. If your application employs another technology or a proprietary language, it will still likely be able to be analyzed according to these criteria; however, the exact test cases as suggested here may not apply.

Buffer Overruns

Buffer overruns (BO)—also called buffer overflows—are the most common security hole of all time. But what is a buffer?

A *buffer* is a holding place that data can be moved into and out of. When software is run, the code requests a buffer of a particular size and then places some data into it.

Think of the code as being like a recipe. Suppose a chocolate chip cookie recipe calls for ¾ cups of sugar, but the preparation instructions tell you to measure out the appropriate amount into a single ½-cup measuring cup. If you follow the instructions given, sugar will spill all over the countertop as you attempt to put ¾ cups of sugar into a ½ cup measuring cup. The same thing is what happens in a buffer overflow. A buffer of memory has been requested by part of the code (the ½ cup measuring cup). Another part of the code stuffs the data into the buffer (pours the ¾ cups of sugar into the ½ cup measuring cup). If the data is actually larger than the buffer, as is the case with the sugar, there can be some severe outcomes causing crashes, failures, downtime, and other bad behavior that is best discovered before software is released or a site goes live.

So how does a buffer overrun occur? As I have discussed, one part of the recipe (code) calls for a particular amount (the ¾ cup—the data) but tries to put that amount into a predefined area that is smaller than the amount (the single ½ cup—the buffer). If the input is not checked for whether or not the amount you are trying to push into the container will fit, then the buffer is overwritten, or overrun.

To continue with the chocolate chip cookie recipe metaphor, another place that you can have a buffer overrun is when you place all the different ingredients into the mixing bowl; the bowl might be too small. In that case, although you might have checked each item individually, when they are combined and pass into another component (when you put butter into the mixing bowl from the measuring cup and add sugar with other ingredients), the new area needs to be checked to ensure that there is enough room for what is intended to be placed there. Otherwise, you can end up with sugar, butter, vanilla, flour, and more all over the countertop. Any place that data is accepted into a function or passed around is a potential site for a buffer overflow.

Consequences of Buffer Overruns

But what are the consequences of buffer overflows? Buffer overflows can cause a number of problems in and of themselves. Commonly, they result in a hang or a crash. Another outcome is a denial of service (DoS) to legitimate users. This DoS could be that the service has been slowed down to such a degree that it is just unusable, that it has stopped taking requests, or that the machine has crashed. Either way, the customers cannot use the service. Since a buffer overrun will most likely start to consume resources at an abnormal rate, it can lead to a denial of service in very quick time. There are other results from a buffer overrun, such as loss of data or data corruption, but these types of problems may go undetected for a long time, only to surface when infrequent actions are performed (such as restorations or upgrades).

If a malicious user knows what type of bad input is going to be effective and where to place it, he can do a lot of damage. Consider Figure 9.4.

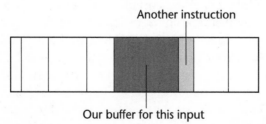

Figure 9.4 Map of the memory allocated for various data.

The middle shaded area in Figure 9.4 is the buffer. If you do not check the size of the data you attempt to place in it, then you could walk right off the end into the shaded area directly to the buffer's right in the figure, which is supposed to contain another instruction. So, suppose you set aside a 10-byte buffer. You attempt to input 11 characters, such as `12345678901`. You have overflowed the buffer, but have not done anything terribly malicious yet. However, if you can find out at what memory address that other instruction is located and then make sure you have your own instructions replacing it, you can do something really bad.

So, suppose a person does know the memory address for that instruction. That person could then stuff in the input `1234567890<script> alert('Hello')</script>`. The information put into the buffer in this case was only input to get out of the buffer area and into the area that should contain the instruction the program is about to run. That initial buffer is of no interest. However, once a person knows it is possible to walk out of that buffer and can reference the first character of his instruction, he can start controlling what the program does next. And once somebody else has that level of control, you no longer own your machine.

Now, there were a lot of *if*s and steps involved to get you to the point I mentioned in the previous paragraph, and your test team probably does not have the time to invest to see exactly how each and every buffer overflow can be exploited. However, somebody out there does. When a buffer overflow is found, campaign to have it fixed. The size and potential for damage and ultimate exploitation are really secondary issues and beside the point; the fact that a buffer overflow exists is reason enough to fix it.

WARNING

Even a 1-byte overflow can be exploited to the point of having complete control of a machine.

Testing for Buffer Overruns

How do you prevent buffer overruns? There are some relatively common ways to prevent buffer overflow problems.

- Carefully and thoroughly inspect the specifications before development or testing begins for data limits to be specified. Just by reading carefully you can often tell that there is a problem, or at least that there is some ambiguity and the potential for failure.

- Nevertheless, many issues will get through the inspection phase, so developers have a responsibility to protect the software against these problems. The code needs to check that the data to be put into the buffer is of the right size to be contained in it. Many bugs are eliminated simply by doing this check.

- However, just because the check is done does not mean it was done properly, so check the size of the data and check it correctly through proper memory calculations. Problems occur when developers make assumptions, such as *all characters are single byte* or *all Unicode characters are 2 bytes*, or when they assume that the size was checked by someone else. And checking the size of the data is only one side of a thorough check. Verifying that the proper size buffer has been requested is the other side of careful coding.

- Developers can also prevent buffer overflows by using all APIs correctly. This advice sounds elementary, but it is crucial that developers using APIs understand the proper usage, not just the way to make their desired results occur.

Just as these are ways that developers can prevent buffer overflows, ignoring these are ways that buffer overruns can be caused. Having code conventions requiring memory checks to be done does not solve the problem of poorly implemented checks. Developer code reviews may help catch many of these problems prior to code being checked in. But because developer code reviews may not catch all these problems and because even well-written code can have problems, Test needs to test for these conditions.

Checking the User Context

The user context is another layer related to buffer overruns. The *user context* is the account in which the program is running on the server. If a user is able to elevate his privileges to that of the account under which all code is running, the user can now run code or control the functions of the server with the permissions of that account. If the user can gain the administrator privilege, the user now controls your entire machine, and perhaps all of your machines. If a user is able to cause a buffer overrun, gain access to a machine, and is left only with the permissions of a user, he can do far less damage than if handed the permissions of an administrator. In general, there is no reason to have code running as administrator or with admin privileges. Precautions against this elevation are to rename the administrator account and follow other good administrative practices, including changing the SQL database sa password.

Buffer Overrun Testing Techniques

Testing for buffer overruns should be done not just through the application user interface, but also through the use of tools that will directly set data beyond the expected size.

Some common sources of buffer overruns include:

- Parameters on the ends of URLs
- Command-line arguments
- File contents
- Network packets
- Simple user input
- URL, query, or command-line attributes and parameters—need to verify that these are the proper length and value
- HTTP headers—content cannot be more than 32 b
- Any transition from managed code to native code
- Parsers—especially if they are looking for a particular character or string as a trigger; pieces of the data stream then can cause a buffer overrun

This is not an exhaustive list, so testing tools will need to be employed. Attacks can and will occur through the interface as well as through the use of tools. Some of these tools are listed in Appendix J. Developers and testers need to be educated in the proper usage of these tools, as well as have them at their disposal.

A common way to check for a buffer overrun is to just hold down a key for a very long time. This method is really the brute force technique and will catch only some of the potential cases. Everyone has heard the story of the tester who fell asleep on his keyboard only to discover the server-crashing bug from overflowing a buffer. What you need to do is test these inputs in a smart way and hit the appropriate boundaries, verifying that problems do not exist.

This brings up the best practice of making your tests obvious. If you want to input 256 characters and know what comes out, how can you do this without having to count every one, possibly miscounting the characters or getting fingerprints all over your screen? You could copy the string and paste it into Word and get a count of the characters, but another technique might be more effective and a better practice, especially if you do not have as many tools quickly at your disposal.

In the following paragraph there are 250 characters:

```
WWWWWWWWWWWWWWWWWWWWWWWWWWWWWWWWWWWWW
WWWWWWWWWWWWWWWWWWWWWWWWWWWWWWWWWWWWW
WWWWWWWWWWWWWWWWWWWWWWWWWWWWWWWWWWWWW
WWWWWWWWWWWWWWWWWWWWWWWWWWWWWWWWWWWWW
WWWWWWWWWWWWWWWWWWWWWWWWWWWWWWWWWWWWW
WWWWWWWWWWWWWWWWWWWWWWWWWWWWWWWWWWWWW
WWWWWWWWWWWWWWWWWWWWWWWWWWWWWWWWWWWWW
WWWWWWWWWWWWW
```

Does that look any different from the following?

WWWWWWWWWWWWWWWWWWWWWWWWWWWWWWWWWWWWW
WWWWWWWWWWWWWWWWWWWWWWWWWWWWWWWWWWWWW
WWWWWWWWWWWWWWWWWWWWWWWWWWWWWWWWWWWWW
WWWWWWWWWWWWWWWWWWWWWWWWWWWWWWWWWWWWW
WWWWWWWWWWWWWWWWWWWWWWWWWWWWWWWWWWWWW
WWWWWWWWWWWWWWWWWWWWWWWWWWWWWWWWWWWWW
WWWWWWWWWWWWWWWWWWWWWWWWWWWWWWWWWWWWW
WWWWWWWWWWWW

(Hint: There are only 249 characters in this latter paragraph.)

To make your input better, you can use a repeated string of 10 characters and create 250 characters of your ultimate test case by repeating the segment. It might look like the following:

1234567890123456789012345678901234567890123456789012345678901234567890123456789012345678
9012345678901234567890123456789012345678901234567890123456789012345678901234567890123456
7890123456789012345678901234567890123456789012345678901234567890123456789012345678901234
5678901234567890123456789012345678901234567890

Then, all you need to do to generate your 256 characters is input 6 extra characters on the end and make it obvious that they are there, such as by using **ABCDEF**.

For some instances, you will want to try thousands of characters, perhaps even several megabytes worth of characters, to ensure that your software will not be crippled by malicious users. Because of this, you probably will want to use Word or some other application where you can paste in a string and find out exactly how many characters long it is. However, having some good techniques for the bulk of your testing allows you to test more of the code base more efficiently and effectively.

TIP

Once you have generated specific data that is of interest in testing your particular application, save them to be used later. Creating test repositories of this type of data is immensely helpful, not only when running cases by hand, but also in brainstorming test cases, and for automation. It also allows data to be created once, by one person, yet utilized by the entire team.

You need to know the limits (any expected maximum or minimum) that are set on each data input field and output field as well as the database object in order to effectively test these boundary conditions and ensure the robustness of your application.

Windows 2000 Server (ISA Component) Bug

The *New York Times* reported a bug in Windows 2000 Server (ISA component) that resulted in the server crashing. All that a user had to do was request a Web page with an unusually large address in the location box—it had to be at least 3,000 characters long. Once the server was challenged with this, the ISA server component would not let computers inside the network view pages outside the network, and vice versa. Through the Microsoft-provided interface of Internet Explorer this is not possible—IE has a URL limit of 2,047 bytes, but Netscape Navigator will send up to 30,000 bytes, even though some standards allow for 1K and others for 4K. IIS was likely never checked for an overflow of incoming data exceeding the size that Internet Explorer was capable of sending, and this made an easy exploitation once it was employed. Checking for a simple buffer overrun here would have saved many companies a lot of money and prevented administrators from having to apply security patches.

The best practices just illustrated that will save you time and effort are:

- Make your test cases obvious.
- Use input and indicators that will immediately tell you what is going on.

Your approach to test for buffer overruns is to identify the expected size of data anticipated in a field and then to try to force an amount larger than that. For example, a field may allow a user to enter 256 characters. If the database component expects up to 255 bytes, then entering any number of single-byte characters up to 255 will be successful, but entering 256 single-byte characters could have serious consequences. So right off you know that the interface and the database disagree on the size of this piece of data. That bug is fixed and the size is set to be 255. But another exercise of the handling to try here is to see if the field accepts double-byte characters. If it does, entering 255 DBCS characters could have worse effects than entering the single-byte characters. If entering that many double-byte characters is blocked, try entering around 128 DBCS chars (half of 255) or entering characters from the GB18030 code page (which contains 4-byte characters). There may be code blocking the 255 DBCS chars that is not blocking at the proper boundary.

Some applications can be invoked through the command-line interface. If they take arguments, you may need to identify several boundaries. If the user types in `runApplication` followed by 300 characters, the application could crash. However, if the user types in `runApplication` followed by 600 characters, the input may not be accepted. In this case, there is a secondary arbitrary boundary within the limitation that would have to be identified. If the value can be UTF-8 encoded or accepts the GB18030 code page, then a third test to try involves a range of these characters that are encoded in 3 bytes or 4 bytes, accordingly. The questions that you need to answer are:

- Where can data be input?
- Where is data read from?
- What type of data is expected and how much?
- How else can I get at that piece of data?

Similar issues exist with parameters on URLs, and they should be tested not only for the expected size of data, but also for unexpected and improper usage.

A buffer overrun could also come from a property that is read in by the application. Suppose the review section of the online bookstore allows users to upload pictures of themselves (view the reviewer). If the code looks at a property of the attachment—one that is not set through the UI of our application—then a malicious user could create a file with that property set to any value he wanted. There could be a property that the file accepts but your application does not. The file would be uploaded through the UI provided, the application would read the property, and the property would cause a buffer overflow. In fact, the application would actually be in a state to run malicious code at that point.

NOTE

One example of this sort of buffer overrun involved a FrontPage bug where a file opened in FrontPage that had a long style applied crashed the application when the application tried to edit the style.

For each component all the places where data can be put in and what other associated properties are read should be enumerated. Some data read in by the application could be from registry keys, cookies, HTTP headers, or other non-UI sources. These need to have special attention because they are really back doors into the code and are easily faked with tools. HTTP headers are easily manipulated and faked using various tools. Any other file property can just as easily be created or manipulated by a malicious user and should never be trusted or relied upon.

In order to perform a buffer overrun test, you need to understand several things:

- What is the limit on the field? Is this limit in bytes or characters?
- Is there a required minimum for the field?
- Is there a limit somewhere in the UI? (The database may allow the field to be larger, but the UI may not allow you to input more; in that case, try another way to get at that field such as manually populating the database.)

- What type of input does this field accept? Lower ASCII only, numbers only, SBCS/DBCS, UTF-8?

- Is there another way to alter this value? Look for a second or third way to get into this state or at this data.

- What else could try to look at this value? Does it have a different assumption of what this value can be? Many times there is no UI to set a value, but there may be other ways to get it set, or unset. The method for setting it may or may not be of importance; you can go into the database by hand and create particular values that are of interest to us. You need to identify first which fields are of interest and what those should be set to in order to check your error-handling code. Some of these failures may be red herrings because they were not created in a valid manner, but they are still valid to consider. Is a regkey or cookie read in by the system? Can this be altered to an unexpected value? Is that error handled?

- Verify input for buffer overruns and validity. If NULL is not an acceptable value for the property, fail gracefully. Other unexpected input should be handled as well.

Tools can catch some of these issues in unmanaged code. All developers need to be aware of these problems to ensure that simple buffer overruns do not exist. Data needs to be checked when being pulled from memory to make sure that it is what was expected and that it was not overwritten by something else. No programming language is completely safe. Some companies will brush overflows under the rug, saying that their managed code simply cannot have these problems, but there can still be unsafe functions running in these applications. Any language can be put into practice in an unsafe way, and therefore, Test needs to be aware of how to identify these problems. The recent XP UPnP bug that got so much press was a buffer overrun. As Bruce Schneier put it in his online newsletter *Crypto-gram*, "This vulnerability is a buffer overflow, the easy-to-use low-hanging-fruit automatic-tools-to-fix kind of security vulnerability." The press oversimplified the problem, but you need to use all the resources at your disposal to eliminate these elementary bugs. User-supplied input should be documented for each component so that it can be traced through the system.

Table 9.1 contains some test cases and samples to use to construct test cases.

Using these 10 character strings, you want to put together strings that exercise the code limits for your particular application. For example, if you have a text box that is limited at 20 characters, you will want to paste the 10 character string into the box twice and try performing the action, as well as other variations on the test case.

Table 9.1 Sample Test Cases for Buffer Overrun Testing

TEST INPUT	TEST CASE
1234567890123456789012345678 9012345678901234567890123456 7890123456789012345678901234 5678901234567890123456789012 3456789012345678901234567890 1234567890123456789012345678 9012345678901234567890123456 7890123456789012345678901234 5 67890123456789012 34567890ABCDE	255 character string
ｱｱｱｱｱｱｱｱｱｱ	String of 10 single-byte DBCS characters; try pasting in the number of characters or bytes that your property supports, and try more than it supports
滾滾滾滾滾滾滾滾黑	String of 10 true double-byte DBCS characters; try pasting in the number of characters or bytes that your property supports, and try more than it supports
∩∩∩∩∩∩∩∩∩	String of 10 2-byte encoded UTF-8 characters; try pasting in the number of characters or bytes that your property supports, and try more than it supports
滌滌滌滌滌滌滌滌滌o	String of 10 UTF-8 encoded 3-byte characters; try pasting in the number of characters or bytes that your property supports, and try more than it supports. This one is particularly of interest because many experienced developers will know to expect double-byte characters, but may not realize that some characters can be encoded into 3 bytes.

Parsing Problems

Parsers often relate to buffer overruns because many parsers are looking for a particular value when stepping through input and may make assumptions when it is found. An example of this is parsing through a path to a file. The parser may correctly parse through the drive name, the folders, slashes, and more folders, but as it hits the actual file name it may be expecting a period followed by a three-letter extension. A four-letter extension (or more) could cause a buffer overrun. In this case, the path could be extremely long and still be handled appropriately. However, if the part following the period was not what the parser expected, there would be a buffer overrun. In this case, the path of C:\Documen~1\user1234567890123456789012345678901234567890\file.txt would be fine, but C:\Documen~1\user123456789012345678901234567890123 4567890\file.txt1 would not. In fact, C:\file.txt1 would not be fine either, and it is a much shorter path. Perhaps your software makes decisions based on file type, extension, or content type. If your software wanted to make sure that no user could upload an executable file to the server in place of a reviewer's picture, it may rightly check that there is not the .*exe* extension at the end of the file. But what about other, potentially valid and executable cases for this file type? Consider Table 9.2, where sample filenames are suggested for test input, and reasons to try them are given.

Starting from a simple list like the one in Table 9.2, you can immediately generate many test cases once the expectations for each value are understood.

Table 9.2 Sample Test Cases for Testing Parsers Related to Filenames

FILE NAME	EXTENSION DESCRIPTION
Foo.exe	.exe—This would be the base case of a period followed by the letters exe and then the null terminator—the usual case.
Foo.exe.	.exe.—Period followed by the letters exe, followed by another period.
Foo.exe	.exe.—Period followed by the letters exe, followed by a space.
Foo. exe	. exe—Period followed by a space, followed by the letters exe.
Foo.e xe	.e xe—Period followed by the letter e, the space, and the letters *xe*.
Foo.exeasdf	.exeasdf—The first three letters may be the only ones expected, and the file may end up being run anyway.
Foo.e_xe	.e_xe—Period followed by the letter e, the underscore, and the letters *xe*.
Foo.{098f2470-bae0-11cd-b579-08002b30bfeb}	{098f2470-bae0-11cd-b579-08002b30bfeb}—The GUID of the exe from the Registry.
Foo. e x e	. e x e—A period followed by the DBCS Romanji characters for e, x, and e. Here there could be assumptions made by components that remove unknown characters, leaving the base case intact, and a file executes by essentially degrading a "safe" unknown extension to an unsafe valid one.
Foo	Here there is no extension, but the tester would need to make sure there is a valid content type associated with the file to see if a fall-though behavior is picking up on that.

This simple parser that makes decisions based on a file extension is just one example of a parser that could be employed along with the ways that it can be deceived into allowing undesirable data though. Other parsers may be more complex, with greater ranges for their tolerance of input. In part, some parser issues can be minimized by properly escaping the appropriate content so that it is not executed or is otherwise neutered to keep it from causing problems. Instead of passing the period to the parser, the period could be escaped to %2E or U002E or some other representation. In general, however, the parser's particular assumptions must be known and error handling must be present, even if everyone agrees that there is no way that the error code will be exercised. Each component should document what information is being parsed as it relates to the feature, as well as any assumptions that are being made about what the parser is looking for in that data stream.

One common assumption made by developers when creating parsers is that one should look at the second character of a path to determine if the path is a local one or not, with the intent to disallow any code from accessing the local machine. The assumption that they are relying on is that all local paths will be in the form of a drive letter followed by a colon and a backslash; however, there are many ways to work around this format. A reference to a file named foo.txt directly in the root of the C: drive on the local machine can be made by referencing the localhost, which is 127.0.0.1, so that our full reference would be \\127.0.0.1\C$\foo.txt. Or it could reference \\.\C$\foo.txt, or even file://C:\foo.txt. Another way around the standard format is to reference the NT-specific local references, which looks like \\?\C:\foo.txt.

Parsing problems often arise when one is parsing the domain name in a location or URL. In this case, the assumption is that there will be a period (at least one) if it is an external address. Making a decision based on this omits the potential for other references for external sites. Table 9.3 shows behavior that would result from this parser assumption if you wished to allow a user to access any item referenced inside your domain, but to stop references to items outside the domain.

Table 9.3 Sample Test Cases for Parsing Machine References

CATEGORY	FORMAT	EFFECT
URL	http://www.oursamplecompany.com	Blocked
IP	http://127.127.127.1	Blocked
Octal equivalence	http://0177.0177.0177.0001	Blocked
Hexadecimal	http://0x7F.0x7F.0x7F.0x01	Blocked
Hexadecimal alternative	http://0x7F7F7F01	Allowed
Decimal	http://2139062017	Allowed

The information in Table 9.3 means that two of the variations used to refer to Web sites (as dictated by the Web standards) would be allowed through when we did not wish them to be allowed. This type of misbehavior comes from faulty assumptions.

Another issue that I consider to come under parsing problems are URL canonicalization issues, which is a very fancy term for a very simple concept. You and I use many relative terms to reference things every day. I could tell you to go next door to borrow a cup of sugar so we can make cookies, and you would know that I meant next door to the house that we are currently in. Without challenging the command, you would go next door and ask for a cup of sugar. *URL canonicalization* is using the computer's built-in assumptions to trick it into doing something. You may know very well never to go to 1600 Pennsylvania Avenue and ask for a cup of sugar. But perhaps you would not realize that was where you were headed if you were just thinking of heading next door for the sugar, and we happened to be next to 1600 Pennsylvania Avenue. In a similar way, you could be in a directory that you have full access to that happens to be under another directory that you do not have as much access to. Figure 9.5 shows two folders—one inside the other.

From a security-testing perspective, you want to figure out how to trick the computer into letting you open a file that lives in the Foo directory. If you simply tried to access `http://oursampleapp.com/bar/barfile.htm`, you would be blocked. If you tried to access `http://oursampleapp.com/bar/foo/foofile.htm`, you would be allowed. But if you tried to make the computer think that you should have access to a directory and then told it to get something from next door, in the hope that it would not notice the permissions problem, you would try asking for this `http://oursampleapp.com/bar/foo/../barfile.htm`. You could also try to force it to let you write an item there, alter an item, delete an item, or execute an item. In this case, you would try to trick the computer by telling it to go next door and get us a file; essentially, you are telling it to make a directory traversal. The computer equivalent of telling the computer to perform this operation is .. which says to look in the folder above the one we are in. There are many other references like this one that the computer can make assumptions from and that parsers might allow through as legitimate input.

NOTE
Testers should understand where parsers are parsing data for their components. Parsers are used everywhere, so this list could be a long one, but only a few items on that list may actually be of concern to each feature area's owner. The important part is to understand all special characters used by your application or any of its components.

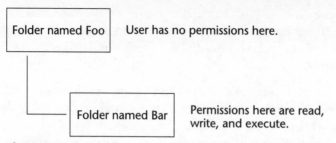

Figure 9.5 One folder with no permissions granted containing a folder that a user has full permissions to.

Some of the parsers that could be involved in your application are:

- XML
- SOAP requests
- HTTP requests
- HTML filtering
- SQL queries
- ISAPI filters
- CGI programs

Table 9.4 shows some inputs that should be verified as not causing problems, some of which should have characters escaped. Each of these cases has a particular reason why it might be problematic in your application.

Table 9.4 General Parser Test Cases

TEST INPUT	UNICODE POINTS	TEST CASE
	[U+0020]	The space can be misread as the end of a stream with the input on the other side as a switch or parameter; one example of this would be the old Windows path, where spaces would be dropped in the command line so that `C:\Documents and Settings` would become `C:\Docu-men~1` to avoid the problem.
!	[U+0021]	Problematic in a URL.
"	[U+0020]	Reserved character in many languages.

Table 9.4 *(continued)*

TEST INPUT	UNICODE POINTS	TEST CASE
#	[U+0022]	Reserved character in some contexts; fragment identifier in a URL.
%	[U+0025]	Reserved character in some contexts.
&	[U+0026]	Can trigger multiple CGI processes with a single request.
'	[U+0027]	Reserved char in C and unwise to leave unescaped; problematic in a URL.
.	[U+002E]	Can be a delimiter expected, as in a file name.
/	[U+002F]	Path delimiter.
:	[U+003A]	Can allow an alternate stream access in a URL.
;	[U+003B]	Can be read as a parameter delimiter.
<	[U+003C]	First character in HTML and script tags; very dangerous and needs to be handled carefully.
>	[U+003E]	Last character in HTML and script tags; very dangerous and needs to be handled carefully.
\	[U+005C]	Illegal in a URL.
ö	[U+00F6]	Extended character that frequently causes problems.
§	[U+00A7]	Extended character that frequently causes problems.
ß	[U+00DF]	Extended character that frequently causes problems.
€	[U+20AC]	Euro character, which often causes problems.
::	[U+003A][U+003A]	Two colons.
..	[U+002E][U+002E]	Two periods can cause a directory traversal.

(continued)

Table 9.4 *(continued)*

TEST INPUT	UNICODE POINTS	TEST CASE
./	[U+002E][U+002F]	Trailing period on a directory name is not expected.
$$	[U+0024][U+0024]	Two dollar signs.
++	[U+002B][U+002B]	Two plus signs.
%0	[U+0025][U+0030]	Can cause problems in Perl script.
\n	[U+005C][U+006E]	New line in JavaScript.
\b	[U+005C][U+0062]	Bold formatting in JavaScript.
%20	[U+0025][U+0032][U+0030]	Wire escaped space.
Ü¢£	[U+00DC][U+00A2][U+00A3]	High literals.
::$DATA	[U+003A][U+003A][U+0024] [U+0044][U+0041][U+0054] [U+0041]	Specifies a data stream.
~!;:?/*	[U+007E][U+0021][U+003B] [U+003A][U+003F][U+002F] [U+002A]	String of known problem characters.
/../	[U+002F][U+002E] [U+002E][U+002F]	Potential file traversal input.
\..\	[U+005C][U+002E] [U+002E][U+005C]	Potential file traversal input.
%2F%2E%2E%2F	[U+0025][U+0032][U+0046] [U+0025][U+0032][U+0045] [U+0025][U+0032][U+0045] [U+0025][U+0032][U+0046]	Potential file traversal input.
%C0%AF	[U+0025][U+0043][U+0030] [U+0025][U+0041][U+0046]	Becomes 11000000 in 10101111 binary, which maps to 00000101111 in UTF-8, which is 0x2F, or the forward slash.
&lt;	[U+0026][U+006C] [U+0074][U+003B]	HTML representation for the less-than sign.
	[U+0026][U+006E][U+0062] [U+0073][U+0070][U+003B]	HTML representation for the non-breaking space.
 	[U+003C][U+0062] [U+0072][U+003E]	HTML tag for a break.
&#65;	[U+0026][U+0023][U+0036] [U+0035][U+003B]	HTML decimal representation for the capital letter *A*.
&#x0041;	[U+0026][U+0023][U+0078] [U+0030][U+0030][U+0034] [U+0031][U+003B]	HTML hexadecimal representation for the capital letter *A*.

Table 9.4 *(continued)*

TEST INPUT	UNICODE POINTS	TEST CASE
<script>alert ('Hello')</script>		JavaScript that, if executed, will pop up an alert that says "Hello!"
<SCRIPT LANGUAGE= "VBScript"> MsgBox "Hello!" </SCRIPT>		VBScript that, if executed, will pop up an alert that says "Hello!"
blah<script>(unencode ("blahblahblah")) </script>		Data input (the *blah*s) followed by script.
0xf	[U+0030][U+0078][U+0066]	May be assumed to be the hexadecimal reference to a number; in this case, it would be *15*.
0xa	[U+0030][U+0078][U+0061]	May be assumed to be the hexadecimal reference to a number; in this case it would be *10*.
å	[U+00E5]	Mostly significant if first char in a string; essentially this is a Ctrl+z.
乗	[U+4E57]	Trailing byte is 5C on the 936 code page.
薄	[U+8541]	Lead byte is E5 on the 932 code page.
ﾌｳｵﾂｲ	[U+FF66][U+FF69][U+FF6B] [U+FF6F][U+FF68]	String of five single-byte DBCS characters.
黑鷛鶴滬潴滚	[U+9ED1][U+9E19][U+FA2D] [U+6EEC][U+6EF8][U+6EFE]	String of five double-byte DBCS characters.
¥\\¥	[U+FFE5][U+005C] [U+005C][U+FFE5]	The Yen sign, can be confused with the backslash.
ç	[U+0063][U+0327]	Lowercase letter c with combining cedilla—can be divided back into two chars improperly.
é	[U+0065][U+0301]	Diacritic combined with a character makes two code points seem to be a single character.
सुस्वागतम	[U+0938][U+0941][U+0938] [U+094D][U+0935] [U+093E][U+0917]	Unicode-only Hindi characters—these exist only in Unicode and not on any code page.

(continued)

Table 9.4 *(continued)*

TEST INPUT	UNICODE POINTS	TEST CASE
तम	[U+0924][U+092E]	Unicode-only Hindi characters—these exist only in Unicode and not on any code page.
	[U+0081]	First character that requires 2 bytes of encoding.
ँ	[U+0901]	First character that requires 3 bytes of encoding.
滬	[U+6EEC]	Character in the middle of the 3-byte encoding range.
ﾮ	[U+FFEE]	End of the 3-byte encoding range.
	[U+000D][U+000A]	Carriage return/line feed (CRLF)—also use two sets of these in a row; this is a non-printable entity so there is no visible character to show.
	[U+FEFF]	Byte order mark (BOM)—especially as the first charac-ter of a file; this is a nonprintable entity so there is no visible character to show.
	[U+2028]	Line separator mark (LSEP); this is a nonprintable entity so there is no visible character to show.

If your application accepts references to files, try calculating the alternative versions of your IP address (or an external IP) to try entering in any place a file can be referenced. This technique should be tried any place a parser is looking for particular strings in order to make a decision as to whether content should be allowed or not. Start by altering the aaa.bbb.ccc.ddd octal format.

- **Hexadecimal.** Take each octet and type it into a calculator separately under Decimal mode, and then change the mode to Hexadecimal. Piece each set together again, preceding each with 0x. The end result of this will be in a format like 0x7F.0x7F.0x7F.0x01. For the alternative, remove all but the first 0x and the periods, giving a result like 0x7F7F7F01.

- **Octal.** Take each octet and type it into a calculator separately in Decimal mode, and then switch to Octal mode. Each set must have four digits, so if you end up with less, add in a 0 at the beginning of the set. The end result of this will be in a format like 0177.0177.0177.0001.

- **Decimal.** Take the *aaa* octet value and multiply it by 16777216. Take the *bbb* octet value and multiply it by 65536. Take the *ccc* octet value and multiply it by 256. Add these all together and add the *ddd* octet value to it. The end result of this will be in a format like 2139062017.

Tools for testing parsers:

- Character viewing and creation tools, such as Character Map
- Network-monitoring tools to view data as it goes across the wire

Conversion Problems

Converters are very similar to parsers and have some of the same potential problems. All the converters that are used must be listed so they can be tested by all components that call into them or receive data from them. The potential problems that result from conversions are:

- Data can end up converted to the wrong character or can end up corrupted. If the data is wrongly converted, it may show up as question marks, boxes, merged characters, split characters, downgraded characters, or true corruptions that were not the actual input. Some data conversions or corruptions are that way by the design of your product and are expected to occur and should be documented as such. It may be a bad design, but the design needs to be understood by developers and testers in order to create it and test it appropriately.
- More data than is expected could be passed into the converter, or the converter could pass out more data than expected, either way resulting in a potential buffer overrun. Tools such as Character Map allow you to enter precise characters and evaluate the output characters to make sure they match what was put in, or otherwise were converted as expected. Some converters will perform several functions or be used by several components, so their testing can be shared among area owners.

Some of the converters could be:

- Converting data from one code page to another, converting data from Unicode to a single code page, or vice versa
- HTML conversions to plaintext, or vice versa

TIP If conversions are being done from one code page to another, then conversions need to be tested from one code page to a different one, and from Unicode (if supported) to a single code page, and then in several round-trips together.

Table 9.5 lists some sample test cases to try and to combine into other test cases:

Table 9.5 Sample Test Cases for Testing Conversions

TEST INPUT	UNICODE POINTS	TEST CASE
Iiİı	[U+0049][U+0069] [U+0130][U+0131]	Two Latin letter I's followed by two Turkish letter I's—these should not be equated with each other.
öÜß	[U+00F6][U+00DC][U+00DF]	High literals.
¿¾Õ	[U+00BF][U+00BE][U+00D5]	Regional literals.
©®¾¿Õ	[U+00A0][U+00A9][U+00AE] [U+00BE][U+00BF][U+00D5]	Literals.
åE5å	[U+00E5][U+0045] [U+35][U+E5]	The code point of 0xE5 for the first character should not be split out to be displayed as E5.
€\$\	[U+20AC][U+005C] [U+0024][U+005C]	
â€™	[U+00E2][U+20AC][U+2122]	
Ü¢£	[U+00DC][U+00A2][U+00A3]	High literals.
1	[U+FF11]	Japanese double-byte number—use this range wherever an application is expecting a number.
0	[U+FF10]	Japanese double-byte number—use this range wherever an application is expecting a number.
A	[U+FF21]	Japanese double-byte letter—use this range wherever an application is expecting a letter—especially in place of a switch or application-provided data.
z	[U+FF5A]	Japanese double-byte letter—use this range wherever an application is expecting a letter.
¥\\¥	[U+FFE5][U+005C] [U+005C][U+FFE5]	The Yen sign can be mistaken for a backslash.

Table 9.5 *(continued)*

TEST INPUT	UNICODE POINTS	TEST CASE
<script>alert('Hello')</script>		Here, the two less-than signs are replaced with their double-byte counterparts. A converter could convert the double-byte less-than sign to the lower ASCII less-than sign, after which the browser would execute the now-valid script.
		[FA/68] on 932 code page—which will equal [ED/4C], which is [U+4E28].
		[FA/55] on 932 code page—which will equal [EE/FA], which is [U+FFE4].
厓		[FA/8D] on 932 code page—which is [U+5393].
晙		[FA/D7] on 932 code page—which is [U+6659].
mil		[A2/4F] on 950 or [U+33D5].
-		[A2/A4] on 950 code page—which will equate to [F9/F9], which is [U+2250].
†		[A2/A6] on 950 code page—which will equate to [F9/EA], which is [U+256A].
卅		[A2/CE] on 950 code page—which will equate [A4/CA] or [U+5345].
가		[B0/A1] on 949 code page—or [U+AC00].
耀		[E9/A5] on 949 code page—or [U+8000].
～		[A1/AB] on 936 code page—or [U+FF5E]
सुस्वागतम	[U+0938][U+0941] [U+0938][U+094D] [U+0935][U+093E][U+0917]	Unicode only Hindi characters—these exist only in Unicode and not on any code page.

(continued)

Table 9.5 *(continued)*

TEST INPUT	UNICODE POINTS	TEST CASE
तम	[U+0924][U+092E]	Unicode only Hindi characters—these exist only in Unicode and not on any code page.
	[U+FEFF]	Byte order mark (BOM)—especially as the first character of a file; this is a nonprintable entity so there is no visible character to show.
	[U+2028]	Line Separator mark (LSEP); this is a nonprintable entity so there is no visible character to show.

Tools that will be used for testing converters and conversion problems are:

- Character-viewing tools such as Character Map
- Network-monitoring tools to view the exact code points that are being passed back from the server to the client or between servers.

Shared Data

Any place that one user can provide information that another user can then access is a potential security hole. Any input that one user provides that determines the output for another user is really data that is being shared. In any situation data needs to be checked to ensure it is safe to both your server and other users. In the sample application of the online bookstore, data is shared when one user enters in a review of a book and saves it. Another user is then being handed data based on the first user's input—he sees what the first user wrote. A back door into this might be to select to reply to the user's commentary.

Consider another scenario where one user creates a name (*firstname lastname*) that, when put together, forms a script executing malicious code. For example, someone creates a user with the first name of `<script>alert` and a last name of `('Hello')</script>`. When the two strings are automatically put together, it executes, popping up an alert, or something more malicious. In this case, the username field is filled in by one user and then passed to another user—shared data.

NOTE This exact problem was discovered in Hotmail. The FROM field was not escaped, so malicious users could send script in the FROM field to unsuspecting users. The fix was to escape the FROM field properly, thereby preventing the script from executing.

The obvious place to look for this problem in the sample application is on the read commentary page, but there could also be an issue on the reply to commentary logic. Back doors to the same data, such as the reply to commentary logic in the online bookstore application, need to be investigated. These issues should be identified from the beginning in the designs and state modeling diagrams. Further, there are some generic test cases that should be run to identify if the escaping mechanisms are done properly.

Data can also be user supplied when it is passed to the server. It is then shared with the server. Measures can be taken to ensure that data is safe. Data can be stripped (for example, removing all less-than signs and any other characters that are considered unsafe), or the potentially dangerous data can be escaped so that instead of a less-than sign being passed in, a %3C is passed and then symmetrically unescaped back to the less-than sign at the appropriate time or passed as is to the browser, allowing the browser to equate the escape sequence with the symbol.

Tools that will be used for testing shared data problems are:

- Character viewing tools such as Character Map
- Network-monitoring tools to view the exact code points that are being passed back from the server to the client or between servers

Escaping

Any time data is shared there is the possibility of having malicious data shared. *Escaping* is a mechanism to take suspicious data and convert it into safe data, while still retaining the content information. It is a very useful technique that allows almost any input to be accepted and rendered without the fear of having malicious input executed. The whole point of dynamically rendered Web sites is to share information, usually from user inputs, but at the same time, this sharing can lead to problems. In the online bookstore application, for example, users can create a book review with script in the review text. Much of the original user input can be allowed to be displayed through proper escaping so that it is displayed and not executed. The problem you need to contend with is the browser's willingness to identify and immediately execute any HTML or script that it can, even handing off what has been downloaded to other programs. Because of this tendency, malicious, or potentially malicious, script needs to be removed prior to its being received by a user. Embedded HTML and scripts can cause many issues here. There could also be an IFRAME link to a page containing malicious script, or, if the relative path can be guessed, a reference to a second file stored on the server that contains malicious content.

Encoding, Escaping, Encrypting—What's the Difference?

Encoding is the process of taking bytes and converting them into characters. There are many different encoding mechanisms, and, along with the code page that they apply to, these are more commonly called *charsets*.

Escaping is identifying character ranges that are not handled (again, the upper ASCII and DBCS characters fall into this category, as well as problem characters or reserved characters that should not be allowed through) and converting them to safe characters to later be converted back to the original data. In this scenario, a set of characters—such as < > ? / \ . and :—is identified as not being allowed in a URL. These specific characters, and the ranges of disallowed characters, are then converted to strings of allowed characters in order to safely transmit them without data loss. This process must be symmetrically done. The result of escaping is to take a character, such as the backslash, and represent it with a string of safe characters:

- ◆ *Character:* \
- ◆ *Escaped sequence:* %5C

Encrypting data means that data is altered with a special mechanism to make it unreadable or undecipherable to anyone but the holder of that mechanism's key. Encrypting through SSL or other means provides no protection to the user or the server from malicious input, but it protects the data in transit from being read. This sort of encryption is similar to the encryption on a cell phone. It prevents other cell phone users from hearing your conversation, but it doesn't prevent the person on the other line from saying bad things or protect you from hearing them. The only problem it solves is that of another person's listening in.

You need to ensure that certain common problems do not exist. Many times script filters have poor parsing and look only for certain tags (for example, <Script>), ignoring other tags (for example, <SCRIPT>), or look only for JavaScript and aren't as vigilant for VBScript, Perl, Mocha, or others.

One of the problems with escaping (or encoding) is ensuring that it is symmetrical. Symmetrical means that the number of escapes performed equals the number of unescapes performed on any piece of data. Consider the problematic forward slash, a common target for escaping.

- **Characters:** cat/dog
- **Single escaped:** cat%2Fdog—Here the backslash is escaped.
- **Double escaped:** cat%252Fdog—Here the percent sign is escaped to the value 25, and then marked as an escaped value with the percent sign; the other two values are not seen as problematic and are not escaped.

■ **Fully double escaped:** cat%25%32%46dog—If the single escaped value is completely escaped again, the % becomes the value 25, the 2 becomes the value 32, and the F becomes the value 46, each indicated as an escaped value by the presence of the percent sign in front.

In this preceding example, the algorithm looked only for particular characters to escape and then only escaped them. Another, more expensive, algorithm could escape every character once, almost guaranteeing that there would be no problems after the escaping was done. In that case, the following would be seen:

■ **String:** cat/dog

■ **Single escaped:** %63%61%74%2F%64%6F%67

In this second example, the string is now three times as long and will cost the server cycles to both escape and to unescape and is more bytes of data to move around and store.

NOTE
There are drawbacks to any technique, but having a knowledge of even not-so-perfect techniques helps you to best identify solutions and weaknesses and vulnerabilities in the application.

Deciding to Escape Data

When examining any feature, look at several input mechanisms carefully. All data should be treated as suspect and potentially dangerous, to either you or your customers. Input can be inserted:

■ By direct injection (access to the database)

■ Through the Web UI

■ Through another file pulled in (containing data or a property that causes an unexpected state)

■ Through the use of a tool

■ Through errors

The last item in this list is often ignored. It is possible that a user could specify input that causes an error containing either the input supplied or a subset of that input. When it becomes dangerous is if those user-defined strings are not handled as input. For instance, a malicious user could provide a link in his book review. The unsuspecting user could click on the link—which is the obvious case. The not so obvious case is if the error that is returned to the unsuspecting user contains either a part or the whole of the data that the malicious user specified. Now, the malicious user could format his URL in such a way that the error that is passed back to the unsuspecting user contains HTML, script, or other code that is not, in this error case, treated as potentially dangerous user-specified input. The script executes, and the unsuspecting user is left with a security breach. Any string that is built from user input has the potential to contain malicious content. Thus, anything that contains user-specified data needs to be handled carefully, and escaped accordingly.

Data verification can be done on the client side, on the server side, or both.

- Client-side verification of anything should be done only to protect the user who is entering it and should never be relied upon for security because it is easily bypassed. Appropriate uses for client-side script include field verification to ensure that a user has filled out all required fields and validly formatted data because this saves the user time and saves the round-trip cost to your server. Inappropriate uses for client-side script would include passing the percent discount that should be applied to a user's purchase. Doing that on the client side makes it too easy for a malicious user to manipulate that data to give himself a 100 percent, or 200 percent, discount.

- Server-side verification should be used for security checks.

Escaping data is one way to prevent the execution of code. Filtering out data is a more severe way to handle it because it involves an actual loss of data that was input, but when all else fails, it is the lesser of the evils and may be necessary.

Commonly Escaped Characters and Escaping Test Cases

Table 9.6 contains characters that are problematic and that should be escaped. These characters are all considered illegal or potentially problematic in various contexts:

Extended range, double-byte, and Unicode characters may or may not be escaped, depending on where they are used. The concern with them is if they are not escaped, they may later be downgraded to a reserved character. Be aware of extended DBCS characters that could be degraded to one of these reserved characters.

Table 9.6 Sample Test Cases for Escaping Mechanisms

TEST INPUT	UNICODE POINTS	TEST CASE
<	[U+003C]	Start of HTML or script
>	[U+003E]	End of HTML or script
!	[U+0021]	HTML comment
"	[U+0022]	Start of HTML argument
#	[U+0023]	Can be a delimiter; problematic in a URL
%	[U+0025]	Can indicate an escaped character
+	[U+002B]	Reserved character in a query component; problematic in a URL
)	[U+0029]	Problematic in a URL
(	[U+0028]	Problematic in a URL
&	[U+0026]	Reserved character in a query component; problematic in a URL
'	[U+0027]	Reserved character in SQL
.	[U+002E]	Especially as last character of a file name
/	[U+002F]	Especially as last character of a file name; also a C reserved char or reserved in a query component; problematic in a URL
:	[U+003A]	Reserved character in a query component; problematic in a URL
;	[U+003B]	Can indicate a parameter delimiter in a URL
\	[U+005C]	Path delimiter
-	[U+—2D]	Reserved character for SQL

Table 9.7 contains some sample cases to try to see if your escaping is working properly.

Table 9.7 Sample Input to Test that Escaping is Working Properly

INPUT	REASON
<script>alert('Hello')</script>	This is the typical script for a JavaScript alert.
<SCRIPT>alert('Hello')</SCRIPT>	Here, I have changed some cases in order to bypass any exact string matches.
<Script>alert('Hello')</script>	Here, I have mixed cases in case the checking mechanism looks for all one case.
<script>alert('Hello') </script>	Here, I have used double-byte opening angle brackets to see if they are downgraded to their dangerous single-byte equivalents and then executed.
BLAH%22><script%20for= window%20event=%22onloa d()%22>document.write (%22Security%20bug!%22); document.close();</script>0 Security%20bug!%22); document.close();</script>. write(%22Security% 20bug!%22);document.close(); </script>	This is an example of input specifically designed to exploit a particular hole in a form. The input is closely followed by escaped HTML.
&lt;	The HTML entity name for the less-than symbol.
&#65;	The HTML decimal reference for the capital letter A—not dangerous in and of itself, but if the letter A appears instead of the entity named here, then other dangerous things can happen, such as a script executing.
&#x0041;	The HTML hexadecimal reference for the capital letter A—not dangerous in and of itself, but if the letter A appears instead of the entity named here, then other dangerous things can happen, such as a script executing.
0xf	Could be assumed to be a hexadecimal reference to a number, in this case, *15*.
0xa	Could be assumed to be a hexadecimal reference to a number, in this case it would be converted to *10*.
.	This is a DBCS period that could be downgraded to the potentially dangerous Lower ASCII period.

Table 9.7 (continued)

INPUT	REASON
/	This is a DBCS forward slash that could be downgraded to the potentially dangerous Lower ASCII forward slash.
:	This is a DBCS colon that could be downgraded to the potentially dangerous Lower ASCII colon.
!	This is a DBCS exclamation point that could be downgraded to the potentially dangerous Lower ASCII exclamation point.
'	This is a high-bit ASCII single left quote that could be downgraded to the potentially dangerous Lower ASCII single quote.
'	This is a high-bit ASCII single right quote that could be downgraded to the potentially dangerous Lower ASCII single quote.
"	This is a high-bit ASCII double opening quote that could be downgraded to the potentially dangerous Lower ASCII double quote.
"	This is a high-bit ASCII double closing quote that could be downgraded to the potentially dangerous Lower ASCII double quote.
<	This is a DBCS less-than sign that could be downgraded to the potentially dangerous Lower ASCII less-than sign.
>	This is a DBCS greater-than sign that could be downgraded to the potentially dangerous Lower ASCII greater-than sign.
'	This is the DBCS prime symbol that could mistakenly be converted to the potentially dangerous Lower ASCII single quote.
"	This is the DBCS double prime symbol that could mistakenly be converted to the potentially dangerous double quote.

Tools to assist in testing escaping:

- Character viewing and generating tools
- Network-monitoring tools
- SQL Profiler

Cross-Site Scripting

Improperly developed Web sites and Web applications are susceptible to *cross-site script* attacks, whereby scripts are run in the domain of the Web site instead of just locally on the machine. Essentially a cross-site scripting attack consists of a malicious user getting his code to run on someone else's Web page in that person's browser in the context of the Web server. An end result of cross-site scripting could be a malicious script deleting a user's account off the server or making purchases for him. Cross-site scripting attacks allow for cookies to be read or set, and browser plug-ins, scripts, native code, or even controls can be started and can run untrusted data. With this code running, user input such as a credit card number, home address, or other sensitive information can be captured and therefore compromised. Any browser with a scripting engine can be compromised through this type of attack, and any Web server using HTML forms is at risk for being open to this.

One way to check for cross-site scripting vulnerability is to fill out a form with some easily recognizable data (for example, *11111111111* or *AAAAAAAAAA*) in all fields. On saving or manipulating the form, check the form source for this data being stored in hidden fields or other areas. Appending a parameter to your URL (*?cmd=AAAAAAAAAA* or *;AAAAAAAAAA*), hitting Enter, and then searching the resulting source can also tell you if the parameter is wrongly injected into the source, allowing a potential cross-site scripting attack. Other holes are created through assumptions, such as what domain the code is coming from. In these cases, the URL standards need to be carefully followed, and the IE functions need to be used to determine what domain is being referenced rather than going off and writing your own functions.

The real problem at the heart of any cross-site scripting attack is that the Web page displays data that has not been validated by the server. This risk is created through poor coding and poor architecture of the application. Cross-site scripting is most usually a shared data problem because the data is provided by a malicious user. The typical points of attack are:

- Through query strings issued to the database
- By way of data posted to the server
- Through URLs or pieces of URLs, cookies, or other user-supplied data that is persisted in some way (usually in the database)

WARNING

To exploit a server, all that a malicious user needs is for one server inside the firewall to not check a field in a form for special characters.

The same precautions that protect the application and user from other attacks also work here. Data should be verified as safe before using it, by escaping, filtering input, and filtering output if necessary. Again many of the vulnerabilities can be eliminated with proper escaping of input and particular characters.

If all data is handled properly through verification, escaping, and filtering, cross-site scripting is generally not a problem.

Tools for testing cross-site scripting are:

- Character-viewing and -generating tools
- Network-monitoring tools

SQL Injection

SQL queries can be injected by a malicious user in an attempt to gather information, edit other user's information, or just cause problems in the database through actions such as dropping tables. These attacks happen when a user inputs data, the Web server sends the data to the database without validating it or securing it, and the database proceeds to execute the commands. These queries can be injected from forms, from the location bar, or through tools.

NOTE If you cannot get directly to the database, then you most probably cannot get to it through tools without otherwise compromising the configuration of the network topology.

When this exploit is successful, a user gets a query to run on the server. The result can be:

- Table dropping (deletion of databases or tables in the system)
- Data loss or modification
- Modification of any stored procedure, query, or rule
- Log deletion or modification
- User management (add users, remove users, and modify permissions)

Because the SQL application runs under the Local System account, any SQL hack immediately opens the system to the malicious user. Without detailing how to exploit this security hole, I will just say that there are other ways in which unexpected results will show up from test cases (especially those from the characters that should be escaped). The single tick apostrophe, double quote, semicolon, dash (and two dashes), and percent sign are all suspicious characters used in this type of an attack. Again, if all data is properly verified and handled, this exploit should not be a problem. The precautions here are the same major ones that have been listed throughout: the escaping, verifying, and filtering of data. Table 9.8 lists many of these characters that are specifically problematic for SQL server databases.

Table 9.8 Sample Test Input for SQL Injection Testing

INPUT	UNICODE POINT
'	[U+0027]
"	[U+0022]
;	[U+003B]
-	[U+002D]
--	[U+002D][U+002D]
%	[U+0025]
Blah%'; DROP TABLE Foo; --	

Tools to use in testing SQL databases are:

- Network-monitoring tools
- SQL Profiler—lets you see traces of requests and responses
- SQL Server Enterprise—lets you watch tables being loaded and dropped

Error Handling

There are many places where error handling can compromise security. You may not want to throw back explicit errors in many situations. Malicious users who are attempting different approaches to compromise your system can then use these detailed and accurate errors to adjust their attacks. Often these errors are not the ones contained in the string table of error messages, but rather are bubbled up from components such as the database itself. They usually originate from a syntax error in the database or other low-level component. Giving the malicious user the exact issue provides them with feedback on what they need to do to make their attack successful. A very general error in many cases may be more appropriate. However, this idea does need to be balanced against usability concerns that too general error messages do not give users enough information to navigate around an error. Well-written messages should not create an issue with either aspect. Databases and other low-level components of your application are likely to bubble up very specific errors, practically guiding a malicious user to the exact point of exploitation. Catching these and handing back general failure messages instead may prevent you from providing a roadmap to malicious users.

Elevation of Privileges

If there is only one type of user and all users are treated the same, then your application has a simple privilege scheme. In the sample online bookstore application, suppose that a user can view his order history of all the books he has ordered from your site. He would not want other users to see his orders, yet he wants the ability to view them. In a simple privilege scheme, this same rule applies for all users—they are to have the ability to see their own orders and nobody else's. A more complex scheme might have the application allow users to set up book clubs where they share their reading lists and purchase history with other members of the group. That scheme allows three kinds of users: the purchaser, members who can see the purchases of others in their group, and all other users. The privilege scheme can get complex very rapidly.

To prevent malicious events, commands submitted to the server should use the POST method. Using the GET method to perform actions other than queries opens your users to attack. If the GET method is allowed in these places, then a malicious user can create a link that a genuine user can click on that will perform the action without the knowledge of the genuine user. This action may be changing a password, deleting an account, or any other action that your application will accept the GET method to initiate. The POST method, on the other hand, transmits the command separately from the response, thereby preventing the user from being so easily duped. It is still possible to cause a user to unknowingly perform the same actions; however, it would require the malicious user's getting the genuine user to invoke script, which should only be an issue if your Web application is not properly handling shared data. Check with the area developer to verify where the POST method and where the GET method should be used. Use network-monitoring software to then identify that the correct rules are being followed.

Security breach attempts should be logged in the event log. These logs will then be used to monitor for any suspicious activity such as brute force password attempts or faulty requests made to the server. However, this in and of itself could become a security problem if the log grows so large as to fill the entire hard drive and therefore throttle it. Be sure that your level of error logging is appropriate and that checks are made for free hard drive space to prevent running out of resources.

Test cases you can try here involve not signing in (being unauthorized) and then attempting to access specific valid URLs, as well as going in with an account that should have limited authorization to certain components and then attempting to surpass the valid use of the account.

CROSS-REFERENCE
The other type of elevation of privileges comes through the elevation to the level at which the server application is running. This type of elevation is discussed earlier in the chapter in the section "Checking the User Context."

Denial of Service

Denial of Service (DoS) is any action that results in users not being allowed legitimate access to their account or data. There are two major ways that this can happen:

- Typically DoS is thought of as a brute force network attack (for example, a ping flood or other massive attack).

- However, DoS could also be due to a few well-placed expensive queries. If a particular query is very expensive, a hacker may make several of those requests in a very short period of time. The end result could be a CPU utilization of 100 percent for an extended period of time, a system shutdown, a restart, a denial of new requests, a start of the garbage collector in managed-code environments, or (in some cases with ASP) a restart of certain services.

You need to make sure that your system configuration is tolerant of these pressures, but also that you do not provide such an easy way to tax the system.

Some other situations that lead to DoS are as follows:

- Failures can also cause a denial of service. If appending a particular parameter to the end of a URL causes the server's World Wide Web Publishing Service to fail, many users have just been denied access.

- Users can send several large files in an attempt to fill the server hard drives and subsequently have them fail.

- Users can attempt to cause many small errors to be triggered and logged, thereby filling up the error log and perhaps a hard drive somewhere.

Planning for these types of cases and having several lines of defense against such an attack is critical.

One key to testing for DoS attacks is to understand very costly actions and request several of them in quick succession, or to find a way to turn an anticipated expensive transformation into an extremely expensive (and unexpected) one. Step through the logic for your component and look at the data traces through the system. Talk with the developer to see which specific actions are going to be more costly for the server and how you can make those actions even more expensive. Many of these actions will be those that require contact all the way through to the database, then back to the client with one or more conversions, parsings, calculations, or other evaluations involved, or much data thrown away.

Another way to test for DoS is to queue up two actions that are "opposite." For example, you can take a very expensive action that instantiates many objects that the application anticipates will be used in the next action and then perform the nonstandard second action that instead throws those objects away. The TCP/IP syn flood attack was similar to this. When the client machine contacted the server, the server allocated resources before the initial handshake was finished. The attack here was for the client machine to then just keep initializing the handshake without ever finishing it; the server would keep allocating resources until it ran out of resources and crashed.

TIP

It is far better to fail closed than to fail open. A server has been crashed and has to be restarted, but at the same time no user data, or corporate sensitive data, has been compromised. It is the best possible outcome for this scenario.

HTTP throttling is another aspect of DoS attacks and will need to be addressed. HTTP throttling can come from all the server connections being tied up with non-genuine requests, or through the server bandwidth being full of non-genuine requests and responses. This situation could happen through many machines simultaneously starting to request lists of images off the server so that the server trying to honor those requests has all of its ports in use and all of the bandwidth filled, essentially blocking genuine users from being able to access the application.

Some general areas where denials of service can arise and should be examined are:

- Many simultaneous requests (for example, ping flood, ping of death)
- Open ports—especially undocumented ones
- Malformed packets
- Unexpected packets (overlapping, out of sequence ranges, and so on)
- Null packets
- Packets with size reported not equaling actual size (for example, small packets reporting that they are large could hang a server waiting for the transmission to end)
- Request actions that require list expansion or directory walking (for example, deeply nested folders, or directory name expansion and distribution lists)
- Request actions outside the normally expected range (for example, attempt to attach and save an item with a 1-GB attachment)
- Resource throttling

Tools to assist in testing for denials of service are:

- Performance-monitoring tools
- Network-monitoring tools

Testing for Privacy Issues

Some data should not be shared (for example, passwords being sent, IP addresses stamped on user's book reviews, and so on). User data should be treated as secure and confidential. To prevent exposing private data, you need to ensure that only the required information accompanies a user's input when it's saved to any source, which means ensuring that:

- The user's IP address is not attached.
- The user's computer path is not stamped on files that are uploaded.
- The user's identifying information is not attached to any item.

Features may carry contradictory criteria as defined by the user. A user may want others on his trusted friends list to be able to see his real name, but want this information blocked from people he does not know. Having conditions like this quickly expands the number of test cases that you need to run. Using a network-monitoring tool to view the data passed allows you to investigate if any personal data is being sent where it should not be. Viewing the source easily lets you see if data is being passed around even if it is not being rendered in the browser.

Within the user's session, there are even privacy issues. Evaluate whether or not items should be passing down the no-cache header to force the browser not to cache data on the client machine. If the site contains images or information that the users would not want found on their personal machine (such as sexually explicit material, medical information, or other sensitive data), then give serious consideration to not caching these items. Cookies stored on the local machine may contain potentially sensitive information such as a credit card number or a password. HTML or XML that is received by the client machine could also be stored. After running the application as a user would, go through the cache item by item and look for anything that users would not reasonably want left on their machine, or on a machine they were just using, such as a kiosk at the local library. The application will incur a performance hit, but you gain a marketing edge and a stronger privacy statement by taking into account such user concerns. Using a network-monitoring tool to view the data passed allows you to investigate if any headers are not set appropriately.

You need to ensure these files are not being cached on the client or on any intermediary proxy. The headers will be respected, but they need to be set appropriately so that security and performance can be kept in balance.

There are some common security problems and interactions that can be tested for:

- What is cached on the client side?
- Do cookies contain sensitive data or data that can be combined to be sensitive?
- Should the code stipulate Cache-control: no-cache headers? You can answer this question in two ways. The first is to use a network-monitoring tool and watch that each request that should send down the no-cache header does, in fact, send one down. The second is to check that once a user has logged out the browser cache does not contain any identifying information from the session. To confirm that the whole application is covered, perform a full pass of user scenarios, watching the headers passed down and ensuring clean-up of all data. After logging out of the application, look through the browser cache, examining it for graphics that the user may not want left behind, XML or HTML cached that contains user-sensitive information, or cookies that contain sensitive information. If you have used unique strings for your sensitive data, such as AAAAAAAAAAAAAAA, search through the hard drive for the sensitive strings that represent the user name, ID, or other sensitive information, without turning up false positive matches.

Tools to assist in investigating privacy issues are:

- Network-monitoring tools

Prevention includes proper caching of data, not storing sensitive data (or giving the user the option to opt-out of having it stored), or simply not even passing around sensitive or personally identifiable data. All features involved with any aspect of privacy should be listed and assessed by Program Management and Test.

NOTE The standard that needs to be applied for privacy issues can be found in the P3P (the Platform for Privacy Preferences) and the European Safe Harbor agreement. In the United States, the COPPA laws may also help guide how user information is gathered, stored, and further used.

Component Interaction Testing

One crucial piece of proper security testing that is not usually pulled into focus remains to be discussed. With any system, there are seams where components come together. The seams where code comes together are areas often rich in bugs. The interfaces where features come together may possibly provide a security hole, and these interfaces need to be analyzed and tested.

Testing each component for the security is expected; however, studies over the decades have shown that the security of a component in isolation is usually fairly well off from the design stage when security is considered throughout the product development. It is when two components interface that security problems are discovered, mostly due to faulty assumptions. The real issues do not lie insular in each component, but rather in the seams where two components meet.

Because the real issues exist where the components meet, you as a tester need to adjust your approach. Do not just approach an application to test each component, but rather to look at how to leverage one component against another. You are not testing a database; you are testing how using your application can open security holes involving the database. You are not testing the dependencies, but you are testing how a user can interact with the dependencies and components to cause unexpected and unwanted results.

Consider an item without a UserID field. The input UI may allow it, the database may not have any requirements on it, but a rendering component could fail because of this unexpected condition. You are not testing the database code, but you are testing the interactions of all the components consumed because all of it taken together composes an application. Putting the focus on these interactions is essential from the beginning. The basic level of testing a component is just the beginning. Testing these components in combination is far more important, for you are not just testing objects in isolation, but leveraging one against another to compromise security. As with any other testing, you need to plan and take one step at a time.

Many of the same issues that are addressed for testing a component in isolation also apply to testing component interactions. If the designs are clear and well understood from the beginning, though, the components should interface better and with fewer problems. After the feature owner has audited his individual area for security issues, he needs to investigate how his area interacts with other areas. (For example, is information retrieved from other components or does it pass information to other components?) Applying the same security concerns to the concept of component interactions as are applied to individual components helps to identify and close the security holes. Enumerate the application components in order to investigate their interactions. Many of these components are dependencies, but they need to be listed as components that can potentially interact. A sample list for our bookstore might be:

- Database
- Authentication mechanism
- Rendering logic
- Browser (Netscape Navigator, Internet Explorer) and the display of content in the browser
- Operating system on client and on server (Windows Server, IIS, unmanaged code, Linux, Sun Solaris, Apache)
- Other server components
- Language itself (C, C++, Java, HTML, script, and so on)

Other components can be introduced that you have no real control over. Some of these are:

- **The Internet.** The Internet itself, by definition, allows traffic to be watched; requiring SSL can offset this risk.
- **Specific tools.** Tools that will ping flood or serve up insincere requests to our servers in an attempt to cause failures.
- **Other applications.** Other applications that are trying to interact (for example, plug-ins, multimedia, and so on).

These are just part of the risks of having a Web application. They can be mitigated, but never fully prevented. If your network traffic is sensitive and the Internet component is problematic, then SSL could mitigate that risk. If tools are identified as being problematic, you need to research which ones your application is at risk from. Some powerful tools, such as Microsoft's Homer (also known as Application Center Test), respect a regkey that can be set on the server to ignore any request served up from that tool. This prevents malicious users from taking this powerful tool and using it against a site in a malicious manner. Other applications, such as multimedia players or plug-ins, can contain security holes that open either your server or your customers' systems to potential risks. Very little can be done to prevent this other than the common-sense steps of forcing users to save content to their hard drive, educating them to use virus-scanning software, educating them not to give their password or credit card information to anyone, and providing them with an information page listing links to places from which to install security patches and upgrades.

Securing the Application through Administration

Since administrators will eventually be rolling out the application and monitoring its health, there needs to be some coordination between those performing the development and test efforts and the administrators. Security works only if it is easy. Make the security of your application easy by making the default setting the most secure setting. Consider the following ways that Development and Test can work together to make the security work of administrators easier:

- Clarify and document all processes that are applicable (installation steps, upgrade procedures, and so on).

- Document which ports are necessary to leave open for the application to work so that all others can be closed. All ports except those noted should be blocked *in both directions* at the router.

- Document the appropriate access control levels of folders and directories so that they can be set and set correctly.

- Remove CGI support from servers that do not use it.

- Listing all the components involved can help the administrators search for, identify, and install all appropriate service packs and security patches for each component used. Not having the appropriate service packs and security patches installed is the most common reason for a compromised system.

- Provide a granular and current list of all components. Such a list greatly assists in keeping the systems secure.

- List particular settings such as log levels. Such settings help ensure that the systems are properly maintained.

- As testing progresses, particularly through the stress and mean time to failure tests, create a profile of a healthy server and an unhealthy server. Sketching out the warning signs of an unhealthy server can help an administrator know when to take a server offline and maintain it prior to a crash or when to call for more experienced help.

A comprehensive troubleshooting guide (TSG) should be compiled for those who will be monitoring the servers on a daily basis. It should contain information on what the expected behavior and settings are, as well as a profile of an unhealthy server and instructions for troubleshooting the server or notifying the appropriate individuals who can investigate the problem.

TIP

Just prior to shipping, the test organization needs to take the TSG that was created and implement a topology exactly by their book to ensure that it works as expected. This topology needs to mirror the real environment down to the number of machines, the type of machines, and the router and networks involved.

Testing for Other Security Issues

Although they all fall into one of the categories discussed earlier in this chapter, there are some common security problems and interactions that you need to test for that are still good to call out separately to give ideas for test cases.

■ One common way to test security in Web applications is with URL parameters that contain commands for the application. Much like a command-line utility that allows switches to be passed in, a browser allows a URL to be input that can contain parameters and even commands. These commands and parameters often relate to DoS attacks. Mismatches between the command and the correct usage or data could cause unwanted outcomes if they are not handled correctly on the server. Misusing the parameters or using them in unexpected places can reveal security holes or can cause the server to be thrown into unexpected states or even to crash. Test the parameters in unexpected ways to ensure that errors are handled properly. Collect a full list of all parameters with assistance from developers and designers. Document valid parameters, data, and the actions they command.

■ Obfuscation can make it more difficult to get at things (for example, file storage, folder paths—using user name instead of user ID). Storing items in predictable locations can immediately open your application to particular security issues, but relying on unguessable locations does not secure your application. If a malicious user knows exactly where a genuine user's data is stored, it makes that data a much easier target. If, however, the data is not stored in an easily guessable location, it makes for just one more hurdle a malicious user must overcome. It is not a technique to rely on to make your system secure, but it will help prevent some simple scenarios from harming your users. If you are using predictable locations or names to store data, error handling needs to be considered and tested if the anticipated name is already taken. For example, if data is stored by the name of the book club, and two book clubs have the same name, you need some way to allow duplicate book club names, yet have unique data storage locations. If numbers are expected, try the DBCS range of Latin-looking numerals.

- Hidden form fields and client-side data verification should be used only to protect the user; server-side verification should be used to protect the server. Client-side script does not provide security, only a shell of it and some validation. However, it can save a round-trip with the data and more quickly alert users that they have entered invalid data.

- Cookies have gotten a lot of attention as a potential security problem. *Cookies* are small bits of information written to the client machine to help maintain state within and across sessions. Cookies can be exploited to obtain the user's information. Because they can be exploited in this way, care needs to be taken to not include sensitive user data in cookies. Cookies may annoy and confuse users; they have received a lot of bad press so users are more wary about sites that want to pop cookies onto their machines.

NOTE

Internet Explorer 6 has the ability to recognize cookies marked to not allow script to access them, making them far safer than in the past.

Since HTTP is stateless, cookies are one mechanism that applications use in order to personalize the user's experience, so they can have a valid use, but storing personal data in these cookies is a practice that needs to be avoided. Test needs to try altering cookie content to ascertain the effects on the server application. Some questions you can ask when testing cookies:

- Can the user have a satisfactory experience with few effects if they do not accept cookies?

- Is there an alternative code path for this scenario or a downgraded experience?

- Can the cookies be altered?

- Can malicious users get any benefit by faking cookie data?

- Do the cookies contain any sensitive user data?

File sharing is often the cause of many security issues and is the source of many Trojan horse and virus distributions. As was mentioned in the section on escaping, browsers can automatically retrieve and then execute code. You need to take several steps to prevent malicious files from masquerading as safe files, to prevent malicious files from affecting the users. Two such steps are:

1. **File blocking.** Blocking files based on the extension or other criteria

2. **File filtering.** Filtering those files whose extensions are considered safe, but whose content type or other criteria is not

Area owners whose components can save or retrieve files should understand how these areas are covered in their component. Filter files based on extension and content-type.

In addition, attachments may be opened in a secure namespace to avoid malicious execution when opened.

ActiveX controls are one place to be wary. Since these controls are executables whose methods and interfaces can be accessed using script, these can be used to execute code or read and write files. ActiveX controls can be called from a script in an HTML page, using the OBJECT tag (for example, `<OBJECT CLSID="clsid:{#1111111111}">`). Since all class IDs are listed in the registry, a malicious user can quickly look up the ID of any given ActiveX control. The ProgID can also be used to reference the control from script.

Because of the potential for problems, this technology needs to be tested carefully and particular precautions need to be employed, such as having the controls signed. ActiveX controls need to be carefully virus scanned with the most recent virus signatures to ensure that viruses are not spread to customers.

CGI applications can also be problematic because they can also be used to gain control of the server itself. Buffer overruns are a common way to gain access to a server through a CGI program. Because of the potential for exploitation, CGI support should be removed from systems not making use of it. CGI samples should be removed as well as compilers and interpreters in the CGI bin.

NOTE
The Department of Justice had a server defaced through this exact exploitation. This type of exploit is headline catching, and the Department of Justice perhaps got lucky. It would have been just as easy for an attacker to steal data, set in place other security vulnerabilities, or destroy information as opposed to just defacing the Web site.

The server's configuration has an enormous impact on the security of your data and software. If users can go to their browser connected to your site and use the *File → Edit with FrontPage* command or *File → Edit with Word* (see Figure 9.6), and the *Save As...* location points to your server, then you have a configuration problem that must addressed. Your server is wide open for alterations by anyone who has a browser and FrontPage or Word, or even just Notepad, installed.

Also, every piece of software that you are dependent on, from the operating system to the databases, needs to be catalogued. The system administrators must keep all servers current on all security patches and fixes released by the software makers. If your servers are not current, then you will still be subject to these preventable problems.

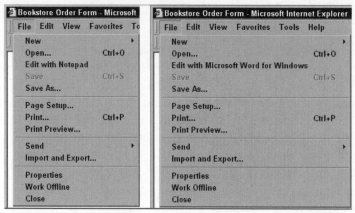

Figure 9.6 Menu options when server configuration allows direct editing of Web pages.

Closing Security Thoughts

I want to end this chapter with a few final security thoughts that you can keep in mind as you approach testing your Web applications:

- The more dependencies you have, the more potential points of failure there are.

- There are some states that you cannot imagine how a server got into or are very difficult to reproduce. For issues such as these, you can manually edit items in the database, inject errors, and use tools to create states that you may otherwise not anticipate hitting. The way to address this type of issue is proper verification and error handling, such as checking values prior to parsing. Tools such as ones that consume all available memory or inject random corruptions into the heap are handy for testing for these issues.

- Be aware of hibernating bugs, places where you can see a potential for problematic scenarios, but cannot work through every step of an exploit to achieve it. Talking with other professionals, other testers, or the developer may help uncover those elusive steps and thereby get the bug fixed.

- Some factors that increase some aspects of your security are the use of technologies and techniques such as SSL, file filtering, script stripping, and escaping. However, just adding and using these features is not enough if they are not implemented well, so they should be tested for effectiveness. If you think any one of these will solve your security issues, then you likely don't fully understand all of your security issues. You cannot build secure systems without understanding the potential threats.

■ Many companies have shipped Web products and in doing so they have found many traps and pitfalls. Learn from these lessons and put preventions in place specifically to close holes your application is susceptible to. Although these preventions are there to increase security, unless they are designed properly and tested correctly, they provide no added security. Security should have layers, but useless layers only give a false sense of security.

Even after analysis and testing, there will be holes and bugs left in either your software or the software dependencies that you have. Because of this fact, the last part of security is planning. Management needs to answer the question what will happen *when* security is breached, not just *if*. How will you go about ensuring that you learn from the mistakes of others? Plan for the scenarios and be prepared for the inevitable.

PART FOUR

Being a Tester

CHAPTER 10

Automation

One machine can do the work of fifty ordinary men. No machine can do the work of one extraordinary man.
—Elbert Hubbard

T oo frequently automation is seen as a magic bullet in testing efforts instead of the tool that it is. No tradesman carries only one tool, and no tester should rely on a single tool or technique. Automation, the subject of this chapter, is one more piece that will help a team deliver high-quality software.

What Is Automation?

Perhaps it would be best to begin with a quick discussion of what automation is from a testing perspective and to define a few key terms and concepts involved with it. *Automation* is the use of any tool to perform those actions that would have otherwise been done manually. Generally, this is the use of scripts or other pieces of code to drive your application. This can be done through the user interface as visible in the browser, or it can be done through direct commands sent from a client to a server to mimic those that the browser would send. Two categories that automation can fit into are as follows:

- **Build verification tests (BVTs).** An automated suite of tests run against a new build of the software to certify that it is stable enough for testing or other purposes. Basic system functionality is certified here. BVTs can also be used on code changes prior to checking them in, to verify that nothing has regressed.

- **Regression testing.** This is testing a scenario that has previously worked. Regression testing is done to ensure that no new code has had adverse effects in other areas, breaking code that previously worked at some point. Bugs that have turned up in this process are regressions.

Automation will run the exact same test in the exact same way thousands of times without complaint. However, automation will never try to do something differently from what it is scripted to do. Because of this, automation is considered to be a suite of *regression tests*—the tests have been conceived and performed previously with successful results. Automation will only catch when bugs are introduced into previously working code. There are exceptions to this, such as when large arrays of data are iterated through for input, or when test tools that create code based on the software or its requirements are used. However, far and away, the bulk of automation falls into the regression category.

What Can Automation Do for You?

Automation is an excellent way to ensure that the software of today is just as good as it was yesterday. In other words, automation is to catch regressions and to loop through many different inputs. By the time that your application is stable enough to write automation against, bugs that automation could have been the first to find have most likely been found and fixed. Many of the bugs attributable to the automation effort are found while writing the automation scripts themselves. Very few new bugs will be found by automation, although new bugs can be found when automation is run in new configurations or when it runs through arrays of data.

Still, automation has a seductive sound to management. It will save time! Reduce the number of testers! Reduce the number of machines! Automation means that we can produce high-quality software faster and cheaper and without as many people involved! Many automation projects fail to deliver what was anticipated of them because those implementing it did not understand that automation is just another piece of the test process, just another tool that can be used.

Automation, large or small, has a place in almost every test project. It will not save any product from poor execution or provide any guarantees, and it can be a time sink if it is allowed to get out of hand. Whereas almost any test effort that is put into place will provide better software than if it were not in place, automation carries no such guarantees. A poorly executed automation effort will end up costing more time and manpower than none at all. However, the benefits are significant if realized. Understand that automation is only there to identify regressions and be the "monkey tester" that doesn't mind running the same test day after day in exactly the same way. Having this task out of the way allows the human software testers to go beyond following simple steps and put their creativity and intelligence to use ferreting out new bugs. Only between 5 percent and 20 percent of bugs are found by automated regression tests. Considering that it can cost upwards of ten times as much to automate a test case as to run it manually one time, without taking into account the upkeep and maintenance that must be done on the test code, the cases to be automated should be selected carefully.

Types of Automation

Automation can take many different forms.

- Starting from the beginning of a software project, the first phase will likely involve direct calls into any APIs that are under development. Developers or architects can provide a list of interfaces along with their expected outputs to allow Test to write very basic automation to call into these, pass in valid data to receive valid output, or pass in invalid data to receive appropriate errors. The reason that these will come first is that these will be the first pieces of code available. Development efforts that require developers to write unit tests can usually be shared with the Test side, providing a partially completed set of API automation. Early on, there will likely be an overlap in the Development and Test efforts. As developers develop scripts to verify the most basic functionality for check-in tests, these can be shared with Test. Vice versa, if Test develops basic verification scripts first, these should be shared with the development team to be run on code changes prior to check-in to ensure basic functions still work as expected. Since Test will likely be in a lull during this phase of the project, and developers will be very busy getting the low levels of the new product into place, it is not unreasonable that Test would take over the role of producing these API tests. For example, in one project, several testers were taken for this type of task, while the rest spent time reviewing specifications, backfilling automation of the legacy code, and ramping up on new technologies. This approach allowed the APIs to become stable, established a baseline of working functions, and prevented regressions.
- Later phases of automation will depend on higher-level functionality being in place, perhaps in the form of the product being able to take requests from a browser and return responses properly, or the product UI being available to use. Many times, automation will not use the UI as displayed in a browser, but will make calls to the servers passing the pertinent information, such as a browser version; accept language, parameters,

and any data to be processed; and then parse the response for the pieces of the response to be validated, or look for error codes. This type of automation can be very fast to write and fairly straightforward to maintain, but it does not test the rendering or the layout. However, since the display and layout are parts that any human tester will notice immediately, that may not be important for your automation to focus on. As resources such as string resources become available and have a UI that is to display them, automation will likely be written to verify that the localized versions of the product are referencing the right resource strings. As the UI is finalized and other components come into place, the layout may be verified from build to build.

In one case, I implemented automation on one project that was highly successful not because of the amount of automation, but because of the cases that were selected. In approaching it, I started with the basic smoke tests, verifying that the application was operable enough to release to the rest of the development team. The automation then went on to verify functionality based on user scenarios, checking the pertinent mathematical operations for proper output as well as other application properties.

More automation will only make for a larger maintenance overhead as well as higher startup costs if it is not done right. Well-done automation will save teams many hours and contribute to the entire development effort.

■ Other types of automation include performance, scalability, and stress testing. These automation areas are not focused on the application's behaving correctly, but rather take some measurement of the server's health or other performance measurement. This measurement may be in the form of CPU utilization, response time, or bytes over the wire, and may help determine that the application's health is appropriate given the test case. The automation may consist only of the various requests that the client browser would send to the server, along with the appropriate parameters and data to properly model a user's interaction. Sending a certain number of requests per minute simulates the system's usage by a certain number of simultaneous users. Increasing the modeled number of users helps to determine the server's behavior under severe loads and moreover its failure points. Holding a set number of modeled users for a long period of time helps determine the mean time to failure (MTTF) for a system.

NOTE
■■■■ The important part of each test is to verify the right thing, and automated testing is no different. Verifying that any response is returned is not useful because the response could be an error. Verifying that the response contains an exact string that you are looking for, such as a value, is of a lot more importance.

Planning Automation

- What is the point of your automation?
- What do you want it to do?
- What do you want to get out of it?

The most critical part of automation is the plan. Planning should range from the high-level overview down to more specific details documenting each stage of the automation effort and how the automation should be written. As the team acts on each stage of the plan during each phase of development, it might be determined that enough automation has been done at a given level and resources may be redeployed in favor of more manual testing or more testing of other areas.

NOTE Planning involves not just creating a schedule and identifing the tasks, but also considering resources.

Some things to consider as you plan automation are the following:

- What machines will the automation be run on? Without having machines dedicated to running the automation, machines will be removed from server topologies or from testers who need client machines. Plan ahead for which machines will be available and what the requirements of these automation clients will be.

- Who will write the tests? Will automation be written by a particular person or team, or will it be written by each individual feature owner? This difference carries with it a significant difference in many of the testing activities around the automation. If each individual will be responsible for his own automation, then libraries will likely be necessary, providing support, education, standards, and documentation.

- Who will be running the automation? Will each individual be responsible for running his automation, or can the task be centralized, perhaps with the person who owns the lab? Again, decentralization may make sense for your project, or a centralized effort may be a better approach.

- Will there need to be databases or other supports put into place, such as source code controls or status Web sites? Not having the proper supports in place can cause any effort, no matter how good the individuals involved, to fail. Some forethought into what the automation effort will need—aliases for individuals to communicate, senior members available for consultation or mentorship, brown bag sessions, documentation, servers, or tools—will give your project better odds of success.

- Is there a dedicated lab for automation (client machines or servers)? If there is not an automation lab, the sensitivity in the automation system may be magnified by being run on many different machines that are not closely configured.

- If the automation relies on external data, can that data be located on an internal share instead of relying on it being put on the local machine? If the necessary data to run the tests or library files that might be referenced by the scripts are located on each individual client machine, then there is overhead necessary to keep each client up-to-date. If, however, each automation client refers to a single common location, then all clients will always be up-to-date and identical.

Your automation plan needs to have discrete sections so that a section of the plan can be carried out at a time as soon as the code is ready to be tested. The sections don't have to cover every detail, such as exact test cases to be automated because that level of information will likely change as the project is carried forth. Rather, sketch out a general path of how the project will proceed and detail resources, processes, and methodologies. This plan also helps indicate when in the process of creating the product such automation will begin, keeping the automation from starting too early or too late.

- Just as you cannot try to run tests too early or the tests will fail because the software is not ready or is not fully implemented, automation cannot be started too early. The product code will be going through too many changes, requiring corresponding automation changes. The product stability may not be there, or features may only be partially ready for extensive testing.

- If automation is started too late, time has been lost and the appropriate fixes may not be able to be made without severe schedule changes or potential instabilities being introduced.

To strike that window when the product is ripe for testing, but time has not been lost, a plan must be in place in order to act with clear purpose. For example, in the online bookstore example I've discussed throughout this book, you could identify several opportunities for automation.

- Smoke tests, or BVTs, would be one very important piece. In the testing plan, these would begin early on. As important functionality is put in place and becomes stable, BVT test cases are added to verify those pieces of important product functionality. A subset of these could be used for basic check-in tests that the developers would run prior to checking in code.

- Basic tests for each functional area or component would be another area for automation. The most fundamental cases might be required to be automated within a week of functionality being available. Any Priority 1 test cases, those that would be run most frequently, might be required within a month of the functionality becoming stable. User scenarios and other frequently run cases might be required before the next full test pass that would include this functionality.

In other words, set a schedule for when pieces of automation should be done and what level of automation is appropriate.

Some automation packages and home-grown harnesses take advantage of features that allow the owner of the case to be emailed when automation passes, or paged if there is a failure. You will have to determine what is the optimal approach for each situation as it comes up. If automation takes several days to run, and email is dodgy, then perhaps a page would be best. Having the system page a person with either a Pass or Fail can help in this situation and prevent somebody from having to sit in front of a machine all weekend.

Deciding What Should be Automated

Have a reason behind every case that is automated. The reason could be to make a suite of BVT level tests to determine basic build stability. Suites can have cases added on to create acceptance-level test suites or comprehensive test passes (where all Priority 1 or Priority 1 and 2 cases are automated). But the important thing to remember is to have a rationale that drives why you decide to automate a certain test.

Some common reasons for automating are as follows:

- If a particular case is to be run frequently, then it may make sense to automate it.
- If a particular case is of high enough importance, then it may make sense to automate it. (Such a case is likely be covered by the previous point, but it bears repeating.)
- Frequently, performance tests and stability tests need to be automated in order to properly determine performance and stability.
- API-level automation will likely be the starting point of an automation effort because the APIs are usually the first components completed when projects are started from scratch.

- Automation can also be used to run through vast arrays of input when test cases can be thought of, but running them by hand would take too much time. An example of this would be to take every identified problem character or problem character combination and iterate through them in every input field to see if script errors appear or if the output is not as expected. These might only be run once, but a quick script that loops through an input and a verification of the proper output can take over this task more efficiently.

When starting to consider automation for your project, think about what platform the user will likely be running the application on. If your product is aimed at a university, then Unix workstations may be the most common client. If your product is aimed at graphic designers, then you may have a substantial user base of Macintosh users. This information has a huge effect on the tools that you can choose from to verify your application. Consider what languages you currently localize the product into and if you may offer any others in the future. Certain packages or individual tools may be limited to supporting only certain code pages, not supporting Far East languages or DBCS character sets, or not supporting Unicode.

Selecting Tools

Once you have settled on a plan for what you want to automate (and have a clear idea of what platforms you are dealing with), you are ready to begin selecting the tools you will use to automate your testing.

Deciding between Tools Packages and Individual Tools

There are a lot of automation tools available in the marketplace, and tools are often developed within the company or team. In a general sense, there are two approaches to selecting tools.

- **There are individual tools aimed at one specific usage or purpose.** It may make sense to select a particular tool for each piece of the automation effort—one tool to script and control the interface, one tool to send direct requests to the server, one tool to verify that the code is written in a standard manner, and any other piece that is identified as necessary or desired. Selecting one tool for each piece of the automation or test plan may make the cost of purchasing the tools cheaper and your solutions more flexible, better fitting your purposes. However, it could cost your team through added confusion from having many different interfaces that testers need to contend with, having to write in different languages and having little coordination between and among the tools. However, selecting each tool on its merits to do one very specific job may get the whole project done better.

■ **There are end-to-end packages that are designed to fit into each other and also fit into development and project management tools.** It may make sense to invest in a particular package that gives your test effort end-to-end solutions to create tests, verify links, verify standard code techniques, and more. Going with a single package allows for certain integration between the tests, perhaps even the ability to hook into a test case manager and defect database. It is also going to be very expensive to purchase.

Depending on your test team's composition, the software, the test plan, available funds, and time, you will find one of these approaches likely makes more sense than the other.

Weighing Your Options

Before deciding which tools and approaches to use, you definitely need to try out the various tools to see if they will support what you want to do with them. Compare their stability, accuracy, ease of use, and any other factors that you are interested in. What is the future of the company, or the tools themselves? What is the level of support available? What if they are internally developed? Some companies charge a flat licensing rate; others charge per installation. If you have many client machines all running automation scripts, per installation licensing can get very expensive very quickly. Many Web sites are available with message boards, ratings, and communities devoted to discussing and helping others with various tools.

Stickyminds.com is a great starting point as a warehouse of information on all aspects of testing. Message boards and discussion sites such as this one collect the information that other people have discovered and found important, and save you time. Yahoo! Groups has many groups set up for all kinds of testing tools, practices, and topics, and you can even start your own group if your particular interest is not covered. You are not looking to these resources to tell you what to do or what tools to use; rather you are looking for insight from other people on what the strengths, weaknesses, and particulars are for tools or processes you are considering.

Weighing the strengths of each tool and the ultimate cost will help you make the decision as to what direction the team should go in.

Download or request trial copies from the companies you are interested in—a 10-day copy might be enough, but hopefully a 30-day evaluation period is available. Create a couple of BVT-level tests and put the system into use as you would if the trial copy were selected as your solution. Have it run the cases every morning and log the results, or send mail and see not only how the tool does its job, but also how it fits in with the talents of the organization that will be coding against it and how it meshes with the current procedures. The evaluation process is not fast, and should not be rushed, but it also should not be started too late.

NOTE

Selecting the right technical solution is only half the problem. If the tool does not fit in with the processes and procedures, then it will still not be a good fit. It may bring welcome change to current poor practices, but those poor practices need to be identified prior to the tool's introduction. Otherwise, the risk of change for the sake of change and the allure of novelty may make for a bad, and expensive, decision.

Attempt to automate several different areas of the product that are each very different in their technology so that the tool's abilities can be determined. Some tools have limitations that may not be found until they are leveraged directly against a particular technical area of the software. One automation package that our team had evaluated had the simple limitation that it could not allow one to double-click inside a table cell that was in another table. This type of HTML appeared in only one place in our product, but it was an area that was slated to be automated. In the end, this limitation was one factor in our ultimate tool purchase decision.

Test automation suites can be very expensive. Many teams waste money by purchasing a software suite and then not developing an effective plan on what to *do* with this new tool. Your team may find that a few free tools can serve all your purposes. Most likely you will want a tool to crawl all your links to ensure that there is a valid page behind each one and there is no link rot. There are free tools to verify that the HTML is standard, that accessibility guidelines have been met, that the script is standard, and more.

CROSS-REFERENCE

A list of various tools and packages can be found in Appendix J.

Writing the Automation

Ideally, any automation project will start small and clean. Start with one individual, or possibly two, to build the framework. The first parts of the automation effort will likely not feel very rewarding or look to management like much is being done. However, a foundation needs to be laid so that common functions are available, the tool that is employed is known to be able to be used in a fashion that suits the project, and the processes can be worked out. The early automation writers will need to carefully take notes as they work, document-ing processes such as setting up the environment to write automation, setting up the environment to run automation, and documenting the peculiarities of the way things work for the project. Having a very quick automation script that can be run to ensure that the environment configuration is correct saves a lot of time in the future debugging false failures. Documenting how to get started writing the most basic of scripts will help get any other tester who has to write or maintain scripts started out right. If the scripts get checked into a source code control system, detailed instructions should be provided to ensure that these get checked in correctly. More likely than not individuals who do not write automation will still need to execute it. Documenting the configuration changes and how to run the automation will save a lot of time in the long run.

Documentation is one of the most important tasks that should be done for any testing effort. I personally like to see documentation written for the average Joe Tester to walk in off the street and generally be able to follow a set of detailed directions on how to configure or install something. Step-by-step instructions, including screen shots and perhaps commentary, will save a lot of time in the future. When other individuals or teams need to set up something, they can be referred to the directions instead of taking up the time of a knowl-edgeable tester to walk them through it.

TIP

A best practice I have learned is to provide a reference of one or two individuals to contact if the directions are out of date or do not work for somebody. Writing these instructions is not out of line with the individual tester's responsibilities or main duties—just start writing down each step the next time you perform a particular task. It will not add much overhead and will save many people a lot of time in the future.

Deciding Where to Start

As I have indicated, one great place to start an automation effort is with build verification tests (BVTs) or smoke tests. These are usually quick and dirty, just designed to verify the most basic of functions to prove that the most basic sce-narios are operable. If the product is operable only at an API level, then that is what the BVTs will test. If the product is fully usable by a customer and is hav-ing additional functionality added (for example, a second release of an exist-ing product), then BVTs may consist of verifying functionality through the user interface as well as lower-level components. If you start this way, you lay out a very small and manageable piece of automation to begin with. Pick out ten or so cases to start with. Should you complete these ten cases and decide that the test architecture is faulty or that it could be done better, it is very easy to go back and rewrite the few automated cases that are in place.

The best way to get started is to have a single person involved, perhaps coordinating with others who also have experience in automating projects that use similar technologies, to get their input on the automation architecture and to review the code. Structure the future of the tests as the groundwork is laid out; externalize variables properly, "componentize" the tests to match the features in the software. For example, if you were approaching the online bookstore example used throughout this book, you might decide on a few smoke tests laid out in the following way:

1. Access the main page.
2. Verify that all images and certain pieces of text are displayed on the main page.
3. Search for the book named *Web Testing Companion*.
4. Verify that one result is found, the author, ISBN, and so on, are correct.
5. Open comments on the book.
6. There should be three comments.
7. Select the book for purchase, using the user account *user00*.
8. The application should prompt for the password, should be using SSL, and so on.
9. Purchase the book.
10. The application should show the appropriate price of $50, no tax, and the appropriate shipping charge of $5.
11. Open the purchase history.
12. The application should show that this book was purchased today, and that no others were purchased.
13. Close session.

NOTE Notice that you aren't just detailing what actions should be performed, but also what the expected outcome is. Without the proper verification, there is no way to ensure that the application is actually working. Code may be exercised, but the output could be completely incorrect.

Adding More Detail

One of the largest advantages to automation is that just the process of writing the automation can chase out more bugs than running the cases ever will. This advantage becomes most apparent in the interactive process of writing the cases in more and more detail, fleshing out the automation cases until there is automation code running.

For example, if you start with our first case from the example using the online bookstore in the last section (accessing the main page of the online bookstore), you could fill it out more, specifying precisely what needs to be done as follows:

Test Case

1. Open the browser (Internet Explorer or Netscape Navigator).
2. In Location, type in *www.oursampleapplication.com.*
3. SendKey ENTER.
4. Our sample bookstore Web site should be found.

Verification

1. logo.jpg is requested and a 200 OK response is returned; the logo is displayed in the browser window.
2. welcome.htm is requested and the 200 OK response is returned.
3. Text displayed is "Sample Bookstore: Here for all your book needs".

Here you have several detailed steps, similar to those in any test case, of what needs to be done to get to a certain point and actually interact with the software. However, how you accomplish these steps and then automate them may vary. You could start by actually opening a Web browser. You would need to locate the location bar either by sending particular keystrokes programmatically to the computer as part of the automation, letting the focus default to that location, sending the cursor to a particular coordinate on the screen, or programmatically setting the value of the location bar to the desired address. The verification could be done through several means. You could bypass any user interface whatsoever and simply pass a request to the server for a particular graphic and then wait for a response and make sure that it's a 200 OK. You could take a screen shot of the main bookstore page and store that as a baseline, comparing all future test runs against that one. This type of verification carries with it the requirement that future test runs of this automated case be on the same platform with the same browser settings, color depth (at least a similar one), and resolution. If you have dedicated automation client machines, this solution may be a perfect one. In a situation where automation is run on just any machine, this same solution may report many false failures and not be a good solution.

To verify that the text sent back to the browser was appropriate, you could set the focus of the browser into the browser frame of interest, invoke the Find dialog, and search for the string of text you wanted. You could also choose to view the source, or save it to a text file, and then search for various pieces of text that way, or you could programmatically grab particular values or hooks that developers set in the code to allow for easy verification.

Once your team has identified which areas to automate and which cases are appropriate for automation, the actual mechanisms that will be employed to drive the application can vary. Depending on the tool you are using to drive the application, the particular technologies involved, and the type of automation (verifying each pixel versus verifying properties on the page), one way will make more sense for your efforts than another. Whichever way you determine to be best, it should be standardized, with libraries written so that others can take advantage of common code and functions. Different application components may have different automation techniques employed. Not locking yourself into one set method everywhere allows you the freedom to select the best mechanism for each area.

Determining Verifications

One of the most difficult parts of automation is verification. The test cases tell you what to put in and where, and then what action to invoke on that data, but sometimes the output is more complex. Should your verification be searching the resulting HTML for a tag or looking at a value of an object? Possibly, you may want to verify the visual layout and results either by pixel location or screen shots. These are the most fragile, but can be very useful when used right. Know what you are trying to test and what constitutes a Pass; all else will constitute a Fail. In other words, for every test it needs to be very clear what the signs of a success and a failure are.

There may be standard verifications, such as specifically looking for errors (script or runtime) and failing a case if they are seen. However, a script error may not be of the level to fail a build and may not, therefore, need to be fixed prior to letting others test the software.

Simply verifying that a test case passed by looking for a 200 OK response from the server is probably not going to be good enough verification. Establishing that a particular HTML tag such as <HEAD> exists in a requested page is too broad to verify that a case has passed. Instead, verify for output based on particular input. Recall Step 10 in the example test cases for the online bookstore mentioned previously in this chapter; in that step a particular price is expected to be associated with the book, a particular amount is to be associated for the shipping cost, and other specifics are made explicit. The general verifications (verifying that the tag <HEAD> exists in the response or that a 200 OK response is returned) are not adequate because that content would be passed back for almost any response from the server. We need a much narrower definition of a passing response, and therefore must make the criteria more specific. Pairing specific input with a particular output will ensure that the functions under Test are behaving as expected.

Should the cost of the book change, or the cost of shipping change, having each of those values externalized in variables allows for a quick alteration to update any test case that uses those pieces of data.

Naming Conventions

Part of the planning should include developing a naming convention for the scripts and functions. Such conventions greatly help in searching for scripts and functions and identifying if an existing one serves a purpose that you are about to write a script for. Some teams break up the naming convention by module. One example would be taking the first three characters of a module's name to indicate which module a script or function tests—if there is a catalog component, the catalog specific scripts may start with CAT, common functions may start with COM, and so forth.

These names could continue to give more abbreviations of the area of the module, or a single word on the action that will be addressed. Tests of a catalog might include searching and placing items in a shopping cart. You might want to name cases for these areas such as CATSRCH and CATCART, then enumerate the individual cases.

The case's priority could also be included. If you grade test cases based on a tier system (colors, letters, or numbers), you can just add that into the case name. CATSRCH01 could become CATSRCH1_01 for the first Priority 1 catalog search case created.

Naming test cases in some easily recognizable way offers a few advantages.

- First, test cases can be clearly attributed to an owner, either a developer or a tester, simply by the component name.

- Second, such naming prevents various areas from naming cases in similar manners and creating confusion, or creating multiple scripts that perform the same function.

- Third, these sorts of names allow a person, at a glance, to see in which order failures should be investigated. The failure of a case named CATSRCH3_01 will likely be investigated after the failure of CATSRCH1_01 because the latter is a higher-priority case.

Your team might have other pieces of information that are important to capture at a glance, so work the system to your own advantage. For example, a case named CATSRCH1_01 could be looked up in a chart or database to see full descriptions of what the case does.

Automated cases come from manual cases. Likely, a case will be identified as important to be manually run before an attempt is made to automate it. A little forethought now will prevent confusion later. Manual test cases need to be named in a logical manner. The automated test cases should match the manual test cases names, and should be enumerated in the same way so that tracking a case and mapping it are easy tasks. There is no reason to develop two naming conventions.

Planning for the Future

Planning for automation doesn't just involve planning in the short term. A useful and effective automation plan considers several issues that involve peering a little further down the road.

Who will be writing the automation in 3 months? 6 months? A year from now? Make sure that the client configuration and any setup steps are as simple as possible and well documented. It will save more time than it takes. When a new member of the testing team is hired or if contractors are brought in, a few days of setting up and examining the system should be enough to get them on their feet and going on to write automation when handed the test cases that need to be automated. If the automation-writing effort will be pushed out further to others, set aside time for training, learning, and producing the tests. Some teams prefer to have one or two individuals devoted to automation. Other teams prefer to give the responsibility to every individual. The process of writing automation should improve the individual tester's understanding of the implementations and the feature areas. Thus, it can make sense to assign this to the feature owner or to grow the team so that after being a feature owner for a period of time individuals begin to automate their areas as well, enforcing good testing practices first and programming second. It depends on the makeup of the team and the individual desires of its members as to which approach is best suited for the project at hand. Code reviews prior to check-in or sample code walk-throughs not only help to educate the team and disseminate information to those in attendance, but also keep expensive overhead in check, making sure that scripts are applied judiciously and making sure that code as well as processes are able to be maintained.

Automation is notoriously fragile. The slightest change in the product can break hundreds of hours of work. A pixel change in an image can fail test cases, as can a change in the ALT text of an image. Stay informed of proposed product changes so you will know if there will be corresponding automation changes to be made. Know when product changes are being implemented so that you can be prepared for the reports of the tests failing and for the fixes that will need to be implemented.

Keeping scripts small and atomic allows you to test only one condition at a time. It also allows you to string several scripts or functions (depending on the framework of the automation) together to accomplish larger tasks. In addition, if there is a change in the product's functionality, then only the atomic scripts that compose the larger tests will need to be updated. The same small atomic case that was broken may be referenced in 500 other scripts. Fixing that one atomic script that corresponded to the product's functionality change, in turn, fixes all 500 dependent scripts. If there is a central location for common functions, it makes it much easier to string these in many different ways and prevents duplicate automation code being written for the same task, which helps greatly in maintaining the automation scripts.

Planning for the next release is necessary, but be careful with such planning. I know I have fallen into the trap of upgrading a purchase or effort, thinking I would get more usage or life out of it. It sounds great to be thinking ahead and to plan on taking the scripts as they are written now and use them in the next release and to save money for future releases. But how much of your product is going to change between now and then? If your user interface, labels, hooks, technologies, or more changes between releases (and they most likely will), how easy will it be to maintain the current scripts? This isn't to say you should toss everything away from one release to the next, but keep in mind that much will be changing underneath you. Be realistic about the lifespan of the automation you are writing now and how closely tied it is to the product code that currently exists. If you are comparing screen shots from release to release, and one graphic or one pixel changes, you need to change the screen shot at the very least, if not some of the code. For example, while I was working at a company that was bought by another, my team and I quickly saw many of our graphics change. This change meant that small branding changes were made all over the product, and many of our verifications had to be updated.

TIP

Externalizing and compartmentalizing all of the strings, graphics, and inputs as variables stored outside the actual cases will make for easier maintenance in the long run and allow you to leverage more in the short run.

Just remember that you need to properly plan from the product's inception in order to test and automate well. For Web testing, this most likely means making sure there are tag IDs for all objects that will need to be accessed through the automation scripts. Accessing IDs through the automation script is one way to automate your Web application. This means that `<A HREF= "main.asp">` becomes `<A HREF= "main.asp" ID=Main_Page>`. Test will have to coordinate these needs with the developers to make sure the tags are all inserted at the time that the code is written and the objects are created. The benefits of this method are that there are no dependencies, no third-party tools are needed, anyone can access or change the ID if necessary, it will work for international versions and localized versions, and there are very few differences in how this works between Internet Explorer versions. The drawback is that since you will likely be using IE's DOM to access them, it works great through IE, but does not interoperate in the same way with Netscape Navigator. Microsoft's Internet Explorer has support for another mechanism that makes automating with it very easy. Active Accessibility provides more information than just the object IDs, allowing the plug-in to grab values, labels, and more for objects where it is provided.

Continuing the Automation Effort

So you've got a small suite of tests selected and written, you're running them on every build to verify the build is good enough to continue testing, and you're ready to move on.

Evaluate the plan. It could stand some revisions at this point for several reasons:

- The automation effort may be going easier than expected and paying off in a big way. In this case the automation effort would likely be extended beyond the original plans.

- Automation may be going slowly. There may be more education to be done and a sharper learning curve to overcome.

- Automation may simply not be showing itself to be worth a large investment on this project. In this case the automation effort would likely be scaled back or would otherwise change configuration.

Regardless of whether the automation effort is expanded or scaled back, the next step to successful automation efforts is in attacking the right tests.

Having each component owner browse through all his test cases and identify cases that are prime for automation is a good start. The newer plan may call for only Priority 1 cases to be automated, or may call for only the end-to-end user scenarios to be automated. The area owners are the best ones to identify which cases are candidates for automation.

While this effort is going on, the current automation owner, who is most familiar with the automation architecture and the plans, needs to work to provide the automation framework of commonly used functions. There may be common functions that are going to be needed by more than one component, for example, starting up the browser and opening the bookstore Web site or logging on to the secure part of the application. It doesn't make sense for every person involved to be writing the same set of functions slightly differently—that makes for more scripts to be maintained in several different ways and takes more time up front to create them. Instead, let one person drive the initial effort and set the framework in place.

NOTE **It is possible for more than one person to own this piece and work together to provide this framework of functions to the team, but they need to work closely with clear communication to ensure that they are not duplicating work and are creating the framework in a consistent manner. Too often, having more than one person writing these initial seeds of the structure results in an inconsistent and mismatched foundation upon which nothing solid can be built.**

Even if there is a single person tasked with laying this framework out, several people need to be involved in daily checkpoints and planning to ensure that the framework is an extensible and flexible one.

So we have a framework, and each person involved has a set of cases to start automating. What next? Here there are again two different approaches:

- A test team can take the approach that each owner is also responsible for his component automation.
- A test team can take the approach that one person (or group) needs to be the automation expert and write automation for the rest.

The composition and interest of the team helps determine which approach will be best. Some testers have an interest in eventually becoming developers. Working on a collaborative effort according to clear specifications and maintaining code others have written can be a good exercise to give them a taste of that type of work. These people may have little interest in devising new test cases, but may be excellent at taking a set of detailed steps and writing code to automate them. On the other hand, there are also many testers who enjoy the more creative side of developing the test cases by thinking through the product architecture, testing, collaborating with developers to identify weak areas, working with business analysts to identify customer needs, or eventually moving into managing people or projects. All of this work needs to be done, the question is who is the best person to do it and how can it best be distributed to take advantage of the talents and interests of members of the team. The team and management need to work to identify the right approach for the project given the resources available.

Rating the Effect

There are many ways to rate the effect of an automation effort:

- Some teams judge automation efforts based on the total number of scripts automated.

- Some base their judgments on the percent of total scripts that can be run by means of automation. This evaluation works only if the initial test cases were thorough in their coverage of the product.

- Other teams measure the effect of automation by how long it took to run all the test cases manually and how long it takes to run them with the automation, yielding a percent time saved measurement. There are some faults to this measurement, but it can be an interesting number anyways.

- Another way that thoroughness can be determined is through code coverage. Since there is a balance on any project between the amount of automated testing and manual testing, identifying the code covered by automation and by the combination of automation and manual test can be very insightful, helping the team to identify dead code, inactive code, or code that is rarely exercised. Identifying the difference between these will also help to grade the effectiveness of each test. Judging a test's effectiveness by code coverage can be misleading, and it can be difficult to get good measurements if there are many or complex DLLs. Code coverage can be taken too far, and out of context, as any metric can be. There is a place for it, however. The concern with code coverage is that it rewards for test code exercising as much of the application's code as possible, and it does not capture how proper the verification is. Each test script written needs to verify proper functionality not just touch as many functions as possible. Theoretically, the higher the percentage of code covered the better and more effective the test cases that are being run. Remember that code coverage does not tell you where you need to test, it tells you where you have been.

- I also suggest a chart to track automation status and history. Not every tester, and definitely not every developer or manager, will have an enlistment in the automation source tree, if there is one, and not every person involved will track the status that carefully. A listing, either in a file or on an internal Web site, quickly allows for these involved people to see what types of cases are routinely failing. An even more integrated approach would be to have the automation itself log status in such a way as to allow a Web page to display real-time results along with the case name, description, and the tester, or even the developer owner. A quick and very visual red or green flag can indicate a pass or fail. (This visual flag is a nice solution, but text will still be required, both for easy searching of a page and for those who may be colorblind.)

Being able to track a history in several ways is very useful. Viewing archived data by build will show how many automated cases of various levels failed. For example one useful display of data would be to view automation failures by build juxtaposed against the tiers of test cases. Consider Table 10.1.

In Table 10.1 you can clearly track your build failures, and even chart them out if that makes for a better display of our information.

- You could chart this table as a bar graph, tracking the rise and fall of various classes of automation failures.

- You could chart this as a pie graph, looking at the percent of total automation that failed.

- You could even chart it as a line graph, if that's just how you prefer to see the data.

In the case of Table 10.1, you can see that you have gone from 25 percent of BVT cases failing in build 4420 to 100 percent passing in build 4422; so as long as our BVT cases have stayed the same, we can read this as having increased the stability of our builds. Our Priority 1 cases have decreased their failure rate from 47 percent to 5 percent over the course of the builds. This is one indicator of higher stability in the software. However, it is completely possible that there were problems in the automation scripts and that no product code was changed between the builds. In that case, you can't correlate the higher passing rates to better product stability, but to initial faulty automation falsely reporting errors in the product.

- Another historical way to view the automation effort would be by case. CATSRCH1_01 may be a Priority 1 case, but may have failed on the last 30 builds. Is there something wrong with the case or is the functionality really broken in our product? Tracking the automation status in this way can point out more precisely if the small handful of failures lies in a single feature and therefore share a common core bug, if they are distributed throughout the product, or if they can be traced to faulty automation code.

Table 10.1 Tracking Various Types of Test Case Pass Rates over Many Builds

	4420	4421	4422	4423
BVT	3 fail/12	1 fail/12	0 fail/12	0 fail/12
Prio 1	28 fail/60	28 fail/60	12 fail/60	3 fail/60
Prio 2	38 fail/120	38 fail/120	24 fail/120	12 fail/120
Prio 3	52 fail/320	52 fail/320	50 fail/320	48 fail/320

WARNING

Since numbers are numbers and are susceptible to interpretation, you need to view them from several perspectives to get an accurate picture of the state of the software.

Constantly evaluate the effect of automation. If the effort is beneficial to the team, then continue down the same path. If it is highly expensive and has proven to have a steeper learning curve, then it might be best to assign one person to make the first forays into the automation effort and have the rest of the team follow after the groundwork is laid. It might even make sense for management to hire a specialist, either full time or as a contractor, to get the automation going and train the team in proper practices. Without evaluating the cost and the benefits, there is no way to judge if the effort is going well or if it needs to be adjusted.

Implementing Good Practices in Automation Development

Since the automation effort will likely start small with one, or possibly two, individuals writing the foundation of functions and initial scripts, bugs will be worked out of the process and prevent the entire team from hitting the same roadblocks while still making headway towards automated suites. There are many good practices to consider that could fit in with your team's project. Laying out coding standards for the automation will help ensure that no matter which team member wrote a piece of the automation, any other member can maintain it or make use of it. Coding standards can be particularly crucial if there are testers trying to evolve their position into that of developer. They need the experience of writing to team standards and having their code reviewed not only on the basis of if it is correct, but also on if it meets those standards. Whether conscious of the fact or not, some may write obfuscated code because it looks more impressive and ensures that ownership stays with them. Staking out a claim in this manner is not uncommon but should be guarded against because it is a sign of a poorly implemented and poorly managed effort. There may be need for complexity in some places, but more often than not there are very simple ways to accomplish the goals. Good practices that help avoid the obfuscated code issue include the use of many meaningful comments and clearly written and formatted code.

- Since we are not as concerned about code bloat or the size of installation space, take the time and effort to insert good comments. Good automation efforts will lay out requirements for comments such as logging comments on entering and exiting functions. It could be as simple as logging a few lines to a text file such as `+++ Starting function searchCatalog` when a function is entered and `--- Exiting function search Catalog` when it is exited. Failures, errors, or asserts would be logged in easy-to-see manners, such as !!!!!!! FAILURE !!!!!!! Not only is this easy to see when skimming a text file, but it is a unique string and easy to search for. Often in automation debugging is done through the use of logs. Commentary becomes the trail by which failures are tracked down. Logging the entrance and exit of functions as well as other important pieces will give important information when you are attempting to debug failures.

■ Writing readable code will also help here. Don't try to do something in one line in a convoluted way that can be broken out to a few simple steps. Automation generally doesn't consume the CPU or memory too heavily and doesn't take up much bandwidth, unless it is performance related, so it can afford to be heavier than product code would be. Write code for the purpose it is intended. The purpose here is to automate a user action or set of inputs, not to devise an ingenious method for doing something, resulting in confusing anyone attempting to maintain the code.

Final Automation Reminders

Of the points I've covered in this primer to automation, here are some key ones to remember as you consider automation in your testing efforts:

■ Starting the automation effort before the product can support the testing will only make more work through extra maintenance and rework. Starting the automation effort too late will not leave enough time to complete the goals. Clear triggers and best guess estimations of time to completion give any project the best odds for success.

■ For each phase of the development of the application, the test cases you intend to automate or the product feature areas that need to have test cases developed and automated have to be clear.

■ Not all tests can be automated easily, and not all tests should be automated. Look for the ability to reuse code, the frequency with which the test should be run, the importance of the test case, and the risk associated with poor quality in the component, to decide if automating that feature or that test case is worth the time and effort of writing *and maintaining* the script.

■ Be prepared and set expectations for other test activities to slow down while in an automation mode, either for one person, or for the entire team.

■ It is important to identify what the goals are and what a successful effort is. Otherwise, you have no measurement if you are done and no way to grade how close you have come to the goals to reflect back on for the next project. Since automation is only one small piece of the total test effort, its role and expectations should be explicitly called out in any master test plan guiding the team.

Finally, automation complements smart testers and takes the daily drudgery of performing the same action over and over away from them. Automation will dutifully repeat test after test for days on end, never failing to perform them in precisely the same way. Automation never gets tired or burnt out or forgets to do a step. But automation is no replacement for a smart tester. Automation can only verify that the software is as good today as it was yesterday. This does not give any reading on quality, but tells you only that the actions that could be performed on previous builds can be performed on the latest build. The whole key to having a successful automation effort is to keep it in perspective. The point is not to automate everything, or to use the automation tools to their fullest. The goal is to ship high-quality software for the lowest cost possible. Automation is one method to use to get there. Just because one approach worked for one company, or one group in your company, does not mean that it is the right approach for your group. Do what works for you.

CHAPTER 11

Test Planning and Design

When all you have is a hammer, every problem
starts to look like a nail.
—Maslow

P erhaps the best way to set the stage for the discussion of test planning and design in this chapter is to indicate to you both what this chapter is and what it is not.

What This Chapter Is

I still need to discuss some basics of test planning and the flow of the work that will progress through the software development process. I want to touch on some basics and some highlights here about what methods may be employed and the general layout of what will happen and when.

What This Chapter Is Not

This chapter is not a complete guide to planning a testing project. Being able to plan a project and manage the testing activities over the product's life cycle is not something that can be completely taught in a book, and certainly not in a single chapter. Fully discussing test planning or design is a subject that takes up many books, and test planning is an ability honed over many years of experience. I want to give only a general overview to help you, as an individual tester, recognize the stages of development and understand the decisions being made, not provide a fully instructive course on test designing or planning.

Why Plan?

One hard truth of testing is that not everything can be done at once. Each phase of the effort needs to be clearly defined and purposeful. There needs to be a clear trigger that opens the gate for each phase to start, and once the goal of that phase is reached, it can be evaluated to decide if the effort is complete or if more work on that phase would be of value. There is a time to start each piece of the plan and a time to hold off until a more appropriate point in the project. Taking the testing one step at a time not only allows the software to be mature enough to work with, but also allows each team member involved to become proficient in each step before beginning the next and ensures that work is performed at the right time instead of too early or too late.

What to Plan

It is very difficult to have a whole plan laid out only to realize that not all of it can be acted on immediately. The danger of such effective planning is that many try to rush ahead because the path is clear, endeavoring to look busy on the tasks that are laid out.

NOTE

Management, who should be the first to see that rushing the tasks only results in poor execution, is sometimes the culprit here because they often want to move on a task as soon as it can be identified.

But moving ahead too quickly is completely wrong, and the work done by those who rush ahead needs to be redone when the time is right because the activities will not be successful at that stage. Because of this, the plan needs to identify the phases of testing as well as what keys and criteria need to be in place that will open the gates to those phases.

In order to identify and sketch out the test activities, there needs to be a plan. There will, in all likelihood, be several plans. The process of planning the activities is different from the test plan. Inevitably something in the way of a plan will need to be written down, documenting the identified activities that will need to happen. In small efforts involving a single person, an effective planning process may be limited to a few notes that are written about what needs to happen. In other projects, there will need to be a master test plan describing the overall test activities for the entire project and calling out smaller pieces that will be documented individually, as well as the resources to be allocated. Features or efforts (such as performance or security) may have their own test plans. From these, the test cases could be created. Depending on the process that the effort is following, there may be a lot of overhead and team involvement or it may be very autonomous and directed completely by the area owner. The test plans will not only call out the activities that will take place, but also the resources that will be involved in each activity, and the parties who will be responsible for the planning and work.

Methodologies

Many teams adopt a methodology to help them create better software or to match customer requirements. Some customers, particularly government agencies or international customers, may require that companies follow one of the ISO certification paths. Other companies may select a methodology based on what promises them the most benefits or sounds trendy enough to gain customers. And still other teams look at methodologies as having something to offer them, as a safety net, to help ensure that they have done the best job possible on their software.

Any methodology is just a collection of best practices formulated into a coherent picture. As I have discussed throughout the book, not every best practice is going to work for every team, project, or application. Some even contradict each other, depending on where they are applied and by whom. The methodologies are merely sets of best practices that have worked for somebody in the past. Given your particular set of people, the technologies used, and the approach to the software, certain best practices may make more sense to you than others. Take what works, alter what may help, and discard the rest.

Certain methodologies may dictate what tools are to be used. The tools provided by any particular methodology may work "out of the box" for your purposes, or they may need to be altered slightly. A pen is a tool. A piece of paper is a tool. Using them to write out a grocery list before going to the market is a best practice. You may find that using a pencil is better for you, or using a PDA may be the right solution. It all describes the same general best practice of knowing what you want from the market before you go there, but the tools used to track that information are different. There is nothing wrong with altering the way the practice or the tools work, as long as, once it is altered, it works better for the team than if it were not there at all. Process must not get in the way of the real work. It must help you toward the end of creating better software and not merely be red tape.

TIP Anything that is difficult or tedious to do will not be done or will not be used in the way that it is intended.

Take, for example, the best practice of including all pertinent information in a bug report the first time it is logged. This practice is an issue that many teams struggle with. A simple tool to help a team follow this practice is to make available bug templates that contain the formatting for the bug so that all the information will be filled in when applicable. The tool in this example helps the tester to use this process because it reduces the amount of work that tester has to do. The individual can alter the tool (text file) easily so that it applies to their particular aspect of the product without diminishing the effect on the outcome (having full bugs logged).

Formal Methodologies

One thing my father taught me was to never force mechanical equipment. "Something will break and frustrate you," he would say, and he is a big advocate of avoiding frustration. If a tool doesn't work or can't easily be adapted to work for you, don't bother. If a process doesn't work for you, discard it and find something else. I want to give you more tools and illustrate potentially useful processes so you can more accurately identify problems and solve them better than if you didn't have that information. Good tools make you more effective. Tools that are poorly matched to their task only take up your time and frustrate you. And good tools become poor tools when they aren't used right or when they are not used in the right place. No tool, in and of itself, is good or bad, and no process is inherently beneficial or detrimental.

There are many formal methodologies that can be followed, each promising perfect software and more profits at the end. Just because they have a name does not make them any better (or any different, in some cases) from what your organization may all ready be doing. Considering that there are excellent pieces of software that have shipped without a single formal methodology being employed, they certainly are not necessary. And many software projects that employ these techniques never manage to be completed, so they are no guarantee of quality or even success. However, they are a collection of best practices, some of which may be very useful to your organization.

Below is just a sampling of some of the more popular methodologies in use in software development efforts. There are many other methodologies out there, and many more that will be devised.

Rational Unified Process (RUP)

The Rational Unified Process (RUP) is a commonly implemented practice for software projects. The unified methodology calls out four distinct phases of creating software and generally follows this methodology:

1. Software is designed through detailed design documents.

2. Software is constructed.

3. Software is tested.

4. Software is released.

It describes six main best practices:

- Manage requirements.
- Develop iteratively.
- Develop in components.
- Verify the software quality.
- Visually model the software.
- Apply source code control mechanisms.

The entire process relies on having many tools to support the various phases and aspects. Rational, the company that developed and espouses the methodology, also sells these tools. From my experience with them, I can say that they are tools that can have a place in an organization; however, it is very difficult to follow the methodology closely without all the tools because they fit together and are tightly integrated with the RUP process. Some excellent tools such as Rose, Purify, and Robot are able to be used as standalone tools or as part of their larger suites of tools that fit in with their methodology. RUP takes into account both QA efforts and test efforts. It has many best practices that can be taken and applied to a variety of organizations outside the tools or the master process they support.

One organization that I was a part of started implementing parts of RUP. It did bring more order to the chaos of the development effort so that instead of each small development team coding at their own pace, checking in, and abandoning that code to write new features, the team was pulled into better communication through having a defined path laid out for them. It provided a template where the teams filled in the blanks for their particular pieces of work to be done.

CROSS-REFERENCE

More information about the Rational Unified Process can be found at the Rational Web site at http://www.rational.com/products/rup/index.jsp.

Capability Maturity Model (CMM)

Carnegie Mellon's Software Engineering Institute devised the *Capability Maturity Model (CMM)* as a way to evaluate the maturity of the software process being used in any development effort. It describes five basic levels that an organization can fall into, ranging from a chaotic "Initial" maturity level all the way up to an "Optimized" level, involving continuous process improvement through quantitative feedback. There are many academic papers on this methodology and tools available to evaluate the software development organization. This methodology is very much aimed at identifying where the software process is right now and what needs to be done to improve it. Again, it is aimed at QA because it is a mechanism aimed at improving quality and not at testing to identify bugs.

The benefit that this offers to organizations is a defined criteria for evaluating the value of the entire development effort. Since the criteria is identified by an outside group, it may not accurately describe your organization. The second advantage is that it describes how to improve an organization, moving it from a low level to a higher one. Examining the criteria should let you lift certain criteria and have an idea at how to go about making improvements in your particular organization.

CROSS-REFERENCE
■■■■■■ **More information about CMM can be found at the SEI's official site: http://www.sei.cmu.edu.**

Six Sigma (6σ)

Six Sigma is usually identified with manufacturing rather than software, but it is gaining a following in software as well. The Six Sigma methodology is different from the rest in that it does not try to map any development effort or dictate sets of processes. Instead, it provides a framework for individuals to use to refine the processes they have in place already, to identify the processes that work well, and to pull out the ones that do not. It is intended to help identify the best practices for the organization and to measure the current processes' effectiveness as well as their variations. It is not so much a methodology to apply as a means to analyze particular problems in an organization and their solutions.

At its heart it is very simple, requiring organizations to clearly identify their problems, causes, and paths to solutions while tracking the improvement that can be attributed to them. It completely depends on the implementer as to how effective it is. Much of what it calls out would already be done by a good manager if there are good managers in the organization with the power to effect processes. One nice aspect of Six Sigma is that a project can be conducted almost under the radar of others in the team if desired. An individual tester can use the framework to analyze his own work and expand the process bringing others under the umbrella of processes that have proven themselves.

Six Sigma defines five stages to process improvement and requires the results to be measured so that a metric of improvement can be assessed at the project's end. The five stages of this are:

1. Define
2. Measure
3. Analyze
4. Improve
5. Control

Within each of these stages, Six Sigma encourages evaluating particular factors, clearly identifying problems, their causes, and possible solutions. A single manager can use it behind the scenes to evaluate the project and the processes being employed. A single analyst can use it to analyze how the entire team is going about producing software. The best practices that it specifies to evaluate the current processes are easily altered to fit almost any problem. Again, this methodology can be a red tape or process-heavy effort, or it can be very transparent, simply guiding the steps of a team or a project. More often it is used to identify current problems and work on solving them, but it can be used for preventing problems in projects as well. Since it is more a collection of best practices and an approach to identifying problems and their solutions than a tool specific process, it is very flexible.

CROSS-REFERENCE
More information about Six Sigma can be found in many places on the Internet; one of the more comprehensive collections of information can be found at http://www.isixsigma.com.

Extreme Programming and Extreme Testing

Extreme Programming and Extreme Testing represent a methodology that consists of a collection of best practices that are mostly applied in small to medium-sized efforts with few people. This methodology is far less formal and more recently developed than others we've discussed. Some of the practices that it puts forth are:

- Paired programming (and paired testing)
- Developers documenting unit tests prior to coding

- Tests written for every bug found that will catch the same bug if it regresses

- Liberal use of automation

Extreme can be a lightweight effort or it can take up many resources if people are paired up and are not the type who work well in that environment. Because of some of the paired collaborative efforts, where each person contributes and learns from the other, it has gained wide use in academic environments where classes can be broken out into pairs for projects.

CROSS-REFERENCE
More information on Extreme Programming can be found at http://www .xprogramming.com.

ISO Standards

The International Organization for Standardization devised many standards that organizations can choose to meet, and those same organizations can have external auditors assess their ability to meet the standard. Certification of an organization to one of these standards can mean more customers or the ability to sell to certain governmental or international entities. The ISO 9001 standard was not initially written with software in mind, so the 9000-3 standard was written to help guide software organizations in how to apply it to themselves. The ISO standards are heavy on documenting definitions, requirements, resources, procedures, and designs. Many of these documents are produced in non-ISO 9001 efforts; the key here is that they are formatted in a certain way and include very specific pieces of information that are required by the process. It has its purpose in certain organizations, but other organizations may end up treating it as a paper to be filled out instead of sandpaper refining their project and processes. If the organization is going to treat the documents as merely more papers to be filled out without a feedback mechanism, then employing such documentation is wasted overhead. If the organization is intending to learn from the exercises that are required, then the effort will likely pay off.

CROSS-REFERENCE
The ISO standards can be found at the official Web site (http://www.iso.org) and are further referenced in Appendix K.

My Advice

Read as much as you can, document your current practices, abstract each practice, distill each to its essence, then pick and choose the ones that work best for your project. You may faithfully follow one for one project and find a completely contrary one for the next. Neither one is wrong as long as they move you towards the ultimate goal which is to make better software more cheaply.

The most important point here is to choose and continue to use what works well for the team. Don't discard something just because you don't know much about it, and don't take everything in one methodology just because it's all part of the same package. Evaluate each piece that you add to your effort and apply what works.

I heard this story from a friend who was interviewing at a company. He said that he asked them if they did code reviews among the developers. "No, that's for ISO 9003. We're a 9001 company," was the reply. Could code reviews have helped that company? Possibly. Should they be dismissed just because they belong to a different package? No! Good processes must be lauded as useful, and poor processes need to be kept in check.

Any sort of bad process needs to be stopped as soon as it is recognized. Gateway identified that there was a break-even point of 13 minutes for customer service calls. It then implemented a process whereby any customer service representative who was on a single call for more than 13 minutes would be ineligible for their monthly bonus that month. The result of this was that representatives did whatever they had to in order to keep the calls to less than 13 minutes, including pretending the line was not working, hanging up, or just sending the customer new parts, all of which are expensive alternatives to a few long phone calls. Customer satisfaction fell, and the referral business went from 50 percent to 30 percent. When Ted Waitt, the founder and former CEO of Gateway, took back over the company, he revoked this process. How long would it have stayed in place had he not stepped in? Why did it stay there even as long as it did? Their customer satisfaction ratings began a quick climb after he revoked the process. In other words, avoid stupid processes. Even if one comes about from good intentions, revoke it as soon as possible or otherwise alter it into a more workable solution. Finally, when finishing one project and starting another, don't forget what went well in the last project. Try to apply those practices where you can.

The processes that your organization uses may be formal or may be very informal. The important thing is that all processes be clearly communicated to all the people involved.

Approaches

Aside from using a methodology, there are several approaches that may be used to try to produce an effective testing effort. Likely a mixed bag of these will be used, the balance of them changing from project to project.

Scenario-Based Testing

Scenario-based testing is one way to document the software specifications and requirements for a project. Scenario-based testing takes each user scenario and develops tests that verify that a given scenario works. Scenarios focus on the main goals and requirements. If the scenario is able to flow from the beginning to the end, then it passes. Scenario-based testing works well for some of the following situations:

- In certain applications, such as internal IT applications or applications that will be used only by specific users in a company, such as those taking phone orders for a catalog, this approach may suffice. Random users off the street are not given access to such internal or specific applications, so random malicious users may not be as large of a consideration.

- The approach works well for usability tests, too. If a usability specialist has a user scenario, he can then walk potential users through the interface given that set of interactions. The aim of this is to turn up poor designs or user expectations that may not have been realized.

- If the development department is focused on chasing every last bug out of their own code and thorough unit testing, then it may just be hooking the components together and ensuring that the interfaces between them work well that is left to the test team. However, as we know, this focus does leave the possibility for many security holes and failures to occur outside the scope of simple verification.

- Scenario-based testing is excellent for end-to-end testing. Having a full scenario ensures that the full user interaction with the software is seamless and that the components on a development level are not seen from the perspective of the user.

The scenario-based test might read like this:

1. User accesses Web site and clicks Catalog link.
2. User enters the name of a book, *Web Testing Companion,* and clicks Search.
3. User is brought to the info page about the book.
4. Verify that the book has one review by Joe User.
5. Verify that the price is $50.
6. User clicks Buy Now link.
7. User is shifted to the secure section of the Web site and is given the purchasing form.
8. User types in valid name, address, credit card, selects 2 copies of the book; price total is $100, with an additional $5 for shipping.

9. User clicks Log Out and is back at the nonsecure portion of the Web site.

10. Verify that no user information is stored on the machine at this time.

11. User can close browser and leave the machine.

12. Verify that the order is properly placed in the database.

13. Verify that two copies are reserved for the user.

14. Verify that an email is sent to the user confirming the order complete with tracking info and the total amount charged, as well as an estimated date of arrival (calculated from shipping estimates and inventory backlog).

This example is a completely verification-based set of tests, ensuring that a user can complete the desired actions from end to end. It can be drawn up in other ways, such as a table with a first column for the user action, and a second column for the system's response to provide more detail. To avoid writing out the same scenario hundreds of times, a second section can be provided at the bottom for alternate inputs, especially if it touches many components in the software and crosses many areas. Essentially, this is verifying that all the pieces go together as expected. Individual test cases can be seen in here (a set of test cases for opening the bookstore Web site, a set of test cases for searching in the catalog, a set of test cases for verifying prices, and so forth).

Eventually, however, all projects need to verify that these user scenarios work well, as most problems do not come from an individual component but rather from combining them and letting them interact.

Model-Based Testing

Interaction is what model-based testing is all about. Model-based testing takes the application and models it so that each state of each input, output, form, and function is represented. Since this is based on detailing the various states of objects and data, this type of testing is very similar to charting out states. Many times a tool is used to automatically go through all the states in the model and try different inputs in each to ensure that they all interact correctly. This procedure can work very well because the automation takes care of much of the verification. However, entering every state and modeling the software is an extensive effort not to be underestimated. Pieces of this approach are easily adapted into test case development without modeling the entire product prior to specifications being implemented by the developers. What this ultimately does is push Test to be involved in the application-planning state, and instead of "putting the application together" in their head during spec review periods and testing the interactions there, they put it together in the model and let the machine test the component interactions. Model-based testing can give the test organization a voice in the development process and backup data to force others to see issues prior to implementation. In a perfect world, Test should not need a tool to let them voice concerns and aggressively pursue the best designs, but in some organizations this type of testing can lend them the muscle and the power to move forward in the process.

The test cases generated from model-based testing will be more atomic than those you generated in scenario-based testing, for example:

- **Test case**: CATSRCH1_01.
- **Setup**: You will need to be at the catalog search page to start.
- **User action**: Type in *Web Testing Companion* and click Find.
- **Expected outcome**: Book should be found—input is valid.
- **Other input**: Try not inputting any characters, inputting a number, a space, or a symbol, and clicking Find.

Since each of these test cases is written in this atomic fashion, they should be able to be pieced together, almost like tile, to cover the various code paths. The Find function is being tested here. Another set of cases ensures that the proper entries have the correct supporting information associated with them. Using code coverage as a measurement helps identify if there are code paths that are not being tested. These atomic cases are then easy to hand to any person familiar with the automation system to be automated. Once automated, or even while still in the written form, the atomic cases can be strung together to create user scenarios.

NOTE Model-based testing and scenario-based testing are really two sides of the same coin. Several model-based test cases strung together really create a user scenario, and user scenarios, when broken up, will render the more atomic model-based test cases. The balance is determined by what is more important to your testing effort and what works best given the tools, personnel, technology, and product.

Writing Test Plans

Books have been written on how to write test plans and how to plan your testing effort. I just want to discuss some of the higher points of this writing here and leave the rest to deeper reading when you need to delve further into this side of the effort.

Coordinating the Test Plan with Project and Development Plans

With all the formulas and methods out of the way, there is still the task of planning the testing effort. These plans will likely start at a very high level, covering the entire test project from a "satellite" view. It will likely call out the resources and milestones and some key events such as beta releases and conferences that may be crucial to making a market window. A test manager or other person at this level will most likely be the one creating this map to get from the beginning of the project to the goal of a shipped piece of software drawing on the development documents and specifications to help plan events and triggers. It has to match the development roadmap and complement it (see Figure 11-1).

1. The Master Test Plan will likely describe components and the estimated timeframe during which they will become available from the developers, answering the questions of what can go wrong and what will be done when that happens.

2. The owners of each of these components or the leads whose team owns the large components will then need to write out more detailed test specifications for component test plans. These serve to break out areas within the component and document that area as well as its interactions with other areas. These plans may be reviewed by a manager or there may be open reviews where the developers involved and other testers are invited to give feedback and ideas on what else should be considered.

3. Feature test plans are then broken out from the component test plan by each individual feature's owner. These are likely to be collaborative efforts, with the lead and peers reviewing the plan and making suggestions on areas to concentrate on.

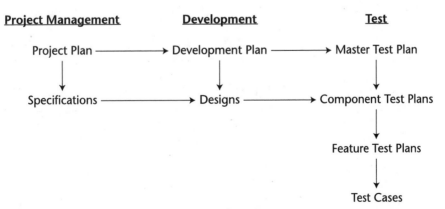

Figure 11-1 General flow of information influencing test plans and test cases.

4. Test cases are then individually broken out of the feature test plans. Again, leads, peers, and the developers involved will likely play a role in recommending areas to test and specific test cases. Often these discussions get very specific, and some great test cases come from them. Although test cases are not the specific topic of conversation for the higher-level feature test plan I am discussing in this chapter, they are the next step. Test cases need to cover valid input for any feature, valid input that is unexpected or known to be problematic, as well as invalid input. Invalid input needs to be covered because the purpose of test plans is not just to test what works, but also to make sure that things that are supposed to fail do actually fail, and fail in the right way.

Table 11-1 draws these steps together into tabular form.

Table 11-1 Ownership of Various Pieces That Will Together Constitute the Test Plans

WHAT IS IT?	WHO IS RESPONSIBLE?	WHO ELSE MAY BE INVOLVED?	WHAT DOES IT DEPEND ON?
Master Test Plan	Test manager	Development manager, business analyst, vice president, or other high-level position	Development Plan and Project Plan
Component Test Plan	Test leads or individual area owners	Leads, managers, possibly the developers who are actually developing the component	Master Test Plan, other Component Test Plans, developer designs, and specifications
Feature Test Plans	Individual area owners	Leads, peers (to review), and the developer responsible for the feature	Component Test Plan, developer designs, and specifications
Test Cases	Individual area owners	Input from peers, lead, and developer of the feature specifications	Feature Test Plan, developer designs, and specifications

The project plans affect the development plans, which in turn affect the test plans. There may be overall roadmaps, objectives, or other guiding statements, but somehow this effort will be documented and staked out. Analysts will develop specifications for various components, which will affect the development designs. The component test plans, which fit into the Master Test Plan, are written mapped to a development component design. From here features within the component are detailed if the components are large enough, then test cases are drawn out and detailed as to planned inputs and proper outputs.

Designing the Test Plan for Use within the Test Team

The Master Test Plan is not just a guide for management, but should be applicable to the individual tester as well. It should be relatively clear what the makeup of various time slots is—some weeks may be reserved for regression testing, some for stabilizing the product, some for international testing, and some for running all cases of a particular priority. This clarity regarding what time is to be spent where has a couple key benefits:

- The Master Test Plan should give each individual tester enough information to really feel like an informed member of the team instead of someone who just shows up and does a bit of work.

- The Master Test Plan should help you, as the owner, have a schedule of your tasks in your head and understand how they fit in with the whole team effort. You may have a list of things you would like to get around to doing, such as reconfiguring parts of the test lab, filling out more test cases for a new area, spending some time with ad hoc testing of your component, and more. You should have a fairly clear idea of when you are likely to get to each of those tasks—based off the schedule you should see of other teamwide efforts. You should have a general idea of when a very busy week of work is on the horizon and when the scheduled tasks look light. You should see from the developer communications giving feedback to the test organization roughly when particular components will become available and when they will really be stable for active testing. None of this work is just for the sake of work. Each piece needs to have a purpose and to be used to its fullest to achieve that purpose.

Other Concerns When Writing the Test Plan

Some teams see commonalities between each of the different features, such as accessibility, globalization, and more. These areas may be considered to be *common areas* because each tester needs to run these types of tests against his own area. A general set of test cases may be developed for testers to run against their area to ensure that the right general tests are being applied to each area. Other features have interactions for which it may be difficult to separate out the owners. The test plans should call out who owns the testing of each piece to ensure that no area is skipped or that several people are not testing the same cases on a single area.

Some teams may consider issues such as performance, automation, security, or other global issues to be a component requiring its own test plan. Others may write a general test plan and refer to the component test plans for the specific criteria and test cases to be performed by the area owner. Neither one is wrong, and the direction will depend on the software, team, and personnel involved.

Communicating Within the Plan

As I indicated in the previous section, members of the test team should know what their role is and what their team's role is in the product's development. They also need to understand what they should expect from the others involved. It is only when individuals have met the expectations of others that trust can be built between them or in the organization. And it is only through setting realistic and well-understood expectations, for both the person delivering and the person receiving, that those expectations can be met in a consistent manner.

The test team should be involved in inducting the new developers, analysts, project managers, and others because they are most usually the keepers of the processes and can clearly communicate them to these new members. Many of these nontesters have not worked with a formal testing effort before and do not know what to expect from the test group, or what the test group expects from them. Issues such as bug assignments, check-in processes, and the like should be explained to ensure that the new employees know the best way to work together as a team. This communication is the only way to have your team set up for success, instead of relying on a sink-or-swim, long road to discovery of what others readily can communicate. If you, as an individual tester, are unsure of what is expected of you, or what you should be expecting of others, it is your responsibility to clarify those relationships. It is also your job to work to understand these expectations. Nobody will hand you a sheet at the beginning of the day with precisely bulleted points for what you need to do, whom to talk with, and what to give them. It is your job to work this out through clear communication with your management and your peers.

Where Will You Start?

Likely, when you are hired into a team, and especially as a novice tester, you will be executing somebody else's plan. It's not that you are incapable of producing such plans, but just that there are others who will likely produce better ones (simple truth be told). Execute what is there, and make notes as to what could be done differently and what is done well. It will soon enough be your turn to step up to full ownership, from the initial inception and to plan the testing effort of your component from scratch. Using your notes and experience will help you turn out an effective and professional set of plans on your first try.

As you proceed through executing somebody else's plans, you will think of new test cases to try. Some may not be applicable, but are still good test cases for some other piece of software, just not yours at hand. You should not discount your aptitude as a tester for finding what otherwise is a good test case.

The test plans need to take into account the resources available and enumerate the activities that the organization will be involved in. The plans, both high-level and low-level, need to clearly indicate those who will be responsible for the work as well as a definition of what work will be accomplished and within what expected timeframe. Without a clear communication of the plans, they cannot be effective. The most ineffective plan is the one nobody knows exists.

CHAPTER 12

On Being a Professional Tester

I'm Mr. Wolf. I solve problems.
—Mr. Wolf, Pulp Fiction

P eople often become software testers by accident. I have not met a single person who has said "I always wanted to be a tester" or "I went through college just to be a tester." More likely testing is a profession that those who practice it stumble upon.

- Sometimes they are on their way to something and see testing as a stepping stone, allowing them to get into a company they want to work for, or into the profession they truly desire to be in (most likely development, but also management).

- Other times they are trying to leave something, perhaps a profession that has a high degree of uncertainty. They may have taken a few courses to gain the rudiments of technical knowledge and are trying to get into something, anything, with more stability, and software is their identified goal.

There is nothing wrong with any of these reasons, or the simple twist of fate that lands many in the field of software testing. Problems arise when individuals "check out" and are not putting effort into their job or treat it as though it is *only* a stepping stone. Those that stay in testing find it fits their personality or their particular talents.

Any job worth doing is worth doing well. Even if the job is a transition for you into a more desired position, do it well anyway; and it will serve you tenfold, paying you back in your reputation, your knowledge, and your satisfaction with the position. This chapter is specifically aimed at a discussion of what qualities set the professional apart from the rest of those holding the same title. I have found many people who want to build their career as a professional tester, but do not see the avenues by which to accomplish this. Because it is more of a profession by accident than design, those that have stepped into the roles may not have planned for a full career path or know the directions that are open to them as they grow.

What Makes a Professional?

Professionals are identified by the quality of their work and the way they go about it. They have the following qualities:

- They are constantly analyzing the work, the methods, and the approach in an effort to improve it, taking the initiative where they see a path. If you are part of a test effort and you regularly install the lab machines, instead of priding yourself on being so indispensable because you are the only one who can do it, raise your visibility by putting together a short set of instructions exactly detailing, perhaps with screen shots, how you install the machines each day. People who are able to analyze their work and recall what they do are worth much more than those who can just push a button. You are not writing yourself out of a job; you are writing yourself up to the next level.

- They watch the way that others do their work and learn from their successes and mistakes, incorporating this knowledge into their own work. If you constantly see the same individuals being rewarded or recognized for the work they do, pay attention to how they do it. It is unlikely that they have the exact same job description as you, but likely many tasks will be the same. Perhaps they do not open more bugs than anybody else, but rather when they open a bug, it is precise, detailed, and correct. Perhaps an individual's bugs always have the appropriate documentation, such as network traces and dumps. Perhaps, even a step further, the individual goes ahead and analyzes the information, including information in the bug report, such as which frame the items of interest are in. Being able to spot a problem where a wrong font is applied is easy, and UI bugs can generate inflated bug numbers. Tougher bugs with detailed analysis are far more valuable to the cause of creating high-quality software.

- Professionals understand not only what to do and what not to do, but why things are done a certain way. This knowledge is what allows them to analyze their work and improve. Without it they would blindly carry out orders; instead, developing an understanding of the constraints and ideal goals actually enables them to take control and innovate. This understanding might not be inherent, but acquired because a professional has taken the time to ask a question and understand the answer at some point in the past. If a professional understands what the ultimate goal of a particular process is, he might see a better path to get there. If issues are arising because teams are not communicating well, a professional works to solve them. A professional might understand where the problems are coming from and guard against them in his own interactions, or may go further and recommend to management ways that the problem can be fixed.

Developing Your Tester Modus Operandi

Being a good tester is not just about what you know; it is also about how you do it. It is a mindset and an attitude. Keep a couple key concepts in mind as you make decisions about how you operate as a tester:

- The very nature of the job is an adversarial one, and because of that a good tester needs to be sensitive to the way in which he works with others. Test needs to have a strong backbone to set hard limits with other teams and management, but they need to do so in a very positive manner. Test is not effective if they are not involved. If the testers themselves make their interactions with others painful, they will quickly be left out of the loop. The difference between an out-of-hand declaration of "No" and a probing question to understand another's position on a matter is the difference between a very difficult situation and a good working relationship. A request from another person or team is usually for a particular service that will go towards a goal that they are interested in. You may not like the particular service that they have requested, or the path that they see you taking to help them towards the goal may not be the optimal one you would choose. Understand not just what service they are requesting, but what that goal is. Often times, it turns out that you have a common goal and that you, or somebody else, would be doing much of that work anyway. The remainder of the work that was unplanned is the piece to negotiate over. Either way, instead of just saying "No," you have worked to at least understand what their desire is. The information gained from that alone is worth the effort. Another request might come to you for the same service. In that case, you can refer that person to the first person because their goals are very similar and they could benefit each other.

- Being professional or committed to quality does not mean that you are the person who arrives first or even stays the latest. You may work well by thoroughly approaching the work in the correct manner during a solid 8-hour work day. Or you may really enjoy being at work and stay until 10:00 P.M. every evening and bounce through the door the next morning at 8:00 A.M. The point is that there is not a solid correlation between number of hours worked and quality of the job done. Certainly, if you are surfing the Web all afternoon and barely spending 2 hours during your work week with your attention on the tasks in front of you, your level of quality is likely to be low. However, there are plenty of other people who cannot accomplish in 12-hour work days that which I've seen others easily get out of their 8-hour day. Do not mistake motion for progress in your own or someone else's work.

There are never any hard-and-fast rules. Everything you do is a judgment call on your part. Sometimes you'll be right, and sometimes you'll be wrong. When you're right, figure out what went well; and when you're wrong, figure out what didn't. The next several sections of this chapter discuss some areas of professional development you may want to focus on as you begin or continue your work as a tester.

Planning

Carrying out your business in a professional manner is a necessity and will only help you. Use some sort of calendaring tool for reminders and scheduling. This tool may just be a notebook, or a PDA, or a software program. Know the purpose of each meeting and have applicable materials prepared for it. Be on time to meetings and be prepared. This preparation and punctuality reflect well on you and show consideration for your colleagues' time. Being on time and prepared is one of the best ways to immediately make your work more professional and thorough.

Take a look at your next day's schedule before you leave at night. Print out any materials you can for the following day, or make a note of what will need to be prepared for those meetings. One rigid method will never work for everyone, but give it a go and see if it works for you. Before I leave at night, I look forward to the next day and mentally chart out my meetings. Are there any preparations I need to make? Do I need to have any last minute communications with anyone? Are any materials required or is there any supporting material that I could provide? Preparing for the next day the evening before is a good way to finish collecting your thoughts, wrap up all the loose ends, and use the momentum you have going from the current workday to give you a head start on the next day. Alternately, carve out the first fifteen minutes when you arrive at work to get a good way through your coffee, check your mail, prepare for meetings, or otherwise schedule your day and organize your thoughts.

Organizing

*It is best to do things systematically, since we are only
human, and disorder is our worst enemy.*
—Hesiod

Organize information—save the useful data and get rid of the rest. You can't
do anything efficiently without organizing your thoughts and the work at
hand. Save and store email in logical places. If somebody sends out an email
with a wonderful description of how to do something or how something
works, file it away in your account for later reference. Not everything will
need to be saved, and not everything is useful, you certainly will not reference
everything you store away. But having the pieces logically arranged and available to you will serve as an archive of data that can prove invaluable.

Write down the tasks you need to accomplish, track them, and cross them off
when they are finished. This procedure can help motivate you by showing you
what you have accomplished and what still needs to be done.

Keep track of due dates. Understand what your responsibility is in any
assigned task. What is expected from you as an output? By when? Who should
you coordinate with and what resources are at your disposal? What is the priority of the task in relation to other tasks going on? Knowing this information
will let you make a good decision when you are faced with choices.

Being Prepared

If you are prepared, then you are able to feel confident.
—Robert J. Ringer

Try carrying a notebook and pen and taking notes. At some point, you will be
told specific pieces of information and will want to carry instructions out in a
complete fashion. Carry your notebook (or PDA or any other method you
work best with) to meetings, even if they are unimportant and you do not
anticipate valuable information coming from them. Informal hallway meetings are common, and snips of very important data can transpire here that you
will not want to risk forgetting or have to hunt down a pen and paper at that
point. Even the most unrelated of meetings may trigger thoughts for new test
cases or scenarios that you will want to ensure are run. There is no need to rely
on a perhaps faulty memory when you can have clear notes to refer to. Many
teams do not have such things documented, but they should be.

TIP

Take the initiative to clearly and carefully document things not only for yourself, but also for others in the team. Contributing this to the team immediately makes you a more valuable member, saves the rest of the team time, and can really go a long way to helping you develop a deeper understanding of the product.

If there is a process to be documented, just the investigation of what the unwritten process is can bring about positive changes in a poor process. If you have questions, write them down before you forget them so you can be sure to get them answered. Raising these questions may turn up great bugs. And even if they don't, at least you have answers to learn from. Try using a divided notebook, earmarking each section for a different topic:

- One for questions
- One for processes you are directed in
- One for tracking tasks and due dates
- One for tracking how you spend your time

Simple things like tape flags in different colors can help you track what needs to be done or what information should not be forgotten. Implementing a little bit of process here, something that works for you personally, can save a lot of effort on a daily basis and allow you to be more effective and efficient.

Knowing Where You're Going . . . and Where You've Been

The whole world steps aside for the man who knows
where he is going.
—Chinese Proverb

Track your activities. You can do this in any number of ways.

- Some people keep a section in their notebook for this, and as they change activities, they write down what new activity they are starting on.
- Others have a grid in half-hour chunks broken out and a note on their calendar that reminds them to break every half hour to make a note of what task they are currently involved in.

Each approach has its benefits and can really work well for different types of people. There are other possibilities that may work better for you, so give one a try and evolve it as best fits you.

Writing down activities as you are involved in them will also be to your benefit. Many people balk at tracking their activities or giving updates to their managers, either verbal or written. Use these to your advantage. Tracking your activities provides you with a record of your successes and a timeline of accomplished tasks. If you are not tracking your own successes, it is likely that many of these will be lost. When you want recognition or are up for a promotion, these are the most useful pieces of information to support you. If your work is ever called into question regarding whether a task was completed or if it was timely, then it is easy to provide factual data quickly to support your position. Most managers want to have you do well. The better you are doing, the more work the manager's team is getting done. The better you make your manager look, the more you will be appreciated. Don't be afraid to forward your manager emails that recognize your successes. If your manager is ever challenged on what the team is doing, he can easily be your advocate. If you hide your tasks, your manager can never be sure that the work is completely being done, or is being done well. Certainly not everything needs to be communicated, but there will be a certain balance of what your manager needs to know to best manage the project, while minimizing random emails.

Let your manager know when there are changes in the status of pieces of the project assigned to you. If some task preempts another task, let your manager know that there are changes in your work schedule. Let your manager know if there is not enough information, if the information given is ambiguous, if there are not enough resources or improper resources, or if the due date cannot be met. It is not too terrible that a due date cannot be met, but you must alert your manager and any dependents in a timely matter so that rescheduling can take place.

NOTE

Letting your manager, and others involved, know you do not have enough information or are not prepared to take on a certain task solo is perhaps the most difficult thing you can do. It may feel like you are admitting failure or stupidity, but it is really just a report that tasks are not flowing according to the predicted timeline, and the sooner this is recognized, the better. There is always more out there to learn about the technology, testing, techniques, or the application. Being able to say "I don't know" or "I don't know yet" in response to someone's questions or telling your manager you need some of his time to better understand what is being asked of you is only a show of honesty. Nobody can learn something for you or can teach you something if you do not meet them halfway, but they cannot read your mind to see if you have lingering questions or not enough information. It is up to you to tell them.

Some deadlines are not achievable, and some projects grow significantly while in progress, pushing out their completion date. Perhaps the priority of the tasks shifts or other resources are added to meet the deadline. Correctly anticipating that the work will turn out to be more than originally suspected and notifying management is a sign of professional maturity. Agreeing to a delivery that you do not think is possible only sets you up for failure. Work with others to determine what is possible and by what date. Without any other notification, management will assume that you will meet the assigned deadline. The key is that you can account for your time when reviews and promotions come around, and you can accurately list achievements and activities that you have been involved in rather than forgetting what might possibly later turn out to be the most important ones.

Sharing

There are two rules to success in life.
1. Don't tell people everything you know.

I disagree with this quote. Sharing information is one of the best ways to gain visibility and to immediately make you an important part of the test team. Some testers feel that they need to hoard information or tools or other pieces of their work that they feel are valuable. This practice is not limited to testers, and it can sometimes be understood because some short-term goals seem to conflict with being open with your teammates. After all, you are in competition with them for recognition and compensation. In the long run, however, you will be much better served by being more open. Out of simple enlightened self-interest, share tools, knowledge, and techniques, and you will be well served by the practice.

Being Visible

A man is not idle because he is absorbed in thought.
There is a visible labor and there is an invisible labor.
—Victor Hugo

One complaint of many testers is that they do not get any visibility and feel forgotten. High-quality work will bring you visibility. This quality will show in several ways:

- Entering good bug reports gains you a reputation for detailed and high-quality work.

- Contributions in meetings or email threads shows you are not "along for the ride," but are actively contributing to the project and the shape of the work.

- Well-thought-out, well-written emails that are appropriate for the audience may not be noticed immediately, but will gain you the reputation you are trying to establish.

- Writing good test cases and test plans leads others by the example you set.

- Making good decisions when confronted with options and then communicating those well to the appropriate audience are more appreciated than you may think.

- It is fine to be thoroughly entranced by technologies other than those your current project is using, but don't let those take precedence at work over the tasks that matter. You are being judged on your work as it applies to the project, not on how much you know or what you might be capable of.

Tend to the work at hand, and focus on being present for your work rather than just going through the motions. If you didn't respect the work you were doing or the people you were working with, then you wouldn't want to put forth the effort. Although you won't think well of everyone you come in contact with, you should have pride in the decisions you make and your actions on them. If you drive your own career through the quality of your work in the ways I've just outlined, issues of visibility will take care of themselves.

Asking Questions

The greatest fool may ask more than the wisest man can answer.
—Charles Caleb Colton

No question is stupid, but they can be asked of inappropriate sources. You wouldn't go to the vice president of the company to ask what XML was because that question would more easily be answered (and probably more thoroughly) by doing a quick search of technical sites on the Web. Once you understand what the technology is, a very applicable question to ask of somebody such as a developer would be *how* the application you are working on makes use of XML. Constantly asking questions without thinking will gain you a bad label very quickly. Some see any communication with management or key individuals as visibility, but not all visibility is positive. Before firing off that email to the whole organization to ask if a server is down, is there a better source to ask. Many questions are commonplace. Has the question been asked all ready? Are there archives or other places to look to find the answer? Can you develop a queue of questions to avoid continuously knocking on the same person's door every 10 minutes?

Consider that each resource has two factors:

- A cost factor
- An effectiveness factor

A book has a very low cost factor ($50 for always being able to access the information). Comparatively, a vice president has a very high cost factor. His time is very limited, and his cost per hour is very likely higher than yours or your colleagues'. When tracking down resources, we need to take into account both the cost and the effectiveness of each resource with respect to the issue at hand.

If there is a question that you need to track down (for the sake of this example the question could be *How do we make use of XML in our product?*), then you need to start tracking it down while thinking in terms of cost and effectiveness. You may initially identify that your peers (other individual testers) represent the right cost and effectiveness for this question. However, after going from office to office asking the same question, taking up time, interrupting tasks, and not receiving full answers, it would definitely be time to identify a new resource. Taking into account both the cost and effectiveness will help you identify the most appropriate source for results.

NOTE

One tester confided in me that the manager wanted to be the first line of contact for any question. In retaliation, this person told me how each and every question that came to mind generated an email to the manager. Through the discussion I had with this tester, however, I think the tester saw how much that would turn into a career-limiting move and that there were better ways to use resources such as the Web, books, and email lists to answer questions and filter out some of the questions that the manager was trying to route away from the tester's peers. Your manager should always be open to your questions, as this manager was, but be sure that you are meeting others halfway by asking good questions and putting forth an effort to understand the answers.

Using Common Sense

A man goes to the doctor and wants his arm checked as he thinks it is broken. The doctor asks, "How did you break it?"

The man replies he has no idea, "but it hurts when I poke here OUCH! And here OUCH! And here OUCH!" as he pokes around his arm and elbow.

"You've not suffered a broken arm, but rather a broken finger."

Use common sense. Using common sense applies to developing new test cases, rolling out new processes, logging bugs, making decisions, and any general day-to-day interactions. It sounds so easy, but it is not as common as the term sounds.

For example, although your management may seem to be rewarding you for finding a high number of bugs, what they really want is to have a better piece of software at the end of the day. Your efforts must be aimed at this real purpose. Don't go logging every permutation of a bug that stems from the same root cause. Inevitably there will be seemingly unrelated bugs that share the same root. These duplicates are inevitable. This warning is aimed at discouraging you from logging a bug that a particular action fails when using the application in English and Japanese and Chinese and German and all subsequent languages. These tester fouls only take up precious time. Part of becoming a professional is to see beyond any intermediary reward system to the true goal of the organization. In this case, the intermediary reward comes from logging a lot of bugs, which isn't really what is wanted. The real goal is to develop and ship better software. Part of developing yourself into a professional is to work towards this real goal. And as you gain experience and examine your experiences, you can start to determine best practices in your own area according to what fits you, your team, your project, or your application.

NOTE It is not always the person who has the most experience who can perform the best. Many of those new to the field can perform in an exemplary fashion because they examine their own work and that of others, and they can apply that which they have learned.

Applying Best Practices

Professionals use all available resources to identify the best practices to employ for their work and their project. What is a best practice for one person or one company is not necessarily the best way to approach an issue in another instance. *Best* is meaningful only in the context of the project. However, there are many practices that transfer from one project to the next. Don't forget what you learned in other projects or in other areas. Think of it as packing up your bags and carrying them with you to be unpacked at the next destination. There is a lot of knowledge that should transfer with you, even from seemingly unrelated activities. Certifications don't teach anything; they seek to measure. They are one component that might help set goals for you to work towards, or provide a framework for your own studies. Testing organizations, or any professional organization, will not teach you anything. You will have access to resources and come in contact with many others who are interested in finding the paths you are working towards. Having lots of affiliations just means you're able to write checks and become a member of these groups. Joining an organization and actually making use of it or contributing to it is where the value is.

Taken as a whole, professionals are constantly striving for more knowledge and to put that knowledge to good use improving themselves, their project, and those around them.

Evolving As a Professional Tester

Everything changes, everything grows. That which does not stagnates and dies. Just as the technologies that you will work with change rapidly, you cannot keep your career alive without constantly updating your area of knowledge and your skill set. You can evolve as a professional tester by way of many methods. As I have indicated, professionals are constantly analyzing their own work, so one way you can evolve is to develop purely within your workday and within your workplace by examining the software and testing methods you are applying. More probably, however, you will look to outside the workplace and workday to expand your abilities. You have many outside sources at your disposal to help you evolve:

- Books, either on testing or on the particular technologies being used in your current project, can be a great source of increasing your knowledge.

- More and more Web sites and magazines are being dedicated to software testing, and of course, to software technologies.

- Many discussion groups exist not only for the networking of individuals, but for sharing general knowledge and thoughts about the work. Some larger companies even have internal aliases for discussing different technologies, tools, or interests.

- In many areas there are local groups that bring in speakers and provide networking opportunities for individuals. Conferences allow you yet another opportunity for this sort of learning.

- You can pursue pertinent certifications. The mark of a professional tester is not how many of these you participate in or how many letters you can tack on to the end of your title, but that you pursue those that give you the most benefit and use to the best of their offering. If the CSTE certification has nothing to do with your work, is out of your financial means, or otherwise not appropriate, then do not pursue it. If there is a Microsoft Certified Professional certification or Linux Administration or networking certification that can further your understanding or career, then pursue those. You should know what certifications exist and whom it could be appropriate for because one day you could benefit from it.

- There are also many organizations you can join. If you are interested in the usability and UI side of testing, perhaps joining ACM's Special Interest Group for Computer Human Interactions would benefit you. If you deal with accessibility issues, joining a special education forum may give you insight into new tools, common issues, or what works and what doesn't for that constituency. Many national, or worldwide, professional organizations have local chapters with regular meetings. Not only are these a good way to be exposed to many different techniques, people, and backgrounds, they are an excellent networking opportunity.

At the very least, read. Read articles, books, papers, or research. Many libraries and bookstores carry technical books that you can browse, allowing you to keep down the cost of reading the snips of many different, yet important, areas. Your organization may be happy to pay for a subscription to one of the magazines devoted to the profession, and it just takes you to ask and detail the benefits of having the resource. Your team may benefit greatly from having a small library of books available. The cost of a single technical book is roughly $50. If one tester saves 2 hours of time by having access to one particular piece of information or a technique given in that book, then that book has more than paid for itself. If that book happens to provide previously unidentified test cases or otherwise prevents problems, it has paid for itself several times over in its benefit to the organization. If you happen to find a few more bugs, perhaps a few serious ones, it is just one more item that you can list to support positive reviews; then, $50 is a bargain for what it can bring to you.

NOTE

Some teams or companies have cut their budgets for this type of material. Teams need to realize that cutting corners in these sections of the budget is not going to help them. It may not be the best use of money to buy ten copies of the same book. On the other hand, it could be a great use of money to buy ten copies and set up study groups, either for the sole purpose of studying various professional writings or to support individual efforts towards certifications.

As a professional, you may not use all the tools out there, but you should at least know that they are available to you. As your position or product changes, you can change the tools you use to be more effective.

I want to leave you encouraged to continue forward in your career. I want to leave you surefooted on your path, confident in your knowledge and decisions. And I want to leave you with information that you can build on. Technical information will go out of date, better techniques and process will evolve, and tools will be replaced. If you can just take away the ideas from this last chapter and apply them, then the rest will fall into place.

PART FIVE

Testing Reference Appendices

Code Pages

P regenerated Windows code pages are excellent data for input as they allow you to paste in an excellent set of test data for almost any text entry field. Here they are presented printed for reference, but these are also available on the companion Web site for you to download and make use of.

NOTE Some characters in this appendix are not able to be printed and the replacement character has been printed in their place.

874 Code Page

Covers Thai.

LOWER ASCII RANGE

```
0x20:  !"#$%&'()*+,-./:0x2F
0x30:0123456789:;<=>?:0x3F
0x40:@ABCDEFGHIJKLMNO:0x4F
0x50:PQRSTUVWXYZ[\]^_:0x5F
0x60:`abcdefghijklmno:0x6F
0x70:pqrstuvwxyz{|}~□:0x7F
```

EXTENDED RANGE

```
0x80:€□,ƒ„...†‡^‰S<ŒZ□:0x8F
0x90:□''""•---~™s>œ□zŸ:0x9F
0xA0:□ขฃคฅฆงจฉชซฌญฎฏ:0xAF
0xB0:ฐฑฒณดตถทธนบปผฝพฟ:0xBF
0xC0:ภมยรฤลฦวศษสหฬอฮฯ:0xCF
```

NOTE

0xDB–0xDE and 0xFC–0xFF are unmapped. Lines 0x80 and 0x90 were added by Microsoft.

Due to combining issues, some points are shown individually below.

0xD0	ะ
0xD1	ั
0xD2	า
0xD3	ำ
0xD4	ิ
0xD5	ี
0xD6	ึ
0xD7	ื
0xD8	ุ
0xD9	ู
0xDA	ฺ
0xDF	□
0xE0	เ
0xE1	แ
0xE2	โ
0xE3	ใ
0xE4	ไ
0xE5	ๅ
0xE6	ๆ
0xE7	็
0xE8	่
0xE9	้
0xEA	๊
0xEB	๋
0xEC	์
0xED	๎
0xEE	฿
0xEF	๏

0xF0	°
0xF1	๑
0xF2	๒
0xF3	๓
0xF4	α
0xF5	α
0xF6	๖
0xF7	๗
0xF8	๘
0xF9	๙
0xFA	๚
0xFB	๛

1250 Code Page

Covers Albanian, Croat, Czech, English, German, Hungarian, Latin, Polish, Romanian, Slovak, Slovene, and Sorbian.

LOWER ASCII RANGE

```
0x20: !"#$%&'()*+,-./:0x2F
0x30:0123456789:;<=>?:0x3F
0x40:@ABCDEFGHIJKLMNO:0x4F
0x50:PQRSTUVWXYZ[\]^_:0x5F
0x60:`abcdefghijklmno:0x6F
0x70:pqrstuvwxyz{|}~□:0x7F
```

EXTENDED RANGE

```
0x80:€□,□„…†‡□‰Š‹ŚŤŽŹ:0x8F
0x90:□''""•––™š›śťžź:0x9F
0xA0: ˇ˘Ł¤Ą¦§¨©Ş«¬®Ż:0xAF
0xB0:°±˛ł´µ¶·¸ąş»Ľ˝ľż:0xBF
0xC0:ŔÁÂĂÄĹĆÇČÉĘËĚÍÎĎ:0xCF
0xD0:ĐŃŇÓÔŐÖ×ŘŮÚŰÜÝŢß:0xDF
0xE0:ŕáâăäĺćçčéęëěíîď:0xEF
0xF0:đńňóôőö÷řůúűüýţ˙:0xFF
```

NOTE Lines 0x80 and 0x90 have been added by Microsoft.

1251 Code Page

Covers English and Russian.

LOWER ASCII RANGE

```
0x20:  !"#$%&'()*+,-./:0x2F
0x30:0123456789:;<=>?:0x3F
0x40:@ABCDEFGHIJKLMNO:0x4F
0x50:PQRSTUVWXYZ[\]^_:0x5F
0x60:`abcdefghijklmno:0x6F
0x70:pqrstuvwxyz{|}~ :0x7F
```

EXTENDED RANGE

```
0x80:ЂЃ‚ѓ„…†‡€‰Љ‹ЊЌЋЏ:0x8F
0x90:ђ''""•——˜™љ›њќћџ:0x9F
0xA0: ЎўЈ¤Ґ¦§Ё©Є«¬®Ї:0xAF
0xB0:°±Ііґµ¶·ё№є»јЅѕї:0xBF
0xC0:АБВГДЕЖЗИЙКЛМНОП:0xCF
0xD0:РСТУФХЦЧШЩЪЫЬЭЮЯ:0xDF
0xE0:абвгдежзийклмноп:0xEF
0xF0:рстуфхцчшщъыьэюя:0xFF
```

NOTE Lines 0x80 and 0x90 have been added by Microsoft.

1252 Code Page

Covers Albanian, Basque, Breton, Catalan, Danish, Dutch, English, Faroese, Finnish, French (with restrictions), Frisian, Galician, German, Greenlandic, Icelandic, Irish Gaelic (new orthography), Italian, Latin, Luxemburgish, Norwegian, Portuguese, Rhjaeto-Romanic, Scottish Gaelic, Spanish, and Swedish.

LOWER ASCII RANGE

```
0x20:  !"#$%&'()*+,-./:0x2F
0x30:0123456789:;<=>?:0x3F
0x40:@ABCDEFGHIJKLMNO:0x4F
0x50:PQRSTUVWXYZ[\]^_:0x5F
0x60:`abcdefghijklmno:0x6F
0x70:pqrstuvwxyz{|}~□:0x7F
```

EXTENDED RANGE

```
0x80:€□‚ƒ„...†‡ˆ‰S‹ŒZ□:0x8F
0x90:□''""•---˜™s›œ□zŸ:0x9F
0xA0:¿¢£¤¥¦§¨©ª«<®¯¬:0xAF
0xB0:°±²³µ¶•₁⁰>>¼½¾¿:0xBF
0xC0:ÀÁÂÃÄÅÆÇÈÉÊÌÍÎÏ:0xCF
0xD0:ÐÑÒÓÔÕÖ×ØÙÚÛÜÞß:0xDF
0xE0:àáâãäåæçèéêëìíîï:0xEF
0xF0:ðñòóôõö÷øùúûüÞÿ:0xFF
```

NOTE ▪▪▪▪ **Lines 0x80 and 0x90 were added by Microsoft.**

1253 Code Page

Covers English and Greek.

LOWER ASCII RANGE

```
0x20: !"#$%&'()*+,-./:0x2F
0x30:0123456789:;<=>?:0x3F
0x40:@ABCDEFGHIJKLMNO:0x4F
0x50:PQRSTUVWXYZ[\]^_:0x5F
0x60:`abcdefghijklmno:0x6F
0x70:pqrstuvwxyz{|}~□:0x7F
```

EXTENDED RANGE

```
0x80:€□‚ƒ„...†‡ˆ‰š‹Œ Ž :0x8F
0x90: ''""•—―˜™š›œ□žŸ:0x9F
0xA0: ΅Α£¤¥¦§¨©?«¬®―:0xAF
0xB0:°±²³´µ¶·ΈΗΙ»Ό½ΥΩ:0xBF
0xC0:ΐΑΒΓΔΕΖΗΘΙΚΛΜΝΞΟ:0xCF
0xD0:ΠΡΣΤΥΦΧΨΩΪΫάέήί:0xDF
0xE0:ΰαβγδεζηθικλμνξο:0xEF
0xF0:πρςστυφχψωϊϋόύώ? 0xFF
```

NOTE ▪▪▪▪ **Lines 0x80 and 0x90 were added by Microsoft.**

1254 Code Page

Covers English and Turkish.

LOWER ASCII RANGE

```
0x20:  !"#$%&'()*+,-./:0x2F
0x30:0123456789:;<=>?:0x3F
0x40:@ABCDEFGHIJKLMNO:0x4F
0x50:PQRSTUVWXYZ[\]^_:0x5F
0x60:`abcdefghijklmno:0x6F
0x70:pqrstuvwxyz{|}~□:0x7F
```

EXTENDED RANGE

```
0x80:€□‚ƒ„…†‡ˆ‰Š‹Œ□Ž□:0x8F
0x90:□''""•–—˜™š›œ□□Ÿ:0x9F
0xA0: ¡¢£¤¥¦§¨©ª«¬®¯:0xAF
0xB0:°±²³´µ¶·¸¹º»¼½¾¿:0xBF
0xC0:ÀÁÂÃÄÅÆÇÈÉÊËÌÍÎÏ:0xCF
0xD0:ĞÑÒÓÔÕÖ×ØÙÚÛÜİŞß:0xDF
0xE0:àáâãäåæçèéêëìíîï:0xEF
0xF0:ğñòóôõö÷øùúûüışÿ:0xFF
```

> **NOTE**
> Lines 0x80 and 0x90 were added by Microsoft.

1255 Code Page

Covers English and Hebrew.

LOWER ASCII RANGE

```
0x20:  !"#$%&'()*+,-./:0x2F
0x30:0123456789:;<=>?:0x3F
0x40:@ABCDEFGHIJKLMNO:0x4F
0x50:PQRSTUVWXYZ[\]^_:0x5F
0x60:`abcdefghijklmno:0x6F
0x70:pqrstuvwxyz{|}~□:0x7F
```

EXTENDED RANGE

```
0x80:€□‚ƒ„…†‡ˆ‰Š‹Œ□Ž□:0x8F
0x90:□''""•–—˜™š›œ□žŸ:0x9F
0xA0: ¡¢£₪¥¦§¨©×«¬®¯:0xAF
0xB0:°±²³´µ¶·¸¹»¼½¾¿:0xBF
```

NOTE
Lines 0x80 and 0x90 were added by Microsoft.

Due to the bidirectional issues in Hebrew when placing characters on the same line, individual code points and their corresponding characters are placed in the following listing.

```
0xC0:  ֖
0xC1:  ֿ
0xC2:  ֻ
0xC3:  ֽ
0xC4:  ֒
0xC5:  ֘
0xC6:  ֙
0xC7:  ַ
0xC8:  ֜
0xC9:
0xCA:  □
0xCB:  ֞
0xCC:  ֿ
0xCD:
0xCE:  ֡
0xCF:  ֢

0xD0:  |
0xD1:  ֨
0xD2:
0xD3:  ׃
0xD4:  װ
0xD5:  ױ
0xD6:  ײ
0xD7:  ׳
0xD8:  ״

0xE0:  א
0xE1:  ב
0xE2:  ג
0xE3:  ד
0xE4:  ה
0xE5:  ו
0xE6:  ז
0xE7:  ח
0xE8:  ט
0xE9:  י
0xEA:  ך
0xEB:  כ
0xEC:  ל
0xED:  ם
0xEE:  מ
0xEF:  ן
```

```
0xF0:  ]
0xF1:  ס
0xF2:  ע
0xF3:  ף
0xF4:  פ
0xF5:  ץ
0xF6:  צ
0xF7:  ק
0xF8:  ר
0xF9:  ש
0xFA:  ת
0xFD:  ‏
0xFE:
```

NOTE

0xFD is the nonprintable left-to-right mark. 0xFF is the nonprintable right-to-left mark.

1256 Code Page

Covers English and Arabic.

LOWER ASCII RANGE

```
0x20: !"#$%&'()*+,-./:0x2F
0x30:0123456789:;<=>?:0x3F
0x40:@ABCDEFGHIJKLMNO:0x4F
0x50:PQRSTUVWXYZ[\]^_:0x5F
0x60:`abcdefghijklmno:0x6F
0x70:pqrstuvwxyz{|}~□:0x7F
```

EXTENDED RANGE

Due to the bi-directional issues in Arabic with placing characters on the same line, individual code points and their corresponding characters are placed in the following listing.

NOTE

Lines 0x80 and 0x90 in the following list were added by Microsoft.

```
0x80:  €
0x81:  ـ
0x82:  ,
0x83:  ƒ
0x84:  „
0x85:  ...
0x86:  †
0x87:  ‡
0x88:  ^
0x89:  ‰
0x8A:  □
0x8B:  ‹
0x8C:  Œ
0x8D:  ڊ
0x8E:  ן
0x8F:  □

0x90:  ں
0x91:  `
0x92:  '
0x93:  "
0x94:  "
0x95:  •
0x96:  –
0x97:  --
0x98:  ڊ
0x99:  ™
0x9A:  □
0x9B:  ›
0x9C:  œ
0x9D:
0x9E:
0x9F:  □

0xA0:
0xA1:  ٬
0xA2:  ¢
0xA3:  £
0xA4:  ¤
0xA5:  ¥
0xA6:  |
0xA7:  §
0xA8:  ¨
0xA9:  ©
0xAA:  □
0xAB:  «
0xAC:  ¬
0xAD:
0xAE:  ®
0xAF:  ¯
```

```
0xB0:  °
0xB1:  ±
0xB2:  ²
0xB3:  ³
0xB4:  ´
0xB5:  µ
0xB6:  ¶
0xB7:  ·
0xB8:  ¸
0xB9:  ¹
0xBA:  º
0xBB:  »
0xBC:  ¹/₄
0xBD:  ¹/₂
0xBE:  ³/₄
0xBF:  ؟

0xC0:  □
0xC1:  ء
0xC2:  آ
0xC3:  أ
0xC4:  ؤ
0xC5:  إ
0xC6:  ئ
0xC7:  ا
0xC8:  ب
0xC9:  ة
0xCA:  ت
0xCB:  ث
0xCC:  ج
0xCD:  ح
0xCE:  خ
0xCF:  د

0xD0:  ذ
0xD1:  ر
0xD2:  ز
0xD3:  س
0xD4:  ش
0xD5:  ص
0xD6:  ض
0xD7:  ×
0xD8:  ط
0xD9:  ظ
```

0xDA: ع
0xDB: غ
0xDC: ـ
0xDD: ف
0xDE: ق
0xDF: ك

0xE0: à
0xE1: ل
0xE2: â
0xE3: م
0xE4: ن
0xE5: ه
0xE6: و
0xE7: ç
0xE8: è
0xE9: é
0xEA: ê
0xEB: ë
0xEC: ى
0xED: ي
0xEE: î
0xEF: ï

0xF0: "
0xF1: ñ
0xF2: ،
0xF3: '
0xF4: ô
0xF5: '
0xF6: ،
0xF7: ÷
0xF8: ·
0xF9: ù
0xFA: ·
0xFB: û
0xFC: ü
0xFD:
0xFE:
0xFF: ☐

NOTE

0xFD is the nonprintable left-to-right mark. 0xFE is the nonprintable right-to-left mark.

1257 Code Page

Covers Estonian, Latvian, and Lithuanian.

LOWER ASCII RANGE

```
0x20: !"#$%&'()*+,-./:0x2F
0x30:0123456789:;<=>?:0x3F
0x40:@ABCDEFGHIJKLMNO:0x4F
0x50:PQRSTUVWXYZ[\]^_:0x5F
0x60:`abcdefghijklmno:0x6F
0x70:pqrstuvwxyz{|}~□:0x7F
```

EXTENDED RANGE

```
0x80:€ ‚ƒ„…†‡ ‰Š‹ Š˝ ˜ :0x8F
0x90: ''""•–—˜™š›œ ¯ Ÿ:0x9F
0xA0: ¢£¤¦§Ø©R«¬®Æ:0xAF
0xB0:°±²³´µ¶·ø¹r»¼½¾æ:0xBF
0xC0:ĄĮĀĆÄÅĘĒČÉŹĖĢĶĪĻ:0xCF
0xD0:ŠŃŅÓŌÕÖ×ŲŁŚŪÜŻŽß:0xDF
0xE0:ąįāćäåęēčéźėģķīļ:0xEF
0xF0:šńņóōõö÷ųłśūüżž˙:0xFF
```

NOTE

0xA1 and 0xA5 are not mapped. Lines 0x80 and 0x90 were added by Microsoft.

1258 Code Page

Covers English and Vietnamese.

LOWER ASCII RANGE

```
0x20: !"#$%&'()*+,-./:0x2F
0x30:0123456789:;<=>?:0x3F
0x40:@ABCDEFGHIJKLMNO:0x4F
0x50:PQRSTUVWXYZ[\]^_:0x5F
0x60:`abcdefghijklmno:0x6F
0x70:pqrstuvwxyz{|}~□:0x7F
```

EXTENDED RANGE

```
0x80: €‚ƒ„…†‡ˆ‰‹Œ : 0x8F
0x90: '""''•–—˜™š›œ žŸ : 0x9F
0xA0: ¡¢£¤¥¦§¨©ª«¬®¯ : 0xAF
0xB0: °±²³´µ¶·¸¹º»¼½¾¿ : 0xBF
0xC0: ÀÁÂÃÄÅÆÇÈÉÊËÌÍÎÏ : 0xCF
0xD0: ÐÑ?ÓÔÕÖ×ØÙÚÛÜÝ ß : 0xDF
0xE0: àáâãäåæçèéêëíîï : 0xEF
0xF0: ðñóôõö÷øùúûüýþÿ : 0xFF
```

NOTE

0xA1 and 0xA5 are not mapped. Lines 0x80 and 0x90 were added by Microsoft.

CROSS-REFERENCE

Double byte code pages can be found on the companion Web site to this book.

Unicode Ranges

The table (Table B.1) that makes up this appendix contains a description of what is contained in the various ranges of Unicode. This can help when you are trying to generate characters or identify problems in your application, when used with particular languages. These entries are arranged in order of range ([U+####] is for the Unicode hex number).

Table B.1 Unicode Ranges and Their Associated Languages/Contents

BEGINNING OF RANGE	END OF RANGE	LANGUAGE OR CONTENTS
[U+0000]	[U+007F]	Controls and Basic Latin
[U+0080]	[U+00FF]	Controls and Latin-1 Supplement
[U+0100]	[U+017F]	Latin Extended-A
[U+0180]	[U+024F]	Latin Extended-B
[U+0250]	[U+02AF]	IPA Extensions
[U+02B0]	[U+02FF]	Spacing Modifier Letters
[U+0300]	[U+036F]	Combining Diacritical Marks
[U+0370]	[U+03FF]	Greek
[U+0400]	[U+04FF]	Cyrillic
[U+0500]	[U+050F]	Cyrillic Supplementary
[U+0530]	[U+058F]	Armenian

(continued)

Table B.1 *(continued)*

BEGINNING OF RANGE	END OF RANGE	LANGUAGE OR CONTENTS
[U+0590]	[U+05FF]	Hebrew
[U+0600]	[U+06FF]	Arabic
[U+0700]	[U+074F]	Syriac
[U+0780]	[U+07BF]	Thaana
[U+0900]	[U+097F]	Devanagari
[U+0980]	[U+09FF]	Bengali
[U+0A00]	[U+0A7F]	Gurmukhi
[U+0A80]	[U+0AFF]	Gujarati
[U+0B00]	[U+0B7F]	Oriya
[U+0B80]	[U+0BFF]	Tamil
[U+0C00]	[U+0C7F]	Telugu
[U+0C80]	[U+0CFF]	Kannada
[U+0D00]	[U+0D7F]	Malayalam
[U+0D80]	[U+0DFF]	Sinhala
[U+0E00]	[U+0E7F]	Thai
[U+0E80]	[U+0EFF]	Lao
[U+0F00]	[U+0FBF]	Tibetan
[U+1000]	[U+109F]	Myanmar
[U+10A0]	[U+10FF]	Georgian
[U+1100]	[U+11FF]	Hangul Jamo
[U+1200]	[U+137F]	Ethiopic
[U+13A0]	[U+13FF]	Cherokee
[U+1400]	[U+167F]	Unified Canadian Aboriginal Syllabics
[U+1680]	[U+169F]	Ogham
[U+16A0]	[U+16FF]	Runic
[U+1700]	[U+177F]	Tagalog, Hanunoo, Buhid, Tagbanwa
[U+1780]	[U+17FF]	Khmer
[U+1800]	[U+18AF]	Mongolian
[U+1E00]	[U+1EFF]	Latin Extended Additional
[U+1F00]	[U+1FFF]	Greek Extended
[U+2000]	[U+206F]	General Punctuation
[U+2070]	[U+209F]	Superscripts and Subscripts

Table B.1 *(continued)*

BEGINNING OF RANGE	END OF RANGE	LANGUAGE OR CONTENTS
[U+20A0]	[U+20CF]	Currency Symbols
[U+20D0]	[U+20FF]	Combining Diacritical Marks for Symbols
[U+2150]	[U+218F]	Number Forms
[U+2190]	[U+21FF]	Arrows
[U+2200]	[U+22FF]	Mathematical Operators
[U+2300]	[U+23FF]	Miscellaneous Technical
[U+2400]	[U+243F]	Control Pictures
[U+2440]	[U+245F]	Optical Character Recognition
[U+2460]	[U+24FF]	Enclosed Alphanumerics
[U+2500]	[U+257F]	Box Drawing
[U+2580]	[U+259F]	Block Elements
[U+25A0]	[U+25FF]	Geometric Shapes
[U+2600]	[U+26FF]	Miscellaneous Symbols
[U+2700]	[U+27BF]	Dingbats
[U+2800]	[U+28FF]	Braille Patterns
[U+2900]	[U+29FF]	Supplemental Arrows-B, Misc. Math Symbols-B
[U+2A00]	[U+2AFF]	Supplemental Mathematical Operators
[U+2E80]	[U+2EFF]	CJK Radicals Supplement
[U+2F00]	[U+2FDF]	KangXi Radicals
[U+2FF0]	[U+2FFF]	Ideographic Description Characters
[U+3000]	[U+303F]	CJK Symbols and Punctuation
[U+3040]	[U+309F]	Hiragana
[U+30A0]	[U+30FF]	Katakana
[U+3100]	[U+312F]	Bopomofo
[U+3130]	[U+318F]	Hangul Compatibility Jamo
[U+3190]	[U+319F]	Kanbun
[U+31A0]	[U+31BF]	Bopomofo Extended
[U+3200]	[U+32FF]	Enclosed CJK Letters and Months
[U+3300]	[U+33FF]	CJK Compatibility
[U+3400]	[U+4DB5]	CJK Unified Ideographs Extension A

(continued)

Table B.1 *(continued)*

BEGINNING OF RANGE	END OF RANGE	LANGUAGE OR CONTENTS
[U+A000]	[U+A48F]	Yi Syllables
[U+A490]	[U+A4CF]	Yi Radicals
[U+4E00]	[U+9FFF]	CJK Unified Ideographs
[U+AC00]	[U+D7A3]	Hangul Syllables
[U+DC00]	[U+DFFF]	Low Surrogates
[U+D800]	[U+DB7F]	High Surrogates
[U+DB80]	[U+DBFF]	Private Use High Surrogates
[U+E000]	[U+F8FF]	Private Use Area
[U+F900]	[U+FAFF]	CJK Compatibility Ideographs
[U+FB00]	[U+FB4F]	Alphabetic Presentation Forms
[U+FB50]	[U+FDFF]	Arabic Presentation Forms-A
[U+FE20]	[U+FE2F]	Combining Half Marks
[U+FE30]	[U+FE4F]	CJK Compatibility Forms
[U+FE50]	[U+FE6F]	Small Form Variants
[U+FE70]	[U+FEFF]	Arabic Presentation Forms-B
[U+FF00]	[U+FFEF]	Halfwidth and Fullwidth Forms
[U+FFF0]	[U+FFFF]	Specials

Language Guides

M any times testers want to enter characters for globalization testing from different languages. Cutting and pasting is one way to do this, but entering the characters using an input method editor is another way. Although some testers guess at characters and what they are typing, this short guide to entering a few words may lend more confidence to this activity.

Arabic

Arabic is the official language of Algeria, Bahrain, Egypt, Iraq, Jordan, Kuwait, Lebanon, Libya, Morocco, Oman, Qatar, Saudi Arabia, Sudan, Syria, Tunisia, United Arab Emirites, and Yemen, but is also a major language in Chad, Djibouti, Ethiopia, Iran, Israel, Syria, Turkey, and Western Sahara. The United Nations made it the sixth official language of the organization in 1974. Worldwide, it is spoken by over 42.5 million people.

Arabic is another complex script language as it is written right to left. Some segments can be written as left-to-right text, causing it to actually be bidirectional (BiDi).

The ISO standard for this language is 8859-6. The Windows code page that correlates to this language is 1256, which covers English and Arabic.

ARABIC

IME	Arabic					
Keyboard layout	Arabic (101)					
Keystrokes	l	v	p	f	h	W
Input characters	م	ر	ح	ب	ا	ً
Unicode positions	[U+0645]	[U+0631]	[U+062D]	[U+0628]	[U+0627]	[U+064B]
Code page points - 1256	0xE3	0xD1	0xCD	0xC8	0xC7	0xF0
Names	Arabic Letter MEEM	Arabic Letter REH	Arabic Letter HAH	Arabic Letter BEH	Arabic Letter ALEF	Arabic Letter FATHATAN
Display	مرحبا					
Pronunciation	Mar-haba—meaning *Hello*					
Unicode ranges	U+0600–U+06FF Arabic U+FB50–U+FDFF Arabic Presentation Forms					
Fonts	**Windows:** Andalus, Arabic Transparent, Arial, Courier New, Microsoft Sans Serif, Simplified Arabic, Simplified Arabic Fixed, Tahoma, Times New Roman, Traditional Arabic **Macintosh:** AlBayan, Baghdad, Cairo, Geeza, Kufi, Nadeem, Tahoma, Tuluth (each carries a different encoding with it) **Unix:** Arial, Arabic Newspaper, Bitstream Cyberbit, ClearlyU Arabic					

English, French, German, Italian, and Spanish

NOTE Many times teams will do much of their Western European globalization testing in German so that many localization issues regarding string expansion are covered. To help with this arrangement of the work, German input has been broken out separately.

Basic Latin (Latin Alphabet No. 1) covers many languages—Albanian, Basque, Breton, Catalan, Danish, Dutch, English, Faroese, Finnish, French (with restrictions), Frisian, Galician, German, Greenlandic, Icelandic, Irish Gaelic (new orthography), Italian, Latin, Luxemburgish, Norwegian, Portuguese, Rhjaeto-Romanic, Scottish Gaelic, Spanish, and Swedish. French is listed as having restrictions in this list as there are three additional characters that it requires, which are included in the ISO 8859-9 standard.

These languages are covered by the ISO 8859-1 standard and roughly correlates to the 1252 Windows code page that covers English, French, German, Spanish, Portuguese, Italian, Dutch, Danish, Swedish, Norwegian, and Finnish. It is also referred to as Latin 1.

In the example used in the English table, the "H" is input by holding down the shift key while typing the *h* key on the U.S.-English keyboard. (It is a great assumption that everyone reading this book will be using a U.S.-English keyboard, but we have to start somewhere.) All the following keystroke inputs are based on that keyboard. The Shift key acts as a modifier, altering the keyboard input. The Shift is not typed and is not displayed by itself, but it affects keys with which it is coupled. There are other modifiers more common in other languages, such as the right-Alt key.

The Macintosh system needs no special fonts altered or installed in order to support Danish, Finnish, French, Gaelic, German, Norwegian, Portuguese, or Spanish.

ENGLISH

IME	English				
Keyboard layout	US				
Keystrokes	shift-h	e	l	l	o
Input characters	H	e	l	l	o
Unicode positions	[U+0048]	[U+0065]	[U+006C]	[U+006C]	[U+006F]
Code page points—same on all code pages	0x48	0x65	0x6C	0x6C	0x6F
Names	Capital Letter H	Small Letter E	Small Letter L	Small Letter L	Small Letter O
Display	Hello				

GERMAN

IME	German (Germany)								
Keyboard Layout	German								
Keystrokes	shift-g	r	[	-	space	d	i	c	h
Input characters	G	r	ü	ß		d	i	c	h
Unicode positions	[U+0047]	[U+0072]	[U+00FC]	[U+00DF]	[U+0020]	[U+0064]	[U+0069]	[U+0063]	[U+0068]
Code page points	0x47	0x72	0xFC	0xDF	0x20	0x64	0x69	0x63	0x68
Names	Capital Letter G	Small Letter R	Small Letter U with Diaeresis	Small Letter Sharp S	Space	Small Letter D	Small Letter I	Small Letter C	Small Letter H
Display	Grüß dich								
Pronunciation	Grüß dich–German informal greeting								
Unicode ranges	U+0000–U+007F Controls and Basic Latin U+0080–U+00FF Controls and Latin-1 Supplement U+0100–U+017F Latin Extended-A U+0180–U+024F Latin Extended-B								
Fonts	**Windows:** Angsana New, Arial, Arial Black, Arial Narrow, Batang, BatangChe, Book Antiqua, Bookman Old Style, Browallia New, Century Gothic, Comic Sans MS, Cordia New, Courier, Courier New, Dotum, Fixedsys, Garamond, Georgia, Gulim, GulimChe, Gungsuh, GungsuhChe, Haettenschweiler, Impact, Lucinda Console, Lucinda Sans Unicode, Microsoft Logo, Microsoft Sans Serif, MingLiU, Monotype Corsiva, MS Dialog, MS Dialog Light, MS Gothic, MS Mincho, MS PGothic, MS PMincho, MS Sans Serif, MS Serif, MS SystemEx, MS UI Gothic, Palatino Linotype, Small Fonts, Sylfaen, System, Tahoma, Times New Roman, Trebuchet MS, Verdana **Macintosh:** Apple Chancery, Capitals, Charcoal, Chicago, Gadget, Geneva, Helvetica, Hoefler Text, Monaco, New York, Palatino, Sand, Skia, Tahoma, Techno, TektonPro, Textile, Times **Unix:** Caslon, ClearlyU								

Latin with Diacritics

In the example in the table, there are two inputs—*c* and the combining cedilla. The cedilla is a combining character, a keyboard modifier similar to the Shift key. It modifies the state of the keyboard driver. Although nothing is typed into the screen when the cedilla is typed, it combines with the letter c to create the Small Latin Letter C with Cedilla.

NOTE The cedilla, and other similar combining marks, are also referred to as dead keys, combining characters, nonspacing marks, or floating diacritics because they do not output a separate displayed character in the text.

Unicode UCS-2 provides for a number of these combining characters, but as processing these is more complex than not processing them, there are three levels of support outlined in ISO 10646.

- **Level 1.** Disallows combining characters from being processed
- **Level 2.** Allows for combining marks in Arabic, Hebrew, Indic, and Thai
- **Level 3.** Allows for combining marks in Cyrillic, Greek, and Latin

An interesting note is that the Small Latin letter C with cedilla does exist as a single code position in the 1252 code page (and a few others). The position that it occupies is 0xE7, and it has a Unicode value of [U+00E7].

LATIN WITH DIACRITICS

IME	English		
Keyboard layout	US		
Keystrokes	Right Alt key and ,	'	c
Input characters	ç	ç	
Unicode positions	007 0027	ç 0327	0063 0063
Code page points—same on all code pages	0xE7 0xB8	0x63	
Names	Small Latin Letter C with Combining Cedilla	Small Latin Letter C with Combining Cedilla / Combining Cedilla	Small Latin Letter C
Display	ç		
Unicode ranges	U+02B0–U+02FF Spacing Modifier Letters U+0300–U+036F Combining Diacritical Marks U+20D0–U+20FF Combining Diacritical Marks for Symbols		
Fonts	Angsana New, Arial, Arial Black, Arial Narrow, Batang, BatangChe, Book Antiqua, Bookman Old Style, Browallia New, Century Gothic, Comic Sans MS, Cordia New, Courier, Courier New, Dotum, Fixedsys, Garamond, Georgia, Gulim, GulimChe, Gungsuh, GungsuhChe, Haettenschweiler, Impact, Lucinda Console, Lucinda Sans Unicode, Microsoft Logo, Microsoft Sans Serif, MingLiU, Monotype Corsiva, MS Dialog, MS Dialog Light, MS Gothic, MS Mincho, MS PGothic, MS PMincho, MS Sans Serif, MS Serif, MS SystemEx, MS UI Gothic, Palatino Linotype, Small Fonts, Sylfaen, System, Tahoma, Times New Roman, Trebuchet MS, Verdana		

Chinese

Chinese is the most widely spoken language in the world; however, because it is divided into dialects, it can appear as though it were smaller. Close to 1.5 billion people speak Chinese throughout the People's Republic of China, Taiwan, Hong Kong, Malaysia, Singapore, Vietnam, Brunei, Cambodia, Thailand, and the United States. It numbers almost twice as many speakers as English.

One of the things that makes Chinese difficult is that there are two separate alphabets, depending on if you are referring to Simplified Chinese (used in the People's Republic of China and Singapore) or Traditional Chinese (used in Taiwan and Hong Kong and sometimes just referred to as Chinese). Each of these has a different standard that applied to it prior to the development of Unicode.

Simplified Chinese (CHS) was standardized by the GB 2312-80, which was developed from the ISO 646 standard, and contains some *Hanzi* corrections. One of the problems that existed with the GB 2312 standard was that all copies of this code page were done by hand, so there was the possibility of slight alterations from one copy to the next, or of slight changes. Microsoft's Windows 936 code page is the more typical standard for this language. The government of China recently reworked the Chinese code pages into a more comprehensive one called GB 18030 (or more accurately GB 18030-2000). This code page is much larger than the typical double-byte character set since it goes up to 4 bytes, making for many great test cases if your application will be supporting this code page.

Chinese Traditional (CHT) was standardized by the code page known as Big Five, which is also the name of the encoding applied to that particular code page. The Windows 950 code page takes Big Five and adds in row 89 of the ETen extensions to support Taiwanese as well.

When testing Chinese, you have several accept languages to check on MS Internet Explorer. For Chinese Traditional, you can select Chinese (Taiwan) [zh-tw], Chinese (Hong Kong) [zh-hk], Chinese (Macau) [zh], or just Chinese [zh]. For Chinese Simplified, you will want to select Chinese (PRC) [zh-cn] or Singapore [zh-sg].

When testing with Netscape Navigator, you will need to use Chinese [zh] or Chinese/Taiwan [zh-tw] for Chinese Traditional, and Chinese/China [zh-cn] for Chinese Simplified.

Fonts and encoding will need to be set appropriately for what you are testing.

CHINESE

IME	Chinese (PRC)
Keyboard layout	Chinese (Simplified)—MS PinYin98
Keystrokes	ni [space] [enter] hao [space] [enter]
Input characters	你 好
Unicode positions	[U+4F60] [U+597D]
Code page points—936	[C4/E3] [BA/C3]
Display	你好
Pronunciation	Ni hao—meaning *Hello* in Mandarin

Unicode ranges

U+2E80–U+2EFF CJK Radicals Supplement
U+2F00–U+2FDF KangXi Radicals
U+2FF0–U+2FFF Ideographic Description Characters
U+3000–U+303F CJK Symbols and Punctuation
U+3100–U+312F Bopomofo
U+3190–U+319F Kanbun
U+31A0–U+31BF Bopomofo Extended
U+3200–U+32FF Enclosed CJK Letters and Months
U+3300–U+33FF CJK Compatibility
U+3400–U+4DB5 CJK Unified Ideographs Extension A
U+A000–U+A48F Yi Syllables
U+A490–U+A4CF Yi Radicals
U+4E00–U+9FFF CJK Unified Ideographs
U+F900–U+FAFF CJK Compatibility Ideographs
U+FE30–U+FE4F CJK Compatibility Forms

Fonts

Windows: Simplified—GB2312: MS Hei, MS Song, NSimSun, SimHei, SimSun, SonTi
Traditional—Big5: MingLiU, PMingLiU, MS MingliU
Macintosh: Simplified—Hei
Unix: Simplified—Arphic, Bitstream Cyberbit
Traditional—Arphic

Czech, Polish, Hungarian, Slovak

ISO 8859-2 correlates to 1250 and is referred to as the Central European page or Latin 2. ISO 8859-2 also covers Albanian, Croat, Czech, English, German, Hungarian, Latin, Polish, Romanian, Slovak, Slovene, and Sorbian.

Albanian is primarily spoken in Albania, but also with a significant number of speakers in Yugoslavia, Italy, and Greece. Czech is the national language of the Czech Republic and has 10 million speakers. Polish is the national language of Poland. Croatian is primarily spoken in Yugoslavia.

CZECH, POLISH, HUNGARIAN, SLOVAK

IME	Czech								
Keyboard Layout	Czech								
Keystrokes	shift-d	o	b	r	7	space	d	e	n
Input characters	D	o	b	r	ý		d	e	n
Unicode positions	[U+0044]	[U+006F]	[U+0062]	[U+0072]	[U+00FD]	[U+0020]	[U+0064]	[U+0065]	[U+006E]
Code page points—1250	0x44	0x6F	0x62	0x72	0xFD	0x20	0x64	0x65	0x6E
Names	Latin Capital Letter D	Latin Small Letter O	Latin Small Letter B	Latin Small Letter R	Latin Small Letter Y with Acute	Space	Latin Small Letter D	Latin Small Letter E	Latin Small Letter N

Display: Dobrý den

Pronunciation: Dob-ray den—meaning *Hello* in Slovak and Czech

Unicode ranges:
U+0000–U+007F Controls and Basic Latin
U+0080–U+00FF Controls and Latin-1 Supplement
U+0100–U+017F Latin Extended-A
U+0180–U+024F Latin Extended-B

Fonts:
Windows: Angsana New, Arial, Arial Black, Arial Narrow, Batang, Book Antiqua, Bookman Old Style, Century Gothic, Comic Sans MS, Cordia New, Courier, Courier New, Garamond, Georgia, Gulim, GulimChe, Haettenschweiler, Impact, Lucinda Console, Lucinda Sans Unicode, Palatino Linotype, Tahoma, Times New Roman, Verdana
Macintosh: Apple Chancery, Capitals, Charcoal, Chicago, Gadget, Geneva, Helvetica, Hoefler Text, Monaco, New York, Palatino, Sand, Skia, Tahoma, Techno, TektonPro, Textile, Times
Unix: Caslon, ClearlyU

Greek

Greek is the national language of Greece, but is also spoken in Albania, Canada, Cyprus, Italy, Macedonia, Turkey, and the U.S. Over 12 million people worldwide speak Greek.

The ISO standard that covers Greek is ISO 8859-7. The Windows code page 1253 correlates with this, covering English and Greek.

GREEK

IME	Greek						
Keyboard layout	Greek						
Keystrokes	shift-g	e	i	;a	s	o	y
Input characters	Γ	ε	ι	ά	σ	ο	υ
Unicode positions	[U+0393]	[U+03B5]	[U+03B9]	[U+03AC]	[U+03C3]	[U+03BF]	[U+03C5]
Code page points–1253	0xC3	0xE5	0xE9	0xDC	0xF3	0xEF	0xF5
Names	Greek capital letter GAMMA	Greek small letter EPSILON	Greek small letter IOTA	Greek small letter ALPHA with TONOS	Greek small letter SIGMA	Greek small letter OMICRON	Greek small letter UPSILON
Display	Γειασου						
Pronunciation	ya'soo—meaning *Hello*						
Unicode ranges	U+0000–U+007F Controls and Basic Latin U+0080–U+00FF Controls and Latin-1 Supplement U+0370–U+03FF Greek						
Fonts	**Windows:** Arial, Arial Black, Arial Narrow, Batang, BatangChe, Book Antiqua, Bookman Old Style, Century Gothic, Comic Sans MS, Courier New, Dotum, DotumChe, Garamond, Georgia, Gulim, GulimChe, Gungsuh, GungsuhChe, Haettenschweiler, Impact, Lucinda Console, Lucinda Sans Unicode, Microsoft Sans Serif, Monotype Corsiva, MS Gothic, MS Mincho, MS PGothic, MS PMincho, MS UI Gothic, Palatino Linotype, Sylfaen, Tahoma, Times New Roman, Verdana **Macintosh:** Tahoma **Unix:** Arial, Bitstream Cyberbit, Caslon, ClearlyU, Lucinda Sans Unicode						

Hebrew

Hebrew is spoken primarily in Israel and the United States, but also in the Gaza Strip and the West Bank.

Hebrew is a complex script because it is a right-to-left (RTL) written language, also called bidirectional (BiDi) because segments of the text are written left to right. Notice that although the order in which the characters are put in is SHIN–LAMED–VAV–MEM, the order in which they appear when typed is reversed.

The ISO standard that covers this is ISO 8859-8. The Windows code page that correlates with this is 1255, which covers English and Hebrew.

HEBREW

IME	Hebrew			
Keyboard layout	Hebrew			
Keystrokes	a	k	u	o
Input characters	ש	ל	ו	ם
Unicode positions	[U+05E9]	[U+05DC]	[U+05D5]	[U+05DD]
Code page points - 1255	0xF9	0xEC	0xE5	0xED
Names	Hebrew Letter SHIN	Hebrew Letter LAMED	Hebrew Letter VAV	Hebrew Letter Final MEM
Display	ש ל ו ם			
Pronunciation	Sha-LOHM—meaning *Hello*			
Unicode ranges	U+0000–U+007F Controls and Basic Latin U+0080–U+00FF Controls and Latin-1 Supplement U+0590–U+05FF Hebrew			
Fonts	**Windows:** Aharoni, Arial, Courier New, David, David Transparent, Fixed Miriam Transparent, FrankRuehl, Levenim MT, Lucinda Sans Unicode, Microsoft Sans Serif, Miriam, Miriam Fixed, Miriam Transparent, Narkisim, Rod, Rod Transparent, Tahoma, Times New Roman **Macintosh:** Caesarea, Carmel Book, Gilboa, Ramat Sharon, Sinai Book **Unix:** Arial, Bitstream Cyberbit, Caslon, Lucinda Sans Unicode			

Hindi (Devanagari)

Hindi is the national language of India. It is also spoken in Fiji, Guyana, Mauritis, Suriname, Trinidad, Tobago, and the U.S., and has 182 million speakers worldwide. Indic languages have no OEM code pages associated with them. These characters exist in the Unicode UCS set only. This makes them ideal for testing your application's dependence on ANSI code pages (ACP dependencies)—you will see questions marks (????) if there are problems.

HINDI (DEVANAGARI)

IME	Hindi								
Keyboard layout	Hindi Traditional								
Keystrokes	m	g	m	d	b	e	i	l	c
Input characters	स	ु	स	्	व	T	ग	त	म
Unicode positions (hex)	[U+0938]	[U+0941]	[U+0938]	[U+094D]	[U+0935]	[U+093E]	[U+0917]	[U+0924]	[U+092E]
Names	Letter SA	Vowel Sign U	Letter SA	Sign Virama	Letter VA	Vowel Sign AA	Letter GA	Letter TA	Letter MA
Display	सुस्वागतम्								
Pronunciation	suswagathem—meaning *Welcome*								
Unicode ranges	U+0900–U+097F Devanagari								
Fonts	**Windows:** Latha, Mangal **Unix:** Sibal Devanagari								

Japanese

Japanese is the official language of Japan, but is also a language widely used in Brazil, South Korea, Peru, Taiwan, and the United States, with over 125 million speakers worldwide.

Japanese was initially standardized by the Japanese Industrial Standard. Their standardization is called JIS X 0208, and the most recent form was JIS X 0208-1997 and describes the JIS-encoding method applied to this set. This standard is the most widely used within Japan.

EUC-JP (Extended Unix Code for Japanese) is another encoding method applied to Japanese text that covers JIS X 0208-1990 8-bit double-byte characters and JIS X 0212-1990 7-bit double-byte characters.

The ISO standard that covers this language is ISO 2022-JP, which is also the name of the encoding method applied there. The Windows 932 code page takes the ISO 2022-JP standard and adds in some of its own extensions and changes the encoding method to a Shift-JIS. Windows code page 932 is the only place where this encoding method is used, so sometimes the MS 932 code page gets confused with its applied encoding method and both are referred to as Shift-JIS.

When testing this language, you will probably want to set your browser accept language to Japanese (JP) and set your browser encoding and font settings appropriately.

JAPANESE

IME	Japanese
Keyboard layout	Japanese Input System (MS-IME 2000)
Keystrokes	kon nichi ha <space> <space> <enter> <enter> <enter>
Input characters	今 日 は
Unicode positions	[U+4ECA] [U+65E5] [U+306F]
Code page points - JIS	[3A/23] [46/7C] [24/4F]
Code page points - 932	[8D/A1] [93/FA] [82/CD]
Names	Hiragana Letter HA
Display	今日は
Pronunciation	kon-nichiwa—meaning *Hello*
Unicode ranges	U+2E80–U+2EFF CJK Radicals Supplement U+2F00–U+2FDF KangXi Radicals U+2FF0–U+2FFF Ideographic Description Characters U+3000–U+303F CJK Symbols and Punctuation U+3040–U+309F Hiragana U+30A0–U+30FF Katakana U+3200–U+32FF Enclosed CJK Letters and Months U+3300–U+33FF CJK Compatibility U+3400–U+4DB5 CJK Unified Ideographs Extension A U+4E00–U+9FFF CJK Unified Ideographs U+FE30–U+FE4F CJK Compatibility Forms U+FF00–U+FFEF Halfwidth and Fullwidth Forms
Fonts	**Windows:** MS Gothic, MS Mincho, MS Mincho, MS PGothic, MS PMincho, MS UI Gothic, Terminal **Macintosh:** ChuGothic, HonMincho, MaruGothic, SaiMincho, TohabaGothic, TohabaMincho **Unix:** Bitstream Cyberbit, Caslon

Korean (Hangul)

Korean is the national language in both North and South Korea, although it is also spoken in Japan, China, and Guam as well as the US. There are over 75.5 million speakers of Korean worldwide.

Korean was standardized by the Korean Standard Code standard KS C 5601, with the most recent version being 5601. The Windows standard code page 949 took KS C 5601 and added some extensions.

KOREAN (HANGUL)

IME	Korean			
Keyboard layout	Korean (Hangul) (MS-IME98)			
Keystrokes	du	qh	tp	dy space
Input characters	여	보	세	요
Unicode positions	[U+C5EC]	[U+BCF4]	[U+C138]	[U+C694]
Code page points - 1361	[B5/61]	[A5/A1]	[AD/41]	[B6/61]
Code page points - 949	[BF/A9]	[BA/B8]	[BC/BC]	[BF/E4]
Names	Hangul Symbol IEUNG YO	Hangul Symbol PIEUP O	Hangul Symbol SIOS E	Hangul Symbol IEUNG YO
Display	여보세요			
Pronunciation	Annung haseyo—meaning *Hello*			
Unicode ranges	U+AC00–U+D7A3 Hangul Syllables U+3130–U+318F Hangul Compatibility Jamo U+1100–U+11FF Hangul Jamo			
Fonts	**Windows:** Batang, BatangChe, Dotum, DotumChe, Gulim, GulimChe, Gungsuh, GungsuhChe, Terminal **Unix:** Bitstream Cyberbit			

Russian (Cyrillic)

The Russian Federation has 125 million native Russian speakers. Throughout other countries, there is a total of 170 million speakers, making it the seventh most popular language (by number of speakers). Primarily found in the former Soviet Union republics, it is spoken throughout Armenia, Azerbaijan, Bashkortostan, Belarus, Estonia, Georgia, Kazakhstan, Kyrgyzstan, Latvia, Lithuania, Moldova, Russia, Turkmenistan, Ukraine, and Uzbekistan with close to 300,000 speakers in the U.S. and Canada alone.

The Cyrillic alphabet was standardized in ISO 8859-5. The Windows code page 1251 correlates with ISO 8859-5, covering English and Russian.

RUSSIAN (CYRILLIC)

IME	Russian											
Keyboard layout	Russian											
Keystrokes	shift-p	l	h	f	d	c	n	d	e	q	n	t
Input characters	З	д	р	а	в	с	т	в	у	й	т	е
Unicode positions	[U+0417]	[U+0434]	[U+0440]	[U+0430]	[U+0432]	[U+0441]	[U+1090]	[U+0432]	[U+0443]	[U+0439]	[U+0442]	[U+0435]
Code page points - 1251	0xC7	0xE4	0xF0	0xE0	0xE2	0xF1	0xF2	0xE2	0xF3	0xE9	0xF2	0xE5
Names	Cyrillic Capital Letter ZE	Cyrillic Small Letter DE	Cyrillic Small Letter ER	Cyrillic Small Letter A	Cyrillic Small Letter VE	Cyrillic Small Letter ES	Cyrillic Small Letter TE	Cyrillic Small Letter VE	Cyrillic Small Letter U	Cyrillic Small Letter Short I	Cyrillic Small Letter TE	Cyrillic Small Letter IE

Display: Здравствуйте

Pronunciation: ZzDRAST-vet-yah—meaning *Hello*

Unicode ranges:
U+0000–U+007F Controls and Basic Latin
U+0080–U+00FF Controls and Latin-1 Supplement
U+0400–U+04FF Cyrillic

Fonts:
Windows: Arial, Arial Black, Arial Narrow, Batang, BatangChe, Book Antiqua, Bookman Old Style, Century Gothic, Comic Sans MS, Courier New, Dotum, DotumChe, Garamond, Georgia, Gulim, GulimChe, Gungsuh, GungsuhChe, Haettenschweiler, Impact, Lucinda Console, Lucinda Sans Unicode, Microsoft Sans Serif, Monotype Corsiva, MS Gothic, MS Mincho, MS PGothic, MS PMincho, MS UI Gothic, Palatino Linotype, Sylfaen, Tahoma, Times New Roman, Verdana
Macintosh: Tahoma
Unix: Albertus, Andale Mono, Arial, Bitstream Cyberbit, Caslon, ClearlyU, Courier New, Lucinda Sans Unicode, Tahoma, Times New Roman, Verdana

Turkish

Turkish is the national language of Turkey and claims 59 million speakers worldwide.

Although ISO 8859-3 covers Turkish, the characters are deprecated there. The full Turkish set of characters is covered in ISO 8859-5. The Windows code page that correlates with this is 1254, also called Latin 5, which covers English and Turkish.

TURKISH

IME	Turkish					
Keyboard layout	Turkish Q					
Keystrokes	Shift-t	]	r	k	.	e
Input characters	T	ü	r	k	ç	e
Unicode positions	[U+0054]	[U+00FC]	[U+0072]	[U+006B]	[U+00E7]	[U+0065]
Code page points—1254	0x54	0xFC	0x72	0x6B	0xE7	0x65
Names	Latin Capital Letter T	Latin Small Letter U with Diaeresis	Latin Small Letter R	Latin Small Letter K	Latin Small Letter C with Cedilla	Latin Small Letter E
Display	*Türkçe*					
Pronunciation	Turkish–name of the language					
Unicode ranges	U+0000–U+007F Controls and Basic Latin U+0080–U+00FF Controls and Latin-1 Supplement					
Fonts	**Windows:** Angsana New, Arial, Arial Black, Arial Narrow, Batang, Book Antiqua, Bookman Old Style, Century Gothic, Comic Sans MS, Cordia New, Courier, Courier New, Garamond, Georgia, Gulim, Gulim-Che, Haettenschweiler, Impact, Lucinda Console, Lucinda Sans Unicode, Palatino Linotype, Tahoma, Times New Roman, Verdana **Macintosh:** Apple Chancery, Capitals, Charcoal, Chicago, Gadget, Geneva, Helvetica, Hoefler Text, Monaco, New York, Palatino, Sand, Skia, Tahoma, Techno, TektonPro, Textile, Times **Unix:** Caslon, ClearlyU					

Vietnamese

Vietnamese is primarily spoken in North and South Vietnam, but also in Cambodia, Laos, France, China, New Caledonia, Vanuatu, Thailand, Senegal, Australia, Côte d'Ivoire, and the U.S., totaling over 67 million speakers.

The Windows code page 1258 covers Vietnamese and English.

VIETNAMESE

IME	Vietnamese								
Keyboard layout	Vietnamese								
Keystrokes	x	i	n		c	h	a	5	o
Input characters	x	i	n		c	h	a´		o
Unicode positions	[U+0078]	[U+0069]	[U+006E]	[U+0020]	[U+0063]	[U+0068]	[U+0061]	[U+0300]	[U+006F]
Code page points—1258	78	69	6E	20	63	68	61	CC	6F
Names	Small Latin Letter X	Small Latin Letter I	Small Latin Letter N	Space	Small Latin Letter C	Small Latin Letter H	Small Latin Letter A	Combining Grave Accent	Small Latin Letter O
Display	xin cha`o								
Pronunciation	ksin chao—meaning *Hello*								
Unicode ranges	U+0000–U+007F Controls and Basic Latin U+0080–U+00FF Controls and Latin-1 Supplement U+0100–U+017F Latin Extended-A U+0180–U+024F Latin Extended-B U+0300–U+036F Combining Diacritical Marks U+20A0–U+20CF Currency Symbols								
Fonts	**Windows:** Arial, Courier New, Microsoft Sans Serif, Palatino Linotype, Tahoma, Times New Roman, Verdana **Unix:** Arial								

Estonian, Latvian, Lithuanian

ISO 8859-4 covers Danish, English, Estonian, Finnish, German, Greenlandic, Latin, Latvian, Lithuanian, Norwegian (with restrictions), Slovene, and Swedish. Windows code page 1257 is known as the Baltic page as it covers English, Estonian, Latvian, Lithuanian. Characters such as the õ shown in the table are found only in Estonian and in no other language, so although the other languages covered in the 8859-4 standard fit under other code pages, there was the requirement that a specific Baltic one be developed.

Estonian is primarily spoken in the Republic of Estonia. Lithuanian is primarily spoken in the Republic of Lithuania. Latvian is primarily spoken in the Republic of Latvia.

ESTONIAN, LATVIAN, LITHUANIAN

IME	Estonian				
Keyboard layout	Estonian				
Keystrokes	shift-j	]	d		
Input characters	J	õ	u	d	u
Unicode positions	[U+004A]	[U+00F5]	[U+0075]	[U+0064]	[U+0075]
Code page points—1257	0x4A	0xF5	0x75	0x64	0x75
Names	Latin Capital Letter J	Latin Small Letter O with Tilde	Latin Small Letter U	Latin Small Letter D	Latin Small Letter U
Display	Jõudu				
Unicode ranges	U+0000–U+007F Controls and Basic Latin U+0080–U+00FF Controls and Latin-1 Supplement U+0100–U+017F Latin Extended-A U+0180–U+024F Latin Extended-B				
Fonts	**Windows:** Angsana New, Arial, Arial Black, Arial Narrow, Batang, Book Antiqua, Bookman Old Style, Century Gothic, Comic Sans MS, Cordia New, Courier, Courier New, Garamond, Georgia, Gulim, GulimChe, Haettenschweiler, Impact, Lucinda Console, Lucinda Sans Unicode, Palatino Linotype, Tahoma, Times New Roman, Verdana **Macintosh:** Apple Chancery, Capitals, Charcoal, Chicago, Gadget, Geneva, Helvetica, Hoefler Text, Monaco, New York, Palatino, Sand, Skia, Tahoma, Techno, TektonPro, Textile, Times **Unix:** Caslon, ClearlyU				

System Guides to Configuring Your Machines

This appendix contains guides that can help you configure your client machine to be the most effective at catching problems. These guides are also available online at the book's companion Web site. Online the guides are illustrated with screen shots to better guide you through machine configuration.

Setting Up Your Windows System for International Content

In order to test international content, you will need to install the various fonts and the Input Method Editors (IMEs) necessary. These are available on the operating system CDs or may be available from various software-maker Web sites. Many fonts are available from various companies or as free downloads online.

Selecting and Installing Fonts

To install the default fonts on Windows 2000:

1. Go to Start → Settings → Control Panel.
2. Open the Regional Options control panel (Regional and Language Options in Windows XP).
3. The Language Settings for your System section of the General tab allow you to select the languages in which you can read and write documents.

Selecting languages here roughly translates to configuring the fonts and other settings to allow for reading and writing documents in other languages. Select the languages that you will be testing to install the appropriate components.

4. Click OK on both dialogs to finish the configuration.

Installing and Configuring Input Method Editors (IMEs)

In Windows 2000:

1. Go to Start → Settings → Control Panel.

2. Open the Regional Options control panel (Regional and Language Options in Windows XP).

3. Select the Input Locales tab on the Regional Options control panel to install and configure your IMEs.

4. Your system will most likely only have English selected and installed. Select Add... to add additional IMEs.

5. If the IME you want is not listed, go back to the General tab and click the Advanced button. Make sure that all the appropriate code pages associated with your desired language IME are selected and loaded. Not having the right ones selected will cause languages such as Greek, Hindi, and Chinese to not show up, so be sure that the appropriate code pages (including the 8859-x pages) are selected.

6 Selecting the Properties... button on the Input Locales tab allows you to change the keyboard configuration for the selected IME. Unless you specifically know what settings you want to adjust, leave these all with the default. When installed, they will be listed in the system tray next to the clock. Clicking on it will allow you to switch between various IMEs and select an IME to use.

Installing the System Debugger

In Windows 2000 and Windows XP:

1. Go to Start → Settings → Control Panel.

2. In Control Panel → Add/Remove Programs → Add/Remove Windows Components, make sure that Windows Script Debugger is installed.

NOTE **Your company may have other debuggers available to be installed on the test computers, but installing the Windows Script Debugger is a cheap and easy way to make all of your test machines meet the basic configuration requirements.**

3. Follow the Next> button on through to install the debugger. You may have to restart your machine to finish the setup.

Setting Your System for High Contrast Mode

High Contrast mode is a mode that you can switch your system into for higher visibility. It allows those with reduced vision or minimal vision to have text highly contrasted against the background so that they can see it more clearly. It also increases the font and window sizes.

To toggle your Windows operating system into and out of High Contrast mode, hold down the left Alt and Shift keys and hit the Print Screen button. The system may ask if you want to toggle into High Contrast mode. If it does so, click OK and your display will be redrawn in High Contrast mode. Do the same to toggle back out of the mode.

TIP **Many bugs involving text strings expanding beyond their boundaries can be found in this mode. Make sure guidelines are put in place regarding which of these types of bugs to fix and how the fixes can be implemented.**

Configuring Browser Settings

If you are going to be testing Web applications, then configuring your browser settings is an activity you will need to perform. In the next sections are the steps for configuring the two most common browsers. Many other browsers have similar controls to adjust them.

Making International Adjustments

Without tuning your client browser properly, you will not set yourself up to successfully test your application for globalization or localization.

Internet Explorer

To prepare Internet Explorer:

1. You can select your encoding method by going to View → Encoding and then selecting the proper encoding method for your application or test pass.

2. Navigating to Tools → Internet Options will bring up a dialog. Click the Languages... button on this dialog to select the accept language.

3. Some Web applications may have fall-through behavior, whereby secondary and tertiary accept languages are used if the primary one cannot be matched by the application. Many other applications simply try to honor the primary selection and default to English (or another assumed language) if the primary cannot be matched. Click the Fonts... button on the Internet Options dialog to select the script and fonts to use. You may need to change this when the document encoding changes.

Netscape Navigator

If you are totally unconfigured for foreign content, you may see corruption or other unexpected content when trying to view international content, such as Japanese text. If you are not configured properly, there are likely question marks indicating that the program does not understand the content in the context you are requesting. If you remember the discussion about code pages in Chapter 7, question marks indicate you have tried to decode the message with the wrong secret decoder ring. Something that appears to be corruption may not actually be. You cannot be sure yet. You must now tell Netscape Navigator which decoder ring to use in order to view the information properly.

1. First, go to View → Character Set to select the proper character set to work with. In this case of Japanese text, you need to change the encoding to Japanese (Shift_JIS). This change may clear everything up, or you may need to explicitly configure other settings such as the font.

2. Since Netscape does not take advantage of Windows font linking, the associated fonts may or may not default in (you may have to give it a second to find it). If it does not default in or you are unsure if the selected font is correct, refer to the particular language's page to see the list of fonts that support that language. The character set must first be selected from the View → Character Set menu option before the encoding or font can be set. Otherwise, at the midpoint of the steps, the character set will not match the encoding, and Navigator will helpfully undo the incompatible settings, which will run you around in circles until you discover the cause. If your application is using Unicode (UTF-8 or UTF-7), you will

need to specify the font to use. However, if your Web application depends on other settings, you may have to change those corresponding settings in your configuration.

3. The last configurations that you will likely want to investigate are available in the Edit menu. Go to Edit → Preferences... You must first select the language, so select Navigator → Languages. Set your accept language to Japanese (or whichever language you are trying to view). Now that the language is set, you can select a font that covers that language. Go to Appearance → Fonts to select the font.

Making Accessibility Browser Adjustments

Accessibility, in this context, refers to adjustments you can make to your browser to duplicate how real users may be running their systems.

Internet Explorer

Consider making the following accessibility adjustments in IE:

- To change the font face or size in IE, go to Tools → Internet Options. On the General tab, there is a button at the bottom labeled Fonts... that will open the dialog to specify the font face and encoding method.

- In IE the font size is not in points, but in relative smallest to largest size, adjusted by the View → Text Size menu.

- To change the font color, background color, or link colors, use the Colors... button on the General tab of the Internet Options dialog.

- Another accessibility adjustment to test would be overriding the document-specified formattings or style sheets. This feature can be accessed by the Accessibility... button on the General tab of the Internet Options dialog.

- Under Tools → Internet Options, select the Advanced tab. Under the Accessibility heading you can choose to always expand the ALT text on images. Under the Multimedia heading you can turn off images, sounds, video, and animations.

Netscape Navigator

You can make the following accessibility adjustments in Netscape Navigator:

- To change the font face in Netscape, go to Edit → Preferences → Appearance → Fonts. For accessibility reasons, some users may want to override the document fonts with their own font face or size. Testing this should be a part of the accessibility testing. The font color, background color, and link colors can be changed here, as well in the Color node.

■ Under Preferences → Advanced, Netscape allows you to deselect images, JavaScript, Java applets, and stylesheets to test how your application will behave under these conditions.

Bypassing a Proxy Server

Since proxy servers cache data and interfere with testing, they may need to be bypassed for testing purposes.

Internet Explorer

To bypass a proxy server:

1. In the Internet Explorer window, go to Tools → Internet Options.
2. Select the Connections tab and click the LAN Settings... button.
3. For your LAN settings, you will have your proxy server and most likely port 80 listed. Having your system automatically try to detect the settings may cause problems because the proxy will probably not be bypassed, so uncheck the auto-detect boxes when setting this up manually. If you are not sure what your proxy server is, check with your system administrator to make sure that this is configured correctly. If it applies, choose to bypass internal (local) addresses.
4. Save all of these and close all of your IE browser instances. When you restart IE, the new settings will be applied.

Netscape Navigator

To bypass a proxy server:

1. In the Netscape window, go to Edit → Preferences.
2. Expand the Advanced category and select Proxies.
3. Select the Manual configuration and click the View... button.
4. Again, list your proxy server for your company; the port is probably port 80, although checking with your system administrator will tell you absolutely what should be entered in each of these spaces.
5. In the area for domains that should not use the proxy server, list *.*yourdomain*.com, as well as <localhost> if appropriate. The asterisk in front of the domain acts as a wildcard and will cover all subdomains of the domain(s) you specify.

6. Click OK here and OK on the Preferences window to save your settings.

7. Closing all Netscape browser windows and restarting the computer will allow you to start using this configuration.

Other Browser Settings

Both Internet Explorer and Netscape Navigator have other settings that you, as a tester, may want to try testing. Some of these affect the way the browser works, while others affect the way the browser displays information.

Internet Explorer

In the Security tab of Internet Options, you can select security zones or individually turn on or off the various functions such as cookies, script, Java applets, or ActiveX controls. Knowing what your application depends on can help you find the required settings for these so that users can be guided to stable settings, and you can test with only supported configurations.

In the Advanced tab of the Internet Options dialog, you will want to set the URLs to be UTF-8 encoded unless your application does not support this or unless you are also using this as a testing configuration. Be sure that you do not have *Disable script debugging* selected. Also, make sure that the browser is set to *Display a notification about every script error*.

Netscape Navigator

In addition to some of the configurations mentioned, Netscape Navigator can be further configured through Edit → Preferences. Selecting the Advanced area allows you to configure the browser cookies, applets, script settings, and other settings.

Taking Screen Shots

Many bugs you log will be better explained with a screen shot to accompany them. You might need to be able to take screen shots on the Windows or Macintosh platforms.

Windows

Just hit the Print Screen key on your keyboard to capture the entire display and place it onto the clipboard. Some hardware configurations such as the addition of switchboxes can interfere with this and may require a different key command, such as holding down the Ctrl key or Alt key and then hitting the Print Screen key. If these two do not work for you, check the switchbox manufacturer's suggestions.

To paste this clipboard copy to a useful place, open MS-Paint and hit Ctrl+v to paste the capture to a new image. From here you can edit the screen capture and save it in various formats.

An alternative is to use Alt+Print Screen to capture only the current active window.

Macintosh

If you are using Macintosh OS 9:

1. Hold down the Command+Shift+4 keys together, and you will get crosshairs. Move the crosshairs to one corner of the area you would like to grab. Alternately, hold down the Command+Shift+3 combination to take a screen shot of the entire screen.

NOTE
The Command key is the one that has an image that looks a little like a pretzel and can be found on the lower-left side of your keyboard. It is also called the Open Apple key by some old-time Apple users because there is also the image of an apple on the key.

2. Hold down the mouse button, drag the crosshairs to the opposite corner, and release the mouse button. You will probably hear a clicking sound (if your sounds are turned on). The capture has now been saved to the default folder on the hard drive.

3. Open the active drive, and your shot will be labeled as Picture 1 or another similar name. Open your graphic-editing program and open the shot that you took. Save it in your desired format (.jpg, .png, .gif), and name it.

If you are using Macintosh OS X, you will actually need to launch a separate application called Grab.

1. Open the Utilities folder and double-click on the Grab utility. This will start it and place it in the tray.

2. When you are ready to capture a screen shot, switch to the Grab program by single-clicking on it in the tray. Your target application should not change other than not looking active.

Transferring Files between Operating Systems

Because you, as a tester, will be involved with using many different operating systems and many different machines, you may find it necessary to transfer files between them. There are many ways to transfer files between computers of various operating systems, but the easiest way that I have found is to use any Web-based email program, either your internal email system or an external free email program such as Hotmail, Yahoo, or Lycos. Simply open a browser and log in to your mail. Create a new email message to yourself and add your graphic as an attachment. Retrieve this on whichever preferred platform you are working from. Alternately, you can set up a share or an FTP site that the Macintosh machines can reach as well as the Windows-based PCs. This method may mean a reliance on the IT department, and if you have none, then the easiest method may be an email solution.

3. Hold down the Command+z combination to bring up a small informational window. To take a shot, you will just click anywhere outside the window. Your screen shot will immediately open in the Grab application.

4. Click on File → Save as..., which allows you to save the file off as a .tiff image. These files can then be opened with any other graphic conversion program to convert them to another format.

HTTP Response Codes

The response codes in this appendix are standardized by the W3C, and the text is taken from RFC 2616.

Codes are divided into five groups based on classification. Each group has a different initial digit, indicating the type of response. Most of the time, users do not see the responses because they are absorbed by the browser or other servers.

1xx—Informational

This class of status code indicates a provisional response, consisting only of the Status-Line and optional headers, and is terminated by an empty line. There are no required headers for this class of status code. Since HTTP/1.0 did not define any 1xx status codes, servers MUST NOT send a 1xx response to an HTTP/1.0 client except under experimental conditions.

A client MUST be prepared to accept one or more 1xx status responses prior to a regular response, even if the client does not expect a 100 (Continue) status message. Unexpected 1xx status responses MAY be ignored by a user agent.

Proxies MUST forward 1xx responses, unless the connection between the proxy and its client has been closed, or unless the proxy itself requested the generation of the 1xx response. (For example, if a proxy adds a "Expect: 100-Continue" field when it forwards a request, then it need not forward the corresponding 100 (Continue) response(s).)

STATUS CODE	ERROR MESSAGE	DESCRIPTION
100	Continue	The client may continue with its request. This interim response is used to inform the client that the initial part of the request has been received and has not been rejected by the server. The client SHOULD continue by sending the remainder of the request, or, if the request has already been completed, ignore this response. The server MUST send a final response after the request has been completed.
101	Switching Protocols	The server understands and is willing to comply with the client's request, via the Upgrade message header field (section 14.41), for a change in the application protocol being used on this connection. The server will switch protocols to those defined by the response's Upgrade header field immediately after the empty line that terminates the 101 response. The protocol should only be switched when it is advantageous to do so. For example, switching to a newer version of HTTP is advantageous over older versions, and switching to a real-time, synchronous protocol may be advantageous when delivering resources that use such features.

2xx—Successful

The request has succeeded.

STATUS CODE	ERROR MESSAGE	DESCRIPTION
200	OK	The request to the server was successful. The resource was successfully retrieved. The information returned with the response is dependent on the method used in the request, for example: GET—An entity corresponding to the requested resource is sent in the response HEAD—The entity-header fields corresponding to the requested resource are sent in the response without any message-body POST—An entity describing or containing the result of the action TRACE—An entity containing the request message as received by the end server
201	Created	The request has been fulfilled and resulted in a new resource being created. The newly created resource can be referenced by the URI(s) returned in the entity of the response, with the most specific URL for the resource given by a Location header field. The origin server MUST create the resource before returning the 201 status code. If the action cannot be carried out immediately, the server should respond with 202 (Accepted) response instead.

(continued)

(continued)

STATUS CODE	ERROR MESSAGE	DESCRIPTION
202	Accepted	The request has been accepted for processing, but the processing has not been completed. The request MAY or MAY NOT eventually be acted upon, as it MAY be disallowed when processing actually takes place. There is no facility for re-sending a status code from an asynchronous operation such as this. The 202 response is intentionally non-committal. Its purpose is to allow a server to accept a request for some other process (perhaps a batch-oriented process that is only run once per day) without requiring that the user agent's connection to the server persist until the process is completed. The entity returned with this response SHOULD include an indication of the request's current status and either a pointer to a status monitor or some estimate of when the user can expect the request to be fulfilled.
203	Non-Authoritative Information or Partial Information	The returned meta-information in the entity-header is not the definitive set as available from the origin server, but is gathered from a local or a third-party copy. The set presented MAY be a subset or superset of the original version. For example, including local annotation information about the resource MAY result in a superset of the meta-information known by the origin server. Use of this response code is not required and is only appropriate when the response would otherwise be 200 (OK).
204	No Content	The server has fulfilled the request, but there is no new information to send back. If the client is a user agent, it SHOULD NOT change its document view from that which caused the request to be sent. This response is primarily intended to allow input for actions to take place without causing a change to the user agent's active document view. The response MAY include new meta-information in the form of entity-headers, which SHOULD apply to the document currently in the user agent's active view. The 204 response MUST NOT include a message-body, and thus is always terminated by the first empty line after the header fields.

STATUS CODE	ERROR MESSAGE	DESCRIPTION
205	Reset Content	The server has fulfilled the request, and the user agent SHOULD reset the document view that caused the request to be sent. This response is primarily intended to allow input for actions to take place via user input, followed by a clearing of the form in which the input is given so that the user can easily initiate another input action. The response MUST NOT include an entity.
206	Partial Content	The server has fulfilled the partial GET request for the resource. The request must have included a Range header field (section 14.36) indicating the desired range. The response MUST include either a Content-Range header field (section 14.17) indicating the range included with this response, or a multipart/byte ranges Content-Type including Content-Range fields for each part. If multipart/byte ranges is not used, the Content-Length header field in the response MUST match the actual number of OCTETs transmitted in the message-body. A cache that does not support the Range and Content-Range headers MUST NOT cache 206 (Partial) responses.
207	Multi Status	

3xx—Redirection

This class of status code indicates that further action needs to be taken by the user agent in order to fulfill the request. The action required MAY be carried out by the user agent without interaction with the user if and only if the method used in the second request is GET or HEAD. A client SHOULD detect infinite redirection loops, since such loops generate network traffic for each redirection.

Note: previous versions of this specification recommended a maximum of five redirections. Content developers should be aware that there might be clients that implement such a fixed limitation.

STATUS CODE	ERROR MESSAGE	DESCRIPTION
300	Multiple Choices	The requested resource corresponds to any one of a set of representations, each with its own specific location, and agent-driven negotiation information (section 12) is being provided so that the user (or user agent) can select a preferred representation and redirect its request to that location. Unless it was a HEAD request, the response SHOULD include an entity containing a list of resource characteristics and location(s) from which the user or user agent can choose the one most appropriate. The entity format is specified by the media type given in the Content-Type header field. Depending upon the format and the capabilities of the user agent, selection of the most appropriate choice may be performed automatically. However, this specification does not define any standard for such automatic selection. If the server has a preferred choice of representation, it SHOULD include the specific URL for that representation in the Location field; user agents MAY use the Location field value for automatic redirection. This response is cachable unless indicated otherwise.
301	Moved Permanently	The requested resource has been assigned a new permanent URI, and any future references to this resource SHOULD be done using one of the returned URIs. Clients with link editing capabilities SHOULD automatically re-link references to the Request-URI to one or more of the new references returned by the server, where possible. This response is cachable unless indicated otherwise. If the new URI is a location, its URL SHOULD be given by the Location field in the response. Unless the request method was HEAD, the entity of the response SHOULD contain a short hypertext note with a hyperlink to the new URI(s).

STATUS CODE	ERROR MESSAGE	DESCRIPTION
301 *(continued)*	Moved Permanently	If the 301 status code is received in response to a request other than GET or HEAD, the user agent MUST NOT automatically redirect the request unless it can be confirmed by the user, since this might change the conditions under which the request was issued. Note: When automatically redirecting a POST request after receiving a 301 status code, some existing HTTP/1.0 user agents will erroneously change it into a GET request.
302	Found	The requested resource resides temporarily under a different URI. Since the redirection might be altered on occasion, the client SHOULD continue to use the Request-URI for future requests. This response is only cacheable if indicated by a Cache-Control or Expires header field. The temporary URI SHOULD be given by the Location field in the response. Unless the request method was HEAD, the entity of the response SHOULD contain a short hypertext note with a hyperlink to the new URI(s).
303	See Other	The response to the request can be found under a different URI and SHOULD be retrieved using a GET method on that resource. This method exists primarily to allow the output of a POST-activated script to redirect the user agent to a selected resource. The new URI is not a substitute reference for the originally requested resource. The 303 response is not cachable, but the response to the second (redirected) request MAY be cachable. If the new URI is a location, its URL SHOULD be given by the Location field in the response. Unless the request method was HEAD, the entity of the response SHOULD contain a short hypertext note with a hyperlink to the new URI(s).

(continued)

(continued)

STATUS CODE	ERROR MESSAGE	DESCRIPTION
304	Not Modified	The client request for modification did not take place.
		If the client has performed a conditional GET request and access is allowed, but the document has not been modified, the server SHOULD respond with this status code. The response MUST NOT contain a message-body.
		The response MUST include the following header fields:
		—Date
		—ETag and/or Content-Location, if the header would have been sent in a 200 response to the same request
		—Expires, Cache-Control, and/or Vary, if the field-value might differ from that sent in any previous response for the same variant
		If the conditional GET used a strong cache validator (see section 13.3.3), the response SHOULD NOT include other entity-headers. Otherwise (i.e., the conditional GET used a weak validator), the response MUST NOT include other entity-headers; this prevents inconsistencies between cached entity-bodies and updated headers.
		If a 304 response indicates an entity not currently cached, then the cache MUST disregard the response and repeat the request without the conditional.
		If a cache uses a received 304 response to update a cache entry, the cache MUST update the entry to reflect any new field values given in the response.
		The 304 response MUST NOT include a message-body, and thus is always terminated by the first empty line after the header fields.

STATUS CODE	ERROR MESSAGE	DESCRIPTION
305	Use Proxy	The requested resource MUST be accessed through the proxy given by the Location field. The Location field gives the URL of the proxy. The recipient is expected to repeat the request via the proxy.
306	(Unused)	The 306 status code used in a previous version of the specification is no longer used, and the code is reserved.
307	Temporary Redirect	The requested resource resides temporarily under a different URI. Since the redirection MAY be altered on occasion, the client SHOULD continue to use the Request-URI for future requests. This response is only cacheable if indicated by a Cache-Control or Expires header field. The temporary URI SHOULD be given by the Location field in the response. Unless the request method was HEAD, the entity of the response SHOULD contain a short hypertext note with a hyperlink to the new URI(s), since many pre-HTTP/1.1 user agents do not understand the 307 status. Therefore, the note SHOULD contain the information necessary for a user to repeat the original request on the new URI. If the 307 status code is received in response to a request other than GET or HEAD, the user agent MUST NOT automatically redirect the request unless it can be confirmed by the user, since this might change the conditions under which the request was issued.

4xx—Client Error

The 4xx class of status code is intended for cases in which the client seems to have erred. Except when responding to a HEAD request, the server SHOULD include an entity containing an explanation of the error situation, and whether it is a temporary or permanent condition. These status codes are applicable to any request method.

User agents SHOULD display any included entity to the user. If the client is sending data, a server implementation using TCP SHOULD be careful to ensure that the client acknowledges receipt of the packet(s) containing the response, before the server closes the input connection. If the client continues sending data to the server after the close, the server's TCP stack will send a reset packet to the client, which may erase the client's unacknowledged input buffers before they can be read and interpreted by the HTTP application.

STATUS CODE	ERROR MESSAGE	DESCRIPTION
400	Bad Request	The request could not be understood by the server due to malformed syntax. The client SHOULD NOT repeat the request without modifications.
401	Unauthorized (Password Protected - and authentication was incorrect)	A password or some other security code is required to gain access to the resource. The request requires user authentication. The response MUST include a WWW-Authenticate header field (section 14.46) containing a challenge applicable to the requested resource. The client MAY repeat the request with a suitable Authorization header field (section 14.8). If the request already included Authorization credentials, then the 401 response indicates that authorization has been refused for those credentials. If the 401 response contains the same challenge as the prior response, and the user agent has already attempted authentication at least once, then the user SHOULD be presented the entity that was given in the response, since that entity MAY include relevant diagnostic information. HTTP access authentication is explained in section 11.
402	Payment Required	Reserved for future use.
403	Forbidden	The server understood the request, but is refusing to fulfill it. Authorization will not help and the request SHOULD NOT be repeated. If the request method was not HEAD and the server wishes to make public why the request has not been fulfilled, it SHOULD describe the reason for the refusal in the entity. This status code is commonly used when the server does not wish to reveal exactly why the request has been refused, or when no other response is applicable.

STATUS CODE	ERROR MESSAGE	DESCRIPTION
404	URL Does Not Exist (not found)	The server has not found anything matching the Request-URI. No indication is given of whether the condition is temporary or permanent. If the server does not wish to make this information available to the client, the status code 403 (Forbidden) can be used instead. The 410 (Gone) status code SHOULD be used if the server knows, through some internally configurable mechanism, that an old resource is permanently unavailable and has no forwarding address.
405	Method Not Allowed	The client tried to access a resource using a method (e.g., POST, HEAD, and so on) that is not allowed for that resource. The method specified in the Request-Line is not allowed for the resource identified by the Request-URI. The response MUST include an Allow header containing a list of valid methods for the requested resource.
406	Not Acceptable	The resource was found but could not be delivered because the type of the resource is incompatible with the acceptable types indicated by the *accept* or *accept-encoding* headers sent to the server by the client. The resource identified by the request is only capable of generating response entities that have content characteristics not acceptable according to the accept headers sent in the request. Unless it was a HEAD request, the response SHOULD include an entity containing a list of available entity characteristics and location(s) from which the user or user agent can choose the one most appropriate. The entity format is specified by the media type given in the Content-Type header field. Depending upon the format and the capabilities of the user agent, selection of the most appropriate choice may be performed automatically. However, this specification does not define any standard for such automatic selection.

(continued)

(continued)

STATUS CODE	ERROR MESSAGE	DESCRIPTION
406 *(continued)*	Not Acceptable	Note: HTTP/1.1 servers are allowed to return responses that are not acceptable according to the accept headers sent in the request. In some cases, this may even be preferable to sending a 406 response. User agents are encouraged to inspect the headers of an incoming response to determine if it is acceptable. If the response could be unacceptable, a user agent SHOULD temporarily stop receipt of more data and query the user for a decision on further actions.
407	Proxy Authentication Required	This code is similar to 401 (Unauthorized), but indicates that the client MUST first authenticate itself with the proxy. The proxy MUST return a Proxy-Authenticate header field (section 14.33) containing a challenge applicable to the proxy for the requested resource. The client MAY repeat the request with a suitable Proxy-Authorization header field (section 14.34). HTTP access authentication is explained in section 11.
408	Request Timeout	The client did not produce a request within the time that the server was prepared to wait. The client MAY repeat the request without modifications at any later time.
409	Conflict	The request could not be completed due to a conflict with the current state of the resource. This code is only allowed in situations where it is expected that the user might be able to resolve the conflict and resubmit the request. The response body SHOULD include enough information for the user to recognize the source of the conflict. Ideally, the response entity would include enough information for the user or user agent to fix the problem; however, that may not be possible and is not required. Conflicts are most likely to occur in response to a PUT request. If versioning is being used and the entity being PUT includes changes to a resource that conflict with those made by an earlier (third-party) request, the server MAY use the 409 response to indicate that it can't complete the request. In this case, the response entity SHOULD contain a list of the differences between the two versions in a format defined by the response Content-Type.

STATUS CODE	ERROR MESSAGE	DESCRIPTION
410	Gone	The requested resource is no longer available at the server and no forwarding address is known. This condition SHOULD be considered permanent. Clients with link editing capabilities SHOULD delete references to the Request-URI after user approval. If the server does not know, or has no facility to determine, whether or not the condition is permanent, the status code 404 (Not Found) SHOULD be used instead. This response is cacheable unless indicated otherwise.
		The 410 response is primarily intended to assist the task of Web maintenance by notifying the recipient that the resource is intentionally unavailable and that the server owners desire that remote links to that resource be removed. Such an event is common for limited-time, promotional services and for resources belonging to individuals no longer working at the server's site. It is not necessary to mark all permanently unavailable resources as "gone" or to keep the mark for any length of time—that is left to the discretion of the server owner.
411	Length Required	The server refuses to accept the request without a defined Content-Length. The client MAY repeat the request if it adds a valid Content-Length header field containing the length of the message-body in the request message.
412	Precondition Failed	The precondition given in one or more of the request-header fields evaluated to false when it was tested on the server. This response code allows the client to place preconditions on the current resource meta-information (header field data) and thus prevent the requested method from being applied to a resource other than the one intended.
413	Request Entity Too Large	The server is refusing to process a request because the request entity is larger than the server is willing or able to process. The server may close the connection to prevent the client from continuing the request.
		If the condition is temporary, the server SHOULD include a Retry-After header field to indicate that it is temporary and after what time the client may try again.

(continued)

(continued)

STATUS CODE	ERROR MESSAGE	DESCRIPTION
414	Request-URI Too Long	The server is refusing to service the request because the Request-URI is longer than the server is willing to interpret. This rare condition is only likely to occur when a client has improperly converted a POST request to a GET request with long query information, when the client has descended into a URL "black hole" of redirection (e.g., a redirected URL prefix that points to a suffix of itself), or when the server is under attack by a client attempting to exploit security holes present in some servers using fixed-length buffers for reading or manipulating the Request-URI.
415	Unsupported Media Type	The server is refusing to service the request because the entity of the request is in a format not supported by the requested resource for the requested method.
416	Requested Range Not Satisfiable	A server SHOULD return a response with this status code if a request included a Range request-header field (section 14.35), and none of the range-specifier values in this field overlap the current extent of the selected resource, and the request did not include an If-Range request-header field. (For byte-ranges, this means that the first-byte-pos of all of the byte-range-spec values were greater than the current length of the selected resource.) When this status code is returned for a byte-range request, the response SHOULD include a Content-Range entity-header field specifying the current length of the selected resource (see section 14.16). This response MUST NOT use the multipart/byte-ranges content-type.
417	Expectation Failed	The expectation given in an Expect request-header field (see section 14.20) could not be met by this server, or, if the server is a proxy, the server has unambiguous evidence that the request could not be met by the next-hop server.

5xx—Server Error

Response status codes beginning with the digit "5" indicate cases in which the server is aware that it has erred or is incapable of performing the request. Except when responding to a HEAD request, the server SHOULD include an entity containing an explanation of the error situation, and whether it is a temporary or permanent condition. User agents SHOULD display any included entity to the user. These response codes are applicable to any request method.

STATUS CODE	ERROR MESSAGE	DESCRIPTION
500	Internal Server Error	The server encountered an unexpected condition that prevented it from fulfilling the request. The server was having technical difficulties, or there was some problem with Internet traffic or connections.
501	Not Implemented	The server does not support the functionality required to fulfill the request. This is the appropriate response when the server does not recognize the request method and is not capable of supporting it for any resource.
502	Bad Gateway	The server, while acting as a gateway or proxy, received an invalid response from the upstream server it accessed in attempting to fulfill the request.
503	Service Unavailable	The server is currently unable to handle the request due to a temporary overloading or maintenance of the server. The implication is that this is a temporary condition that will be alleviated after some delay. If known, the length of the delay may be indicated in a Retry-After header. If no Retry-After is given, the client SHOULD handle the response as it would for a 500 response. Note: The existence of the 503 status code does not imply that a server must use it when becoming overloaded. Some servers may wish to simply refuse the connection.

(continued)

(continued)

STATUS CODE	ERROR MESSAGE	DESCRIPTION
504	Gateway Timeout	The server, while acting as a gateway or proxy, did not receive a timely response from the upstream server it accessed in attempting to complete the request.
505	HTTP Version Not Supported	The server does not support, or refuses to support, the HTTP protocol version that was used in the request message. The server is indicating that it is unable or unwilling to complete the request using the same major version as the client, as described in section 3.1, other than with this error message. The response SHOULD contain an entity describing why that version is not supported and what other protocols are supported by that server.

The complete RFC 2616 spec can be found at http://www.ietf.org. The copyright that the content in this chapter is subject to is as follows:

Languages and Mappings

T he mappings between languages used and the code pages that cover them is not direct, but rather loose. This is a general guide for which code pages to use to generate test data for applications that will be localized or globalized for various languages.

ISO 8859

The International Organization for Standardization (ISO) lays out many standards for the computing industry. Each part of ISO/IEC 8859 specifies a character set that is suitable both for data- and text-processing applications and for information interchange.

For information processing, it includes 8-bit single-byte coded graphic character sets as follows:

- **Part 1:** Latin alphabet No.1 (1997)—second edition
- **Part 2:** Latin alphabet No.2 (1998)—second edition
- **Part 3:** Latin alphabet No.3 (1998)—second edition
- **Part 4:** Latin alphabet No.4 (1998)—second edition
- **Part 5:** Latin/Cyrillic alphabet (1998)—second edition
- **Part 6:** Latin/Arabic alphabet (1998)—second edition
- **Part 7:** Latin/Greek alphabet (1998)—second edition

- **Part 8:** Latin/Hebrew alphabet (1998)—second edition
- **Part 9:** Latin alphabet No.5 (1998)—second edition
- **Part 10:** Latin alphabet No.6 (1998)—second edition
- **Part 11:** Latin/Thai alphabet (1998)
- **Part 12:** Unassigned
- **Part 13:** Latin alphabet No.7 (1998)
- **Part 14:** Latin alphabet No.8 (1998)
- **Part 15:** Latin alphabet No.9 (1998)

Each part specifying a Latin Alphabet lists the languages for which it has been designed. These are:

- **Latin Alphabet No. 1.** Albanian, Basque, Breton, Catalan, Danish, Dutch, English, Faroese, Finnish, French (with restrictions), Frisian, Galician, German, Greenlandic, Icelandic, Irish Gaelic (new orthography), Italian, Latin, Luxemburgish, Norwegian, Portuguese, Rhjaeto-Romanic, Scottish Gaelic, Spanish, and Swedish.

- **Latin Alphabet No. 2.** Albanian, Croat, Czech, English, German, Hungarian, Latin, Polish, Romanian, Slovak, Slovene, and Sorbian.

- **Latin Alphabet No. 3.** Esperanto and Maltese, and if needed in conjunction with these, English, French (with restrictions), German, Italian, Latin, and Portuguese. Coding of Turkish characters is deprecated in this code.

- **Latin Alphabet No. 4.** Danish, English, Estonian, Finnish, German, Greenlandic, Latin, Latvian, Lithuanian, Norwegian, Sámi (with restrictions), Slovene, and Swedish.

- **Latin Alphabet No. 5.** Albanian, Basque, Breton, Catalan, Danish, Dutch, English, Faroese, Finnish, French (with restrictions), Frisian, Galician, German, Greenlandic, Irish Gaelic (new orthography), Italian, Latin, Luxemburgish, Norwegian, Portuguese, Spanish, Rhaeto-Romanic, Scottish Gaelic, Spanish, Swedish, and Turkish.

- **Latin Alphabet No. 6.** Danish, English, Estonian, Faroese, Finnish, German, Greenlandic, Icelandic, Irish Gaelic (new orthography), Latin, Lithuanian, Norwegian, Sámi (with restrictions), Slovene, and Swedish.

- **Latin Alphabet No. 7.** Danish, English, Estonian, Finnish, German, Latin, Latvian, Lithuanian, Norwegian, Polish, Slovene, and Swedish.

- **Latin Alphabet No. 8.** Albanian, Basque, Breton, Catalan, Cornish, Danish, Dutch, English, French (with restrictions), Frisian, Galician, German, Greenlandic, Irish Gaelic (old and new orthographies), Ialian, Latin, Luxemburgish, Manx Gaelic, Norwegian, Portuguese, Rhaeto-Romanic, Scottish Gaelic, Spanish, Swedish, and Welsh.

- **Latin Alphabet No. 9.** Albanian, Basque, Breton, Catalan, Danish, Dutch, English, Estonian, Faroese, Finnish, French, Frisian, Galician, German, Greenlandic, Icelandic, Irish Gaelic (new orthography), Italian, Latin, Luxemburgish, Norwegian, Portuguese, Rhaeto-Romanic, Scottish Gaelic, Spanish, and Swedish.

NOTE

For writing French, three characters not included in Latin Alphabets 1, 3, 5, and 8 are also needed. These are included in Latin Alphabet No. 9.

ISO 8859 versus Windows Code Pages

While the ISO standards are very clear, sometimes their mappings to a Windows code page (or any other corporate interpretation) is not so precise. Because of the slight differences that may occur in the interpretations, I refer to the relationship as a correlation rather than a direct mapping. These correlations will be useful when testing various languages and the globalization of your application. The code pages and more are available on the companion Web site to the book.

- 1252 correlates with ISO 8859-1
- 1250 correlates with ISO 8859-2
- 1257 correlates with ISO 8859-4
- 1256 correlates with ISO 8859-6
- 1253 correlates with ISO 8859-7
- 1255 correlates with ISO 8859-8
- 874 correlates with ISO 8859-11

Additional Windows Code Pages

Other important Windows code pages are not strict interpretations of the ISO standards or the original standards that developed them. Many have additional ranges added for better coverage of the language of the people they represent.

- Windows 936 code page is the GB 2312-80 (based from the ISO 646) with the Hanzi corrections. (CHS).
- Windows 932 code page is JIS X 0208-1990 plus the Microsoft extensions by SJIS code. (JPN).

- Windows 950 is the Big Five set plus row 89 of the ETen extension. (CHT/Taiwanese).

- Windows 949 is 5601 plus extensions. (Korean).

- ISCII is a newly developed code page for Indic.

- GB 18030 is the newest revision of the CHS code page and includes 4-byte characters.

Problem Characters and Sample Test Input

This appendix contains sample input that has a high likelihood of causing misbehavior in many different types of applications. The exact usage varies depending on the application—some will be sensitive to these cases in a URL, others through a text input field, and others will be very tolerant of the data and behave correctly. Many applications will have their own sets of problematic input that may contain these and may have some unique ones.

Characters from the Single-Byte Character Sets

Control Characters

The control characters in Table G.1 are often left off of code pages because these first 32 code points are common to them all but are nonprintable entities.

Table G.1 Control Characters

UNICODE POINT	ABBRE- VIATION	KEYSTROKE	NAME	COMMENTS
[U+0000]	NUL	Ctrl+@	NULL	This needs to be tested in every place where data can be input or stored; many systems will crash or fail when this is encountered because they are not expecting this; code needs to handle these situations gracefully.
[U+0001]	SOH	Ctrl+A	START OF HEADING	
[U+0002]	STX	Ctrl+B	START OF TEXT	
[U+0003]	ETX	Ctrl+C	END OF TEXT	
[U+0004]	EOT	Ctrl+D	END OF TRANSMISSION	
[U+0005]	ENQ	Ctrl+E	ENQUIRY	
[U+0006]	ACK	Ctrl+F	ACKNOWLEDGE	
[U+0007]	BEL	Ctrl+G	BELL	(Beep)—caused teletype machines to ring a bell; will cause many common terminal/ term emulation programs to beep.
[U+0008]	BS	Ctrl+H	BACKSPACE	
[U+0009]	HT	Ctrl+I	HORIZONTAL TAB	
[U+000A]	LF	Ctrl+J	LINE FEED	
[U+000B]	VT	Ctrl+K	VERTICAL TAB	
[U+000C]	FF	Ctrl+L	FORM FEED	
[U+000D]	CR	Ctrl+M	CARRIAGE RETURN	

Table G.1 *(continued)*

UNICODE POINT	ABBRE-VIATION	KEYSTROKE	NAME	COMMENTS
[U+000E]	SO	Ctrl+N	SHIFT OUT	Switches output device to alternate character set.
[U+000F]	SI	Ctrl+O	SHIFT IN	Switches output device to default character set.
[U+0010]	DLE	Ctrl+P	DATA LINK ESCAPE	
[U+0011]	DC1	Ctrl+Q	DEVICE CONTROL 1	Also the XON command for a modem soft handshake.
[U+0012]	DC2	Ctrl+R	DEVICE CONTROL 2	
[U+0013]	DC3	Ctrl+S	DEVICE CONTROL 3	Also the XOFF command for the modem soft handshake.
[U+0014]	DC4	Ctrl+T	DEVICE CONTROL 4	
[U+0015]	NAK	Ctrl+U	NEGATIVE ACKNOWLEDGE	
[U+0016]	SYN	Ctrl+V	SYNCHRONOUS IDLE	
[U+0017]	ETB	Ctrl+W	END OF TRANSMISSION BLOCK	
[U+0018]	CAN	Ctrl+X	CANCEL	
[U+0019]	EM	Ctrl+Y	END OF MEDIUM	
[U+001A]	SUB	Ctrl+Z	SUBSTITUTE	
[U+001B]	ESC	Ctrl+[	ESCAPE	
[U+001C]	FS	Ctrl+\	FILE SEPARATOR	
[U+001D]	GS	Ctrl+]	GROUP SEPARATOR	
[U+001E]	RS	Ctrl+^	RECORD SEPARATOR	
[U+001F]	US	Ctrl+_	UNIT SEPARATOR	

IBM PC Keyboard Scan Codes

For special key combinations (for example, Alt+S, F5, and so on), a special two-character escape sequence is used. Depending on the language, the escape character can be either Escape [U+001B] or NUL [U+0000]. I will assume that NUL is being used in Table G.2. Having these codes can be very useful for automation or other places where you need to send particular keys.

Table G.2 IBM PC Keyboard Scan Codes

KEY COMBINATION	ESCAPE SEQUENCE
Alt+A	[U+0000][U+001E]
Alt+B	[U+0000][U+0030]
Alt+C	[U+0000][U+002E]
Alt+D	[U+0000][U+0020]
Alt+E	[U+0000][U+0012]
Alt+F	[U+0000][U+0021]
Alt+G	[U+0000][U+0022]
Alt+H	[U+0000][U+0023]
Alt+I	[U+0000][U+0017]
Alt+J	[U+0000][U+0024]
Alt+K	[U+0000][U+0025]
Alt+L	[U+0000][U+0026]
Alt+M	[U+0000][U+0032]
Alt+N	[U+0000][U+0031]
Alt+O	[U+0000][U+0018]
Alt+P	[U+0000][U+0019]
Alt+Q	[U+0000][U+0010]
Alt+R	[U+0000][U+0013]
Alt+S	[U+0000][U+001A]
Alt+T	[U+0000][U+0014]
Alt+U	[U+0000][U+0016]
Alt+V	[U+0000][U+002F]
Alt+W	[U+0000][U+0011]
Alt+X	[U+0000][U+002D]
Alt+Y	[U+0000][U+0015]

Table G.2 *(continued)*

KEY COMBINATION	ESCAPE SEQUENCE
Alt+Z	[U+0000][U+002C]
PGUP	[U+0000][U+0049]
PGDN	[U+0000][U+0051]
HOME	[U+0000][U+0047]
END	[U+0000][U+004F]
UPARRW	[U+0000][U+0048]
DNARRW	[U+0000][U+0050]
LFTARRW	[U+0000][U+004B]
RTARRW	[U+0000][U+004D]
F1	[U+0000][U+003B]
F2	[U+0000][U+003C]
F3	[U+0000][U+003D]
F4	[U+0000][U+003E]
F5	[U+0000][U+003F]
F6	[U+0000][U+0040]
F7	[U+0000][U+0041]
F8	[U+0000][U+0042]
F9	[U+0000][U+0043]
F10	[U+0000][U+0044]
F11	[U+0000][U+0085]
F12	[U+0000][U+0086]
Alt+F1	[U+0000][U+0068]
Alt+F2	[U+0000][U+0069]
Alt+F3	[U+0000][U+006A]
Alt+F4	[U+0000][U+006B]
Alt+F5	[U+0000][U+006C]
Alt+F6	[U+0000][U+006D]
Alt+F7	[U+0000][U+006E]
Alt+F8	[U+0000][U+006F]
Alt+F9	[U+0000][U+0070]
Alt+F10	[U+0000][U+0071]
Alt+F11	[U+0000][U+008B]
Alt+F12	[U+0000][U+008C]

Character Combinations

Using the control characters mentioned previously in this appendix, each separately, is one type of test case; however, they can sometimes be handled correctly individually yet mean something special when used in certain combinations. Below is one key combination to test that uses the control characters.

[U+000D][U+000A]—CRLF or (CR)(LF), carriage return, and a line feed—means multiple things, such as the end of a packet segment; two of these in a row also need to be tested as input or within a stream of input because many protocols see two in a row as the end of a transmission.

Lower ASCII

Table G.3 provides some information about each potentially problematic lower ASCII character. Depending on the usage and context, these characters can mean very different things. The notations are just suggestions about how a character could be a sensitive or unwise character.

Table G.3   Lower ASCII Problematic Characters

CHARACTER	CODE PAGE POINT	UNICODE POINT	NAME	COMMENT
	0x20	[U+0020]	Space	Also a C reserved char—very useful for turning up problems if first, last, or only char entered; problematic in a URL
!	0x21	[U+0021]	Exclamation mark	Problematic in a URL
"	0x22	[U+0022]	Double quotes	A C reserved char and delimiter; problematic in a URL
#	0x23	[U+0023]	Number sign	May be a delimiter; problematic in a URL
$	0x24	[U+0024]	Dollar sign	A reserved character in a query component
%	0x25	[U+0025]	Percent	A C reserved char or a delimiter

Table G.3 *(continued)*

CHARACTER	CODE PAGE POINT	UNICODE POINT	NAME	COMMENT
&	0x26	[U+0026]	Ampersand	Character in a query component; problematic in a URL
'	0x27	[U+0027]	Apostrophe	A C reserved char and unwise to leave unescaped; problematic in a URL
(	0x28	[U+0028]	Left parenthesis	Problematic in a URL
)	0x29	[U+0029]	Right parenthesis	Problematic in a URL
*	0x2A	[U+002A]	Asterisk	
+	0x2B	[U+002B]	Plus sign	Character in a query component; problematic in a URL
,	0x2C	[U+002C]	Comma	Character in a query component; problematic in a URL
-	0x2D	[U+002D]	Hyphen—minus	
.	0x2E	[U+002E]	Full stop (period)	Especially as last char of a file name
/	0x2F	[U+002F]	Solidus (slash)	Especially as last char of a file name; also a C reserved char or reserved in a query component; problematic in a URL
:	0x3A	[U+003A]	Colon	A reserved character in a query component; problematic in a URL

(continued)

Table G.3 *(continued)*

CHARACTER	CODE PAGE POINT	UNICODE POINT	NAME	COMMENT
;	0x3B	[U+003B]	Semicolon	A valid char in a URL, however can be problematic; may want to escape anyway; reserved within a query component, can be a parameter delimiter.
<	0x3C	[U+003C]	Less-than sign	Can be a delimiter or part of HTML or script; problematic in a URL
=	0x3D	[U+003D]	Equals sign	Reserved character in a query component; problematic in a URL
>	0x3E	[U+003E]	Greater-than sign	Can be a delimiter or part of HTML or script; problematic in a URL
?	0x3F	[U+003F]	Question mark	Reserved character in a query component; problematic in a URL
@	0x40	[U+0040]	Commercial At (at sign)	Reserved character in a query component; problematic in a URL unless part of the authentication
[	0x5B	[U+005B]	Left square bracket	An unwise character to leave unescaped; problematic in a URL; also problematic in RTL

Table G.3 *(continued)*

CHARACTER	CODE PAGE POINT	UNICODE POINT	NAME	COMMENT
\	0x5C	[U+005C]	Reverse solidus (backslash)	Especially as last char of a file name; an unwise character to leave unescaped; problematic in a URL
]	0x5D	[U+005D]	Right square bracket	An unwise character to leave unescaped; problematic in a URL; also problematic in RTL
^	0x5E	[U+005E]	Circumflex accent	An unwise character to leave unescaped; problematic in a URL
_	0x5F	[U+005F]	Low line	An unwise character to leave unescaped; problematic in a URL
`	0x60	[U+0060]	Grave accent	An unwise character to leave unescaped; problematic in a URL; also problematic in RTL
{	0x7B	[U+007B]	Left curly brace	An unwise character to leave unescaped; problematic in a URL
|	0x7C	[U+007C]	Vertical line (pipe)	An unwise character to leave unescaped; problematic in a URL; also problematic in RTL
}	0x7D	[U+007D]	Right curly brace	

(continued)

Table G.3 *(continued)*

CHARACTER	CODE PAGE POINT	UNICODE POINT	NAME	COMMENT
~	0x7E	[U+007E]	Tilde	
	0x7F	[U+007F]	Delete	
«	0xAB	[U+00AB]	Left-pointing double angle	
_	0x1C	[U+001C]	File Separator	

Extended Range Problem Characters

Table G.4 contains potentially problematic extended range characters from the single-byte code pages.

Table G.4 Extended Range Problem Characters

CHARACTER	UNICODE POINT	NAME	COMMENT
ö	[U+00F6]	Latin Small Letter O with Diaeresis	Can be a problem in file names on DBCS systems.
§	[U+00A7]	Section Sign	
ß	[U+00DF]	Latin Small Letter Sharp S	
å	[U+00E5]	Latin Small Letter A with Ring Above	DOS delete marker. Mostly significant if first char in a string; essentially this is a Ctrl+z.
€	[U+20AC]	Euro Currency Symbol	
a	[U+00AA]	Feminine Ordinal Indicator	This can sometimes be interpreted by Novell's NetWare as a disconnect signal or other similar low-level command. If your software will be used with NetWare, you will want to plan your tests to include these.

Table G.4   *(continued)*

CHARACTER	UNICODE POINT	NAME	COMMENT
®	[U+00AE]	Registered Sign	This can sometimes be interpreted by Novell's NetWare as a disconnect signal or other similar low-level command. If your software will be used with NetWare, you will want to plan your tests to include these.
¿	[U+00BF]	Inverted Question Mark	This can sometimes be interpreted by Novell's NetWare as a disconnect signal or other similar low-level command. If your software will be used with NetWare, you will want to plan your tests to include these.
İ	[U+0130] 0xDD on 1254 code page	Latin Capital Letter I with Dot Above	Only found in Turkish on the 1254 code page; this can be seen being converted if the system does not properly handle this.
ı	[U+0131] 0xFD on 1254 code page	Latin Small Dotless Letter I	Only found in Turkish on the 1254 code page; this can be seen being converted if the system does not properly handle this.

Problem Character Combinations

Table G.5 contains problem character combinations from the lower ASCII, the extended range (or upper ASCII), and then combinations of the two.

Table G.5 Problem Character Combinations

CHARACTER	UNICODE POINT	NAME	COMMENT
::	[U+003A] [U+003A]	Two colons	
~1:	[U+007E] [U+0031] [U+003A]	A tilde, a number (any number), and a colon	
..	[U+002E] [U+002E]	Two periods	This can present security problems by allowing access to files otherwise not accessible.
$$	[U+0024] [U+0024]	Two dollar signs	
:€□	[U+003A] [U+20AC] [U+FFFD]	Colon, Euro symbol, and [U+FFFD]	Although FFFD is not a "real" character, this can present problems.
++	[U+002B] [U+002B]	Two pluses	
%0	[U+0025] [U+0030]	Percent sign, number zero	Can cause problems in Perl scripts.
\n	[U+005C] [U+006E]	Backslash, letter n	Escape sequence for new line in JavaScript.
\b	[U+005C] [U+0062]	Backslash, letter b	Escape sequence for bolding in JavaScript.
%20	[U+0025] [U+0032] [U+0030]	Percent sign, number two, number zero	URL encoded sequence for a space.
00:\	[U+0030] [U+0030] [U+003A] [U+005C]	Two number zeros, colon, backslash	
&	[U+0026]	Ampersand	
<	[U+003C]	Less-than sign	
>	[U+003E]	Greater-than sign	
=	[U+003D]	Equals sign	
Ü¢£	[U+00DC] [U+00A2] [U+00A3]	Letter U with diaeresis, cent sign, pound (currency) sign—high literals	

Table G.5 *(continued)*

CHARACTER	UNICODE POINT	NAME	COMMENT
FFFFFFFF	[U+0046] [U+0046] [U+0046] [U+0046] [U+0046] [U+0046] [U+0046] [U+0046]	Eight letter F	Input as a value, especially a regkey.
::$DATA	[U+003A] [U+003A] [U+0024] [U+0044] [U+0041] [U+0054] [U+0041]	Two colons, dollar sign, letters D, A, T, A	Indicates data stream.

Lower ASCII Character Combination Verification Cases

Table G.6 contains test cases to try in order to verify that your application properly handles various lower ASCII characters. Whereas the previous set of character combinations were chosen because of their potential ability to break an application, these are chosen for their ability to prove that the application is properly handling valid lower ASCII input.

Table G.6 Character Combination Verification Cases

CHARACTERS	UNICODE POINT	COMMENT
aAzZ	[U+0061][U+0041][U+007A][U+005A]	Tests that basic alphabetic characters are accepted.
1234	[U+0031][U+0032][U+0033][U+0034]	Tests that common numbers are accepted.
12aZ	[U+0031][U+0032][U+007A][U+005A]	Tests that numbers and letters are accepted, starting with numbers.
aZ12	[U+007A][U+005A][U+0031][U+0032]	Tests that letters and numbers are accepted, ending with numbers.
~!;:?/*	[U+007E][U+0021][U+003B][U+003A][U+003F][U+002F][U+002A]	Tests that common symbols are accepted.

(continued)

Table G.6 *(continued)*

CHARACTERS	UNICODE POINT	COMMENT
/../	[U+002F][U+002E][U+002E][U+002F]	Tests symbols, but in an arrangement that can be interpreted as a file path.
/À®./	[U+002F][U+00C0][U+00AE][U+002E][U+002F]	Used with the previous test, specifically to test parsers— if the previous input is not an allowed sequence, then this should probably not be an allowed sequence.
\\?\C:\foo.txt	[U+005C][U+005C][U+003F][U+005C][U+0043][U+003A][U+005C][U+0066][U+006F][U+006F][U+002E][U+0074][U+0078][U+0074]	Tests the assumption that the local file location has the second character of a colon; NT specific.
\\127.0.0.1\C$\	[U+005C][U+005C][U+0031][U+0032][U+0037][U+002E][U+0030][U+002E][U+0030][U+002E][U+0031][U+005C][U+0043][U+0024][U+005C]	Tests the assumption that the local file location has the second character of a colon; refers to the UNC localhost.
&lt;	[U+0026][U+006C][U+0074][U+003B]	HTML sequence for the less-than sign.
	[U+0026][U+006E][U+0062][U+0073][U+0070][U+003B]	HTML sequence for a non-breaking space.
 	[U+003C][U+0062][U+0072][U+003E]	HTML tag for a break.
&#65;	[U+0026][U+0023][U+0036][U+0035][U+003B]	Decimal HTML sequence for the letter A.
&#x0041;	[U+0026][U+0023][U+0078][U+0030][U+0030][U+0034][U+0031][U+003B]	Similar to previous example, but this is the hexadecimal HTML sequence for the letter A.
0xf	[U+0030][U+0078][U+0066]	May be assumed to be the hexadecimal reference to a number; in this case it would be 15.
0xa	[U+0030][U+0078][U+0061]	May be assumed that this is the hexadecimal reference to another number; in this case it would be converted to 10.

Table G.6 *(continued)*

CHARACTERS	UNICODE POINT	COMMENT
%UFF3C	[U+0025][U+0055][U+0046] [U+0046][U+0033][U+0043]	URL encoded DBCS backslash.
Iiİı	[U+0049][U+0069][U+0130] [U+0131]	Tests the two Latin Latter I's and the two extra Turkish I's.
<script>alert ('Hello')</script>	[U+003C][U+0073][U+0063] [U+0072][U+0069][U+0070] [U+0074][U+003E][U+0061] [U+006C][U+0065][U+0072] [U+0074][U+0028][U+0027] [U+0048][U+0065][U+006C] [U+006C][U+006F][U+0027] [U+0029][U+003C][U+002F] [U+0073][U+0063][U+0072] [U+0069][U+0070][U+0074] [U+003E]	Script will pop up a Hello alert box if it is executed— should not be executed.
'><script>alert ('Hello')</script>	[U+0027][U+003E][U+003C] [U+0073][U+0063][U+0072] [U+0069][U+0070][U+0074] [U+003E][U+0061][U+006C] [U+0065][U+0072][U+0074] [U+0028][U+0027][U+0048] [U+0065][U+006C][U+006C] [U+006F][U+0027][U+0029] [U+003C][U+002F][U+0073] [U+0063][U+0072][U+0069] [U+0070][U+0074][U+003E]	Similar to the previous example, except this will attempt to close a tag before the script.
"><script>alert ('Hello')</script>	[U+0027][U+00322][U+003C] [U+0073][U+0063][U+0072] [U+0069][U+0070][U+0074] [U+003E][U+0061][U+006C] [U+0065][U+0072][U+0074] [U+0028][U+0027][U+0048] [U+0065][U+006C][U+006C] [U+006F][U+0027][U+0029] [U+003C][U+002F][U+0073] [U+0063][U+0072][U+0069] [U+0070][U+0074][U+003E]	Similar to the previous example; this will attempt to close a tag before the script.

(continued)

Table G.6 *(continued)*

CHARACTERS	UNICODE POINT	COMMENT
<Script>alert ('Hello')</Script>	[U+003C][U+0053][U+0063] [U+0072][U+0069][U+0070] [U+0074][U+003E][U+0061] [U+006C][U+0065][U+0072] [U+0074][U+0028][U+0027] [U+0048][U+0065][U+006C] [U+006C][U+006F][U+0027] [U+0029][U+003C][U+002F] [U+0053][U+0063][U+0072] [U+0069][U+0070][U+0074] [U+003E]	Using mixed case in the script, testing for an exact string match.
<sCript>alert ('Hello')</sCript>	[U+003C][U+0073][U+0043] [U+0072][U+0069][U+0070] [U+0074][U+003E][U+0061] [U+006C][U+0065][U+0072] [U+0074][U+0028][U+0027] [U+0048][U+0065][U+006C] [U+006C][U+006F][U+0027] [U+0029][U+003C][U+002F] [U+0073][U+0043][U+0072] [U+0069][U+0070][U+0074] [U+003E]	Similar to the previous example, using mixed case in the script, testing for an exact string match.
<SCRIPT>alert ('Hello')</SCRIPT>	[U+003C][U+0053][U+0043] [U+0052][U+0049][U+0050] [U+0054][U+003E][U+0061] [U+006C][U+0065][U+0072] [U+0074][U+0028][U+0027] [U+0048][U+0065][U+006C] [U+006C][U+006F][U+0027] [U+0029][U+003C][U+002F] [U+0053][U+0043][U+0052] [U+0049][U+0050][U+0054] [U+003E]	Similar to the previous example, using all capitals in the script, testing for an exact string match.
<script> alert('Hello')< /script>	[U+0026][U+0023][U+0036] [U+0030][U+003B][U+0073] [U+0063][U+0072][U+0069] [U+0070][U+0074][U+0026] [U+0023][U+0036][U+0032] [U+003B][U+0061][U+006C] [U+0065][U+0072][U+0074] [U+0028][U+0027][U+0048] [U+0065][U+006C][U+006C] [U+006F][U+0027][U+0029] [U+0026][U+0023][U+0036] [U+0030][U+003B][U+0026]	Similar to the original script example, except this string has the symbols in their decimal HTML reference.

Table G.6 *(continued)*

CHARACTERS	UNICODE POINT	COMMENT
(continued)	[U+0023][U+0034][U+0037] [U+003B][U+0073][U+0063] [U+0072][U+0069][U+0070] [U+0074][U+0026][U+0023] [U+0036][U+0032][U+003B]	

%22><script%
20for=window %
20event=%
22onload()%
22> document.
write(%22Hello%22);
document.close();
</script> Hello%22);
document.close();
</script>.write
(%22Hello%22) ;
document.close();
</script>
	[U+0025][U+0032][U+0032]
	[U+003E][U+003C][U+0073]
	[U+0063][U+0072][U+0069]
	[U+0070][U+0074][U+0025]
	[U+0032][U+0030][U+0066]
	[U+006F][U+0072][U+003D]
	[U+0077][U+0069][U+006E]
	[U+0064][U+006F][U+0077]
	[U+0020][U+0025][U+0032]
	[U+0030][U+0065][U+0076]
	[U+0065][U+006E][U+0074]
	[U+003D][U+0025][U+0032]
	[U+0032][U+006F][U+006E]
	[U+006C][U+006F][U+0061]
	[U+0064][U+0028][U+0029]
	[U+0025][U+0032][U+0032]
	[U+003E][U+0064][U+006F]
	[U+0063][U+0075][U+006D]
	[U+0065][U+006E][U+0074]
	[U+002E][U+0077][U+0072]
	[U+0069][U+0074][U+0065]
	[U+0028][U+0025][U+0032]
	[U+0032][U+0048][U+0065]
	[U+006C][U+006C][U+006F]
	[U+0025][U+0032][U+0032]
	[U+0029][U+003B][U+0064]
	[U+006F][U+0063][U+0075]
	[U+006D][U+0065][U+006E]
	[U+0074][U+002E][U+0063]
	[U+006C][U+006F][U+0073]
	[U+0065][U+0028][U+0029]
	[U+003B][U+003C][U+002F]
	[U+0073][U+0063][U+0072]
	[U+0069][U+0070][U+0074]
	[U+003E][U+0048][U+0065]
	[U+006C][U+006C][U+006F]
	[U+0025][U+0032][U+0032]
	[U+0029][U+003B][U+0064]
	[U+006F][U+0063][U+0075]
	[U+006D][U+0065][U+006E]
		Similar to the previous example, except this has all quotes and spaces URL escaped.

(continued)

Table G.6 *(continued)*

CHARACTERS	UNICODE POINT	COMMENT
(continued)	[U+0074][U+002E][U+0063] [U+006C][U+006F][U+0073] [U+0065][U+0028][U+0029] [U+003B][U+003C][U+002F] [U+0073][U+0063][U+0072] [U+0069][U+0070][U+0074] [U+003E][U+002E][U+0077] [U+0072][U+0069][U+0074] [U+0065][U+0028][U+0025] [U+0032][U+0032][U+0048] [U+0065][U+006C][U+006C] [U+006F][U+0025][U+0032] [U+0032][U+0029][U+003B] [U+0064][U+006F][U+0063] [U+0075][U+006D][U+0065] [U+006E][U+0074][U+002E] [U+0063][U+006C][U+006F] [U+0073][U+0065][U+0028] [U+0029][U+003B][U+003C] [U+002F][U+0073][U+0063] [U+0072][U+0069][U+0070] [U+0074][U+003E]	
<script>(unencode ("<script>alert ('Hello')</script>")) </script>	[U+003C][U+0073][U+0063] [U+0072][U+0069][U+0070] [U+0074][U+003E][U+0028] [U+0075][U+006E][U+0065] [U+006E][U+006F][U+0064] [U+0065][U+0028][U+0022] [U+003C][U+0073][U+0063] [U+0072][U+0069][U+0070] [U+0074][U+003E][U+0061] [U+006C][U+0065][U+0072] [U+0074][U+0028][U+0027] [U+0048][U+0065][U+006C] [U+006C][U+006F][U+0027] [U+0029][U+003C][U+002F] [U+0073][U+0063][U+0072] [U+0069][U+0070][U+0074] [U+003E][U+0022][U+0029] [U+0029][U+003C][U+002F] [U+0073][U+0063][U+0072] [U+0069][U+0070][U+0074] [U+003E]	Similar to previous examples, except this attempts to use the unencode function to get script to execute.

Table G.6 *(continued)*

CHARACTERS	UNICODE POINT	COMMENT
blah<script> (unencode("<script> alert('Hello') </script>"))</script>	[U+0062][U+006C][U+0061] [U+0068][U+003C][U+0073] [U+0063][U+0072][U+0069] [U+0070][U+0074][U+003E] [U+0028][U+0075][U+006E] [U+0065][U+006E][U+006F] [U+0064][U+0065][U+0028] [U+0022][U+003C][U+0073] [U+0063][U+0072][U+0069] [U+0070][U+0074][U+003E] [U+0061][U+006C][U+0065] [U+0072][U+0074][U+0028] [U+0027][U+0048][U+0065] [U+006C][U+006C][U+006F] [U+0027][U+0029][U+003C] [U+002F][U+0073][U+0063] [U+0072][U+0069][U+0070] [U+0074][U+003E][U+0022] [U+0029][U+0029][U+003C] [U+002F][U+0073][U+0063] [U+0072][U+0069][U+0070] [U+0074][U+003E]	Similar to above examples, except this attempts to use the unencode function to get script to execute.
blah'<script> (unencode("<script> alert('Hello') </script>"))</script>	[U+0062][U+006C][U+0061] [U+0068][U+0027][U+003C] [U+0073][U+0063][U+0072] [U+0069][U+0070][U+0074] [U+003E][U+0028][U+0075] [U+006E][U+0065][U+006E] [U+006F][U+0064][U+0065] [U+0028][U+0022][U+003C] [U+0073][U+0063][U+0072] [U+0069][U+0070][U+0074] [U+003E][U+0061][U+006C] [U+0065][U+0072][U+0074] [U+0028][U+0027][U+0048] [U+0065][U+006C][U+006C] [U+006F][U+0027][U+0029] [U+003C][U+002F][U+0073] [U+0063][U+0072][U+0069] [U+0070][U+0074][U+003E] [U+0022][U+0029][U+0029] [U+003C][U+002F][U+0073] [U+0063][U+0072][U+0069] [U+0070][U+0074][U+003E]	Similar to previous examples, except this attempts to use the unencode function to get script to execute and a single quote.

(continued)

Table G.6 *(continued)*

CHARACTERS	UNICODE POINT	COMMENT
blah"<script> (unencode("<script> alert('Hello') </script>"))</script>	[U+0062][U+006C][U+0061] [U+0068][U+0022][U+003C] [U+0073][U+0063][U+0072] [U+0069][U+0070][U+0074] [U+003E][U+0028][U+0075] [U+006E][U+0065][U+006E] [U+006F][U+0064][U+0065] [U+0028][U+0022][U+003C] [U+0073][U+0063][U+0072] [U+0069][U+0070][U+0074] [U+003E][U+0061][U+006C] [U+0065][U+0072][U+0074] [U+0028][U+0027][U+0048] [U+0065][U+006C][U+006C] [U+006F][U+0027][U+0029] [U+003C][U+002F][U+0073] [U+0063][U+0072][U+0069] [U+0070][U+0074][U+003E] [U+0022][U+0029][U+0029] [U+003C][U+002F][U+0073] [U+0063][U+0072][U+0069] [U+0070][U+0074][U+003E]	Similar to previous examples, except this attempts to use the unencode function to get script to execute and a double quote.
<SCRIPT LANGUAGE= "VBScript"> MsgBox "Hello!" </SCRIPT>	[U+003C][U+0053][U+0043] [U+0052][U+0049][U+0050] [U+0054][U+0020][U+004C] [U+0041][U+004E][U+0047] [U+0055][U+0041][U+0047] [U+0045][U+003D][U+0022] [U+0056][U+0042][U+0053] [U+0063][U+0072][U+0069] [U+0070][U+0074][U+0022] [U+003E][U+0020][U+004D] [U+0073][U+0067][U+0042] [U+006F][U+0078][U+0020] [U+0022][U+0048][U+0065] [U+006C][U+006C][U+006F] [U+0021][U+0022][U+0020] [U+003C][U+002F][U+0053] [U+0043][U+0052][U+0049] [U+0050][U+0054][U+003E]	VBScript of the previous example—alert box will pop up if it is executed.

Table G.6 *(continued)*

CHARACTERS	UNICODE POINT	COMMENT
<a href="JavaScript: alert()">link</a>	[U+003C][U+0061][U+0020] [U+0068][U+0072][U+0065] [U+0066][U+003D][U+0022] [U+004A][U+0061][U+0076] [U+0061][U+0053][U+0063] [U+0072][U+0069][U+0070] [U+0074][U+003A][U+0061] [U+006C][U+0065][U+0065] [U+0072][U+0074][U+0028] [U+0029][U+0022][U+003E] [U+006C][U+0069][U+006E] [U+006B][U+003C][U+002F] [U+0061][U+003E]	
‹script›alert ('Hello')‹/script›	[U+2039][U+0073][U+0063] [U+0072][U+0069][U+0070] [U+0074][U+203A][U+0061] [U+006C][U+0065][U+0072] [U+0074][U+0028][U+2018] [U+0048][U+0065][U+006C] [U+006C][U+006F][U+2018] [U+0029][U+2039][U+2044] [U+0073][U+0063][U+0072] [U+0069][U+0070][U+0074] [U+203A]	Symbols have been replaced with their high-bit counterparts.

HTML tags can include script where it may not be anticipated. Because these tags, and others, can include script with their attributes, they cannot be considered safe. The following lines contain some examples of how script can appear in what appear to be safe HTML tags.

```
<img src="JavaScript:alert()">img src</img>
<bgsound src="JavaScript:alert()">bgsound src</bgsound>
<iframe src="JavaScript:alert()">iframe src</iframe>
<table background="JavaScript:alert()">table background</table>
<object data="JavaScript:alert()">object data</object>
<frameset onload="JavaScript:alert()">frameset onload</frameset>
<body onload="JavaScript:alert()">body onload</body>
<body background="JavaScript:alert()">body background</body><span
ID="ActiveX ID"></span>
```

Upper ASCII Character Combinations

In Table G.7 you will find upper ASCII (extended range) character combinations for use in verifying that your application can handle various valid upper ASCII input.

Table G.7 Upper ASCII Character Combinations

CHARACTERS	UNICODE POINT	COMMENT
öÜß	[U+00F6][U+00DC][U+00DF]	High literals
Ü¢£	[U+00DC][U+00A2][U+00A3]	High literals
©®	[U+00A0][U+00A9][U+00AE]	Problem literals
¿¾Õ	[U+00BF][U+00BE][U+00D5]	Regional literals
&><"	[U+0026][U+003E][U+003C][U+0022]	Named entities
©®¾¿Õ	[U+00A0][U+00A9][U+00AE][U+00BE] [U+00BF][U+00D5]	Literals
åE5å	[U+00E5][U+0045][U+35][U+E5]	Can be mistaken for the DOS delete mark
€\$\	[U+20AC][U+005C][U+0024][U+005C]	
â€™	[U+00E2][U+20AC][U+2122]	

Diacritics

Table G.8 contains the combining marks that can cause large problems and have no ANSI equivalent; these are typed in combination with another character to alter them (for example, typed in with c [u+0063] to create ç).

High-Bit Characters

The characters listed in Table G.9 are different from their low-bit counterparts and often end up converted to their low-bit counterparts when the software cannot handle them. For instance, try taking script and substituting in the correlating high-bit characters to see if a filter allows them through and another component downgrades them, with the end result of script being executed. These characters can also be problematic on their own as input.

Table G.8 Diacritics

UNICODE POINT	NAME
[U+0333]	Combining double lowline
[U+033F]	Combining double overline
[U+0327]	Combining cedilla

Table G.9 High-Bit Characters

CHARACTERS	UNICODE POINT	NAME
_	[U+00AD]	Soft hyphen (SHY)
`	[U+2018]	Single opening quote
'	[U+2019]	Single closing quote
"	[U+201C]	Double opening quote
"	[U+201D]	Double closing quote
´	[U+00B4]	Acute accent
¸	[U+00B8]	Cedilla
	[U+00A0]	Non-breaking space (NBSP)
©	[U+00A9]	Copyright
®	[U+00AE]	Registered mark
™	[U+2122]	Trademark
–	[U+2013]	En-dash
—	[U+2014]	Em-dash
...	[U+2026]	Ellipsis
/	[U+2044]	Fraction slash
‹	[U+2039]	Single left-pointing angle
›	[U+203A]	Single right-pointing angle
′	[U+2032]	Prime
″	[U+2033]	Double prime

Characters from Multibyte Character Sets

The rest of the tables in this appendix deal with double-byte characters and single-byte characters from the multibyte code pages.

Boundary Cases

Table G.10 contains characters for testing the first and last characters of the various multibyte code page ranges.

Table G.10 Boundary Cases for the Multibyte Code Pages

CHARACTERS	UNICODE POINT	COMMENT
	[U+3000] [81/40] in 932, [A1/A1] in 949 and 936, [A1/40] in 950	Ideographic space— beginning of first DBCS range on 932 code page
滌	[U+6EEC] [9F/FC] in 932	End of first DBCS range on 932 code page
｡	[U+FF61] [A1] in 932	Beginning of Kana (single- byte range) on 932 code page
｡	[U+FF9F] [DF] in 932	End of Kana
漾	[U+6F3E] [E0/40] in 932	Beginning of Second DBCS range on 932 code page
黑	[U+9ED1] [FC/4B] in 932	End of Second DBCS on 932 code page
□	[U+E4C6] [A1/40] in 936 code page	Beginning of CHS 936 code page
□	[U+E4C5] [FE/FE] in 936 code page	End of CHS 936 code page
□	[U+EEB8] [81/40] in 950 code page	Beginning of CHT 950 code page
□	[U+E310] [FE/FE] in 950 code page	End of CHT 950 code page
갂	[U+AC02] [81/41] in 949 code page	Beginning of Korean 949 code page
詰	[U+8A70] [FD/FE] in 949 code page	End of Korean 949 code page

Testing Individual Bytes that Make Up the Double-Byte Character

Since the double-byte characters consist of 2 bytes read in individually, either one of the bytes could be mistaken for a special lower ASCII character. Because of this, you need to look at the special meaning of the lower ASCII characters and take the code point that they occupy to identify double-byte characters that have that code point as either a leading byte or a trailing byte (see Tables G.11 through G.16).

Table G.11 Lead Byte Is 81

CHARACTER	UNICODE CODE POINT	CODE POINT
—	[U+30FC]	[81/5B] on 932 code page
-	[U+2010]	[81/5D] on 932 code page
\	[U+FF3C]	[81/5F] on 932 code page
+	[U+FF0B]	[81/7B] on 932 code page
_	[U+FF0D]	[81/7C] on 932 code page
±	[U+00B1]	[81/7D] on 932 code page
×	[U+00D7]	[81/7E] on 932 code page

Table G.12 Trailing Byte is 5C (ANSI Backslash Character—Need to Use as First, Middle, and Last Character in a String)

CHARACTER	UNICODE CODE POINT	CODE POINT
—	[U+2015]	[81/5C] on 932 code page
□	[U+E0F7]	[81/5C] on Windows 932 code page
乗	[U+4E57]	[81/5C] on 936 code page
□	[U+EED4]	[81/5C] on 950 code page

Table G.13 Lead Byte Is E5—Special DOS Deletion Mark

CHARACTER	UNICODE CODE POINT	CODE POINT
薁	[U+8541]	[E5/40] on 932 code page
蛬	[U+86EC]	[E5/7E] on 932 code page
夜	[U+591C]	[E5/A8] on 949 code page
女	[U+F981]	[E5/FC] on 949 code page

Table G.14   Trail Bytes Is AD—ANSI Soft Hyphen

CHARACTER	UNICODE CODE POINT	CODE POINT
ボ	[U+4F03]	[81/AD] on 936 code page
撰	[U+85C4]	[F0/AD] on 950 code page

The double-byte Romanji characters are Latin-looking characters that need to be used anywhere that Latin single-byte characters are expected.

Table G.15   Romanji Characters—Latin-Looking Characters from the 932 Page

CHARACTER	UNICODE POINT	COMMENT
◯	[U+25EF]	Boundary
0	[U+FF10]	Use the double-byte numbers where any number might be expected.
1	[U+FF11]	Use the double-byte numbers where any number might be expected.
@	[U+FF20]	Use the double-byte symbols where any symbol might be expected.
A	[U+FF21]	Use the double-byte letters where any letter might be expected.
Z	[U+FF3A]	Use the double-byte letters where any letter might be expected.
a	[U+FF41]	Use the double-byte letters where any letter might be expected.
z	[U+FF5A]	Use the double-byte letters where any letter might be expected.
あ	[U+3041]	Boundary
．	[U+FF0E]	Use the double-byte fullwidth period where any period might be expected.
／	[U+FF0F]	Use the double-byte fullwidth solidus where any forward slash might be expected.
：	[U+FF1A]	Use the double-byte fullwidth colon where any colon might be expected.
！	[U+FF01]	Use the double-byte fullwidth exclamation mark where any exclamation mark might be expected.
'	[U+2018]	Use the double-byte fullwidth left single quote where any quote might be expected.

Table G.15 *(continued)*

CHARACTER	UNICODE POINT	COMMENT
'	[U+2019]	Use the double-byte fullwidth right single quote where any quote might be expected.
"	[U+201C]	Use the double-byte fullwidth left double quote where any quote might be expected.
"	[U+201D]	Use the double-byte fullwidth right double quote where any quote might be expected.
<	[U+FF1C]	Use the double-byte fullwidth less-than sign where any less-than sign might be expected.
>	[U+FF1E]	Use the double byte fullwidth greater-than sign where any greater-than sign might be expected.

Table G.16 shows characters that represent potential problems in NetWare.

Table G.16 NetWare Potential Problem Characters

CHARACTER	UNICODE CODE POINT	CODE POINT
ｴ	[U+FF6A]	[AA] on 932 code page
ｮ	[U+FF6E]	[AE] on 932 code page
ｿ	[U+FF7F]	[BF] on 932 code page
穐	[U+7A50]	[88/AA] on 932 code page
旭	[U+65ED]	[88/AE] on 932 code page
裕	[U+88B7]	[88/BF] on 932 code page

Potential Problem Character Conversions

When the same character shares more than one code point, it can cause problems when converting from the code page to Unicode and then back to the code page. Tables G.17 and G.18 contain some examples of these types of problem characters.

Table G.17 JPN—932

CHARACTER	UNICODE CODE POINT	CODE POINT
丨	[U+4E28]	[FA/68] which will equal [ED/4C]
｜	[U+FFE4]	[FA/55] which will equal [EE/FA]
厓	[U+5393]	[FA/8D]
晙	[U+6659]	[FA/D7]
繊	[U+7E8A]	[FA/5C]
榢	[U+69E2]	[FA/EC]

Table G.18 CHT—950

CHARACTER	UNICODE CODE POINT	CODE POINT
─	[U+2550]	[A2/A4] which will equal [F9/F9]
├	[U+255E]	[A2/A5] which will equal [F9/E9]
┼	[U+256A]	[A2/A6] which will equal [F9/EA]
十	[U+5341]	[A2/CC] which will equal [A4/51]
┤	[U+2561]	[A2/A7] which will equal [F9/EB]
卅	[U+5345]	[A2/CE] which will equal [A4/CA]
╭	[U+256D]	[F9/FA] which will equal [A2/7E]

Miscellaneous DBCS Problem Characters

Table G.19 contains a variety of other characters that may cause problems in your application. These are ones that do not necessarily fall into classifications of types of problems, but they are historically known to cause misbehavior.

Table G.19 Miscellaneous DBCS Problem Characters

CHARACTER	UNICODE POINT	COMMENT
郂	[U+90C2]	936 code page CHS character.
mil	[U+33D5]	936 and 950 code pages.
╵	[U+2574]	950 code page.
～	[U+FF5E]	932, 936, 949, and 950 code pages.
		Full-width tilde; can have a different Unicode mapping to the code page table depending on the platform.

Table G.19 *(continued)*

CHARACTER	UNICODE POINT	COMMENT
＿	[U+FF3F]	932, 936, 949, and 950 code pages.
＃	[U+FF03]	932, 936, 949, and 950 code pages.
＆	[U+FF06]	932, 936, 949, and 950 code pages.
▓	[U+2593]	936 and 950 code pages.
가	[U+AC00]	949 code page.
耀	[U+8000]	The E5 trailing byte of this Korean char can cause problems.
肭	[U+80AD]	932, 936, and 950 code pages.

Multibyte Character Combinations

The problem characters that have been discussed in this section all come from the multibyte character sets; however, thus far I have discussed only individual code points. Table G.20 contains strings of multibyte characters to use both in verification and in testing the ability of your application to handle truly problematic characters.

Table G.20 Multibyte Character Combinations

CHARACTER	UNICODE POINTS	COMMENT
ヲゥォッ	[U+FF66][U+FF69][U+FF6B][U+FF6F]	String of four single-byte DBCS characters
ヲゥォ ッ	[U+FF66][U+FF69][U+3000] [U+FF6B][U+FF6F]	String of single-byte DBCS characters with a DBCS space in the middle
ヲゥォ ッ	[U+FF66][U+FF69][U+FF6B] [U+FF6F][U+FF68]	String of five single-byte DBCS characters
ヲゥォ ッィエ	[U+FF66][U+FF69][U+FF6B] [U+FF6F][U+FF68][U+FF6A]	String of six single-byte DBCS characters
黑鯔鶴滬	[U+9ED1][U+9E19][U+FA2D] [U+6EEC]	String of four double-byte DBCS characters
黑鯔鶴滬潃	[U+9ED1][U+9E19][U+FA2D] [U+6EEC][U+6EF8]	String of five double-byte DBCS characters

(continued)

Table G.20   *(continued)*

CHARACTER	UNICODE POINTS	COMMENT
黑鱅鶴滬淅滾	[U+9ED1][U+9E19][U+FA2D] [U+6EEC][U+6EF8][U+6EFE]	String of six double-byte DBCS characters
ｦｩｵｯ黑鱅ｦｩｵｯ	[U+FF66][U+FF69][U+FF6B][U+FF6F] [U+9ED1][U+9E19][U+FF66][U+FF69] [U+FF6B][U+FF6F]	String of DBCS characters starting and ending with single-byte characters with double-byte characters in the middle
黑鱅ｳｵｯ黑鱅	[U+9ED1][U+9E19][U+FF66][U+FF69] [U+FF6B][U+FF6F][U+9ED1][U+9E19]	String of double-byte characters starting and ending with double-byte characters, with single-byte characters in the middle
¥ \\ ¥	[U+FFE5][U+005C][U+005C][U+FFE5]	Yen signs around two back-slashes

Unicode-Only Characters

Table G.21 contains characters that are not found in any code page, but rather exist only in Unicode. These characters are useful in identifying problems in an application that should be handling Unicode input, uncovering any potential code page dependencies it has.

Table G.21   Unicode-Only Characters

CHARACTER	UNICODE CODE POINT	COMMENT
	[U+2002]	En space
	[U+2003]	Em space
	[U+200E]	Left-to-right mark
	[U+200F]	Right-to-left mark
-	[U+2011]	Non-breaking hyphen
"	[U+201F]	Double high reversed quotation marks
	[U+202A]	Left-to-right embedding

Table G.21 *(continued)*

CHARACTER	UNICODE CODE POINT	COMMENT
	[U+202B]	Right-to-left embedding
☐	[U+FFFD]	Replacement character
	[U+FEFF]	Byte order mark (BOM)
	[U+2028]	Line Separator mark (LSEP)
	[U+0938][U+0941][U+0938] [U+094D][U+0935][U+093E] [U+0917][U+0924][U+092E]	Devanagari characters— can be a problem and unsupported in some areas

UTF-8 Potential Problems

In UTF-8 encoding you have three ranges of characters because the characters can be encoded with 1, 2, or 3 bytes. Testing the boundaries here is very important. Another good test case is to take a long string of the 3-byte encoded Unicode characters and try to overrun buffers with them. This will turn up a number of missed buffer overflows because the error handling may be expecting 2 bytes per character (assumptions based on the double-byte characters), but not 3-byte characters. (See Table G.22.)

Table G.22 UTF-8 Potential Problems

CHARACTER	UNICODE CODE POINT	COMMENT
	[U+0020]	First printable character that requires only 1-byte encoding (Basic Latin—space)
~	[U+007E]	Last character that requires only 1-byte encoding (Basic Latin)
☐	[U+0081]	First character that requires 2-byte encoding (Latin-1 supplement)
	[U+06ED]	Last character that requires only 2-byte encoding (Arabic)
☐	[U+0901]	First character that requires 3-byte encoding (Devanagari)
滬	[U+6EEC]	Character in the middle of the 3-byte encoding range (CJK Unified)
○	[U+FFEE]	End of the 3-byte encoding (Half-width form)

Testing Checklist and Questions

*It is more important to know what sort of person
has a disease than to know what sort of disease
a person has.*

—Hippocrates

Taking information from all the previous chapters, this appendix compiles very detailed and encompassing lists of questions for verifying your site or application. These questions need to be asked of the specifications before the code is written, but they need to be asked again when you are testing. Asking these questions before coding has begun helps identify problems while they are still very cheap to fix, but it also helps to identify where information is missing and more details need to be determined.

NOTE Not all of these will apply, and your application will raise many not listed here, but these questions are a starting point. Always ask yourself the question, "What's missing?"

General

- How will the application be used?
- What is the purpose of the application? Information, entertainment, business, and so on.
- Who is the target audience? Who is the current audience? Who is the potential audience?
- What is the user scenario for using it? There may be several representing various classes of users.

- Will this be used from an Internet kiosk or other machine that the user has no control over? Should the application be verified in kiosk mode?

- Are alternative devices going to use this? (Web TV, PDAs, iMode phones, and so on.)

- What is the estimated user base for the first 6 months? First year?

- Are users paying to access your site or use your application? If so, their expectations may be very different than if it were free.

- Are there partners you are dependent on? Are partners dependent on you? Is there a plan if either your service is down or a partner you rely on is down?

- Is there a new user or first-time user experience that differs from subsequent visits?

- What dependencies does your site/application have? It may require that WinAmp, AOL Instant Messenger, or some other piece of software be installed, or it may make use of system- or browser-provided DLLs. If it does not rely on any system DLLs, then there may be no need to test on various versions of each platform family.

- Does your application install any components or controls? What if the user cannot/does not install it? What if you release a new version—is there an upgrade path for the users?

- If your application installs components or controls, where are they installed? Is there an assumed or hard-coded location? Will that break on a nonstandard configuration (for example, a Windows machine where the active drive is the F:\ drive instead of the more common C:\ drive)?

- If there is a component or control installed, is there an uninstall path for it?

- Does the component or control that is installed set any registry keys? When it uninstalls, all of these need to be cleaned up appropriately.

- What platforms is this supported on? What are the various Windows, Macintosh, and Unix versions, as well as various devices?

- Which browsers are supported? Microsoft Internet Explorer, Microsoft MSN Explorer, Netscape Navigator, Microsoft Pocket IE and Generic IE, Opera, Omni Group Omni Web, Amaya?

- Are there varying levels of support?

- What does the test matrix look like?

- What does the support matrix look like?

- What happens if you access the application from an unsupported platform? Consider a notification mechanism.

- What other requirements does the application have—security settings, script settings, cookie settings, resolution, line speed, and so on?
- Is there an internal coding standard?
- Is this feature necessary?
- Is the role of the feature in the application clearly understood?
- How will a user access this piece of functionality? List all ways to get into this feature.
- How will the user put data into this piece of functionality?
- What are those areas of user-defined input? What are the sizes of those areas (in bytes or characters)? What type of input do they accept?
- Where is the data output displayed?
- What boundaries exist for this data?
- What error states can come of this data or action?
- What states is the data available in? Map the creation, edit, save, display, and delete states.
- How is the user expected to navigate? Are Back and Forward controls provided in the application interface or is the user expected to use the browser buttons? Make this clear, but know what the behavior is when using the browser buttons.
- If the application makes use of frames, what should the behavior be when the user clicks the browser Back or Forward buttons? What about Refresh or Stop?
- Do errors occur when the page loads?
- Do all graphics appear properly?
- Are all similar icons of the same size (visually), giving a clean appearance?
- Is the download time perceptibly slow?
- Do all graphics have width and height tags to correctly place them into a formatted page while they are downloading?
- Are all links active and working? Are they accurate and/or descriptive?
- Are links relative or absolute?
- Should all links or active (hot) areas have the finger pointer (hand) displayed when the cursor is over them?
- Do the mailto links also display the mailing address?
- Can the user print various pages?

Usability

- Does the user interaction for this feature make sense? Will the user easily figure out how to use it?
- Are Help files provided?
- Are error messages to the user helpful?
- Will server errors (such as 404s) be given a more usable interface when delivered to the user?
- Can the user easily find the necessary navigational controls, or are the application controls easily confused with the browser's controls? (For example, if users are looking for the Help pages for your application, do they instead click the Help for the browser?)
- What is the result of each click? Where does it navigate to?
- What happens if the user right-clicks? Is this disabled or is there a special menu that appears? Is it supported?
- Is the information architecture clearly mapped out with content topics mapped to it?
- Would the user try to bookmark the page? Can the user return to a book-marked page of yours? What if the page has been removed? There should at least be a polite general statement and links to the main navigation page of your site/application.
- Will there be usability studies performed with typical users prior to the release?

Accessibility

- After reading Section 508 (the Rehabilitation Act Amendment [RAA]) of the Workforce Investment Act of 1988, do you notice particulars that apply to your application?
- Will your application be made Section 508 compliant?
- Can the application be used without a mouse? This means keyboard-only navigation and the use of the Tab key to navigate. Try placing the mouse behind the computer to force you to try this.
- Is the tab order through the application logical (TabIndex attribute)?
- Does the focus default to the most logical place when a user enters a page?

- Are there any keyboard shortcuts in the product (AccessKey attributes)?

- Are these shortcuts unique on each page compared to any other access key, browser hotkey, or system command? You cannot have duplicates.

- Do all pages, tables, columns, frames, forms, graphics, links, animations, applets, and controls have a descriptive real-language label (ALT text and TITLE text)?

- Do all tables have header attributes? (<TH> with a real-language description.)

- Do all links, buttons, and graphics have tooltips?

- Do all images used as anchors for links have a text-based alternative?

- Is the application able to function with all graphics turned off? With the sound turned off?

- Can the application function when the user has turned off style sheets in the browser?

- Is color or sound the only method of communicating information to the user in any place?

- Are the user's specified colors of fonts, links, and the background applied?

- Are the user's specified font face and size applied?

- Can the application be used while in High Contrast mode?

- Does the application or site provide the appropriate properties for the controls in MSAA?

- If any text edit boxes are used, can you change the value in the box and have MSAA recognize the new input?

- What level of MSAA is the application standardized to (v1.3 or v2.0)? The standardization is a good marketing point and worth at least a mention on the Web page. More information on Microsoft Active Accessibility can be found at http:/www.microsoft.com/enable/.

- Do included video or animations have closed captioning, narration, or text equivalents?

Localization

- What languages will the application be localized into?

- When you view each localization, are all the strings localized? Are all the strings supposed to be localized? (Some strings, such as the company name, may not be translated.)

- If you provide more than one language, how do you determine which one to show to the user? Read the browser's accept language? A user preference when they register?
- Will the localizations from a previous release be reused?
- Will server errors (such as response codes—404) be localized?
- Is there country-dependent formatting?
  - Sorting
  - Number formats (thousand place separator, decimal, and negative)
  - Numerals—ordinal and cardinal numbers
  - Units of measurement (U.S. versus metric)
  - Currency (symbol and placement and the new Euro—some contain more than one symbol; place the symbol before the amount and after as well as with leading and trailing 0s and spaces)
  - Calendar (Gregorian, Lunar, Hebrew, Thai, Korean, Japanese, Chinese)
  - First week of year
  - First day of week (Sunday or Monday)
  - Date format and separator (mm-dd-yyyy or dd-mm-yyyy or mm-dd-yy, and using a period, dash, or slash to separate the fields)
  - Time format (12-hour clock versus 24-hour clock and A.M./P.M. formats)
  - Punctuation (quotes, exclamation marks, question marks, list separators)
  - Address formats
  - Name formats (last name last versus last name first)
  - Phone number formats
- Is there language-dependent formatting such as spell check or sort order? (for example, in Finnish or Swedish, the word *waffle* should be sorted ahead of the word *vegetable*).
- Will complex scripts be supported? Are there different behaviors that should be observed here?
- Does the interface display correctly with RTL localizations?
- Does the interface properly display the extended ASCII range for each language you localize into?
- Does the interface properly display double-byte characters?
- Does the interface properly display Unicode-only characters?

- What encodings are supported (particularly for Russian [Cyrillic versus KOI-8] and Japanese [JIS versus SJIS])?
- Does your application specify fonts to be used? If so, make sure that the fonts you hard-code are able to display the language you are localizing into.
- Will this application be code page dependent?
- Will the application be pseudolocalized prior to release?
- Will all localizable strings be placed in a central location?
- Do all graphics and symbols make sense for the language? Many symbols, graphics, and images do not carry the same meaning in different cultures; for example, flags should not represent a language, and icons such as a mailbox may not exist in all regions.
- Are there other internationally sensitive issues—maps, country names, and so on?

Globalization

- What languages will users be allowed to input information in?
- Will complex script input be supported? Are there different behaviors that should be observed here?
- What encodings are supported? Not just code-page encodings, but Unicode UTF format and conversions as well.
- What code pages are supported? Microsoft? Mac? OEM?
- Will this application be code-page-dependent?
- Does your application need to do any escapings of the input?
- Does the application accept extended ASCII, double-byte, complex script, RTL, or Unicode input?

Performance

- What are the performance criteria that the application needs to meet? (Page load time over various line speeds, bytes over the wire, server-side performance issues, client response times, and so on.)
- What are the baseline numbers for these, as determined by testing?
- What is the typical customer bandwidth? Make sure that metrics are taken with this.

- Will there be automation to quantify the performance numbers?
- Will this automation require developers to provide performance markers in the code? Are these documented?
- Can the server configuration be changed to set the caching on images higher, allowing users revisiting the site from the same machine the ability to use the images from cache instead of downloading them from the server?
- Have all the graphics been optimized for the Web?
- What operations are the most expensive?
- What do the most expensive operations cost?
- What do the cheapest operations cost?
- Is there a base cost that cannot be escaped; any fixed overhead costs?
- What is the cost (in megahertz or other value) of a typical user scenario?
- Is there any instrumentation being used to calculate performance?
- Are other tools being used to calculate performance?
- What are the metrics for quantifiable entities such as:
  - Performance versus users
  - Performance versus time
  - Transactions per second
  - Errors per user interaction
  - Errors per unit of time
  - Kilobytes of data per second
  - Average amount of data downloaded per user visit
  - Round-trip time
  - Round-trip count
  - Client response time
  - Bytes per request
  - Bytes over the wire per transaction
- Has the application been profiled when performing at peak capacity—75 or 80 percent CPU utilization?

Security

- What security problems were present in the previous version? Examine these and understand how they could have been prevented. Make sure that these and any new ones are all documented through the development process.
- Could a malicious user get the server to respond or send an error that gives away information about the server (name, IP address, and so on)?
- When connected to the application/site with IE, can a user go to File → Edit with Microsoft FrontPage or File → Edit with Microsoft Word or File → Edit with Notepad to alter and save the files back to your servers?
- Are cookies used to store user state or other user information? What features read or set a cookie?
- For each cookie, is it persisted or session only? Is it marked as HTTP only (IE6 feature)?
- What if the user does not accept the cookie? What if the user has cookies set to Prompt and then accepts the cookie?
- What information is stored in the cookie? What happens if the user edits any of this information?
- Is any user information passed in a URL (parameter, path, and so on)?
- Are any forms being submitted to the server using the GET method?
- What information do we have of the users? Is any of it sensitive (credit card, SSN, address, and so on)? How could it be used to their detriment? Make sure that this information is not passed in cookies or in the parameters in the URL.
- Do we send any of the sensitive information in the body of the request? If so, could a malicious user grab it with a packet sniffer?
- How could any of these pieces of information be put together to be used maliciously?
- What information is the user expecting to be kept secure? (A user ID may not be something that the user has an opinion about, but in answer to the previous question, having the user's ID plus a time stamp may allow a malicious user to guess at a user's email locations, as the Hotmail bug did.)
- Can a malicious user deny a valid user access to his own data?
- Could a malicious user alter or corrupt data?

- What software do you depend upon? (Windows NT, IIS, Sun Solaris, Apache, SQL, and so on.) What vulnerabilities do these pieces of software have? Make sure you are up-to-date on all patches and security releases. Monitor BugTraq at http://www.securityfocus.com to keep up with recent exploitations.

- What security problems does your competitors' or other similar software have? How can you avoid them? Again, some of this might be available at http://www.securityfocus.com, but also on other sites.

- How are your servers configured? What permissions are set on those directories and files?

- Are users required to log in to the application? What if they are behind a firewall or proxy server?

- Does your application perform any encryption? Does it use SSL?

- Does your application generate passwords for the user? Are they easily guessed?

- Does your application allow users to select their own password? Are there guidelines that they must follow?

- Are there any points where data could be shared or accessed by users other than the creator?

- Is this written in managed code? Are there any unsafe functions? Are there legacy pieces or other components that are unmanaged? Where are the transitions from managed to native code?

- Could a malicious user set up scripts to guess at a password 10,000 times until it is guessed correctly? What safeguards could be put in place to safeguard against that?

- Could a malicious user flood your application with requests? Do you want your application to try to respond to them all, or are safeguards in place for that?

- Could a malicious user send a malformed request? What does your application do with it?

- Could a malicious user send a NULL request? What would your application do with it?

- Could a malicious user send a very large request? What would your application do with it?

- Could a malicious user send a small request and tell the server it was a large request? Does the server hang?

- Could a malicious user open many connections to your server? What would your application do about that?

- What ports are open? How could these be exploited?
- What is the response to a denial of service attack?
- What buffer overruns could exist in the software? You do not have to go through the work of identifying how they can be exploited as long as you fix them when you find them.
- Is there a data conversion in this feature or between two features?
- Is data parsed in this feature or between two features?
- Does your application try to write to the server? Could a malicious user exploit this by convincing the server to write more data than it has space for?
- What kind of logging does your application do on the server side? Does it make note of attacks on the servers, and are they descriptive enough to help identify attacks? Are these logs too granular or too general?
- Is there a user-side cache? Does the application rely on it?
- Always assume that the worst happens. How will the server recover? Have a plan in place for each scenario.
- What gets cached on the client side?
- Do cookies contain sensitive data or data that can be combined to be sensitive?
- Should the code stipulate Cache-control: no-cache headers?
- How can you programmatically access the data in the SQL database?
- Is there a way to do this from the outside?
- Can the administrators or product support personnel read the information in the database?

HTML

- Which HTML version will you create your application with and standardize to (v 3.2 or v 4.0)? What about CHTML?
- What file extension will be used—.htm or .html?
- Is there a default file set up for your folders? This default file will allow a user who tries to navigate to a folder directly to have something to navigate with. What is the name of this file (default.htm, index.htm, home.htm, or something else)?
- Are there tags supported in one browser and not another that you want to take advantage of?

- Are there attributes supported in one browser and not another that you want to take advantage of?

- Will you provide a separate code path for various clients based on their levels of support for HTML tags or attributes?

- Does your application make use of any other technologies such as CSS? What happens if no styles are applied or custom styles are applied?

- Can the client request the page and have something appear?

- Do the graphics show up in their proper place?

- Are the graphic dimensions too large, forcing users to scroll horizontally or vertically?

- Are table dimensions too large, forcing users to scroll horizontally or vertically?

- Can the image's file size be reduced to improve the download time, either by saving it in a different file format or reducing the number of colors in the graphic?

- Are there extra images that are unnecessary?

- Are there images that can be reused throughout the site?

- Are WIDTH and HEIGHT attributes associated with each graphic?

- Is an ALT text supplied for each graphic? Is it useful?

- If the client system is reduced to 256 colors, does the application render too poorly? What about in High Resolution mode (for flat screens)?

- Are the plaintext files of the HTML code bloated due to extra tags? Should these be removed for cleanliness and performance?

Script

- Is script used? Is server-side script implemented? Client-side script? Both?

- Is JavaScript, Jscript, or VBScript used? If JavaScript is used, is it ECMA-262/ISO/IEC 16262 compliant?

- Does your script check to make sure it is fully loaded before any references are made to the document object model? (This can be particularly bad if used in conjunction with frames because there is a larger opportunity for them to be out of sync.)

- Is all script commented out so browsers without scripting engines will ignore it? Can these users still access some amount of helpful information?

- What happens when the application is run maximized? Less than maximized? Minimized?
- If you resize the browser so that the window, frames, or controls will not have enough room to load and be displayed, are there script errors when they are navigated to?
- If there is client-side data validation, what happens if the data is input in a different order than the application is expecting (for example, zip code then state)?

Automation

- Will there be automation written to test this product? This feature?
- Do the developers need to provide any hooks to allow for automation (for example, element IDs for tags to identify objects)?
- Are the most important test cases automated?
- Is there API-level automation that should be done calling directly into the functions that provide no UI?
- Are the typical user scenarios automated?
- Does some part of the automation rely on random data?
- Is the wait time (latency) between user interactions also randomized?

ASP

- Are Active Server Pages (ASP) used in this application?
- What is the performance of these pages?
- Where is the performance bottleneck in your pages?
- Should your pages check if machines are still connected when expensive pages are requested?
- Can the number of requests or the data transferred be minimized further?

Other Technologies

- Are ActiveX controls used? If they are planned in the product, is this product intended to be used anywhere except for Microsoft Internet Explorer on Windows?

- Do the ActiveX controls allow code to be executed? Do they read or write files? Could they be made to?

- Do the ActiveX controls create or delete any persisted data?

- Do the ActiveX controls touch any system files or registry settings? (for example, reading or modifying)?

- Are any other objects created?

- Does the object ShellExecute?

- Does the control expose any personal information? (Think about file names, user login name, paths, and so on.)

- Are all of your ActiveX controls signed?

- Are all of your ActiveX controls virus checked?

- Are Java applets implemented?

- Is CGI used? If not, can it be disabled on the server?

- Are XML requests being sent?

- Can a malformed XML query come from the client?

- What happens if an XML request is sent to the server without the closing tag </...>? Does the server hang waiting for the end of the request?

Server-Side Issues

- What is the required stability and uptime for this application?

- What type of servers are being planned for deployment? Microsoft Internet Server (IIS)? Netscape Web server? Apache Web server?

- What server-side technologies are being planned? ISAPI? CGI? ASP? Scripts? Make sure these are compatible with the server platform planned.

- What is the server architecture?

- What is the server technology?

- Are there other servers involved? (Hardware load balancers, routers, hardware SSL, and so on.)

- What software dependencies does your application have? (OS, components, third-party components, and so on.)

- Is there a test lab for you to test the application in? Does it accurately mirror the intended deployment topology?

- What ports are left open? Are these necessary?

- Is a content expiration set on items? Should some items be cached and others not?

- Is the content expiration set in the response header or in the META data for the page?
- How many users total are expected? How many simultaneously?
- How does the application scale? Up or out? What is the scaling unit, and how many users are supported there?
- What is the anticipated traffic?
- How are backups, restores, failovers, and disasters handled?
- Is there any user management? How are they managed?
- How are the live boxes administered?
- Where is the bottleneck? Is it acceptable? (Disk I/O, network, memory paging, database, and so on.)
- What memory leaks exist? Have you looked for them?
- Is server-side caching implemented?
- Is the architecture redundant and distributed?
- Are server logs analyzed while testing?
- Is there a plan to dogfood this application or have a progressive roll-out to users?
- What happens if the server hard drive space on servers fills up?
- Could a malicious user constantly fire errors into the log to attempt to fill up the hard drive space?
- How are requests received from the client? ASP, ISAPI filters, CGI?
- What user context does the receiving code run under? (Administrator, sa, local system, local user, or so forth.)
- Is the communication between the client and the server (or the server and the other servers) in plaintext or encrypted?
- How does the server know the user is who he says he is?
- How does the user know the server is who it says it is?
- Is data stored securely on the server?

Client-Side Issues

- Can users behind proxies and firewalls use the application effectively? Certain requests can be refused by some older firewalls.
- Is client-side caching relied upon?
- Are there any temp files created? This question could also apply to the server side.

- Do any files created rely on a particular name? What if another file of that name was already created? What if a folder of that name has been created there? I have seen programs handle assumed file and path names well and increment a number on the end. Try creating a file and adding those numbers, or the DBCS number, on the end.

- What are the permissions on these files?

- Does your feature allow scripts to run?

- Can anything be embedded in input areas? (Images dropped in, files, controls with code behind them, and so on)

- Is data stored securely locally?

Forms and Templates

There are some functions and activities that are common across many test efforts. Each of these strikes the same set of issues as they start up. These are some of my personal preferences and suggestions on some of those pieces that can get a team headed in the right direction or that can be added in to an existing effort in order to make improvements.

NOTE All of these files are available for download on this book's companion Web site.

Defect-Tracking Database Fields

This section contains suggestions for a defect database. Have several high-level areas with individual values contained therein. The next four sections outline possible high-level areas, along with potential divisions of these areas. Your own areas and breakdowns will likely be different, but this is a point from which to start.

Opened

- Opened By
- Opened Date
- Build
- How Found

Opened By tracks the person who opened the issue. *Opened Date* tracks what date and time the bug was opened.

Build is the build number that this bug was found on. If this bug was found on a late build number, but can be reproduced on an earlier build number, then that earlier number is generally entered to track the earliest point in time for which the problem was able to be reproduced.

How Found tracks how the bug was identified. Such fields as Ad Hoc, Automation, BVTs, Bug Bash, Code Review, Customer, Dogfood, Localization, Test Case Development, Test Pass, or Usability testing are useful here.

Project

- Project (if multiple projects)
- Component
- Area or Feature
- Approving Body
- Approval State
- Target
- Release Note

Project tracks the specific project that this bug is found in. Some testing houses have several projects going on simultaneously. If they do not have separate databases, then they will want to set a field to separate the various groups' bugs.

Component relates to the specific project's components. If this were an online business, such components might be Sign-Up, Ordering, Help, Content, or others.

Area or Feature is relevant if there is a finer breakdown than the component level.

Some organizations require bugs to be approved by management or require approval after a certain point in the project. The *Approval State* tracks what level of approval there is, and the *Approving Body* tracks who set the state.

Target tracks when the bug needs to be fixed—by milestones or releases, or even by dates.

Release Note is a simple Y/N field (or even a blank/Y field) that allows the documentation team to easily find which bugs need to be addressed on paper.

Status

- Status
- Assigned To
- Issue
- Severity
- Priority
- Updated By
- Updated Date

Status is the current status of the bug. Typically there are three states:

1. **Active.** Active correlates to a bug being open and a fix being planned at some point in the future for it.

2. **Resolved.** Resolved should be only a short state for a bug because it will then be assigned back to the tester who created the database entry for him to close, with either the bug being fixed or another resolution that he agrees with.

3. **Closed.** Closed is what happens when bugs are not being considered relevant any more. They can be closed because they have been fixed, it has been decided never to fix the problem, because they were the result of an external problem, or because they are not reproducible.

Assigned To tracks who the bug is assigned to. Many organizations use at least one catch-all of Active or Developer as a general account to assign bugs to so that they will be picked up by the proper groups. Once a bug is closed, it is typically assigned to Closed so that it does not pop up on anybody's personal queries of assigned bugs.

Issue is the type of problem that this bug represents. Typical options here might be Accessibility, Malfunction, Code Defect, Spec Change, Design Change Request, Customer, Corruption, Globalization, Performance, Localization, Scalability, Resource Leak, Misc, Security, Fit and Finish, or Assert, to track the particular classification of the issue that is encountered.

Priority and *Severity* are typically rated on a 1–4 scale, although some companies use a 1–10 scale or a color system (red, yellow, green). A 1–4 system easily breaks things into buckets, while in a 1–10 system, the difference between a 5 and a 6 might not be apparent. Colors are interpreted differently based on cultures, and those who are color-blind may not understand them. A simple value works best.

Updated By and *Updated Date* simply track who was the last person to edit the bug and when did that edit occur.

Resolved

- Resolution
- Resolved By
- Resolution Date
- Build
- Cause

Resolution tracks the resolution state for any single bug. This can have any of the following aspects:

- **By Design.** This is the design of the product as you want it to be.
- **Duplicate.** There is already a bug tracking this issue (should reference the bug #).
- **External.** This is the result of another piece of software/hardware that is out of our control—may include release notes or Help pages regarding this, though.
- **Fixed.** Programmer has fixed this, and it will be assigned back to the tester to verify.
- **Not Repro.** Cannot reproduce the stated problem; usually assigned back to the tester to create a more compelling case or to follow up directly with the developer to understand the issue.
- **Postponed.** Will fix in a later release.
- **Won't Fix.** Will never fix.
- **Not Yet Implemented.** Not a developer-produced error, but a piece of functionality that has not been added yet as planned—having lots of bugs resolved this way indicates a disconnect in communication between Development and Test.
- **Config.** Problem is valid, but was due to a configuration on the server or the client; may be useful to break this out into two resolutions so you can track who misconfigures their servers/clients and what a typical problem can be (for example, security settings).

Resolved By tracks who set the Resolution on the bug. Some organizations frown on individuals setting bugs to a Resolved state and prefer that committees do this. *Resolution Date* tracks when the bug was set to Resolved or Closed.

Build can be filled in if there was a fix implemented, letting users know when the fix was available in the code.

Cause tracks why this problem popped up. Such options as Bad Design, Broke by Fix, Broken by Localization, No Code, No Previous Spec, or Dev Error can track what caused the bug to happen.

Test Plan

All test plans are slightly different in their scope and form. This section is just a recommendation of some contents to consider when putting together an effective plan that can guide a testing effort.

Project Name:

<Project name—can be product name, release, or other identifying factor>

Component Name:

<Name of the component>

Feature Name:

<General name of the feature>

Development Resources:

<Developers responsible for this piece of the project>

Test Resources:

<Testers responsible for this piece of the project>

Other Resources:

<Other resources involved: management, usability experts, designers, and so on>

Timeline:

<Dates the development is expected to start, coding is expected to finish, testing is expected to begin and end>

Requirements:

<Several paragraphs or specifications about this piece, references to more detail. Discussions of architecture, platforms, clients, and so on can be drawn out here.>

Limitations:

<Specific limitations or what this feature is acknowledged as not accomplishing>

Risks:

<Areas or potentially problematic aspects of this piece of the project>

Plan:

<High-level discussion of what needs to be considered for this piece of the project. Should be fairly detailed, though>

Specific Test Cases:

<There may be some specific test cases outside the obvious that need to be called out, either due to their high risk or their importance.>

Other References:

<Are there previous or planned future iterations on this feature? Are there other documentations or areas that overlap with this?>

Bug Template

I'm a staunch advocate of keeping a small text file template on your desktop to paste bugs into just so that you can easily fill out all pertinent information. The following is similar to the one I use, but broader so that you can alter it for your own specific project.

Server Config:

Platform: <List Windows, Unix, and so on.>

Build: <Give the build number.>

Test Bed: <Give a test bed identification or topology name.>

Client Config:

OS: <List Windows 2000, Macintosh, and so on.>

Browser: <List browser and version IE 5.5, NN 4.76, and so on.>

Description:

<Brief description of the problem, more than the title, but not too much>

Repro:

Filling in this part of the bug template may require the following steps:

0. Sometimes there is a step 0 if you have to alter a configuration of some sort or install an extra piece to get to a basal state.

1. Exact steps here—start with the very first piece (e.g., logging in to the service) if necessary to give the overview of where this issue comes into the user scenario.

2. Continue repro steps.

Result:

<List the exact result of what happens after the last step. This entry should be the bug.>

Expected Results:

<What you were expecting to have happen after the last repro step. This material should clearly identify what the difference is between the expected behavior and the observed behavior.>

Notes:

<There may be more supporting documentation you can provide, such as a description of how this affects the user, or details of the downstream effects of leaving this bug in. If supporting documents are included, name each and describe in a few words what each is.>

Check-In Mail

When changes are made to the code base, there must be some sort of notification. This notification could be through a Web site tracking product changes or through email to the team. This section contains a suggestion of what needs to be covered for information to be effectively transferred.

Bug Number(s)

Include the number of each bug and possibly the bug title.

Build Number

Include the number of the build that contains these changes.

Description of Problem(s) Fixed

Bug number: Description of problem.

Description of Change

Bug number: Description of change implemented to fix the identified problem.

New Feature(s) Implemented

Give the name and description of new feature(s) implemented, as well as a comment if these features are complete and ready for full testing or if they are only partially implemented.

Potential Destabilization

Give a short description of the potential problems or risk areas that have been identified.

Performance Impact

Give a short description of the potential problems or risk areas that have been identified.

Source Files Affected

List all source files touched by this change. Even if some files were not touched, they may need to be rebuilt. Include those here.

Build Instructions

Include any special instructions for building this.

Binary Files Affected

List built files that are altered by these fixes.

Tests Run

List BVTs, unit tests, smoke tests, or other automation that was run here, and the pass or fail results from that. Potentially, changes will break automation. Potential automation breaks, such as changes to the tag IDs or other hooks that have been provided, need to be listed here if they are known. You can also list testers involved in testing if this was submitted to test first.

Code Reviewed By

List the name of the developer who code reviewed the changes.

Build Release Mail

When builds come out, especially during periods of the product cycle when many features are being checked in and stability may not be very high, information needs to be disseminated to the team about the state of the build and the features it contains. The build release mail is a complement to the check-in mail because it wraps all check-in mails together for a particular build and draws certain conclusions for the team to reduce confusion.

Build Number

List the number of the build that contains these changes.

New Feature(s) Implemented

Give the name and description of new feature(s) implemented fully in this build—ready to be tested.

New Feature(s) Available

Give the name and description of new feature(s) that can be accessed in this build, but are not ready to be tested.

Known Blocking Bugs

List Bugs that may block code paths or scenarios and their bug number.

Bug Number(s) Fixed in build

Give the number of each bug and possibly the bug title.

Weekly Status Report 3/19–3/23

Status reports are not just a way for your manager to watch what you are doing; they are your chance to show your accomplishments and keep your manager informed, as well as ensure that you are on the right track. The following is a template you can follow for a weekly status report.

Weekly Status Report (Format 1)

Subject: Weekly Status Report 3/19–3/23

Bugs logged during the week: <bug #s>

3/19

- Activity one (for example, Created 12 new test cases)
- Activity two (for example, Weekly team meeting)
- Activity three (for example, Reviewed test spec with developer responsible)

3/20

- Activity one
- Activity two
- Activity three

3/21

- Activity one
- Activity two
- Activity three

3/22

- Activity one
- Activity two
- Activity three

3/23

- Activity one
- Activity two
- Activity three

Goals for Next week:

1. First goal to accomplish
2. Second goal
3. Third goal, and so on

Notes: Any issues blocked from completion, not finished, or cancelled.

Weekly Status Report (Format 2)

Alternately, the following format may work better for you:

This Week's Accomplishments

- First goal
- Second goal
- Third goal

Last Week's Goals—Pasted in from last week's status report

- First goal
- Second goal
- Third goal

Next Week's Goals

- First goal
- Second goal
- Third goal

Tools

The following lists contain links to various corporate sites as well as organizations, general information, and links for tools that will be of use. Since many of these will change, please check the book's companion Web site for more up-to-date references.

Company and Software Sites

- **All NetTools:** http://www.all-nettools.com
- **Apple:**
  - **Corporate site:** http://www.apple.com/
  - **Downloads:** http://www.info.apple.com/support/downloads.html
  - **Knowledge Base:** http://kbase.info.apple.com/
  - **Mac IE DOM:** http://developer.apple.com/internet/_javascript/ie5macscripting.html
- **eEye Digital Security:** http://www.eeye.com/
- **Empirix:** http://www.rswsoftware.com/
- **HP (Hewlett-Packard):**
  - **Corporate site:** http://www.hp.com/
  - **Downloads:** http://welcome.hp.com/country/us/eng/software_drivers.htm

- **Imagiware:** http://www2.imagiware.com/RxHTML/
- **Intel:** http://developer.intel.com/design/
- **LemkeSoft:** http://www.lemkesoft.de/
- **LogiGear:** http://www.logigear.com/
- **Lynx:** http://lynx.browser.org/
- **Mercury Interactive:** http://www.merc-int.com/
- **Microsoft:**
  - **Accessibility:** http://www.microsoft.com/enable/index.htm
  - **Application Center Test:** http://www.microsoft.com/applicationcenter/
  - **Browser versions and corresponding DLLs:** http://support.microsoft.com/support/kb/articles/Q269/2/38.ASP
  - **Corporate site:** http://www.microsoft.com/
  - **Developer Network:** http://msdn.microsoft.com/
  - **Downloads:** http://www.microsoft.com/downloads/
  - **Keyboard layouts:** http://www.microsoft.com/globaldev/keyboards/keyboards.asp
  - **Knowledge Base:** http://support.microsoft.com/
  - **MS Active Accessibility SDK:** http://www.msdn.microsoft.com/downloads/default.asp?URL=/downloads/sample.asp?url=/msdn-files/027/001/785/msdncompositedoc.xml
  - **MSN Companion:** http://msnc.msn.com/v2/companion/features.asp
  - **MSN Explorer:** http://explorer.msn.com/install.htm
  - **NetMon:** http://support.microsoft.com/support/kb/articles/Q148/9/42.ASP
  - **PocketIE/GENIE:** http://www.microsoft.com/Windows/embedded/internetappliances/whichie.asp
- **Mozilla:**
  - **Main site:** http://www.mozilla.org/
  - **Downloads:** http://www.mozilla.org/releases/
  - **Bugzilla:** http://www.mozilla.org/bugs/

- **Mutek Solutions:** http://www.mutek.com/
- **Netscape:**
  - **Corporate site:** http://www.netscape.com/
  - **Downloads:** http://home.netscape.com/download/
- **NuMega (now Compuware):** http://www.compuware.com/products/numega/index.htm
- **Opera:**
  - **Corporate site:** http://www.opera.com/
  - **Downloads:** http://www.opera.com/download/
  - **Technical support:** http://www.opera.com/support/
- **Omni Group:**
  - **Corporate site:** http://www.omnigroup.com/
  - **Omniweb browser:** http://www.omnigroup.com/products/omniweb/
- **Paessler Tools:** http://www.web-server-tools.com/tools/
- **PowerQuest:** http://www.powerquest.com/
- **Rational:** http://www.rational.com/
- **Segue:** http://www.segue.com/
- **SnagIt:** http://www.snagit.com/products/snagit/default.asp
- **Spinwave:** http://www.spinwave.com/
- **Sun:**
  - **Corporate site:** http://www.sun.com/
  - **Downloads:** http://www.sun.com/download/
- **SysInternals:** http://www.sysinternals.com/
- **VM Gear OptimizeIt (now part of Borland):** http://www.borland.com/optimizeit/
- **Watchfire:** http://www.watchfire.com/
- **Web Performance Tools:** http://webperformanceinc.com/
- **Web Warper's Site Optimizer:** http://webwarper.net/ww/0/wwgz/so.htm?*
- **Winternals:** http://www.winternals.com/
- **XCache:** http://www.xcache.com/

Free Tools

- **Amaya:** http://www.w3.org/Amaya/
- **AnyBrowser.com:** http://www.anybrowser.com
- **Babelfish Online Translator:** http://babelfish.altavista.com/
- **Big Brother:** http://pauillac.inria.fr/~fpottier/brother.html.en–Link validator for most Unix and Windows systems
- **CAST's Bobby:** http://www.cast.org/bobby/—Accessibility checker and HTML validator
- **CSE HTML Validator:** http://www.htmlvalidator.com/
- **DENIM:** http://guir.berkeley.edu/projects/denim/—University of Berkeley design tool
- **Douglas Crockford's Web site:**
  - **JavaScript Validator service:** http://www.crockford.com/javascript /jslint.html
  - **JavaScript Minifier:** http://www.crockford.com/javascript/jsmin.html
- **Dr. HTML:** http://www.doctor-html.com/RxHTML/
- **Evolt.org's Browser Repository:** http://browsers.evolt.org
- **Foundstone's free security tools:** http://www.foundstone.com /knowledge/free_tools.html
- **HTML Tidy:** http://www.w3.org/People/Raggett/tidy/
- **Internet Explorer Components:** http://msdn.microsoft.com/workshop /author/behaviors/reference/methods/installable.asp
- **Lang to Lang:** http://www.langtolang.com/—Translation
- **Microsoft's StrGen:** http://www.microsoft.com/globaldev/tools/tools.asp
- **NetMechanic:** http://www.netmechanic.com/
- **Saltstorm:** http://www.saltstorm.net/depo/esc/—JavaScript compressor
- **SpinWave's free trial page:** http://www.spinwave.com/crunchers.html
- **TaskInfo2000:** http://www.iarsn.com/index.html#/download.html
- **UniPress' HTML Validation Service:** http://www.unipress.com /cgi-bin/WWWeblint
- **W3C HTML Validator:** http://validator.w3.org/

- **Web Accessories for IE5:** http://www.microsoft.com/Windows/IE/WebAccess/ie5tools.asp
- **Web Design Group HTML Validator:** http://www.htmlhelp.com/tools/validator/
- **WorldLingo Online Translator:** http://www.worldlingo.com/products_services/worldlingo_translator.html
- **WWWStat:** http://www-old.ics.uci.edu/pub/websoft/wwwstat/

Relevant RFCs, ISO Standards, and IEEE Standards

This appendix lists many standards that pertain to Web applications and, therefore, to Web testing. Many more will address Web applications in the future, so this appendix is only a starting point to give ideas about what objective references there are for you to refer to. Your particular application may use a variety of other technologies, so I encourage you to search out those standards that pertain to you.

RFCs

Requests for Comments (RFCs) are set out by the IETF and are all available at their Web site at http://www.ietf.org. Some of the ones that most interest those involved in Web development efforts are set out in the following list:

791—Internet Protocol: DARPA Internet Program Protocol Specification

793—Transmission Control Protocol DARPA Internet Program Protocol Specification

821—Simple Mail Transfer Protocol

822—Standard for the Format of ARPA Internet Text Messages

894—Standard for the Transmission of IP Datagrams over Ethernet Networks

913—Simple File Transfer Protocol

931—Authentication Server

977—Network News Transfer Protocol

1009—Requirements for Internet Gateways

1036—Standard for Interchange of USENET Messages

1057—RPC: Remote Procedure Call

1094—NFS: Network File System Protocol Specification

1157—A Simple Network Management Protocol (SNMP)

1173—Responsibilities of Host and Network Managers

1180—A TCP/IP Tutorial

1244—Site Security Handbook

1345—Character Mnemonics & Character Sets

1355—Privacy and Accuracy Issues in Network Information Center Databases

1392—Internet Users' Glossary

1413—Identification Protocol

1421-4—Privacy Enhancement for Internet Electronic Mail: Part I: Message Encryption and Authentication Procedures

1425-7—SMTP Service Extensions

1428—Transition of Internet Mail from Just-Send-8 to 8bit-SMTP/MIME

1437—The Extension of MIME Content-Types to a New Medium

1456—Conventions for Encoding the Vietnamese Language VISCII: Vietnamese Standard Code for Information Interchange

1468—Japanese Character Encoding for Internet Messages

1489—Registration of a Cyrillic Character Set

1510—The Kerberos Network Authentication Service (V5)

1521-3—MIME (Multipurpose Internet Mail Extensions)

1554—ISO-2022-JP-2: Multilingual Extension of ISO-2022-JP

1555—Hebrew Character Encoding for Internet Messages

1556—Handling of Bi-directional Texts in MIME

1557—Korean Character Encoding for Internet Messages

1635—How to Use Anonymous FTP

1738—Uniform Resource Locators (URL)

1746—Ways to Define User Expectations

1806—Communicating Presentation Information in Internet Messages: The Content-Disposition Header

1815—Character Sets ISO-10646 and ISO-10646-J-1

1818—Best Current Practices

1831—RPC: Remote Procedure Call Protocol Specification Version 2

1842-3—ASCII Printable Characters-Based Chinese Character Encoding for Internet Messages

1847—Security Multiparts for MIME: Multipart/Signed and Multipart/Encrypted

1855—Netiquette Guidelines

1866—Hypertext Markup Language—2.0

1935—What is the Internet, Anyway?

1939—Post Office Protocol—version 3

1945—Hypertext Transfer Protocol—HTTP/1.0

1947—Greek Character Encoding for Electronic Mail Messages

1964—The Kerberos Version 5 GSS-API Mechanism

2044—UTF-8, a transformation format of Unicode and ISO 10646

2045-9—Multipurpose Internet Mail Extensions

2068—Hypertext Transfer Protocol—HTTP/1.1

2069—An Extension to HTTP : Digest Access Authentication

2070—Internationalization of the Hypertext Markup Language

2083—PNG (Portable Network Graphics) Specification

2109—HTTP State Management Mechanism

2130—The Report of the IAB Character Set Workshop held 29 February–1 March, 1996

2152—UTF-7—A Mail-Safe Transformation Format of Unicode

2196—Site Security Handbook

2251-5—Lightweight Directory Access Protocol (v3)

2277—IETF Policy on Character Sets and Languages

2279—UTF-8, a transformation format of ISO 10646

2291—Requirements for a Distributed Authoring and Versioning Protocol for the World Wide Web

2302—Tag Image File Format (TIFF)—image/tiff

2354—Options for Repair of Streaming Media

2396—Uniform Resource Identifiers (URI): Generic Syntax

2445-7—Internet Calendaring and Scheduling Core Object Specification (iCalendar)

2504—Users' Security Handbook

2518—HTTP Extensions for Distributed Authoring—WEBDAV

2534—Media Features for Display, Print, and Fax

2616—Hypertext Transfer Protocol—HTTP/1.1

2617—HTTP Authentication: Basic and Digest Access Authentication

2640—Internationalization of the File Transfer Protocol

2713—Schema for Representing Java(tm) Objects in an LDAP Directory

2714—Schema for Representing CORBA Object References in an LDAP Directory

2718—Guidelines for New URL Schemes

2732—Format for Literal IPv6 Addresses in URL's

2781—UTF-16, an encoding of ISO 10646

2795—The Infinite Monkey Protocol Suite (IMPS)

2810-3—Internet Relay Chat: Architecture

2821—Simple Mail Transfer Protocol

2822—Internet Message Format

2828—Internet Security Glossary

2964—Use of HTTP State Management

2965—HTTP State Management Mechanism

2987—Registration of Charset and Languages Media Features Tags

3050—Common Gateway Interface for SIP

3066—Tags for the Identification of Languages

3076—Canonical XML Version 1.0

3092—Etymology of "Foo"

3098—How to Advertise Responsibly Using E-mail and Newsgroups or—how NOT to $$$$$ MAKE ENEMIES FAST! $$$$$

3106—ECML v1.1: Field Specifications for E-Commerce

3143—Known HTTP Proxy/Caching Problems

ISO Standards

ISO has several standards that are of interest to those involved in Web development efforts. Some of these are listed in the section that follows. These, and many others, are available at the ISO site: http://www.iso.org.

646—ISO 7-bit coded character set for information interchange

3166—Codes for the representation of names of countries and their subdivisions

2022—Character code structure and extension techniques

8859—8-bit single-byte coded graphic character sets

9000—Quality management systems—Fundamentals and vocabulary

9001—Model for quality assurance in design, development, production, installation and servicing

9002—Model for quality assurance in production, installation and servicing

9003—Model for quality assurance in final inspection and test

9000-3—Quality management and quality assurance standards—Part 3: Guidelines for the application of ISO 9001:1994 to the development, supply, installation and maintenance of computer software

10646—Universal Multiple-Octet Coded Character Set (UCS)

12207—Software Lifecycle Processes

IEEE Standards

The IEEE also has several published standards of interest to those involved in testing efforts (see the following list). These, and many others, can be referred to at their site: http://www.ieee.org.

730—IEEE Standard for Software Quality Assurance Plans

829—IEEE Standard for Software Test Documentation

1008—IEEE Standard for Software Unit Testing

Numeric References

The numeric references can be used to unequivocally cite a particular character. Some samples are given below, but the general format is to use an ampersand symbol followed by the pound sign, then the decimal numeric reference of the character followed by a semicolon. To refer to the character *exclamation mark*, the decimal numeric reference would need to be *!* in order to have the browser understand the character entity. You can also use the hexadecimal value of a character to reference it; in that case, provide an *x* in front of the numeric value. For the exclamation mark, this numeric reference would be *!*. Because the hexadecimal value can easily be obtained from the Windows Character Map utility, that may be the easiest to use.

Alternately, the character's code can be referenced. This is usually a shortened version of the character's official name.

Below are some of the more common 1252 characters and then samples of symbols and characters from other languages arranged by their Unicode value.

CHARACTER	DECIMAL VALUE &#___;	HEXADECIMAL VALUE &#X___;	NAME
	32	0020	space
!	33	0021	exclamation mark
"	34	0022	quotation mark
#	35	0023	number sign
$	36	0024	dollar sign
%	37	0025	percent
&	38	0026	ampersand
'	39	0027	apostrophe
(	40	0028	left parenthesis
)	41	0029	right parenthesis
*	42	002A	asterisk
+	43	002B	plus sign
,	44	002C	comma
-	45	002D	hyphen or minus sign
.	46	002E	period
/	47	002F	slash
0	48	0030	zero
1	49	0031	one
2	50	0032	two
3	51	0033	three
4	52	0034	four
5	53	0035	five
6	54	0036	six
7	55	0037	seven
8	56	0038	eight
9	57	0039	nine
:	58	003A	colon
;	59	003B	semicolon
<	60	003C	less-than sign
>	62	003D	greater-than sign
	160	00A0	no-break space
¡	161	00A1	inverted exclamation mark

CHARACTER	DECIMAL VALUE &#___;	HEXADECIMAL VALUE &#X___;	NAME
¢	162	00A2	cent sign
£	163	00A3	pound sign
¤	164	00A4	currency sign
¥	165	00A5	yen sign
¦	166	00A6	broken bar
§	167	00A7	section sign
¨	168	00A8	diaeresis
©	169	00A9	copyright sign
ª	170	00AA	feminine ordinal indicator
«	171	00AB	left-pointing double-angle quotation mark
¬	172	00AC	not sign
	173	00AD	soft hyphen
®	174	00AE	registered sign
¯	175	00AF	macron
°	176	00B0	degree sign
±	177	00B1	plus-minus sign
²	178	00B2	superscript two
³	179	00B3	superscript three
´	180	00B4	acute accent
µ	181	00B5	micro sign
¶	182	00B6	pilcrow sign
·	183	00B7	middle dot
¸	184	00B8	cedilla
¹	185	00B9	superscript one
º	186	00BA	masculine ordinal indicator
»	187	00BB	right-pointing double-angle quotation mark
¼	188	00BC	vulgar fraction one quarter
½	189	00BD	vulgar fraction one half

(continued)

(continued)

CHARACTER	DECIMAL VALUE &#___;	HEXADECIMAL VALUE &#X___;	NAME
¾	190	00BE	vulgar fraction three quarters
¿	191	00BF	inverted question mark
À	192	00C0	Latin capital letter A with grave
Á	193	00C1	Latin capital letter A with acute
Â	194	00C2	Latin capital letter A with circumflex
Ã	195	00C3	Latin capital letter A with tilde
Ä	196	00C4	Latin capital letter A with diaeresis
Å	197	00C5	Latin capital letter A with ring above
Æ	198	00C6	Latin capital letter AE
Ç	199	00C7	Latin capital letter C with cedilla
È	200	00C8	Latin capital letter E with grave
É	201	00C9	Latin capital letter E with acute
Ê	202	00CA	Latin capital letter E with circumflex
Ë	203	00CB	Latin capital letter E with diaeresis
Ì	204	00CC	Latin capital letter I with grave
Í	205	00CD	Latin capital letter I with acute
Î	206	00CE	Latin capital letter I with circumflex
Ï	207	00CF	Latin capital letter I with diaeresis
Ð	208	00D0	Latin capital letter ETH
Ñ	209	00D1	Latin capital letter N with tilde

CHARACTER	DECIMAL VALUE &#___;	HEXADECIMAL VALUE &#X___;	NAME
Ò	210	00D2	Latin capital letter O with grave
Ó	211	00D3	Latin capital letter O with acute
Ô	212	00D4	Latin capital letter O with circumflex
Õ	213	00D5	Latin capital letter O with tilde
Ö	214	00D6	Latin capital letter O with diaeresis
×	215	00D7	multiplication sign
Ø	216	00D8	Latin capital letter O with stroke
Ù	217	00D9	Latin capital letter U with grave
Ú	218	00DA	Latin capital letter U with acute
Û	219	00DB	Latin capital letter U with circumflex
Ü	220	00DC	Latin capital letter U with diaeresis
Ý	221	00DD	Latin capital letter Y with acute
Þ	222	00DE	Latin capital letter thorn
ß	223	00DF	Latin small letter sharp s
à	224	00E0	Latin small letter a with grave
á	225	00E1	Latin small letter a with acute
â	226	00E2	Latin small letter a with circumflex
ã	227	00E3	Latin small letter a with tilde
ä	228	00E4	Latin small letter a with diaeresis

(continued)

(continued)

CHARACTER	DECIMAL VALUE &#___;	HEXADECIMAL VALUE &#X___;	NAME
å	229	00E5	Latin small letter a with ring above
æ	230	00E6	Latin small letter ae
ç	231	00E7	Latin small letter c with cedilla
è	232	00E8	Latin small letter e with grave
é	233	00E9	Latin small letter e with acute
ê	234	00EA	Latin small letter e with circumflex
ë	235	00EB	Latin small letter e with diaeresis
ì	236	00EC	Latin small letter i with grave
í	237	00ED	Latin small letter i with acute
î	238	00EE	Latin small letter i with circumflex
ï	239	00EF	Latin small letter i with diaeresis
ð	240	00F0	Latin small letter eth
ñ	241	00F1	Latin small letter n with tilde
ò	242	00F2	Latin small letter o with grave
ó	243	00F3	Latin small letter o with acute
ô	244	00F4	Latin small letter o with circumflex
õ	245	00F5	Latin small letter o with tilde
ö	246	00F6	Latin small letter o with diaeresis
÷	247	00F7	division sign
ø	248	00F8	Latin small letter o with stroke
ù	249	00F9	Latin small letter u with grave

CHARACTER	DECIMAL VALUE &#___;	HEXADECIMAL VALUE &#X___;	NAME
ú	250	00FA	Latin small letter u with acute
û	251	00FB	Latin small letter u with circumflex
ü	252	00FC	Latin small letter u with diaeresis
ý	253	00FD	Latin small letter y with acute
þ	254	00FE	Latin small letter thorn
ÿ	255	00FF	Latin small letter y with diaeresis
Œ	338	0152	Latin capital ligature OE
œ	339	0153	Latin small ligature oe
Š	352	0160	Latin capital letter S with caron
š	353	0161	Latin small letter s with caron
Ÿ	376	0178	Latin capital letter Y with diaeresis
ƒ	402	0192	Latin small f with hook
ˆ	710	02C6	modifier letter circumflex accent
˜	732	02DC	small tilde
Α	913	0391	Greek capital letter alpha
Β	914	0392	Greek capital letter beta
Γ	915	0393	Greek capital letter gamma
Δ	916	0394	Greek capital letter delta
Ε	917	0395	Greek capital letter epsilon
Ζ	918	0396	Greek capital letter zeta
Η	919	0397	Greek capital letter eta

(continued)

(continued)

CHARACTER	DECIMAL VALUE &#___;	HEXADECIMAL VALUE &#X___;	NAME
Θ	920	0398	Greek capital letter theta
I	921	0399	Greek capital letter iota
K	922	039A	Greek capital letter kappa
Λ	923	039B	Greek capital letter lambda
M	924	039C	Greek capital letter mu
N	925	039D	Greek capital letter nu
Ξ	926	039E	Greek capital letter xi
O	927	039F	Greek capital letter omicron
Π	928	03A0	Greek capital letter pi
P	929	03A1	Greek capital letter rho
Σ	931	03A3	Greek capital letter sigma
T	932	03A4	Greek capital letter tau
Υ	933	03A5	Greek capital letter upsilon
Φ	934	03A6	Greek capital letter phi
X	935	03A7	Greek capital letter chi
Ψ	936	03A8	Greek capital letter psi
Ω	937	03A9	Greek capital letter omega
α	945	03B1	Greek small letter alpha
β	946	03B2	Greek small letter beta
γ	947	03B3	Greek small letter gamma
δ	948	03B4	Greek small letter delta
ε	949	03B5	Greek small letter epsilon
ζ	950	03B6	Greek small letter zeta
η	951	03B7	Greek small letter eta
θ	952	03B8	Greek small letter theta
ι	953	03B9	Greek small letter iota

CHARACTER	DECIMAL VALUE &#___;	HEXADECIMAL VALUE &#X___;	NAME
κ	954	03BA	Greek small letter kappa
λ	955	03BB	Greek small letter lambda
μ	956	03BC	Greek small letter mu
ν	957	03BD	Greek small letter nu
ξ	958	03BE	Greek small letter xi
ο	959	03BF	Greek small letter omicron
π	960	03C0	Greek small letter pi
ρ	961	03C1	Greek small letter rho
ς	962	03C2	Greek small letter final sigma
σ	963	03C3	Greek small letter sigma
τ	964	03C4	Greek small letter tau
υ	965	03C5	Greek small letter upsilon
φ	966	03C6	Greek small letter phi
χ	967	03C7	Greek small letter chi
ψ	968	03C8	Greek small letter psi
ω	969	03C9	Greek small letter omega
ϑ	977	03D1	Greek small letter theta symbol
ϒ	978	03D2	Greek upsilon with hook symbol
ϖ	982	03D6	Greek pi symbol
	8194	2002	en space
	8195	2003	em space
	8201	2009	thin space
	8204	200C	zero width non-joiner
	8205	200D	zero width joiner
’	8217	2019	right single quotation mark

(continued)

(continued)

CHARACTER	DECIMAL VALUE &#___;	HEXADECIMAL VALUE &#X___;	NAME
'	8218	202A	single low-9 quotation mark
"	8221	201D	right double quotation mark
"	8222	201E	double low-9 quotation mark
†	8224	2020	dagger
‡	8225	2021	double dagger
•	8226	2022	bullet
...	8230	2026	horizontal ellipsis
€	8364	20AC	euro sign
™	8482	2122	trade mark sign
↑	8593	2191	upwards arrow
→	8594	2192	rightwards arrow
↓	8595	2193	downwards arrow
↔	8596	2194	Left right arrow
♠	9824	2660	black spade suit
♡	9825	2661	black club suit
◇	9826	2662	black heart suit
♣	9827	2663	black diamond suit
あ	12354	3042	hiragana letter a
い	12355	3043	hiragana letter i
よ	12424	3088	hiragana letter yo

Web Site References

T he following appendix lists many useful Web sites that I visited during the course of writing this book and visit frequently in the course of my work as a tester. Many of these are updated frequently with fresh material and technologies so they can serve as excellent resources, especially if they pertain to the particulars of your application. With so many sites being frequently updated, there is the potential for references here to go out of date. Although the links as they appear here are as up-to-date as possible, the companion Web site has more recent information.

Design References

- **The Alertbox (Jakob Nielsen's column):** http://www.useit.com/alertbox/
- **Ask Tog (Bruce Tognazzini's monthly column):** http://www.asktog.com/
- **Constantine and Lockwood's Usage Centered Design:** http://www .foruse.com
- **Government Accessibility Site (provided by the National Cancer Institute):** http://usability.gov/guidelines/
- **Interface Hall of Shame:** http://www.iarchitect.com/mshame.htm
- **Macintosh Human Interface Guidelines:** http://developer.apple.com/ techpubs/mac/HIGuidelines/HIGuidelines-2.html

International Considerations

- **Dr. Berlin's Foreign font archive:** http://user.dtcc.edu/~berlin/fonts.html
- **Fonts for the World:** http://www.linguistsoftware.com/
- **International Accessibility Policies:** http://www.w3.org/WAI/Policy/
- **Keyboard layouts:** http://www.hermessoft.com/newproject/lang.html
- **Languages of the World:** http://www.worldlanguage.com/German/Products/3010.htm
- **Microsoft:**
    - **Microsoft IMEs available for download:** http://www.microsoft.com/windows/ie/features/ime.asp?
    - **Microsoft list of code pages and code points:** http://www.microsoft.com/globaldev/
- **Natural Innovations:** http://www.natural-innovations.com/boo/doc-charset.html—Character reference
- **Time and Date useful info:** http://www.timeanddate.com/worldclock/full.html
- **Unix Fonts:** http://www.ccss.de/slovo/unifonts.htm
- **Yamada Language Center:** http://babel.uoregon.edu/yamada/guides.html—Free fonts

Professional Organizations

- **American Society for Quality (ASQ):** http://www.asq.org/
- **Association for Computing Machinery (ACM):** http://www.acm.org/
- **Institute of Electrical and Electronics Engineers (IEEE):** http://www.ieee.org/
- **International Organization for Standardization (ISO):** http://www.iso.ch
- **Quality Auditing Institute (QAI):** http://www.qai.org/

Reference and Informational Sites

- **Betasoft:** http://www.betasoft.com/
- **Bugnet:** http://www.bugnet.com/

- CNet's Download.Com site:
  - http://www.download.com/
  - http://download.cnet.com/
- **The Counter:** http://www.thecounter.com/stats/—Statistics on users on the Web
- **EchoEcho:** http://www.echoecho.com—Usage statistics and verification tools
- **Internet FAQs Consortium:** http://www.faqs.org/
- **Section 508 Government information site:** http://www.section508.gov/
- **Software Development Magazine online:** http://www.sdmagazine.com
- **Software QA Test Resource Center:** http://www.softwareqatest.com/
- **Software Testing and Quality Engineering Magazine:** http://www.stqemagazine.com/
- **SQA Test:** http://www.sqa-test.com/
- **StatMarket:** http://statmarket.com/
- **StickyMinds:** http://www.stickyminds.com/
- **Testing Stuff:** http://www.testingstuff.com
- **TestingFAQs.org:** http://www.testingfaqs.org/
- **Time zone converter:** http://www.timezoneconverter.com
- **W3C Accessibility Guidelines:** http://www.w3.org/TR/WAI-WEBCONTENT/

Security References

- **Buffer overruns:** http://www-106.ibm.com/developerworks/library/overflows/index.html
- **Church of the Swimming Elephant:** http://www.cotse.com/
- **Cookie Central:** http://www.cookiecentral.com/
- **Cult of the Dead Cow's (CDC) "Tao of Windows Buffer Overruns":** http://www.cultdeadcow.com/cDc_files/cDc-351/
- **Foundstone:** http://www.foundstone.com/
- **Insecure.org:** http://www.insecure.org/
- **L0pht/@Stake:** http://www.l0pht.com

- Microsoft:
  - **Security site:** http://www.microsoft.com/security/
  - **Windows Update site:** http://windowsupdate.microsoft.com/—Checks for service packs of installed software
- **Phrack's article "Smashing the Stack for Fun and Profit":** http://www.phrack.org/show.php?p=49&a=14
- **SANS Institute's "The Twenty Most Critical Internet Security Vulnerabilities":** http://www.sans.org/top20.htm
- SecurityFocus:
  - **Main page:** http://www.securityfocus.com/
  - **Security Focus examples of client side scripting security vulnerability:** http://online.securityfocus.com/bid/1836
- **SQL Security:** http://sqlsecurity.com/
- **Standard port assignments:** http://www.iana.org/assignments/port-numbers

Standards Bodies

- **Institute of Electrical and Electronics Engineers (IEEE):** http://www.ieee.org/
- **International Organization for Standardization (ISO):** http://www.iso.org/
- **Internet Engineering Task Force (IETF):** http://www.ietf.org/
- **World Wide Web Consortium (W3C):** http://www.w3.org/

Technology References

- **15 Seconds:** http://www.15seconds.com/
- **ActiveX:** http://activex.microsoft.com/
- **CGI Reference:** http://hoohoo.ncsa.uiuc.edu/cgi/overview.html
- **HTML Help:** http://www.htmlhelp.com/
- **HTML History:** http://www.blooberry.com/indexdot/html/index.html
- **Real World Browser Size stats:** http://evolt.org/article/Real_World_Browser_Size_Stats_Part_I/17/2295/index.html

- **Supported HTML tags per browser:** http://www.webreview.com/browsers/browsers.shtml
- **Swynk technology for administrators:** http://www.swynk.com/
- **W3C Latest version of HTML (4.01):** http://www.w3.org/TR/html401/
- **W3Schools.com:**
    - **HTML Color names, values and samples:** http://www.w3schools.com/html/html_colornames.asp
    - **Main page:** http://www.w3schools.com/
    - **W3Schools.com's Browser Stats:** http://www.w3schools.com/browsers/browsers_stats.asp
- **XML 101:** http://www.xml101.com/xml/default.asp

Bibliography and Recommended Reading

The following is a list of some excellent books on testing, software, technologies, and other aspects of software development. Some will be more applicable to your application, and many are written for the experienced industry professional, but all of them are excellent.

Alexander, Christopher. *A Timeless Way of Building*. New York: Oxford Univ. Press, 1979.

Beizer, Boris. *Black Box Testing: Techniques for Functional Testing of Software and Systems*. New York: John Wiley & Sons, 1995.

Beizer, Boris. *Software Testing Techniques*. Boston: International Thomson Computer Press, 1990.

Brand, Stewart. *How Buildings Learn: What Happens After They're Built*. New York: Penguin Books, 1995.

Brooks, Fred. *The Mythical Man Month*. Reading, MA: Addison-Wesley, 1995.

Casey, Steven. *Set Phasers On Stun: and Other True Tales of Design, Technology, and Human Error*. Santa Barbara: Aegean, 1993.

Collins, James. *Built to Last*. New York: HarperBusiness, 1994.

Cooper, Alan. *About Face: The Essentials of User Interface Design*. Foster City, CA: Programmers Press, 1995.

Cusumano, Michael. *Competing on Internet Time*. New York: Free Press, 1998.

DeMarco, Tom. *The Deadline*. New York: Dorset House Pub., 1997.

DeMarco, Tom. *Peopleware*. New York: Dorset House Pub., 1995.

DeMarco, Tom. *Slack: Getting Past Burnout, Busywork, and the Myth of Total Efficiency*. New York: Broadway Books, 2001.

DeMarco, Tom. *Why Does Software Cost so Much?* New York: Dorset House, 1995.

Dobens, Lloyd. *Thinking about Quality: Progress, Wisdom, and Demming Philosophy*. New York: Times Books/Random House, 1994.

Dorner, Dietrich. *Logic of Failure: Why Things Go Wrong and What We Can do to Make Them Right*. New York : Metropolitan Books/Henry Holt and Company, 1996.

Dyer, Michael. *The Cleanroom Approach to Quality Software Design*. New York: John Wiley & Sons, 1992.

Evans, Michael W. *Productive Software Test Measurement*. New York: Wiley, 1984.

Fernandes, Tony. *Global Interface Design*. Boston: AP Professional, 1995.

Flanagan, David. *JavaScript: The Definitive Guide*. Sebastopol, CA: O'Reilly & Associates, Inc., 2002.

Gillam, Richard. *Unicode Demystified: A Practical Programmer's Guide to the Encoding Standard*. Boston: Addison-Wesley, 2003.

Grady, Robert. *Practical Software Metrics for Project Management and Process Improvement*. Englewood Cliffs, NJ: Prentice Hall, 1992.

Hakos, JoAnn T. *User and Task Analysis for Interface Design*. New York: Wiley, 1998.

Heckel, Paul. *Elements of User Friendly Design*. San Francisco, CA: SYBEX, Inc, 1991.

Hetzel, Bill. *The Complete Guide to Software Testing*. Wellesley, MA: QED Information Sciences, Inc, 1988.

Huff, Darrell. *How to Lie With Statistics*. New York: Norton, 1954.

Jaskiel, Stefan P. *The Web Testing Handbook*. New York: Software Quality Engineering Pub, 2001.

Johnson, Jeff. *GUI Bloopers: Don'ts and Do's for Software Developers and Web Designers*. San Francisco: Morgan Kaufmann Publishers, 2000.

Jones, Capers. *Applied Software Measurements*. New York: McGraw-Hill, 1997.

Jones, Capers. *Assessment and Control of Software Risks*. Englewood Cliffs, NJ: Yourdon Press, 1994.

Jones, Capers. *Estimating Software Costs*. New York: McGraw Hill, 1998.

Jones, Capers. *Patterns of Software System Failure and Success*. Boston: International Thomson Computer Press, 1996.

Jones, Capers. *Software Assessments, Benchmarks, and Best Practices*. Reading, MA: Addison-Wesley Pub. Co., 2000.

Jones, Capers. *Software Quality: Guidelines and Analysis for Success*. Boston: International Thomson Publishing, 1996.

Kaner, Cem. *Testing Computer Software*. New York: International Thomson Computer Press; Wiley 1999.

Kano, Nadine. *Developing International Software*. Redmond, WA: Microsoft Press, 1995.

Karten, Naomi. *Managing Expectations*. New York: Dorset House, 1994.

Killelea, Patrick. *Web Performance Tuning*. Sebastopol, CA: O'Reilly & Associates, Inc., 1998.

Landauer, Thomas K. *The Trouble With Computers*. Cambridge, MA: MIT Press, 1995.

Laurel, Brenda. *The Art of Human Computer Interface Design*. Reading, MA: Addison-Wesley Pub. Co., 1990.

Levy, Matthys. *Why Buildings Fall Down: How Structures Fail*. New York: W.W. Norton, 1992.

Lunde, Ken. *CJKV Information Processing*. Sebastapol, CA: O'Reilly & Associates, Inc., 1999.

Lunde, Ken. *Understanding Japanese Information Processing*. Sebastapol, CA: O'Reilly & Associates, 1993.

Marick, Brian. *The Craft of Software Testing*. Englewood Cliffs, NJ: PTR Prentice Hall, 1995.

McConnell, Steve. *The Software Project Survival Guide*. Redmond, WA: Microsoft Press, 1997.

McConnell, Steve. *Rapid Development: Taming Wild Software Schedules*. Redmond, WA: Microsoft Press, 1996.

McKay, Everett. *Developing User Interfaces for Windows*. Redmond, WA: Microsoft Press, 1999.

Metzger, Philip W. and Boddie, John. *Managing a Programming Project: Processes and People*. Englewood Cliffs, NJ: Prentice Hall PTR: 1995.

Morrison, Mike. *Database Driven Web Sites*. Redmond, WA: Microsoft Press, 1999.

Mullet, Kevin. *Designing Visual Interfaces*. Englewood Cliffs, NJ: SunSoft Press, 1995.

Musciano, Chuck. HTML: *The Definitive Guide*. Sebastopol, CA: O'Reilly & Associates, Inc., 1998.

Meyers, Glenford. *The Art of Software Testing*. New York: John Wiley & Sons, 1979.

Microsoft Windows User Experience: Official Guidelines for User Interface Developers and Designers. Redmond, WA: Microsoft Press, 1999.

Nguyen, Hung Quoc. *Testing Applications on the Web*. New York: Wiley, 2001.

Nielsen, Jakob. *Usability Engineering*. Boston: Academic Press, 1993.

Norman, Donald. *The Design of Everyday Things*. New York: Doubleday/ Currency, 1990.

Papanek, Victor. *Design for the Real World*. New York: Pantheon Books, 1972.

Perry, William E. *Surviving the Top Ten Challenges of Software Testing*. New York: Dorset House Pub., 1997.

Peters, Tom. *A Passion for Excellence*. New York: Warner Books, 1986.

Peters, Tom. *In Search of Excellence*. New York: Harper & Row; Warner Books, 1982.

Peterson, Ivars. *Fatal Defect*. New York: Time Books, 1995.

Petroski, Henry. *To Engineer Is Human: The Role of Failure in Successful Design*. New York: Vintage Books, 1992.

Petroski, Henry. *The Evolution of Useful Things*. New York: Knopf, 1992.

Raskin, Jeff. *The Humane Interface*. Reading, MA: Addison-Wesley, 2000.

Rosen, Kenneth. *Discrete Mathematics and Its Applications*, 4th Ed., New York: McGraw-Hill, 1998.

Spool, Jared M. *Web Site Usability*. North Andover, MA: Morgan Kaufmann Publishers, 1998.

Tognazzini, Bruce. *Tog on Interface*. Reading, MA: Addison-Wesley, 1992.

Tufte, Edward R. *The Visual Display of Quantitative Information*. Cheshire, CT: Graphics Press, 1983.

Wiegers, Karl. *Creating a Software Engineering Culture*. New York: Dorset House, 1996.

Woods, D.R. *Problem Based Learning*. Self-published by Don Woods, 1994.

Yourdon, Ed. *Death March*. Upper Saddle River, NJ: Prentice Hall PTR, 1999.

Zachary, G. Pascal. *Showstopper!* New York: The Free Press, 1994.

Glossary

CROSS-REFERENCE
More information on other terms is available at the FutureSights, Inc., Web site in their online technical dictionary at http://www.futuresights.com/techsupport/ techdictionary.ihtml.

Acceptance test Minimum criteria that the software must pass to be accepted and moved to the next phase. The next phase could be another level of testing, the addition of features, or the release of the software to customers. When referring to the application being accepted for further testing, this small set of tests may be called *sniff tests*, *entry tests*, or *quick tests*. The idea behind the term *sniff test* is if you smelled the software, would it stink?

Accessibility test Test that determines the software's compliance with accessibility standards designed to allow those with disabilities to use the software, perhaps with the help of third-party tools.

Ad hoc testing Less-structured testing activities that rely on intelligent and experienced testers to find the important bugs. Ad hoc testing is usually an activity reserved for more senior testers or brand-new testers who need some familiarization with the product. Testers also need to use ad hoc testing when they have run through all the test cases or when they can think of good areas that the test cases have missed. Writing individual test cases, maintaining them, and logging their results is a process with a lot of overhead, although it provides a good framework for junior testers.

Alpha release A very early build of the product intended for an internal distribution, which may include marketing. An alpha build should not be deployed in any real-world scenario, but should have some amount of stability and robustness.

ANSI (American National Standards Institute) Previously known as the American Standards Association, ANSI is the standards body that devises the ASCII codes. ANSI released the first version (under the name ASA) in 1963 and began including Western European (non-American) languages in 1967. Currently, it has 180 character codes registered with ISO.

Application under test (AUT) The application that is currently being tested, or the components of the larger application.

ASCII (American Standard Code for Information Interchange) This consists of the actual code points that characters are mapped to, as standardized by the ANSI organization. ASCII allows for 255 items (single byte) and is always a 7-bit code.

Baseline A measure of various actions with a product without any special conditions. This measure can be compared against various benchmarks to see how they differ from the baseline for various specific conditions.

Benchmark A measure of various actions performed with the product under specific conditions. This term usually applies to performance or stability comparisons generated by using different builds with optimizations or features added and comparing the outcomes.

Beta release A build that comes after the alpha release but prior to shipping the finished product and that is declared stable enough for distribution to partners or key customers. Real-world installations should be very limited and should be monitored so that feedback gets to the development teams. Some beta releases are Web releases, and any person interested can download and try the software. These beta releases still need to be of high enough quality to protect consumers and provide them with a positive experience.

Bit combination An ordered set of bits used to represent characters (for example, 0x41, which represents the Latin Capital Letter A).

Black-box testing Test interactions in which the tester interacts with the application either without knowing the internal machinations of the implementation or acting as though the internals are unknown. The result is to more closely simulate real user mistakes and usage.

Blocking bug A bug that prevents further development, testing, or product usage. Once a blocking bug is fixed, more code paths are opened up. Blocking bugs are very common early in the development cycle, which explains the software bug numbers that can be seen at various points in the software cycle.

Brute force testing Testing input without too much thought as to what the input is. This type of testing is akin to beating on the keyboard without learning what patterns of bugs turn up or where the application tends to have bugs. Very time-consuming and usually yielding little reward, it can, however, turn up very unanticipated scenarios.

Buddy test Also called *buddy builds*, *private releases*, or *private builds*. Buddy tests involve builds produced by an individual developer or small group of developers that are handed over to a tester or small group of testers to test prior to merging into the main code base. This type of test may be done for every check-in or only when large changes or highly destabilizing changes are made.

Bug bash A concentrated effort for a period of time by a group of testers (and perhaps others) to focus on the application and only log bugs. These efforts may last a single day, a week, or longer. A bug bash is an effort to "chase out" all the remaining bugs. It provides a chance for testing to not be randomized with other tasks and to focus on the application as a whole.

Build Complete compilation of code being created; includes all changes. A build can be created daily, weekly, or on any other schedule.

Build release document A document certifying the build and documenting all code changes (bugs fixed, new features, features not completed, and so on).

Build verification tests (BVTs) An automated suite of tests run against a new build of the software to certify it is stable enough for testing or other purposes. Basic system functionality is certified here. BVTs can also be used on code changes prior to checking in to verify that nothing has regressed.

Cache The storage of information. Specifically, as it applies to Web testing, the client machine caches pages, graphics, and other files for a period of time. If the machine requests another copy of those items before they expire, the cached copy is used. A proxy server can also cache files for the client machines. The caching can be controlled from the client side, but server-side settings can also influence it. Some of these settings are as follows:

- **public**—Mark responses as cacheable that would otherwise be non-cacheable, or private

- **private**—Must not be cached in a public cache

- **no-cache**—Do not cache anywhere, even in caches deliberately returning stale responses

Canvas size Actual area available to display a Web page within a Web browser given a particular screen resolution. Canvas size can be figured as the screen resolution minus the amount of area that the edges of the window take up when it is maximized. It varies from browser to browser, depending on the operating system and configuration, as well.

Character set The combination of a code page and the encoding method applied to that particular code page.

Charset The more common shortened word for *character set*.

Check-in The process of merging new code into the main code base or code tree.

Check-in tests (CIT) Usually a suite of automated tests run against code that certify it is stable enough to check in. Similar or sometimes the same as build verification tests (BVTs).

Client response time (CRT) The amount of time it takes for the client to be able to respond after the browser has loaded HTML and interpreted and executed script or applets.

Code complete The point at which new feature code implementation has been completed. No outstanding issues should exist at this point. Depending on the organization's definitions, bugs may or may not be allowed to be outstanding at this point.

Code page See *Code table*.

Code point The unique location of a character on a code table. This character will always be here, and the code point serves as a way to reference it (a mapping). This point is referenced in a way such as [4D] or [9F/FC].

Code review The process of walking through new code changes to analyze implementation and syntax. Typically this review is a development on development process, but Test should be involved because much good information can be gained from this procedure.

Code table A table showing the character allocated to each bit combination in a code. Also called a *code page*.

Comparison test Comparing the application under test with previous versions or competing products.

Compatibility test Testing the application with other components, programs, or applications to verify that they interact as expected.

Complex script Writing script with no assumption of a linear layout. Includes such issues as bidirectional layout and contextual shaping.

Control character A code point without a glyph or graphic representation, such as a carriage return or end-of-file marker. Can also be referred to as *non-printing characters* because they cannot be seen.

Customer acceptance test (CAT) Verifying the customers' list of requirements that must be met before they will take delivery (and finish paying for) the product.

Disaster recovery Testing the system's ability to recover from disasters such as server crashes, database corruptions, or other problems.

Dogfood The process of rolling out the software for internal use and requiring employees to replace current internal software with the software under development.

Encode The process of taking bytes and converting them into characters.

Encrypt Altering data with a special mechanism to make it unreadable or undecipherable to anyone but the holder of that mechanism's key.

End-to-end test Testing a full scenario as the user would use it; a test through the entire application following a user scenario.

Entry test See *Acceptance test*.

Escape Identifying character ranges that are not handled and problem characters or reserved characters that should not be allowed through the application, to either the server or another user, and converting them to safe characters to later be converted back to the original data.

Exit criteria A set of requirements that must be met before the application can be allowed to pass into the next phase.

Exploratory test Testing by playing with the software; such testing can be a very good learning experience, revealing what parts of the software are available, but without a senior tester to help guide an exploratory test, many false bugs are likely to be reported.

Font A repertoire of glyphs constitutes a font. In a more technical sense, as the implementation of a font, a font is a *numbered* set of glyphs. The numbers correspond to code positions of the characters (represented by the glyphs). Thus, a font in that sense is character code dependent.

Functional test Testing an individual function for bugs.

Glass-box testing See *White-box testing*.

Globalization Testing that the application can handle global content, layout, and input. Very similar to *internationalization*, and sometimes the terms are interchanged.

Glyph The graphic representation of a character. A glyph is what you would write on paper. You can think of this as the picture of the letter that the computer decides to show you when you request a character.

Hotfix A small, localized patch or fix that is applied to repair a bug. Smaller than a service pack and usually only covers a single issue.

Integration test Testing the way that several functions work together; many times this is done after new code has been written to test how it works with the old stable code or how it works with another developer's new code.

International sufficiency testing Testing the ability of the product to be suitable for various international markets. Such testing does not require knowledge of foreign languages; rather, it's a matter of just testing pseudo-localized builds and the software's ability to handle international content. It can include testing the software for locale dependences, country requirements, and code pages.

Internationalization Making the product able to be localized for various markets. Very similar to *globalization*, and sometimes the terms are interchanged.

ISO (International Organization for Standardization) International standards body that makes recommendations and standards. In 1967, it basically adopted ASCII as is and has since been a guiding body in setting standards.

Language script A national language that exists within a writing system.

Leak testing Testing for memory leaks (client side or server side).

Load testing Testing the application's ability to withstand high loads of requests without breaking, independent of time. See also *Stress testing*.

Localization Testing that the user interface (UI) strings have been translated (and translated correctly) into the language of the target markets. These strings may include error messages, dates, layout, or field order, as well as the rest of the UI strings.

Memory testing The same as leak testing, testing for memory leaks.

Performance testing Testing the application's ability to handle a large, but anticipated, load within a certain acceptable timeframe. This testing is intertwined with stability (reliability) testing and load (stress) testing.

Post mortem Latin for "after the death." In this case, it refers to the practice of examining the processes that were used to produce the application. Many organizations do not employ this practice, but should. Learning from mistakes and getting feedback from those involved can give great insights to the failures and successes of the project. Care should be taken that this is not simply an airing of grievances.

Quick test (QT) A quick-and-dirty test to ensure stability; similar to BVTs. See also *Acceptance test*.

Recovery test Testing the system's ability to recover after a failure. This restoration can be performed with the help of a backup, but the ability of the system to recover and the amount of time it takes to recover is crucial.

Regression testing Testing a scenario that has previously worked. Regression testing is done to ensure that no new code has broken or has had adverse effects in other areas, breaking code that previously worked at some point. Bugs turned up in this process are regressions.

Release criteria (RC) Set of criteria that the product must meet in order to be released from a given milestone.

Release scenario (RS) A set of steps or situations that the product must work through in an acceptable manner to be released from a given milestone. Many times, these steps or situations are only the most common actions and the ways that they will be enacted. Organizations may put an expectation on these, for example, indicating that if the release scenarios pass, then 80 percent of all users should never encounter a bug. (Take note: Saying that 80 percent of all users will never encounter a bug is not the same as saying that most users will see bugs 20 percent of the time.)

Release to Internet (RTI) Pushing the code or application to a live Internet site for use or downloading.

Release to manufacturing (RTM) Releasing the code or application to manufacturing to produce CDs or otherwise package for sale.

Release to operations (RTO) Releasing the code or application to an internal team to deploy to internal consumers or a select audience.

Release to Web (RTW) See *Release to Internet (RTI)*.

Sanity test A quick check to ensure that the build is viable for further testing.

Scalability The ability for a system to scale to accommodate more users without incurring higher costs.

Security testing Testing the security risks of the product and analyzing the possible security holes.

Signoff Certification by management that the software is ready to pass into the next phase, which can be a new milestone or release to operations once the exit criteria are met.

Smoke test Quick-and-dirty test, similar to a BVT, to determine if the software meets the minimum functionality requirements to allow more testing. The term comes from hardware manufacturers—if hardware was plugged in and started to smoke, there was a problem and the hardware failed.

Sniff test See *Acceptance test*.

Specifications Detailed description of how the product will work, what will be used for the work, and what work will be done and not be done, as well as who the primary contacts are. There can be product specifications written by project managers, design specifications written by developers, and test specifications written by the testers.

Stateless No information is retained from request to request. By definition, HTTP is a stateless protocol, although there are techniques, such as cookies, that can be employed to give the user a stateful experience.

Stress testing Testing the amount of stress that can be applied to an application through many requests, expensive requests, or other means before it breaks, independent of time. See also *Load testing*.

Test case An individual atomic test that can be passed or failed. These tests may have dependencies on other test cases that must be passed, or could be blocked by them.

Test design specification (TDS) A fairly high-level test plan document. Unfortunately, *TDS* sounds like *tedious* when spoken. TDS can also be called a *Test plan*.

Test pass A pass through the product, running all cases of a particular type. This pass could involve only priority 1 test cases, a release scenario, or only security cases.

Test plan See *Test design specification (TDS)*.

Test script A test script is typically a test case with exact keystrokes spelled out. A test case can be very tedious and time-consuming to create and can quickly become outdated, but can be useful to hand to junior testers or contractors in order to ensure that tests are performed exactly the right way. However, a test script allows for no creativity, which is the advantage of having a human run the tests rather than automating them.

Unit test Very granular test for a new line of code or a new function placed into the code. Developers should own this part of testing their own code because they know it best. Enforcing unit tests in the development process helps ensure that more stable builds reach Test and Test is not spending its time on build breaks.

Usability testing Testing the application's ability to be easily used by the target audience.

Usage scenario See *User scenario*.

User acceptance Verifying the application against a list of requirements from the user perspective; this process can be very formalized and legal if the software is to be delivered to a customer, or can be more informal involving a list of guesses as to what the user would like to have and then a verification that the software meets those criteria.

User agent The data string passed by a client to a server to identify the type of application that it is (for example, *Mozilla/4.0 (compatible; MSIE 5.5; Windows NT 5.0)*). Some applications are written to hand back different forms, depending on the user-agent string. Not all user agents are browsers; some can be Web spiders.

User interface (UI) The visual part of the software with which the user interacts. It could be anything from a simple command line as in DOS to a Windows-like experience.

User profile A sketch of the typical user, his usage habits, career, techno-savvy, and general level of comfort with the product, along with some examples of how the person might use the product. This profile may also include what his hardware configurations are expected to be. There may be several user profiles for a product to target different areas of the intended audience. The user profile helps developers and testers keep a perspective on their target audience and identify with them, as well as appropriately aim features at their audience and test according to how the software will be used.

User scenario A series of typical user interactions that users perform, described in steps that detail the way that the user will perform them. Several user scenarios may be combined into a release scenario. For example for an online catalog, user scenarios might include browsing for an item, selecting items, and checking out and paying for items. Can also be called a *usage scenario* or similar term.

Virtual user A script run to simulate a user's interactions against a server; a simulated user performing simulated actions derived from a user profile. Having virtual users allows for exact testing configurable to the users' needs. With a small change, a single script can be used to simulate 1, 1,000, or 10,000 users interacting with the server.

Web testing Composed of several areas; primarily broken out by the GUI and the server, but many areas such as performance and security straddle both. Also involves API, HTTP interfaces, objects, data, and more.

White-box testing Testing the application based on the knowledge of how the internals work and are coded. This sort of testing may also be called *glass-box testing* and is the other side of *black-box testing*.

Work breakdown structure (WBS) A document that details the individual tasks that must be done and sometimes associates particular resources (machines, personnel, lab space, time, etc.) with the tasks.

Writing script A system for writing a language of a people.

Zero bug bounce (ZBB) Hitting zero bugs for at least a short period of time; usually means having all bugs cleared up and resolved in some way and then having a few more entered. The bounce may be only a matter of hours.

What's on the Web Site?

This appendix provides you with information about the contents of the companion Web site for this book. The companion Web site can be found at the following URL:

```
http://www.wiley.com/compbooks/ash
```

Here is what you will find in this appendix:

- System requirements
- What's on the Web site
- Troubleshooting

System Requirements

Make sure that your computer meets the minimum system requirements listed in this section. If your computer doesn't match up to most of these requirements, you may have a problem using the contents of the Web site.

For Windows 9x, Windows 2000, Windows NT4 (with SP 4 or later), Windows Me, or Windows XP:

- PC with a Pentium processor running at 120 MHz or faster
- At least 32MB of total RAM installed on your computer; for best performance, we recommend at least 64MB

- Ethernet network interface card (NIC) or modem with a speed of at least 28,800 bps

- A browser installed (preferably Internet Explorer 5+, Netscape Navigator 6+, or other HTTP 1.1 standard browser)

For Linux:

- PC with a Pentium processor running at 90 MHz or faster

- At least 32MB of total RAM installed on your computer; for best performance, we recommend at least 64MB

- Ethernet network interface card (NIC) or modem with a speed of at least 28,800 bps

- A browser installed (preferably Internet Explorer 5+, Netscape Navigator 6+, or other HTTP 1.1 standard browser)

For Macintosh:

- Mac OS computer with a 68040 or faster processor running OS 7.6 or later

- At least 32MB of total RAM installed on your computer; for best performance, we recommend at least 64MB

- A browser installed (preferably Internet Explorer 5+, Netscape Navigator 6+, or other HTTP 1.1 standard browser)

What's on the Web Site

The following sections provide a summary of the software and other materials you'll find on the Web site.

Author-Created Materials

All author-created material from the book along with additional information is on the Web site. This material includes the following:

- Checklists and questions

- Bibliography and suggested reading list

- HTTP Response codes

- Templates of bug reports, build release notifications, test plans, and more

- System setup guides, with full-color graphics not included in the text

- Windows code page examples
  - 874
  - 932
  - 936
  - 950
  - 1250
  - 1251
  - 1252
  - 1253
  - 1254
  - 1255
  - 1256
  - 1257
  - 1258
- Language guides to guide you in using the Windows IMEs
  - Arabic
  - Chinese
  - Czechoslovakian
  - Diacritics
  - English/German
  - Greek
  - Hebrew
  - Hindi
  - Japanese
  - Korean
  - Lithuanian
  - Russian
  - Turkish
  - Vietnamese
- HTML Numeric Character References
- Sample problem characters

- Unicode range guide
- Examples of script error in Web pages
- Links to tools, companies, and more information

Troubleshooting

If you have difficulty using any of the materials on the Web site, check that your system is configured to view various international content. The most common problem with the provided materials will center around international content and problem characters. Without the appropriate fonts and configurations, the Web pages will not be useful.

Because other unforeseen technical problems may still exist, the materials have also been provided in Microsoft Word format and in some cases as plain text files. Systems that do not support Unicode or the UTF-8 encoding method are more likely to have problems with the international pages and the problem characters. Some operating systems are not able to display some characters, and certain older browsers may not display all complex content correctly. If the latter is the cause, upgrading your browser may solve the problem. The documents available for download will solve this issue for you. If you are using an operating system that does not recognize certain characters, you will need to use a different operating system in order to view that data. Appendix D should guide you through dealing with any of these types of issues.

If you still have trouble with the Web site, please call the Customer Care phone number: (800) 762-2974. Outside the United States, call 1 (317) 572-3994. You can also contact Customer Service by email at techsupdum@wiley.com. Wiley Publishing, Inc. will provide technical support only for installation and other general quality control items.

A

acceptance testing, 38
accessibility
  with assistive technology, 129, 130
  browser adjustments, 409–410
  for hearing impaired, 131
  questions, 470–471
  requirements, planning, 130
  with screen readers, 131
  testing, 39, 129–130
  for vision impaired, 130–131
Active Server Pages. *See* ASP
ActiveX controls, 161–162, 479–480
ad hoc testing, 40, 207
alpha testing, 39
application architecture, 144–146
Arabic, 375–376
ASCII (American Standard Code for
    Information Interchange)
  defined, 169
  lower, 168, 169, 173
  upper, 168, 169, 173
ASP (Active Server Pages)
  caching, 159
  CPU monitoring and, 233
  defined, 158
  operating system and, 233
  performance testing, 159–160, 232–233
  questions, 479
  as resource-intensive technology, 233
  testing, 159
  URL construction requirements, 159
asserts, 209
assistive technology, 129–130
auditing, 244, 246, 250
automation
  API-level, 305
  basic test, 305

benefits, 300–301, 322
categories, 299–300
code coverage, 318
code readability, 321
code reviews, 314
coding standards, 320
decisions, 305–306
defined, 299–300
detail, adding, 310–312
development practices, 320–321
documentation, 309
effect, 318–320
effort, continuing, 316–321
external data reliance, 304
framework, 317
good practices implementa-
    tion, 320–321
machines running, 303
manual test cases and, 314
measurements, 215
naming conventions, 313–314
packages, 305
performance testing, 234–235
planning, 303–316
project, starting, 308–309
questions, 479
reasons for, 305–306
reminders, 321–322
revisions, 316
scripts, 318
start decision, 309–310
status/history chart, 318–319
test cases, 311, 313, 319
tools, 306–308
types of, 301–302
verification, 311–313
writing, 308–313